COLLECTOR'S ENCYCLOPEDIA OF

PENDANT AND POCKET

WATCHES

1500 – 1950

IDENTIFICATION
AND VALUES

C. Jeanenne Bell, G. G.

cb

COLLECTOR BOOKS

A Division of Schroeder Publishing Co., Inc.

On the Cover:

Front:

Top, left: Rock crystal skull, gold-mounted watch, James Harmer, London, circa 1715, $9,000.00 – 12,000.00.

Center, left to right: Open face, sunken second, Waltham, $700.00.
Large gilt metal coach watch, Carl Schmidt, German, circa 1585, $24,000.00 – 30,000.00.
Shirley Temple dial watch, Westclock, $400.00 – 500.00.

Bottom, left to right: The Cherub, unsigned, circa 1810, $12,000.00 – 15,000.00.
The Tiger Hunt, Abrecht & Co., Calcutta, circa 1895, $2,500.00 – 3,500.00.
Open face, sunken second, white gold filled case, Howard, $650.00.
Small silver coach watch, Julien le Roy, Paris, 1740, $18,000.00 – 24,000.00.

Back:

Top middle: Yellow gold–filled octagonal, open-face case, missing crown and second hand, Swiss lever movement, $80.00 – 100.00.
Top, right: 18kt. gold hardstone-set watch with special escapement, Bruguet, $12,000.00 – 18,000.00.
Bottom left-hand corner: Hunting case, sterling silver, embellished with niello enamel and yellow gold, Swiss lever escapement, $1,100.00.

Cover design:
Beth Summers

Book design:
Allan Ramsey

COLLECTOR BOOKS
P.O. Box 3009
Paducah, Kentucky 42002-3009
www.collectorbooks.com

Copyright © 2004 C. Jeanenne Bell

The current values indicated in this book should be used only as a guide.
They are not intended to set prices, which vary from one section of the country to another. Auction prices as well as dealer prices vary and are affected by
condition as well as demand. Neither the Author nor the Publisher assumes
responsibility for any losses that might be incurred as a result of consulting
this guide. Any errors or omissions are strictly the responsibility of the author.

Searching for a Publisher?

We are always looking for people knowledgeable within their fields. If
you feel that there is a real need for a book on your collectible subject and
have a large comprehensive collection, contact Collector Books.

Proudly printed and bound in the
United States of America

Contents

Acknowledgments

A BIG THANK YOU

to contributers of pictures and descriptions and to those who allowed this author to photograph their watches:

Antiquarian Horologist — Stephen Bogoff
Fine Antique Timepieces
P.O. Box 408
Mill Valley, CA 94942
(415) 383-8100
www.bogoff.com

Antiquorum USA, Inc. — Lisa L. Jones
609 5th Ave. Suite 503
New York, NY 10017
(212) 750-1103
ljones@antiquorum.com

Bonhams and Butterfields
7601 Sunset Boulevard
Los Angeles, CA 90046
(323) 850-7500
Fax: (323) 850-5843

Dan Dolff
Collector and Watch Judge
Zanybrainy@msn.com

Eric Engh
www.oldwatch.com

Aaron Faber
666 5th Ave.
New York, NY 10103
(212) 586-8411

Global Antiques — Glenn Smith
4140 Lincoln Boulevard
Marina del Rey, CA 90292
(310) 823-8616
Fax: (310) 823-4838

Jack Harvey
JacksStuff@aol.com

J. D. Miller
3639 E. Magnolia Ave.
Knoxville, TN 37914
(865) 523-5079
tandersonco@mindspring.com

Mike Harold
Advisor and consultant for the American watch section

Father Bradley Offutt

Penny Steiner
5802 Sunset Drive
So. Miami, FL 33143
(305) 667-5567
(305) 588-0910
Fax: (305) 667-5747

Professional Horologist — Joseph Conway
(617) 970-6101
the_boston_flash@yahoo.com

Solvang Antique Center — Jeff Rosen
(714) 536-2087
rosenboys2@aol.com

Somlo Antiques
7 Piccadilly Arcade
London SW 1Y6NH
4401714996526
Fax: 440174990603
www.somloantiques.com

Stellar Communications — David Strudler
1372 Toms River Road.
Jackson, NJ 08527-5207
(732) 323-0303
edikted@earthlink.net

The Escapement — Edward B. Ueberall
P.O. Box 522
Pooler, GA 31322
STDWATCH@aol.com
(912) 330-0866

Varner Clock Repair — Oren L. Varner
425 Olive Street
Windsor, MO 65360
(660) 647-2571

The Walters Art Museum — Kate Lua
600 N. Charles St.
Baltimore, MD 21201-5185
(410) 547-9000
www.thewalters.org

Special Thanks to the Following:

Antiquorum, a world renowned auction house, for its kind permission to use so many of the photographs and descriptions from its beautiful and informative catalogs. Thanks to Lisa Jones for being so helpful.

Dr. Theodore R. Crom, internationally known horological expert and author of many books, for his friendship, help, and never-ending patience. He opened up his home, his vast resources, and his heart to me. He is truly my mentor.

Roy Ehrhardt, internationally-known horological expert and author of many books, for his friendship over the years and his generosity in sharing his watch serial numbers.

Mike Harrold, internationally known horological expert and author, for sharing his time and vast knowledge about American watch companies.

Edward B. Ueberall, railroad watch expert and author, for taking time out of his scheduled moving to Savannah, Georgia, to supply us with some of his beautiful photographs and descriptions.

Dedication

This book is dedicated with love and gratitude to The One from Whom all good things cometh; my parents, Anne and Belton Noblitt; my husband, Michael T. Marshall; and my favorite "Uncle" and mentor, Dr. Theodore Crom.

Dr. Theodore Crom.

Introduction

Many people find watches fascinating. Others have an old watch in the family about which they are curious. Appraisers, dealers, and collectors also have times when they need to know how to identify and evaluate an old watch. No matter how intense or casual your interest may be, this book should open your mind and eyes to the miracle of these tiny machines. We will explore the dedication and labor of the men who strove to make these portable time pieces. Their success is evident in our ability to take the accuracy of today's watches for granted. The accuracy that can be purchased for a few dollars was actually purchased by generations of watch makers who spent their lives striving for accuracy and affordability.

The book is divided into four time periods of one hundred years each, and one that spans the first 50 years of the twentieth century. In each century, we will explore what was happening that influenced timekeeping and the development of the watch. Events such as the industrial revolution, expansion of the railroads, and even train wrecks are included. We wil focus on both pendent and pocket watches, because early watches were worn around the neck or the waist. Pants pockets did not come onto the scene until 1625, and waistcoat pockets followed in 1675.

The purpose of this book is to help you identify and evaluate a watch. Instead of discussing each and every part of the movement, I have chosen instead to focus on the parts of the watch that will help you identify the escapement, the country of origin, the type and style of the case, and the materials and methods of embellishment. Being able to associate these things with what was happening in the world usually helps one to remember them.

The eighteenth century includes a section about a few of the characters who played a part in watchmaking history. The chapter about the nineteenth century not only includes a synopsis of the beginnings of the American watch companies, but also includes serial numbers to help circa date these watches. Topics such as metals and makers' marks are also discussed.

Each time period will include numerous photographs of watches and their prices, in various levels of the market place. A timeline of each century is provided to put the development of the pocket watch into historical perspective.

Having written many books on jewelry, this book has been a stretch for me. It has given me, and I hope it will give you, a look at how these tiny machines that began as decorative and amusing novelties for the wealthy evolved into a functional accessories that are indispensible in today's world.

Enjoy, and happy hunting!!

A NOTE FROM THE AUTHOR

The idea for this book started about three years ago when Collector Books asked me to write it. Although I joined the National Association of Watch and Clock Collectors in the early 1970s, it had never occurred to me to write about watches. Of course I had bought and sold watches in my antique jewelry stores; they were in the "is it pretty and does it run?" category. In fact, I put all old watches into three categories: 1. Is it pretty and does it run? 2. Is it collectible; i.e., a railroad watch? 3. Is it pretty *and* collectible?

My first reaction to the request to write this book was, "I don't even collect watches!" Then I started thinking about how many wristwatches I owned that dated from about 1890 through the 1940s. Next I realized that whenever I had gone to the national meetings of the N.A.W.C.C. through the years, I had often purchased pocket and pendant watches. The beautiful movements and elaborate decorations from the eighteenth century had always appealed to me. Pulling my watches out of the safe, I was amazed at the number I had accumulated. Was I a collector or an accumulator? When does the accumulation become a collection? My conclusion was that a "collector" is one that knows something about the history of the items. Hopefully, this book will help accumulators become collectors, jewelry appraisers gain more expertise in appraising watches, and curious individuals find out what the old watch in their family is worth.

Again, enjoy!

A Note About Prices

There can be a big difference between price and value. Price is subjective. If you are going to sell an item, you are allowed to put any price on it that you want. This does not mean that the price that you decide on is the value. The item might have a value much higher or much lower than the chosen price.

To complicate matters, value is transient. An item that was valuable in one time period is not necessarily always valuable. For instance, in the mid-nineteenth century, hair was worth three times more than sterling silver. In the late nineteenth century, aluminum was more valuable than gold. Often, expensive jewelry pieces contained both metals. One very rich man displayed his wealth by covering the walls of his entry hall with embossed panels of aluminum. Today, piles of hair are trashed each day at beauty salons, and cooking pans are made of aluminum. What made these items go down in value? Supply and demand. Synthetic fibers are now used for wigs, dolls' hair, and hair augmentation. Aluminum is now much easier to get out of the ground and process.

The items in this book are priced by the owners or by a price realized at auction. Sometimes these owners are collectors, and sometimes they own retail stores. Many examples were furnished by dealers who only sell on the internet. Other watches were photographed at N.A.W.C.C. conventions and reflect the price one member was asking another member to pay for the piece.

If you are looking for the insurance replacement value of a particular watch, it is unwise to look in a book, think that you see one just like the one that you own, and then use it for your valuation. To be truly comparable, a piece must be the same size, have a case of the same style and materials, have the same number of jewels, and have either the same maker or one of comparable reputation; also, the movement must have the same type of escapement. Even if the watch in question is the same, do not automatically consider the price the value until you have found comparable prices at the same level of the marketplace.

Many online companies that sell watches do not have a retail store or the overhead that goes with staffing, advertising, high insurance premiums, and rent. Consequently, their prices may be closer to wholesale or dealer prices. Of course, you do not have a chance to hold and touch the piece before buying, but some of the dealers will send a watch out on approval.

Auction houses often sell to collectors, dealers, and individuals. Collectors and individuals will often pay more than a dealer, but the dealer has to have a retail mark-up. By looking at comparables from several auction houses or from several different auctions at the same auction house, you can determine a pattern of value.

Retail antiques stores may charge a bit more if they specialize in watches, but with them you not only have the added advantage of handling the piece, but also a convenient place to take the watch for servicing. Only you or your client can determine which level of the market to shop.

Happy hunting!

Chapter I
THE BEGINNINGS
THE SIXTEENTH CENTURY

Most historians agree that the evolution of the watch from the clock began in the second or third quarter of the fifteenth century. This step was made possible by the invention of a spring that provided power while taking up a small amount of space. As with most important inventions, the idea of making the clock into a portable timepiece seems to have occurred simultaneously to more than one person. This particular idea formed in the minds of people in southern Germany, Italy, and France. Consequently, no one knows for sure just who made the first one. For years Peter Henlien, a locksmith from Nurenberg (circa 1500 – 1503), was given credit for this great achievement, but in recent years this has been disputed. But small disagreements such as these are not important. The important thing is that it was made, and thus, the evolution of the early watch into the one we today tend to take for granted began! Unfortunately, almost no examples of these fifteenth century watches have survived. Consequently, our odyssey through the history of watches will begin by examining the watches of the sixteenth century.

Most knowledge is formed in layers, and the invention of the clock-watch (as the early watches were called) was a natural progression that stemmed from the desire to make time personal.[1] Prior to this invention, man had to rely on the town clock or the clock at home (if he was fortunate enough to own one.) When he was away from these clocks, he had to rely on a sundial during the day and rely on the stars at night. If it was a cloudy day or a dark and rainy night, the only clock he had was his inner clock, which we all know is not always reliable.

Fortunately, when one man used all of his abilities to make a good watch, there was always someone else who would try to improve upon his work. Over the centuries, the work and the dedication of countless men resulted in our ability to know time whenever we want, no matter where we are.

THE TIMES

To really appreciate the work and the devotion to craft of these early watchmakers, it is a good idea to know what was happening in the world during this century. It is also easier to remember how watches evolved if we can associate changes in the watch industry with what was happening in the world.

Almost the entire century was one of upheaval. It began in 1517, when Martin Luther nailed his Ninety-five Theses to a church door in Wittenberg. One of the things that he was protesting was the selling of indulgences by the Roman Catholic church. These indulgences enabled someone who had committed a particular sin to be pardoned by the church by paying a fee. Many people agreed with Luther's protests. They were soon known as Protestants. Germany joined in the protests against the abuses of the church. The movement became known as the Reformation. It spread to Switzerland in 1519, with Ulrich Zwingli (1484 – 1531), working in Zurich, and John Calvin (1509 – 1564), in Geneva, as leaders.

Because Protestants who followed Calvin were not allowed to wear worldly things such as jewelry and watches embellished with gems, many Genevese jewelers went to France and Germany to expand their field of expertise to include the craft of watchmaking. After all, this was the time of the "universal man," and one could embrace many fields of expertise. During this century, Germany was the leader in the field of watchmaking and German watchmakers were more than happy to share their knowledge with the jewelers from Geneva. It's easy to see how this sharing of knowledge would have a profound effect on the future watch industry.

The year 1598 was one of jubilation for the Protestants in France. The Edict of Nantes assured the Huguenots equal political rights with the Roman Catholics. This climate of peace allowed the craft of watchmaking to flourish, and enticed other Protestant watchmakers to move to France.

For more perspective on what was happening in the world and the development of watches during this century, a timeline is included. Remember that different sources often disagree with one another concerning watchmaking facts of these early years of the industry. Consequently, I have offered a time span of years for some developments. (See Sixteenth Century Timeline.)

Many of the men who experimented with making the table clock smaller were locksmiths, because they were accustomed to working with small tools. The locksmiths, however, were not jewelers or goldsmiths, so it seems likely that they would use a casing already available. During this time period, it was necessary for people to wear a scent ball around their necks. This insured that the pleasant smelling ball was readily available to put up to the nose when one encountered the unpleasant smells often found on walkways, roads, and even people. Remember, this was a time when one lady was considered odd because she boasted that she took a bath once a year whether she needed it on not.

A brass musk ball, or "musk apple" as it was referred to by Italians, could be opened at the middle in order to put in a supply of musk. The top of the ball was pierced, to allow as much fragrance as possible to escape. A ring on the top of the ball provided a way to attach it to a chain. Consequently, it's not surprising that many of these very early watch cases were ball shaped.

The movements were made of iron, a material that locksmiths were accustomed to working with, and the brass dials had only one short hand to point out the twelve Roman numerals that marked the hours. On the top outside of each numeral was a small, half-round brass protrusion used as touch-pin for telling the time in the dark. These early watches were referred to as clock-watches because they struck the hours and sometimes included an alarm.

The chances of finding a spherical clock-watch from the early sixteenth century are very small, but there is a special one that can be seen at the Walter's Gallery in Baltimore, Maryland. It is the oldest known dated watch, and it was made in 1530. The fact that the original owner was a well-known person in that time period makes the find even more exciting! The inscription reads "PHIL. MELA. GOTT. ALEIN. DIE HER 1530" (Philip Melanchthon. To God alone the honor. 1530). Philip Melanchthon (1497 – 1560) was a protestant reformer of the period.[2]

Plate 1. Top view of Philip Melanchthon's watch dated 1530, which gives a clear look at the dial and the top of the spherical case. Note the touch-pads (on the outer edge of the dial) and the sturdy iron hand.

Plate 2. The open watch with the backside up. Note the three little legs that allow the piece to sit upright on a table at night. Also note the case hinge and clasp. The case is 4.8 cm in diameter.

Plate 3. A side view of the movement.

Plate 4. A top view of the movement.

The patronage of the royals and other wealthy individuals of the time spurred watchmakers to produce more watches. Because watches were as much or more of a novelty as they were a timekeeper, they were referred to as "ticky toys." But they were definitely toys for the wealthy and needed to convey this image. Consequently, jewelers became involved in both case making and engraving. After all, the case was the most visible part of a watch.

CASES AND DIALS

THE CASES

By the middle of the sixteenth century, cases had evolved to oval (or egg) shaped and tambour (or drum) shaped. These shapes were popular throughout the century. Soon, other shapes were introduced. "Cushion"-shaped cases (rectangular, with rounded edges and sides) became popular. Toward the end of the century, octagonal cases made their appearance, and cases made entirely out of rock crystal appeared on the scene. Jewelers and case makers seemed to love the challenges of these new shapes.

Plate 5. Oval shape.

Plate 6. Drum shape.

Photos courtesy of Antiquorum Auctioneers.

Plate 7. Cushion shape.

Other case changes included detachable alarms. This fact is illustrated in an an Italian oil painting dated 1560. It shows an Italian Nobleman proudly holding his watch out to his right side. It is a typical watch of the period and has the hinged pierced cover raised to display the dial. A chain hangs down from the watch. He is standing next to a table on which is displayed the watch carrying case and the detachable alarm mechanism. It is clear that his prized watch could be worn around the neck or waist, used on a table, or combined with the alarm for a morning wake up.

Case embellishments also became more sophisticated. Piercing became elaborate and and included birds, flowers, hearts, and countless other motifs. The piercing was not only on the top of the case but also adorned the sides. The areas not pierced were engraved. By 1560, many of the tambour-shaped watches included round plaques with raised figures in the center. The plaque on the watch in the photo below depicts Adam and Eve in the Garden.

Plate 8. *Photo courtesy of Musee National de la Renaissance, Chateau d' Ecouen.*

THE DIALS

Cases were not the only parts of watches to go through changes. As the century progressed, dials became more highly engraved. Stars were added to the sun rays that were popular throughout this period. Other dials featured designs such as engraved swirls, quatrefoils, birds, or flowers; the designs were too varied to describe them all. By the end of the century, the tails of the hands had become longer and were used to point to the alarm hour. Some dials and hands were embellished with enamel.

Plate 9. Enamel dial.
Photo courtesy of Antiquorum Auctioneers.

WHAT MADE IT TICK?

The mechanics of the watch changed very little during the century. Many watches included not only alarms, but also bells to sound the hour. Unfortunately, the accuracy of the watch had not improved. Many watches made throughout the century also included a sundial and a compass, so one could make sure that the watch was on time.

Plate 10. For a description and realized price see photo at the bottom of page 21.

After looking at the case and the dial, the time has come to look at what made a waatch tick. In the introduction of this book, a promise was made to keep this text as non-technical as possible, and I intend to keep that promise. But to appreciate the evolution of the pendant and pocket watch one needs to know something about the works of early watches.

Just what makes up the tiny machine known as the *movement*? Let's explore this: The first thing it needs is power. This power is supplied by a spring most commonly housed in a container called a "barrel." Unfortunately, as a spring winds down, its strength is less powerful. The watch spring needed something to equalize its power. Two types of equalizers were used, the *fusee* and the *stackfreed*.

THE FUSEE

Fusees had been used in clocks for almost one hundred years before the development of the watch, so it was natural for them to be put to use in early watches. No one knows for sure how old it is, but we do know that Leonardo de Vince made reference to the fusee and is often given credit for its invention. The French favored a tall, fairly small-in-diameter fusee, but this resulted in a thicker movement.

The fusee is a somewhat cone-shaped piece of metal with a spiral track cut into it. It reminds me of a small road winding around a tall mountain. A length of catgut (and after around 1670, a chain) is fastened to both the main spring barrel and the wide end of the cone. As the watch is wound, the gut is drawn off of the barrel and onto the fusee. It starts at the wide end and winds up the spiral to the small end. As the chain winds off of the barrel, the action also winds the mainspring. As the main spring winds down, it receives power compensation from the larger end of the cone. This helps to insure a fairly constant force.

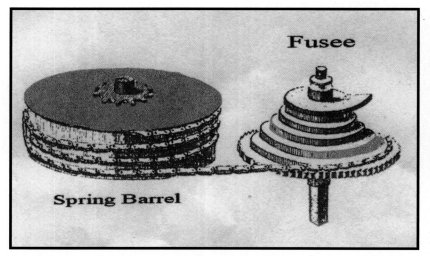

Plate 11. On the right side of this illustration is the fusee with the chain almost unwound. On the left is the barrel housing the spring.

THE STACKFREED

Many German watchmakers preferred to use the stackfreed, as evidenced by the number of German watches containing this type of equalizer.

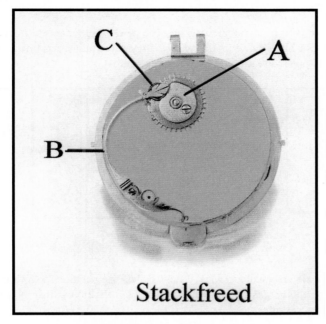

Plate 12. *Photo courtesy of Antiquorum Auctioneers.*

The cam (A) in the center of the watch in the photo above is referred to as a "snail," because of its shape. The stiff spring (B) with a little roller (C) is used to apply pressure to the snail, or cam, which creates friction on the pivots of the mainspring arbor. This friction is varied by the amount of pressure that the stackfreed spring puts against the cam through the little roller. As the snail begins its turn with the fully wound mainspring, it is at its largest radius, and this produces a maximum amount of friction to equalize the main spring. By the time that the mainspring begins to wind down and has less torque, the snail is at its minimum radius to the arbor and gives the least amount of friction.

Once the power was fairly constant, it needed to be controlled by the escapement (with the help of an oscillating balance) so that the hands moved at the appropriate speed to express the correct time. Two of the regulating devices used in these early watches were the *dumbbell*, an oscillating balance bar (see below) and the wheel (see below). Their jobs were like that of a pendulum in a clock.

Plate 13. Balance bar.

The Balance is the silver wheel under the cock.

Plate 14. Wheel.

The Germans made and used the dumbbell, or foliot oscillator, and the French favored the balance wheel. Both types of regulators received their power from the main spring and helped to regulate the escapement.

THE ESCAPEMENT

Watches are often identified by their type of escapement. The type of escapement used in these early watches is known as the *verge and fusee*. It was used for over two hundred years. As with many other things pertaining to watch and clock movements, no one knows for sure who first made it. Let's look more closely at the verge.

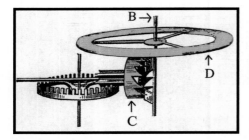

Plate 15. Verge and fusee escapement.

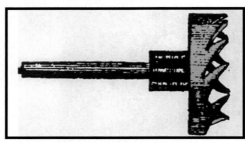

Plate 16. Crown wheel.

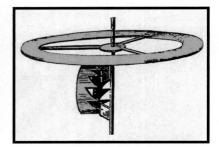

Plate 17. Balance wheel.

The verge is an arbor (B) with two little flags called *pallets*. These pallets are positioned towards the top and bottom of the crown wheel (C), which is perpendicular to the verge. The crown wheel is identifiable by little pointed teeth, similar to the ones on a crown except that they lean slightly to one side.

Now let's use this early drawing of a French watch to see how the parts go together.

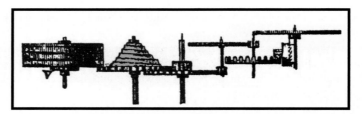

Plate 18. Side view.

Plate 19. Top view.

Drawings of an early French watch movement.

SIXTEENTH CENTURY TIMELINE

1500 — Watches first came on the scene. The first ones were sometimes round, like the musk balls of the period.

1517 — The beginning of the Reformation, by Martin Luther in Wittenberg, Germany.

1519 — Ulrich Zwingli started Reformation in Switzerland.

1522 — Megellan sailed around the world.

1525 – 1550 — Round balance wheel used, as well as the foliot, or dumbbell.

1525 — Watchmaking centers in the French cities of Blois, Dijon, Paris, and Stutagart.

1525 — Fusee and stackfreed used in watches. Early fusee used catgut.

1530 — Earliest known dated watch was made in southern Germany for Philip Melanchthon.

1530 — Watchmakers began to use brass plates, superceding iron.

1544 — First clockmakers guild was established in Paris.

1550 — Oval, or egg-shaped, watches made their appearance.

1553 — Thomas Bayard was mentioned as a watchmaker in Geneva. He was one of the first recorded watchmakers there.

1560 — Larger balance wheel was used.

1570 — Octagonal and hexagonal watches became fashionable.

1575 – 1600 — Rock crystal became a popular material for watch cases.

1575 — Watchmaking started in England.

1577 – 1580 — Francis Drake sailed around the world.

1582 — Gregorian calendar was introduced to Roman Catholics by Pope Gregory.

1587 — Although watches had been made in Switzerland prior to this date, watchmaking as an industry was introduced to this country by Ch. Cusin.

1597 — Clockmakers guild was formed in Blois.

1598 — Edict of Nantes marked the end of the religious wars in France.

Late Sixteenth Century — To counterbalance the hand, the tail of the hand became longer. This allowed the tail to point to the alarm. The engraving on the dial became more elaborate.

SIXTEENTH CENTURY WATCHES

Most watches from this time period are housed in museums or private collections around the world. Occasionally, someone's collection does come onto the market. The Sandberg Collection was a superb collection that was auctioned by Antiquorum. This auction company always has the very finest catalogs with beautiful photographs and a wealth of well-documented and well-researched information about each watch.

With Antiquorum's kind permission, I have included its photographs and descriptions and the realized prices of some of the watches from its auction catalogs. Most of the watches in this section are from the catalog of the Sandberg Collection.

Plate 20. Drum Watch.
German, second quarter of the sixteenth century.
Exceptional and important, gilt metal, tambour-shaped watch with concealed dial and iron movement.

Case. Three-body, drum-shaped, hinged covers, the from pierced with two rows of 12 openings each for the hours, the center pierced and engraved with a six oak-leaf rosette, the edge with laurel leaves, back cover etched in relief with four stylized heart-shaped leaf scrolls, each with a fleur-de-lis inside surrounded by arabesques, the band also in arabesques, small ring pendant. **Dial.** Fixed to the band cover. the edge with twelve touch studs, the hour chapter ring with Roman numerals from I to XII. An inner ring with Arabic numerals from 12 to 24 with a Z in place of 2, the centre engraved with arabesques, single, blued-iron elaborate hand M. 46.6 mm circular, entirely of iron, full plate, three rectangular pillars, two with concave from edges, fusee and gutline with five and half turns, the cone loosely fitted on short, straight fusee wheel arbor, the verge escapement controlled by a foloit, S-shaped cock, pinned from underneath, five-wheel iron train (48. 48/6. 30/5. 30/5. 15/5.), ratchet and click mainspring setup, escape wheel mounted between two arms stemming from a block slipping over one of the pillars, mainspring cover fastened by four riveted pins, hour wheel driven from the fusee arbor. **Movement.** Fastened into the case from underneath by two pivoted, spring-loaded latches.
Diam. 54 mm. Published in the Sandberg book, pages 24 – 25. **$34,564.00.**
Photo and description courtesy of Antiquorum Auctioneers 31 Mar 2001.

Plate 21. Theseus and the Minotaur.
Tambour watch, German, circa 1570.
Extremely rare and important gilt tambour-shaped, single-hand, hour-striking clock watch with iron movement, stackfreed. Foliot and hog's bristle regulator.

Case. Drum-shaped, "fermee" type, hinged top and fixed bottom, the front pierced with 12 openings to see the hours with Minotaur's masks between them, the centre with a very well-executed bas-relief of a knight on horseback, pierced band and bottom cove, the band with scrolls and tendrils, the back with masks and figures in the "grotesque" manner typical of the German Renaissance. **Dial.** Gilt metal, hinged to the case, twelve tactile knob markers for night reading, outer Roman I to XII hour chapter ring, engraved inner quarter-hour divisions and innermost chapter with Arabic 13 to 24 hour numerals in the German style, pinhole for setting the striking, the centre with Mauresque pattern. Blued-steel hand. **Movement.** 40.9 mm, polished iron, full plate, four rectangular pillars, C-shaped stackfreed and going barrel, verge escapement, brass escape wheel, foliot and hog's bristle mounted on a pivoted, adjustable lever, small iron S-shaped cock secured by a screw, five-wheel iron striking train driven by an open spring fixed to a post mounted on the inside of the back plate, count wheel on the back plate, striking on a bell fixed to the inside of the case. Diam. 54 mm, height 23 mm. Published in the Sandberg book, pages 28-29. **$15,815.00.**
Photo and description courtesy of Antiquorum Auctioneers, 31 Mar 2001.

Plate 22. Unsigned.
German, possibly Strasburg, circa 1570.
Highly important, rare gilt bronze, tambour-shape balance spring, single-hand pendant watch with iron movement, double fusee, foliot and a hog's bristle regulator in leather fitted box.

Case. Two-body, drum-shaped, hinged front cover, fixed back, identical front and back pierced with 12 openings for the hours in the front and for the sound in the back, the centers pierced and engraved with Moresque pattern, the edges with repeated engraving, the band pierced and engraved with strap-work, small ring pendant, hook locking. **Dial.** Hinged, gilt metal, the edge with twelve touch studs, the hour chapter ring with radial Roman numerals from I to XII, an inner ring with Arabic numerals from 12 to 24 with a Z in place of 2. The center engraved with wind rose and sun rays. Single blued-iron arrow hand. **Movement.** 50.5 mm, circular, entirely of iron, full plate, bayonet fixing to the dial feet, three rectangular pillars with concave front edges, fusee and gut line with five turns, the cone loosely fitted on short, straight fusee wheel arbor, ratchet and click mainspring set-up, verge escapement controlled by a foliot with pivoted hog's bristle adjustable lever, S-shaped cock, secured by a screw, five-wheel iron train with five-wheel pinions, escape wheel mounted between C-shaped brass bracket mounted over a square post riveted to the back plate, mainspring covers fastened by four riveted pins, hour wheel driven from the fusee arbor striking movement, also with fusee and gut driving four-wheel steel train, gilt count plate on the back plate, striking on a bell screwed to the case by a single hammer.
Diam. 64 mm. **$73,720.00.**
Photo and description courtesy of Antiquorum Auctioneers, 16 Nov 2002.

Plate 23. Oval striking watch.
German school, circa 1580, maker's mark "M.S.," possibly Martin Schmidt, Prague.
Fine and very rare silver and gilt metal, oval, single-hand two-train clock-watch.

Case. Three-body, "fermee" type, hinged gilt metal covers, both pierced and engraved with a Gothic rosette, the front to allow for reading of the dial. the back with an elongated geometrical pattern, the silver band engraved with floral decoration, once with champlevé enamel, swivel pendant, loose ring, small gilt finial at the bottom. **Dial.** Silver, outer I to XII hour Roman chapter with half-hour divisions, quarter-hour ring inside and inner ring for 13 to 24 Arabic hours in the German style, center once with champlevé enamel, engraved with a flower vase with a bird on top, blued-steel hand. **Movement.** Oval. 40 x 49 mm, gilt brass full plate, turned column pillars, fusee and chain, five-wheel iron train, verge escapement, two-arm iron circular balance, small brass S-shaped cock secured by a screw, pierced and curved foot, iron striking train with brass fixed barrel engraved with alternating horizontal lines, iron count wheel on the back plate, gilt hammer striking on round shallow bell mounted inside back cover. Stamped on the back plate "MS," with inverted goblet symbol between the letters.
Diam. 71 x 50 mm. Published in the Sandberg book, pages 30 – 31. **$12,630.00.**
Photo and description courtesy of Antiquorum Auctioneers, 31 Mar 2001.

Plate 24. Octagonal striking watch.
David Haisermann, Augsbourg, circa 1580, maker's mark "DH."
Fine and very rare gilt metal, octagonal, single-hand three-train clock-watch with six-hour striking and alarm, made for the Italian market.

Case. Three-body, octagonal. The front cover faceted, fluted band. Hinged faceted back with the centre pierced and engraved with a Renaissance rosette, octagonal pendant with loose bow, small turned finial. **Dial.** Silver applied ring with Roman chapters, inner rotating gilt alarm dial with Arabic numerals in the German style, small rosette in the centre. Blued-steel arrow hand.
Movement. Octagonal, 50 x 40 mm, gilded full plate, turned baluster pillars, fixed barrel engraved with foliage, verge escapement, two-arm circular foliot, hog's bristle mounted on adjustable lever, gilt metal cock pierced and engraved with floral decoration with clear S-shaped skeleton, secured by a screw. Five wheel train with gilt four-spoke wheels, striking from a fixed barrel with a gilt hammer shaped and engraved like a boar's head, six-hour gilt count wheel mounted on the back plate, alarm also from a fixed barrel with four-wheel iron train, all barrels and the striking train escape wheel bridge florally engraved, striking and alarm on a shallow round bell mounted inside the back cover.
Stamped "DH" on the back plate.
Dim. 73 x 44 mm. Published in the Sandberg book, pages 30 – 31. **$23,930.00.**
Photo and description courtesy of Antiquorum Auctioneers, 31 Mar 2001.

Plate 25. Cushion-shaped watch.
German, circa 1590, maker's mark "PB," possibly Paulus Braun, Augsburg.
Fine and rare gilt metal, hour striking, single-hand three-train clock-watch with concealed dial, alarm, stackfreed, foliot and hog's bristle regulator.

Case. Double-body, tambour-like but with cushioned band and slightly domed covers, the front lid pierced with 24 heart-shaped openings for the hours, the center pierced and engraved with a rosette, the band and the back decorated with arabesques typical for the period, flower blossoms and foliage, short pendant and loose ring.
Dial. Gilt metal, hinged to the case, outer chapter with twelve Roman chapters divided for quarters, with 3 to 24 hour Arabic numerals in the German style, innermost revolving ring for the alarm. Blued-steel hand. **Movement.** 47.2 mm, gilt brass full plate with five pillars, C-shaped stackfreed and going barrel, five-wheel brass train, verge escapement, steel foliot, hog's bristle mounted on a pivoted adjustable lever, small gilt S-shaped cock, striking train driven by a fixed barrel with five-wheel brass train, count wheel on the back plate, alarm driven by a fixed barrel with four-wheel train, the bell mounted to the bottom of the case.
Stamped "PB" on either side of a town's mark on the movement.
Diam. 65 mm. Published in the Sandberg book, pages 36 – 37. **$12,673.00.**
Photo and description courtesy of Antiquorum Auctioneers, 14 Jun 2003.

Plate 26. Jacques Bulcke, France, circa 1590.
Fine and very rare gilt metal oval single-hand watch.

Case. Two-body, "fermee" type, domed hinged polished cover and back, the back with round shutter, fluted band decorated with geometrical pattern. **Dial.** Oval, gilded, central round 24 hour chapter ring with I to XII radial Roman chapters and star half-hour markers, inner ring from 13 to 24, touch pins for night reading, framed by finely engraved flowers, foliage, cornucopias, and vases. Blued-steel beetle hand. **Movement.** 41 x 51 mm, oval, gilt brass full plate, turned baluster pillars, fusee and gut line, short four-wheel train, the first one with six-leaf pinion, the other with five, two-arm steel circular foliot, elongated gilt pinned, pierced, and foliage-engraved cock, wheel and click setup, the border engraved with scrolls and flowers.
Signed on the back plate.
Diam. 72 x 49 mm. Published in the Sandberg book, pages 38 – 39. **$15,180.00.**
Photo and description courtesy of Antiquorum Auctioneers, 3 Mar 2001.

Plate 27. Hans Koch, Munich, sundial attributed to Marcus Purman of Munich, dated 1592.
Highly important and exceptionally fine gilt bronze pre-balance spring, single-hand hour-striking clock-watch, alarm, sundial, compass, stackfreed, foliot and hog's bristle regulator with rack and pinion micro metric adjustment.

Case. Tambour-shaped, hinged top and fixed bottom, the front pierced with 12 heart-shaped openings for the hours, floral engraving in the center, border engraved with floral and foliate pattern, small disc in the center engraved with a rosette holding compass on the other side, which has a sundial in the center with a spring-loaded hinged gnomon and Arabic scale, pierced band and bottom cover, the band with hunting scene, hounds chasing boars, the back with a horseman in the center, flowers and foliage around, border same as the front, small ring pendant. **Dial.** Gilt metal, hinged to the case, outer radial Roman 12 hour chapter ring, engraved inner quarter-hour divisions and innermost chapter with 24 hour (13 to 24) Arabic division with German *Z* for numeral *2*, twelve touch pins in the outermost ring, pinhole for setting the striking, the center revolving alarm disc with Arabic numerals in German style, center engraved with wind rose and sun ray motif. Single blued-steel hand. **Movement.** 54 mm, iron, mounted to the dial by bayonet fixing, full plate, four rectangular pillars, C-shaped stackfreed and going barrel, verge escapement with foliot and hog's bristle mounted on a pivoted, adjustable (rack and pinion) lever, steel train, four-wheel train, small iron S-shaped cock secured by a screw, five-wheel iron striking train driven from a fixed barrel, the last pinion with a fly in a form of a round-shaped brass weight, count wheel on the back plate driven by four pins mounted on the end of the first striking wheel. All wheels in small countersinks, striking on a bell of rectangular cross-section mounted with a screw to the bottom of the case, strikes with a single hammer lifted by pins of the second wheel of the striking train, alarm driven from fixed barrel with steel train and single hammer ringing the same bell.

Maker's mark "HK" punched in the back plate, along with Munich city mark, sundial incused "MP" and engraved with date.
Diam. 72 mm, height 29 mm. **$6,647.00.**
Photo and description courtesy of Antiquorum Auctioneers, 31 Mar 2001.

Plate 28. Nicollas Vallin, London, circa 1595.
Fine and rare gilt metal, oval, single-hand concealed-dial watch.

Case. Two-body, "fermee" type, oval, domed back engraved with an allegorical figure of justice, hinged front cover engraved with a figure of Peace, fluted band engraved with a stylised laurel leaf pattern. **Dial.** Oval, gilt metal, Roman hour chapters hour chapter ring with inner half-hour marks, touch pins for night reading, engraved with a cherub resting his elbow on a skull and an hour-glass on the table behind, in a solemn reminder that our lives are passing away with the hours which may have been adapted from an illustrated "ars moriendi" book-block. Blued-steel "arrow" hands. **Movement.** Oval, 36 x 46 mm, gilt brass full plate, turned baluster pillars, fusee and gut line, short four-wheel train with five-leaf pinions, verge escapement, three-arm steel circular balance, blued-steel balance spring, elongated pinned cock pierced and engraved with asymmetrical floral decoration, wheel and click set-up. Signed on the back plate.
Diam. 67 x 42 mm. Published in the Sandberg book, pages 40-41. **$7,670.00.**
Photo and description courtesy of Antiquorum Auctioneers, 31 Mar 2001.

Plate 29. The Salamander.
Unsigned, probably C. Phelizot, Oijon, dated 1597.
Very fine and very rare silver, octagonal, pre-balance spring, single-hand watch.

Case. Three-body, "fermee," both covers with eight triangular panels, engraved with Cupids playing different musical instruments, inside covers engraved with symbols of friendship, prosperity, and love; the front of the horn-of-plenty: pierced heart, an anchor, clasped hands, and two pairs of initials, "FF" and "II," the back with a burning heart, quivers of arrows, and two sets of initials, "MD" and "PD"; gilt metal band with silver ribbon engraved with rabbits, stag, and hounds, below the back cover there is a silver octagonal dust-protective cover (later called *cuvette*) engraved with a mountain village scene with symbols of love along the edge, gilt metal reverse engraved with coat-of-arms, small finial and loose ring pendant. **Dial.** Silver with radial Roman numerals and half-hour markers, center engraved with a village scene, mounted on octagonal gilt metal dial plate engraved with symbol of love. Gold and green enamel single hand in the shape of a salamander. **Movement.** Octagonal, 28 x 28 mm, gilt brass full plate, turned baluster pillars, fusee and gut line short three-wheel train, verge escapement, circular steel foliot irregular pinned cock pierced and engraved with flowers and wild strawberries, ratchet wheel mainspring set up with large pierced and engraved click matching the cock.
Dated on the dust cover.
Diam. 42 x 31 mm. **$94,214.00.**
Photo and description courtesy of Antiquorum Auctioneers, 16 Nov 2003.

Chapter II
THE STAGE IS SET
THE SEVENTEENTH CENTURY

By the early 1600s the stage was set as far as basic watch mechanics were concerned. For the next 75 years, there would be very few changes in the movement. The balance cock screw was invented sometime in the first quarter of the century, and between the years of 1640 and 1670, chains began to replace the catgut used on the fusee. The Germans made use of the chain as early as 1640, but the Swiss and French preferred the gut line.[3] Meanwhile, because of the involvement of the many jewelers who entered into watch making, the watch became a beautiful piece of jewelry that had the added novelty and prestige of a timepiece.

CASES

Jewelers and case makers made these the glory years for case decorations. In the last decade of the sixteenth century, silver was combined with the gilded brass to make beautiful two-color cases that were often pierced and highly engraved. This combination continued through the early years of the new century.

Crystal cases were also popular, because they provided a beautiful case while protecting the dial and movement. They were truly the first watch crystals, and continued to be in vogue until the middle of the century. Jean Rousseau, a master watchmaker of the period, specialized in making "form" watches out of rock crystal. His cases with animal, cruciform, and tulip motifs are especially beautiful. Rousseau was certainly not the only maker of these form watches. Because form watches were a very popular style, many watchmakers used their skills to make crystal cases and capture their shares of the market.

Plate 30. This is a later watch circa 1660, by Jean Rousseau le jeune (1606-1684), one of Jean Rousseau I 's (1580-1642) seven sons; he followed in his father's trade. It is interesting to note that the elder Rousseau was the great-great-grandfather of the philosopher Jean-Jacques Rousseau.[4]

Watch cases were also made in the form of shells, clovers, pears, stars, teardrops, fleur-de-lis, crosses, and even skulls. One reason that these form watches were so popular was that wearing a watch not only told much about the financial status of the wearer, but the shape of the watch could say volumes about the interests or beliefs of its owner. For instance, the skull head, or death's head, watch was a sign that the wearer was cognizant of the brevity and ultimate end of life. The oldest dated skull head watch was made in Geneva; it is dated 1620. A portrait of Elizabeth of Neuchatel dated 1624 shows her with a death's head watch suspended from the girdle. Ann Boleyn is also said to have worn this style of watch. These three examples show that this motif was popular in Geneva, Germany, and England. This style of watch waned in popularity later in the century only to be revived again in the next century. New collectors, beware!! Good reproductions of the watch case and dial are being made today, but the movement is often the Swiss lever type that was not available until many years later. The makers usually use a mechanical wristwatch movement and convert it to key wind. It was not made to deceive, but someone who is not acquainted with movements could be fooled.

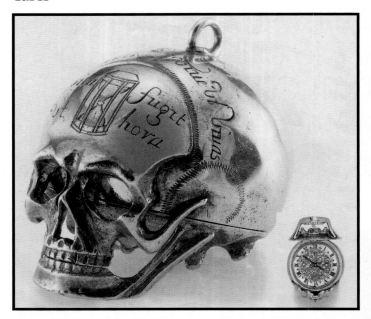

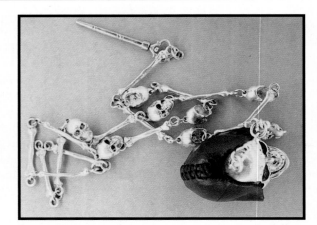

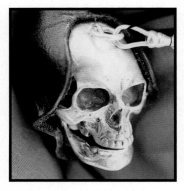

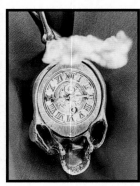

Plate 31. Watch #2 is a silver, pre–balance spring, single hand form watch designed as a skull. Circa 1650. For a complete description and realized price, see plate #69 photo on p. 42.

About 1620, tortoise-covered cases came onto the scene. This new type of case was used by some watchmakers until the early nineteenth century. Because tortoise shell is a natural plastic, it can be heated and molded. For watchcases, it was heated and formed around a gilded brass shell. As hot tortoise shell cools it emits a glue-like film, which, along with the natural contraction of the shell, made for a snug fit. For some cases, openings were made in the heated material and inlaid with gold or silver decorations in order to create beautiful patterns. As the shell cooled, it shrunk around the tiny pieces and held them securely in place. This finished work was known as pique.

Plates 32, 33 & 34. Watch #3 is a limited production copy of a skull watch that was presented to Mary Queen of Scots. The maker has made 300 in the last 30 years. One end of the hand has a stork, a symbol of the "bringer of life." The other end has a vulture, the symbol of the "taker of life." The movement is a modern Swiss lever that has been converted to a key wind. $2,500.00. *Courtesy of Joseph Conway, dealer.*

Pair cases were introduced around 1640, to protect the beautifully enameled cases that were produced at that time and also to keep dust out of the movement. A pair case is just what the name implies, a watch with two cases, an outer one that protects the inner one. Ten years after the introduction of pair cases, cases decorated with *repoussé* also became the vogue, and it was not a coincidence that pair cases became popular to protect this beautiful work. Repoussé is a decorative technique of raising a pattern on metal by beating, punching, or hammering from the reverse side. This technique is also called *embossing*. The repoussé of the 1600s consisted of radial fluting. Believe it or not, before the decade of the 1650s was over, the triple-cased watch had appeared on the market.

Plate 35. For more information, please refer to plate #65 photo on p. 40.

Before pair-cases arrived on the scene, there was another way of keeping dust and dirt from getting into the movement when winding or wearing the watch. This was achieved by putting a round, disk-like cover over a winding hole in the back of the case. This disk rotated so that it could be pushed to either side or the top when the wearer needed to insert the winding key. Because a single case was less expensive than a pair case, some people preferred this option. Others liked the convenience of dealing with only one case. Even though the pair case was by far the most popular case by the 1690s, cases with the shutter-type disk continued to be made by some makers for another 70 years.

By the third quarter of the seventeenth century, some watches had a smooth, or chased, finished case with a shagreen outer case. *Shagreen* usually refers to sharkskin or ray skin, but the term was sometimes used to include skins from other types of fish or even other types of animals. The sharkskin or ray skin was pliable, but hard enough to be durable. It was used to cover a base of gilded brass and was decorated with pins in a technique referred to as *pinwork*. Shagreen case making was a trade unto itself in watch-making. Because shagreen cases were not made of gold or silver, they were exempt from the taxes levied on the precious metal cases and still exhibited a decorative look. Shagreen pin-worked cases were referred to by some as the "poor man's pique."

Plate 36. A pin-worked shagreen case.

Plate 37. Pin-work dyed horn case owned by Dr. Theodore Crom.

ENAMEL EMBELLISHMENTS

In the early years of the century, the type of enamel embellishment used was *Champlevé*. It was used to define the Roman numerals and half-hour markers on the dial. At times the entire dial was decorated in this manner (see below) This form of enamel required digging out the metal to create the desired shape and then filling the indentations with a flux enamel that would then be fired onto the metal. Because each color had to be fired at a different temperature, the craftsmen had to start with the color that had the highest melting point and then go to the next color in declining temperature until all the colors had been fired. For a good example of champlevé enamel, see below.

Plate 38. Champlevé dial circa 1635.
Photo coutesy of Antiquorum Auctioneers, from the Sandberg Collection Catalogue.

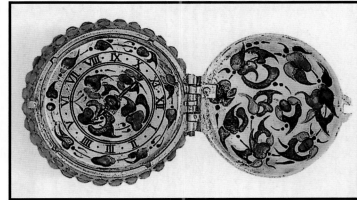

Plate 39. Champlevé dial circa 1640.
Photo courtesy of Antiquorum Auctioneers, Sandberg Collection Catalogue.

Painting on enamel was introduced around 1632, and it wasn't long until this type of enamel became a favored form of embellishment. Watches made in the form of the cross or other shapes and decorated with enameled scenes from the scriptures were a favorite of the religious or those who wanted to appear virtuous.

The cities of Limoge and Bloise, France, and Geneva, Switzerland, became important centers for enamel artists. The most important family of enamel painters in this period was the Toutin family of France. Jean Toutin is the most well-known member of the family. He is credited with developing the technique of enamel painting in about 1632. According to an Antiquorum catalog, "Toutin developed a true miniature method, refining the existing technique (the Limoge school) and extending the range of colors." It is reported that he kept this technique a family secret for a while, but somehow it spread through the painting community. He also made design books that were popular throughout Europe and England, but he is best known for being a master of enamel painting.

Geneva produced the enamel artist Jean Petitot, his brother-in-law, Jacques Bordier, and the Huaud family. In 1671, Pierre I Huaud founded the Huaud school in Geneva. His three sons, Pierre II, Jean-Pierre, and Ami, worked together. This trio of respected enamel painters was referred to as the "Brothers Huaud." For more information on enamel painters of Geneva, please refer to the beautiful book *Clock and Watch Museum Geneva*.

Because the watch was a prestigious sign of status, checking the time became a social production. The wearer was sure to garner attention as he or she picked up the precious timepiece and slowly and carefully opened one enameled case lid and then another. All hard enameled pieces need enamel on the underside (counter enameling) in order to be properly fired. But the enamel artist during these year took it a step further and decorated the inside of the back case with enameled scenes and decorations that would compliment the case and make a fine showing when the watch was ceremoniously wound. The handmade keys were usually also enameled to match the watch. Before 1675, the winding procedure was usually performed twice a day. Around that time a fourth train wheel was added to the movement, making it possible for the watch to run for 26 hours.

It's always good to remember that not everyone shared the urge to be conspicuous. In 1640, just a few years after the development of enamel painting was introduced, Puritan style watches were used in England. The watch cases of these were often oval shaped and very plain.

Plate 40. Enamel by "Brothers Huaud." 1700s.

THE EMERGENCE OF THE POCKET WATCH

These were also the years that saw the evolution of the pendant watch into a pocket watch. Why wasn't the watch worn in the pocket before this time period? The answer is simple: there were no pockets. Pockets were first made and used around 1625, but it wasn't until the waistcoat, which had a waist pocket, became popular in 1675 that the transformation from pendant to pocket watch became complete.

Coincidentally, the same period in which the pocket watch was introduced also ushered in the mechanical development of the century — THE BALANCE SPRING. As with many inventions, several unrelated individuals were working toward the solution to the problem at the same time. As they say, "great minds think alike." This was certainly the case which the development of the balance spring.

The two main characters in the scenario were Dr. Robert Hooke and Christian Huygens. Hooke was a professor of geometry at Gresham College and had somewhat of a reputation when it came to his relationships with women. Huygens was an astronomer and mathematician who was already credited, as was Dr. Hooke, with the invention of the pendulum clock.

Dr. Hooke and Thomas Tompion, also a renowned watchmaker, worked on a spiral spring for years. Hooke was the idea man on this project, and Tompion put these ideas into tangible form. Hooke came up with the idea in 1658, and Tompion made the prototype in 1675.

Huygens completed his watch that same year. As fate would have it, he received the credit and the patent. In this case though, it was also more than fate. His really was the better solution for the proper hairspring. Rhiengard Meis, in his book *Pocket Watches,* notes that the Huygens design was the only one that placed the spring around the balance arbor in spiral form. Dr. Hooke's spirals were either "straight or snake-like springs." Huygens's spiral, or coiled, spring not only made the watch a viable timepiece, it precipitated changes in the look of the watch. For the first time, the watch could be accurate to within a few minutes a day. Consequently, a minute hand and marks could be added to the dial, along with an outside ring that often had Arabic numbers denoting each five minute interval.

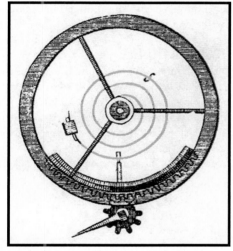

Some watches had minute hands before 1675 (see the 1660 watch with a minute hand and a short balance spring, p. 45). But it took Huygens's development to enable reasonably accurate timekeeping, because the new version allowed the gear wheels to escape one equal oscillation at a time.

The new minute hand was not immediately accepted. People were accustomed to one hand on a watch, and to them, two hands seemed confusing. Watchmakers, always eager to please and to keep their share of the watch-making business, came up with some pretty novel ideas. A popular one was a watch with a "wandering hour dial." It did not have any hands; instead, it had a rotating disk and the hour number was viewed through a semi-circular cutout in the outer dial. By the end of the century it had waned in popularity, but it continued to be made throughout the first quarter of the next century.

Another novel innovation was the so-called pendulum watch. Of course it did not have a real pendulum, only something that gave the appearance of one. Because most people were accustomed to the accuracy of the pendulum clock, watchmakers decided that by attaching a small, bob-like disk to the balance wheel and cutting a semi-circular opening in the dial or the back bridge, when the wheel oscillated back and forth the disk would have the appearance of a pendulum and thus inspire more trust in the watch's accuracy. Also, the result was fun to watch. Examples of this faux pendulum watch can be found as late as 1725.

Plate 41. The balance spring is also known as a *hairspring,* because some springs are the size of a hair. This fine spring is attached at one end to a collet on the balance staff and on the other to a stud on the balance cock or movement plate.

Another change in the look of the watch took place, but this time the waistcoat, not the balance spring, was responsible. The part of the pendant that the watch chain was threaded through was changed to be on the same plane as the watch face (as they are today). This made it easier to slide the watch into and out of the watch pocket.

In the last quarter of the seventeenth century, there seemed to be an explosion of new ideas and developments in watchmaking. As you might remember, clock watches from the sixteenth century had a mechanism to strike a bell on the hour. The problem was that it struck day and night. There was no way to make it strike only when the owner wanted to know the time. This problem was solved in 1686, when Daniel Quare invented a repeating watch. At least, he was the person King James II credited with its invention. As usual, others were working on the same idea at the same time. Quare's invention allowed the wearer to hear the time at will by pressing a lever that activated an hour strike and a quarter-hour strike. These watches were made to order for a select few. It took another one hundred and twenty years, and many other developments, for it to have widespread use.

Plate 42. Wandering hour dial circa 1705. *Photo Courtesy of Antiquorum Auctioneers.*

THE TIMES

At the dawn of the seventeenth century, watches were still only a novelty for the very rich. The price of a plain watch was enough money to comfortably support a common laborer's family for a year.[5]

As usual, what was happening in the world in the seventeenth century had profound effects on the watchmaking industry. In 1618, a series of wars now known as the Thirty Years War began in Germany. This series of wars started over who would be the next Holy Roman Emperor — the protestant Prince Frederick or the Roman Catholic King Ferdinand of Bohemia. Both were princes of Germany.[6] Soon this battle between the two religious factions was joined by supporters of like kind in other countries. Without going into details about who won what battles, the war in Germany finally ended in 1648. The Peace of Westphalia granted parts of Alsace and Lorraine to France. As you might imagine, thirty years of war left Germany in ruins and the people devastated by the loss of loved ones, many of whom were watch and clock makers.

The Edict of Nantes (1598) gave the French Hugenots the right to practice Protestantism. In this climate of freedom, watchmaking flourished and the production of French watches expanded. As French production was rising, German production declined. By the end of the first quarter of the seventeenth century, the French dominated the watch market.

TULIPMANIA

It's sometimes amazing how the seemingly trivial things that are a part of life are incorporated into material items that are used every day. In the seventeenth century, tulips became one of these things; the world seemed to be struck by "Tulipmania." It had its beginnings in 1593, when the botanist Carolus Clustius brought tulips to Holland from Constantinople for research purposes. The Dutch tulip trade started when someone stole some of these bulbs from his garden and planted them. By 1636, "one Viceroy tulip cost approximately as much as ten tons of cheese."[7] Tulips were even bought and sold as a commodity. Because of the popularity and prestige of these flowers, the tulip motif was incorporated into jewelry and watch designs. Cases were made in the shape of tulips. This motif was also used to decorate the center chapter of the dial, which often included tulip-shaped hands.

 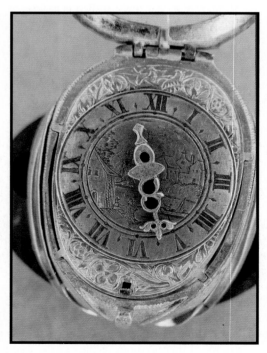

Plates 43 and 44. Tulip watch from the collection of Dr. Crom.

Plate 45.

Plate 46.

Movement of tulip watch.

During much of this century, King Louis XIV was the ruler of France. He ascended to the throne in 1643, at the age of five. In 1664, at the age twenty-four, he assumed the full duties of monarch. His dislike of the Huguenots led to his mistreatment of them, and to his revocation of the Edict of Nantes in 1685. After this, 400,000 Huguenots left the country[8] Many immigrated to England and Switzerland. Because Geneva's strict class system allowed only citizens and *burghes* (the governing class of the city) to become master watchmakers, many moved on to the Jura mountains. Here they began to do piece work for the Geneva watchmakers. The watchmakers who went to London were recognized for their talent, and played a big part in the rise in production of English watches.

Plate 47. Portrait of a woman circa 1612 – 1690. Note the watch in her right hand.

SEVENTEENTH CENTURY TIMELINE

1609 — The Netherlands gained independence from Spain.

1615 – 1630 — Crystals made of rock crystal were used to cover and protect the dial and movement.

1618 – 1648 — Thirty Years War. Germany lost its watchmaking dominance to France.

1620 — Pilgrims founded the New Plymouth.

1620 — Tortoise shell–covered cases came onto the scene and were used until circa 1800.

1624 — Virginia became a Crown colony.

1600 – 1630 — Sometime in these years, someone invented the balance cock screw. Prior to this invention, the balance cock was fastened with a stud and pin.

1625 — Pockets made their first appearance.

1631 — Worshipful Company of Clockmakers was founded in Britain.

1632 — Introduction of colored enamel painting. All watches with this type of embellishment were made after this date.

1635 — Paul Viet of Blois, France, invented enamel dials.

1640 — Because watches needed protection against dirt, dust, etc., pair cases came into vogue about this time.

1640 — Puritan-style watches in England. Many were oval and had a very plain case.

1648 — End of the Thirty Years War. Millions of Germans died, and many of their towns and cities were destroyed. The Peace of Westphalia gave parts of Alsace and Lorrain to France.

1650 — Triple-cased watches made their appearance about this time.

1650 — Gold and silver repoussé cases made their appearance. Repoussé was used on the second case. The inner case was usually plain, and the third, outer case was usually made of shagreen, tortoise shell, or shark skin, which was usually decorated with pins.

1660 – 1670 — Chains began to replace gut cord on fusees.

1670 — A wheel cutting machine was developed by Dr. Robert Hook for Tompion.

1675 — Huygens developed the balance spring. This thin, coiled spring provided more accuracy, which paved the way for the watch to have a minute hand.

1675 — The waistcoat came into fashion; it had a waist pocket in which to carry a watch. It was introduced in England by Charles II.

1675 — Watches became larger, to accommodate the balance wheel and the spring. This resulted in larger balance cocks.

1675 — British watchmakers began to take the lead from the French.

1676 — Mechanisms that enabled watches to repeat the hour (repeaters) were invented by Edward Booth.

1685 — In France, King Louis XIV revoked the Edict of Nantes. This resulted in over 50,000 Huguenot families (approx. 400,000 people) leaving France. Many of the fine watchmakers moved to Switzerland, England, Holland, and Germany. This lead to the decline of French watches.

1685 — Gold cases begin to be hallmarked in England.

1686 — The repeating watch was developed by Daniel Quare.

1687 — The minute hand was incorporated into many watches.

1698 — English makers were required by law to put their names on watches.

1690s — Rural landscapes and scenes from Roman mythology were popular for enameled case embellishments on Swiss watches.

1690 — Wandering hour and sun and moon watches appeared.

1695 — Patent issued to Thompion, William Houghton, and Edward Booth (who also used the last name Barlow). Its description reads like it could have been for a concept such as the cylinder escapement.

SEVENTEENTH CENTURY WATCHES

Photos of watches from the seventeenth century are presented in chronological order.

**Plate 48. Charles Desrue, Nancy, circa 1600.
Very fine and very rare silver and gilt metal,
single-hand oval watch.**

Case. Three-body, hinged polished back cover
with round shutter, the front cover with circular
glazed opening for the dial, the silver band
engraved with bird and floral decoration. **Dial.** Silver applied ring with radial Roman chapters and
half-hour markers, on a gilt metal floral engraved
plate. Blued-steel beetle hand. **Movement.** 35 x
46 mm, oval, gilt brass full plate, turned baluster
pillars, fusee and gut line, short four-wheel train,
verge escapement, steel two-arm circular foliot,
rectangular pinned cock, symmetrically pierced
and engraved with scrolls.
Signed on the back plate.
Diam. 51 x 39 mm. Published in the Sandberg
book, pages 38 – 39. **$9,338.00.**
Photo and description courtesy of Antiquorum Auctioneers, 31 Mar 2001.

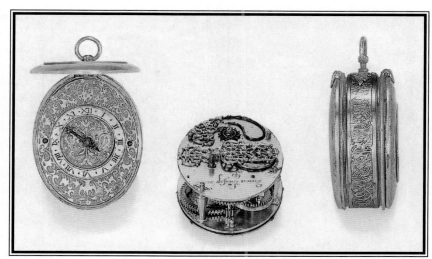

**Plate 49. Circa 1600.
Fine and rare French gilt brass and silver, pre-hairspring antique pocket
watch by Ch. Desrue, Nancy, circa 1600.**

Highly chased **dial** with silver chapter
ring and single blued-steel hand. The
case has traces of the original gilding,
the band has a silver scene of inhabited
folliage. Wonderful gut fusee **movement**
has flat steel balance, beautiful pinned
pierced and engraved cock and set-up
regulator click.
A very fine example.
Diam. 51 x 39 mm. **$18,250.00.**
*Photo and description courtesy of Stephen
Bogoff, Antiquarian Horologist.*

Plate 50. Unsigned, probably Flemish, circa 1610. Very fine and rare gilt metal, single-handed, two-train clock-watch.

Case. Two-body, oval, domed, plain back, band pierced in a baluster pattern for sound, front cover with a small round glazed bezel, small finial at the bottom, short turned pendant, loose ring. **Dial.** Hinged, gilt metal, applied silver ring with radial Roman chapters, half-hour divisions, engraved with coat-of-arms. **Movement.** Oval, 41 x 48 mm, gilt brass balance, blued-steel balance spring, pinned gilt metal cock pierced with foliage, striking from one fixed plain gilded barrel, five-wheel train, blued-steel count wheel on the back plate. Diam. 62 x 52 mm. Published in the Sandberg book, pages 40 – 41. **$11,362.00.**
Photo and description courtesy of Antiquorum Auctioneers, 31 Mar 2001.

Plate 51. Unsigned, German, circa 1620. Fine and rare silver gilt and rock crystal, octagonal, single-hand stackfreed pendant watch.

Case. Two-body, both of elongated, octagonal faceted rock crystal, mounted into a small gilt silver frame, short silver swivel pendant, small gilt silver finial. **Dial.** Circular, silver chapter ring with champlevé enamel radial Roman chapters, centre with translucent dark blue enamel on a flinque ground, with 12 gold stars; mounted on the gilded engraved, hinged plate, gold tulip hand. **Movement.** 21.7 x 27.8 mm, oval, gilt brass full plate, turned baluster pillars, fixed barrel going train, C-shaped stackfreed, verge, escapement, two-arm steel circular foliot with hog's bristle regulator mounted on gilded adjustable arm, gilt brass cock pierced and engraved with asymmetrical foliage.
Signed on the back plate.
Diam. 52 x 28 mm. Published in the Sandberg book, pages 48 – 49. **$21,344.00.**
Photo and description courtesy of Antiquorum Auctioneers, 31 Mar 2001.

Plate 52. Hercules between Virtue and Vice, Pierre Combret a Lyon, circa 1620.
Exceptional and very rare silver and gilt metal, single-hand, oval alarm watch with a concealed dial.

Case. Two-body, "fermee" type, silver hinged, oval, the front cover with magnificent chased and "taille douce" engraving of Hercules at the crossroads, choosing between Virtue and Vice, after an engraving by Etienne Delaune (1518 – 1595), the silver back with King David on the throne and Nathan before him, gilt brass band pierced and engraved with flower and leaf decoration, small finials, chiselled pendant, loose ring. **Dial.** Oval plate, silver with applied gilt metal radial Roman chapters chapter ring, inner revolving alarm disc with Arabic numerals, a small square opening at 12 indicating the hour, engraved outside the chapter ring with a reclining nymph at the top and another nymph and faun below, the sides engraved with fine foliage and flowers. Blued-steel poker hand to set the alarm. **Movement.** 34 x 42 mm, oval, gilt brass full plate, vase pillars, fusee and gut line, short four-wheel train, verge escapement, two arm brass circular foliot, elongated small pinned cock pierced and engraved with flowers, wheel and click setup cock and alarm stop-work cock similarly decorated, alarm from a fixed engraved barrel with two-wheel train with large brass pinion on the second wheel, striking on an oval bell.
Signed on the back plate.
Diam. 76 x 46 mm. Published in the Sandberg book, pages 44 – 45. **$30,682.00.**
Photo and description courtesy of Antiquorum Auctioneers, 31 Mar 2001.

Plate 53. Pigeon A. Clermont, France, circa 1625.
Very fine and very rare silver and gilt metal, oval, single-hand, three-train, astronomical clock-watch with phases of the moon, alarm, and perpetual manual calendar.

Case. Two-body, "fermee" type, oval, polished silver cover and back, the inside of the cover engraved with a branch of blossoms, gilt metal band pierced and engraved with floral decoration, small finial at the bottom, tulip-shaped gilt pendant, loose ring. **Dial.** Silver, oval, hinged, eccentric, gilt metal applied-radial Roman hour chapter ring with half-hour divisions in the lower part, inner silver rotating alarm disc with Arabic numerals and arrow indicating the time, small knob for setting the time, below 12 o'clock aperture for days of the week (in French); at the top, gilt brass ring for the day of the month, on the left, aperture for phases and age of the moon, on the right, aperture for the month and its duration, the entire plate finely engraved with allegories of love with Venus and Cupid. Blued-steel hands. **Movement.** Oval, 44 x 40 mm, gilt brass full plate, turned baluster pillars, fusee and gut line, short four-wheel train with six-leaf pinions, verge escapement, two-arm circular foliot, small pinned cock and engraved with asymmetrical floral pattern, striking from a fixed barrel decorated with pierced and engraved floral pattern, five-wheel train, steel count wheel set on the back plate under a pierced and engraved cock, alarm driven from a fixed and engraved barrel striking on the same bell, ratchet wheel and click setup.
Signed on the back.
Diam. 85 x 52 mm. Published in the Sandberg book, pages 50 – 51. **$29,348.00.**
Photo and description courtesy of Antiquorum Auctioneers, 31 Mar 2001.

Plate 54. Henry Gebart a Strasburg, circa 1630.

Very fine and very rare gilt metal and rock crystal single-hand, fleur-de-lis–shaped pendant form watch.

Case. Two-body, the front and back lobed and carved rock crystal, within a hinged and engraved frame, tulip pendant, loose ring, small finial. **Dial.** Silver disc with Roman chapters and a central engraved town scene, applied to a four-lobed, hinged gilt metal plate engraved with Juno with her peacock and spear attributes. Blued-steel fleur-de-lis hand. **Movement.** Four-lobed, hinged, gilt brass full plate, turned vase pillars fusee and chain for the going train, verge escapement, brass two-arm balance, elongated pinned gilt cock pierced and engraved with fruits and leaves, wheel and click setup with cock similarly decorated.
Signed on the back plate.
Diam. 57 x 35 mm. Published in the Sandberg book, pages 362 – 363. **$20,010.00.**
Photo and description courtesy of Antiquorum Auctioneers 31 Mar 2001.

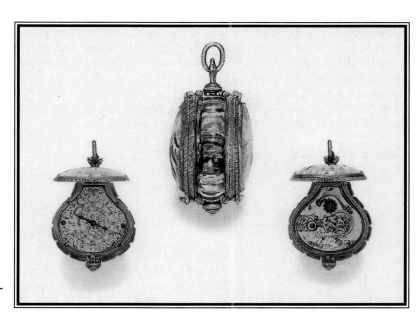

Plate 55. Blampignon. Lyon, circa 1630.
Fine and very rare single-hand rock crystal pendant form watch in the shape of a scallop shell.

Case. Three-body, the hinged covers and band carved in rock crystal and mounted within two gilt frames with geometrical engraving, small finial at the bottom, short pendant, loose ring. **Dial.** Gilt metal, following the shape of the case, engraved Roman chapters, decorated with engraved champleve scrolling. Blued-steel tulip hand. **Movement.** 25 x 25 mm, follows the shape of the case, gilt brass full plate, vase-shaped pillars, and gut line for the going train, verge escapement, two-arm steel circular foliot, elongated pinned cock asymmetrically pierced and engraved, ratchet wheel and click set-up.
Signed on the back plate.
Diam. length 44 mm, width 29 mm. Published in the Sandberg book, pages 366 – 367. **$21,344.00.**
Photo and description courtesy of Antiquorum Auctioneers, 31 Mar 2001.

Plate 56. Henry Beraud Fecit, London, circa 1630.
Very fine and rare silver, single-hand, pendant-form watch with concealed dial, in the shape of a tulip.

Case. Two-body, with six overlapping petals decorated with alternately hatched and polished check-like rectangles, the winding shutter also shaped and engraved as a flower, tulip pendant, loose ring. **Dial.** Silver, oval, hinged, central Roman hour chapter with dot half-hours. Center engraved with a river view with a town on the far bank, the borders florally engraved. Blued-steel tulip hand. **Movement.** 20.6 x 26.5 mm, oval, hinged. Gilt brass full plate, vase pillars, fusee and gutline for the going train, two-arm, plain steel balance. Elongated pinned gilt pierced and engraved with fruit and leaves, worm and wheel setup.
Signed on the movement.
Diam. 38 x 24 mm. Published in the Sandberg book, pages 364 – 365.
$20,010.00.
Photo and description courtesy of Antiquorum Auctioneers, 31 Mar 2001.

Plate 57. J. H. Ester, Geneva, circa 1630.
Very fine and rare silver, gilt metal, and rock crystal single-hand teardrop-shaped pendant form watch.

Case. Three-body, both engraved bezels hinged and fined with rock crystal domes, plain silver band in replacement of a crystal, engraved similarly to the bezels, tulip pendant, loose ring, small finial. **Dial.** Silver ring with Roman chapters and half-hour markers, applied to a teardrop-shaped gilt metal plate engraved with reclining figures and foliage, the center engraved with a rural scene. Blued-steel Fleur-de-lis hand. **Movement.** 22.5 x 30.8 mm, teardrop shaped, gilt brass full plate, turned vase pillars, fusee and gut line for the going train, verge escapement two-arm iron circular foliot, elongated gilt pinned cock pierced and engraved with fruits and leaves, wheel and click setup with similarly decorated cock.
Signed on the back plate.
Diam. 52 x 28 x 21 mm. Published in the Sandberg book, pages 362 – 363. **$28,014.00.**
Photo and description courtesy of Antiquorum Auctioneers, 31 Mar 2001.

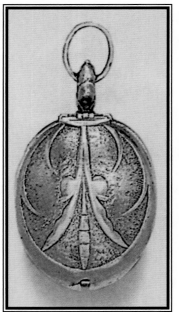

Plate 58. The Tulip.
Henry Grendon at the Exchange, London, circa 1630.
Very fine and very rare lady pendant silver gilt, pre–balance spring, single-hand form watch designed as a tulip.

Case. Two-body, cast, chiseled with three petals, one of which forms the front cover, tulip pendant, loose ring. **Dial.** Silver, hinged, oval, radial Roman hour chapter, inside and outside engraved with tulips and daisies. Single blued-steel tulip hand. **Movement.** 22 x 26 mm, mounted to the dial, fusee and gut line, short four-wheel train with five leaf pinions, pre–balance spring verge escapement with brass balance without a spring, small elongated and regular gilt pinned cock, pierced and engraved with asymmetrical flower and foliate decoration, worm and wheel setup.
Signed on the movement.
Diam. 42 x 25 mm. **$8,855.00.**
Photo and description courtesy of Antiquorum Auctioneers, 14 Jun 2003.

Plate 59. The Holy Family.
F. Baronneau a Paris, painting on enamel attributable to Robert Vauquer, circa 1640.
Magnificent and very rare large 22 ct. gold and enamel pendant watch, with concealed dial.

Case. Double-body, "bassine fermee," with curved-in edge, entirely enamelled with scenes from the life of the Virgin Mary and the Christ Child, from engravings after Simon Vouet (1590 – 1649) depicting the Holy Family after their return from Egypt, when they stayed with Elizabeth, a cousin of the Virgin, and her young son St. John the Baptist. Elizabeth, known as an elderly mother, holds Saint John, who has a cross made of reeds and who points to a small bird which has been tethered by the mother of Jesus. Jesus watches the bird and Saint Joseph stands behind with a book. The theme continues on the cover, with Saint Joseph consulting a book with the words of the prophets and what they foretold. Gold enameled pendant. **Dial.** Silver, with champlevé Roman chapters and inner quarter-hour ring, center chased and engraved with a floral design. Blued-steel tulip hand. **Movement.** 47.5 mm 0, hinged, gilt brass full plate, turned baluster pillars, fusee and gut line for the going train, verge escapement, two-arm steel circular foliot, elongated pierced and engraved gilt cock secured by a screw, ratchet wheel and click setup.
Signed on the backplate.
Diam. 61 mm. Published in the Sandberg book, pages 68 – 69.
$72,210.00.
Photo and description courtesy of Antiquorum Auctioneers, 31 Mar 2001.

Plate 60. Richard Masterson, London, circa 1640.
Very fine and rare silver, single-hand pendant watch in the form of an oval scallop shell, with concealed dial.

Case. Two-body, oval, "bassine fermee" type with curved-in edges, the case entirely chiseled with scallop shell ribs in relief against a matted ground, silver shutter in the form of a scallop shell on the back short tulip pendant, loose ring. **Dial.** Silver, oval, red radial Roman chapters, fine floral engraving inside and outside the chapter ring. Blued-steel tulip hand. **Movement.** 26 x 35 mm. Oval, gilt brass full plate, early Egyptian pillars, fusee and gut line for the going train, verge escapement, two-arm steel circular foliot, elongated pinned cock asymmetrically pierced and engraved with floral decoration, wheel and click setup.
Signed on the movement.
Diam. 30 x 57 mm. Published in the Sandberg book, pages 72 – 73.
$33,350.00.
Photo and description courtesy of Antiquorum Auctioneers, 31 Mar 2001.

Plate 61. La Vierge aux Roses, Blois school enamel, possibly by Christophe Morliere, circa 1640, movement bearing the signature "Goullons a Paris."
Magnificent and extremely rare very large, 22K gold, and enamel single-hand pendant watch, with concealed dial.

Case. Two-body, "bassine fermee," the front lid very finely painted with The Virgin and Child encircled by roses, after an engraving by Simon Vouet (1590 – 1649), the back with a charming scene of the Virgin and the Child in the manger, adored by two angels, also after Vouet, the inside of the lid painted with a garden scene and a classical building in the foreground, inside the back a scene of country festivities with a castle in the background, the band painted with rose buds and blossoms. **Dial.** Silver, champlevé radial Roman chapters, a town scene in the centre. Blued-steel tulip hand. **Movement.** 51 mm 0, hinged, gilt brass full plate, turned baluster pillars, fusee and gut line for the going train, verge escapement with two-arm circular foliot, elongated and irregular cock asymmetrically pierced and engraved with foliage and strawberries and secured by a screw, worm and wheel setup.
Signed on the movement.
Diam. 68 mm. Published in the Sandberg book, pages 64 – 65. **$148,770.00.**
Photo and description courtesy of Antiquorum Auctioneers, 31 Mar 2001.

Plate 62. David Bouquet at London, circa 1640.
Very fine and rare silver and rock crystal, single-hand, lobed pendant watch.

Case. Two-body, "fermee" type, eight lobes on cover and back, mounted to a small hinged and engraved silver frame, fixed silver pendant and small finial. **Dial.** Silver, champlevé radial Roman chapters with half-hour markers and inner quarter-hour ring, the center engraved with a town scene, a tree and fisherman in the foreground, engraved gilt border. Elaborate gilt brass hands **Movement.** 24 mm 0, hinged, gilt brass full plate, narrow Egyptian pillars, fusee and gutline for the going train, verge escapement, two-arm iron circular foliot, elongated silver cock pierced and engraved with asymmetrical floral decoration and a figure of a winged cherub, worm and wheel setup with silver plate.
Signed on the back plate.
Diam. 29 mm. Published in the Sandberg book, pages 72 – 73. **$21,344.00.**
Photo and description courtesy of Antiquorum Auctioneers, 31 Mar 2001.

Plate 63. Sermand, Geneva, circa 1640.
Exceptional gold, enamel, and faceted rock crystal form watch designed as a cross.

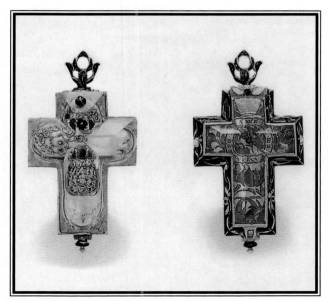

Case. Two-body, rock crystal front and back covers mounted in gold bezels with black champlevé enamel, decorated with gold scrolling pattern and white enamel spots, small enamelled finial, tulip-shaped enamelled pendant. **Dial.** Gold, cross shaped, hinged, with radial Roman hour chapters in the center with half-hour dots, the arms decorated with stylized flowers in translucent red enamel for petals and translucent green for leaves over flinque engraving. Blued-steel hand. **Movement.** Cross shaped, 24 x 34 mm, gilt brass full plate, fusee and gut line. Short four wheel train with five-leaf pinions, verge escapement, steel two-arm circular foliot, elongated cock pierced and engraved with flowers, secured by a screw, ratchet wheel and click mainspring setup. Signed on the movement.
Diam. 55 x 29 mm. Published in the Sandberg book, pages 372 – 373.
$49,880.00.
Photo and description courtesy of Antiquorum Auctioneers, 31 Mar 2001.

Plate 64. La Sainte Famille l'oiseau Salomon Plairas a Blois, circa 1640.
Extremely fine and equally rare large, 20K gold, and painted-on enamel "fermee"-type pre–balance spring single-hand pendant watch.

Case. Two-body, "bassine," with deep back and curved-in edge, the front cover finely painted with the Virgin, the Child, and St. John the Baptist, the back with the Virgin and Child and St. Joseph, with a nightingale sitting on Jesus' finger, rural background painted after Simon Vouet's *La Sainte Famille a l'oiseau*. Inside front cover the Annunciation, inside back cover a landscape, the band with continuous landscape with travelers, river with a large boat. **Dial.** Radial Roman numerals painted on half-hour divisions, center painted with a landscape. Gilt brass tulip hand. **Movement.** Gilt brass, full plate, column pillars, fusee and catgut, verge escapement, circular foliot, irregular pierced and engraved cock secured by a screw, worm and wheel mainspring setup. Signed on the back plate.
Diam. 59 mm. **$10,672.00.**
Photo and description courtesy of Antiquorum Auctioneers, 16 Nov 2002.

Plate 65. Jean and Jacques Rousseau, Geneva, circa 1640. Very fine and rare silver, pre–balance spring, one-hand watch.

Case. Two-body, "bassine" type, with inward-curving edges, entirely fluted including the hinged bezel, small rosette in the center of the back, tulip-shaped pendant, loose ring. **Dial.** Silver chapter ring with Roman numerals and half hour dot divisions applied on gilt metal engraved plate, the center with a town scene, the Outside with floral engraving, single blued-steel hand. **Movement.** 30.1 mm, gilt, full plate, turned baluster pillars, short four-wheel train with five-leaf pinions, fusee and gut-line, verge escapement, bronze balance without a spring, long gilt one-footed cock secured by a screw but still with a pinning block, pierced and engraved with foliage, ratchet wheel and click setup, the hand driven directly (via the hour wheel) from a four-leaf lantern pinion mounted on the extension of the fusee arbor.

Signed on the movement.
Diam. 35 mm. Published in the Sandberg book, pages 58 – 59.
$19,734.00.

Photo and description courtesy of Antiquorum Auctioneers, 31 Mar 2001.

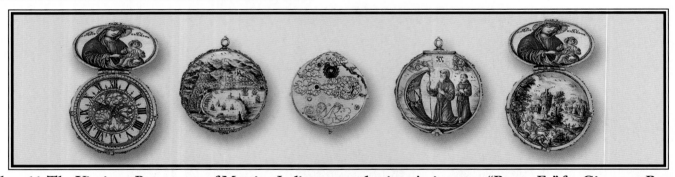

Plate 66. The Virgin as Protectress of Messina Italian, enamel painter's signature "Bruno F.," for Giuseppo Bruno Fecit in Messina, movement engraved with the initials "NK," circa 1640.
Magnificent and highly important 20K gold and enamel pendant watch decorated with scenes from the lives of Saint Francis of Paola and St. John the Baptist, and the harbour of Messina.

Case. Two-part, "bassine fermee," interior and exterior with painted enamel scenes relating to the life of Saint Francis of Paola, who gathered about him a community of followers whose Rule was based on that of the Franciscans. The front cover depicts him, according to legend, calming a storm in the Straits of Messina. He spread his cloak on the waters, also using it as a sail and his staff as a mast, thus enabling his companions to pass safely across. His motto of *caritas* (charity) is shown in a sunburst. The arms on the cloak are those of the Aragon-Pennafort family, under whose protection the island of Sicily fell in the mid-fifteenth century, and where the saint had established a community. The scene on the back of the case is a view of the town of Messina and its cathedral dedicated to the Madonna dell a Lettera, in which, until it was destroyed by Allied bombardment in 1943, there was the Byzantine icon; reproduced inside the front cover. The band of the gold case is enamelled en ronde bosse with flowers and foliage on a matted ground, in a style typical of Sicilian enamelled jewelery of the period. The signature "Bruno F." is visible beneath the scene of Messina. The engraving is by Jean Bazin, after a painting by De Boulogne Le Vieux. The enamel inside the case back shows St. John the Baptist in a landscape which may well be the town of Messina, with its castle and city walls, the inside band repeats the floral motif of the outside one, ring pendant. **Dial.** Gilded, with Roman chapters, quarter-hour divisions, the center engraved with flowers. Single gilt brass hand. **Movement.** 41 mm 0, gilt brass full plates, turned vase baluster pillars, fusee of four turns with original long-hook chain, barrel with cover secured by pins, five-wheel train with second wheel with six-leaf pinion, the other wheels with five-leaves, verge escapement, plain two-arm steel balance without spring, one-footed elongated cock pierced and engraved with asymmetrical floral decoration, ratchet wheel and click setup covered with a gilded plate pierced and decorated similarly to the cock.

Monogram on the movement, enameller's signature on the case back.
Diam. 47 mm. Published in the Sandberg book, pages 76 – 77. **$218,950.00.**
Photo and description courtesy of Antiquorum Auctioneers, 31 Mar 2001.

Plate 67. Venus and Adonis.
Goullons a Paris, circa 1650.
Important and rare 20K gold, painted-on
enamel, single-hand lady's pendant watch.

Case. Two-body, "bassine," with curved edge, the
front lid and the back entirely painted-on enamel, the
principal scenes, on the lid and the back, depicting
Venus and Adonis, the band painted with a continuous hunting and pastoral scene, on the inside of the
lid a riverside fishing scene, on the inside of the back a
pastoral scene, short pendent, loose ring. **Dial.**
Painted enamel on gold, repeating the same motifs as
the band, Roman chapters on outer white enamel ring
with half-hour divisions, inner quarter-hour ring.
Blued-steel hands. **Movement.** 26.6 mm, hinged, gilt
brass full plate, turned baluster pillars, fusee and gut
line, verge escapement, two-arm steel balance without
spring, elongated asymmetrically pierced and foliate-
engraved cock secured by a screw, four-wheel train
with five-leaf pinions, worm and wheel set up with a
silver scale plate mounted on the setup wheel.
Signed on the movement.
Diam. 32 mm. Published in the Sandberg book,
pages 70 – 71. **$25,346.00.**
Photo and description courtesy of Antiquorum Auction-
eers, 31 Mar 2001.

Plate 68. Memento Mori Marc Lagisse, Geneva, circa 1650.
Very fine and rare silver, single-hand pendant form watch in the shape of a skull, with concealed dial.

Case. Double-body, cast in relief, repoussé, and chased, the jaw hinged at the back of the neck to reveal the dial set in the underside of the head. **Dial.** Silver champlevé with radial Roman chapters and half-hour divisions, the center engraved with a riverside
town and a watermill in the foreground. Blued-steel tulip hand. **Movement.** 28.7 mm 0, hinged, gilt brass full plate, turned baluster pillars, fusee and gut line for the going train, verge escapement, two-arm steel circular foliot, elongated cock asymmetrically
pierced, with floral engraving, secured by a screw, ratchet wheel and click setup.
Signed on the back plate.
Diam. height 46 mm, width 35 mm. Published in the Sandberg book, pages 374 – 375. **$25,346.00.**
Photo and description courtesy of Antiquorum Auctioneers, 31 Mar 2001.

Plate 69. Vitafugit Charles Bobinet, Paris. Circa 1650.
Very fine and rare silver, single-hand pendant form watch in the shape of a skull, with concealed dial.

Case. Double-body, cast in relief, repoussé, and chased, the jaw hinged at the back of the neck to reveal the dial set in the underside of the head. The forehead and head engraved with an hourglass and the mottos "Vita fugit, Vt hora," "dum Viuis Viue Vt Vuias," "Caduca despice aeterna respice," and "Incerta Mortis hora." **Dial.** Silver champlevé with radial Roman chapters and half-hour divisions, center engraved with flowers. Blued-steel hand. **Movement.** 28.7 mm 0, hinged, gilt brass full plate, turned baluster pillars, fusee and gut line for the going train, verge Escapement, two-arm steel circular foliot, elongated cock asymmetrically pierced, with floral engraving, secured by a screw ratchet wheel and click setup.
Signed on the back plate.
Diam: height 42 mm, width 30 mm. Published in the Sandberg book, pages 374 – 375. **$17,342.00.**
Photo and description courtesy of Antiquorum Auctioneers, 31 Mar 2001.

Plate 70. Jacob Molly, Geneva, circa 1650
Extremely fine and rare 22K gold, enamel, and amethyst-colored faceted glass, single-hand lady's pendant watch with concealed dial.

Case. Two-body, "fermee" type, hinged, mounted in gold and painted on "ronde bosse" enamel frames, with floral designs. **Dial.** Enamel on gold, radial Roman chapters on while enamel ring with half-hour divisions, the center with flowers and foliage painted on champlevé translucent and opaque enamel. Blued-steel serpent hand. **Movement.** 26 mm, gilt brass full plate, turned baluster pillars, short four-wheel train with five-leaf pinions, fusee and gut line. Verge escapement, steel two-arm circular foliot, elongated gilt brass cock pierced and engraved with floral decoration secured by a screw, worm and wheel mainspring setting.
Signed on the movement.
Diam. 34 mm. Published in the Sandberg book, pages 62 – 63. **$79,950.00.**
Photo and description courtesy of Antiquorum Auctioneers, 31 Mar 2001.

Plate 71. Angely a Monpelier, probably Etienne Angely, French, circa 1650.
Very fine and rare small, 20K gold and agate, single-handed lady's pendant watch with concealed dial.

Case. Two-body, "bassine fermee," both parts made of agate set in gold hinged bezels which are painted on white enamel in "ronde bosse," the top part with pink and black Flowers, the lower with foliage and floral decoration, short pendant, loose ring. **Dial.** Enamel on gold, radial Roman chapters on white enamel ring, centre with translucent red enamel over a flinque ground. Blued-steel arrowhead single hand with serpentine tail. **Movement.** 24.5 mm 10, gilt brass full plate, turned baluster pillars, fusee and gut line, short four-wheel train with five-leaf pinions, verge escapement, steel two-arm circular foliot, symmetrically elongated pierced and engraved cock secured by a screw, worm and wheel mainspring setting.
Signed on the movement.
Diam. 30 mm. Published in the Sandberg book, pages 60 – 61. **$23,346.00.**
Photo and description courtesy of Antiquorum Auctioneers, 31 Mar 2001.

Plate 72. Pierre Drouynot a Poitiers, circa 1650.
Very fine and extremely rare gilt metal, single-hand, hour-striking, three-train coach watch with an alarm, in original fitted traveling box.

Case. Hinged and latched leather traveling box with dial viewing cover. Inner: two-body, "bassine," polished bezel, the back engraved with a small rosette, the band pierced and engraved with flowers and foliage and four anchors, tulip pendant with loose ring. **Dial.** Gilt, floral and mask engraving outside the applied Roman chapter ring with quarter-hour divisions, center rotating gilt alarm disc comprising four flower-engraved divisions with fleur-de-lis blued-steel pointer indicating the time. Blued-steel poker hand for setting the alarm. **Movement.** 63.6 mm, gilt brass full plate with vase pillars, fusee and chain, four-wheel train, verge escapement, plain steel three-arm balance, short balance spring, unusual continental cock with two feet, pierced and engraved with symmetrical foliage, the feet engraved with scallop shells, wheel and click setup covered with a bridge decorated with flowers and foliage. Fixed barrel for the striking, pierced and engraved with foliage, five-wheel train, silver count wheel mounted on the bottom plate, striking with one hammer on a bell, alarm with fixed barrel and three-wheel train, striking on the same bell.
Signed on the movement.
Diam. 90 mm. Published in the Sandberg book, pages 78 – 79. **$25,346.00.**
Photo and description courtesy of Antiquorum Auctioneers, 31 Mar 2001.

Plate 73. Circa 1650.
Fine and rare English 20K gold pre-hairspring pair-case antique pocket watch by John Chatfield, London.

Lovely pique **outer case** with goldwork in particularly fine condition. Polished **inner case** with shutter over winding hole. Lovely engraved **dial** is likely an early replacement, since there are plugged holes in the dial plate. Fine **movement** with asymetrical balance cock, setup regulator, and fusee with gut.
A wonderfully early watch in particularly fine condition.
Diam. 47 mm. **$18,750.00.**
Photo and description courtesy of Stephen Bogoff, Antiquarian Horologist.

Plate 74. Circa 1650.
Fine and rare French, small, silver and leather pique, single-handed antique pocket watch by Gabriel Gamo, Paris.

Polished silver **dial** with single gilt hand. The intricate pinwork is in particularly fine condition. The pre-hairspring **movement** has elegant pierced and engraved cock and sprung click.
Diam. 41 mm. **$18,500.00.**
Photo and description courtesy of Stephen Bogoff, Antiquarian Horologist.

Plate 75. Jean Drouynot a Poitiers, France, circa 1660.
Very fine and rare small, silver, single-hand, pre–balance spring, hour-striking coach clock.

Case. Two-body, "bassine," with deep back with curved-in edge, band pierced and engraved with flowers and foliage, polished back, loose ring pendant, split bezel. **Dial.** Silver, hinged, champlevé bold radial Roman numerals separated by small rosettes, inner quarter hour ring, center engraved with flowers. Blued-steel large fleur-de-lis hand. **Movement.** 64 mm, gilt metal, full plate with baluster pillars, fusee and chain, verge escapement, plain brass balance with flat balance spring (originally pre–balance spring foliat), single-footed cock, worm gear mainspring setup, striking train driven from a fixed barrel, silver count wheel on back plate, striking on a large bell with single hammer.
Signed on the movement.
Diam. 84 mm. **$14,440.00.**
Photo and description courtesy of Antiquorum Auctioneers, 16 Nov 2002.

Plate 76. Genevese, probably Abraham Arlaud I, made for the Islamic market, circa 1660.
Very fine and rare oval, gold, gilt brass, and enamel single-hand pre–balance spring pendant watch.

Case. Two-body, "bassine," with curved band, polished, shutter for winding, bezel split for glass retention, short swivel pendant, loose ring. **Dial.** Oval, *en ronde bosse* enamel on gold, applied gold chapter ring with Islamic numerals, half-hour arrow divisions and small markers for the quarters, applied on an enameled plate centered by a six-petaled flower in translucent green enamel over a flinque ground, framed by white enamel painted with pink and burgundy floral decoration, outside the chapter ring translucent green enamel crescents decorated similarly to the flower. Gold tulip hand. **Movement.** 29.1 x 32.4 mm, hinged, gilt brass full plate finely engraved, bearing the maker's signature in Islamic characters, unusual pierced rectangular pillars, fusee and gut line for the going train, two-arm steel circular foliot, elongated cock pierced and symmetrically engraved with floral decoration, conical foot secured by a screw, ratchet wheel and click setup under the barrel, with calibration on the back plate by a pointer. Signed on the movement in Islamic characters.
Diam. 35 x 45 mm. Published in the Sandberg Book, pages 228 – 229.
$34,086.00.
Photo and description courtesy of Antiquorum Auctioneers, 31 Mar 2001.

Plate 77. Goullons a Paris, circa 1660.
Very fine and rare silver, hour-striking, three-train coach watch with alarm.

Case. Double-body, "bassine," bezel engraved and split for glass retention, the back beautifully pierced and engraved with scrolls and flowers, loose-ring pendant. **Dial.** Silver champlevé, Roman chapters with quarter-hour divisions, outer minute ring with five-minute Arabic numerals, central gilded revolving alarm-setting dial, border engraved with foliage. Gilt brass Louis XV hands. **Movement.** 70 mm, gilt brass full plate with round baluster pillars, fusee with chain, four-wheel train, verge escapement, plain brass three-arm balance with short early balance spring, gilt brass cock pierced and engraved with flowers and foliage. Striking train with fixed gilt brass barrel pierced and engraved with flowers, gilt count wheel on the back plate. Alarm train with gilt brass fixed barrel and steel four-wheel train striking on a bell fixed to the bottom of the case.
Signed on the back plate.
Diam. 97 mm. Published in the Sandberg book, pages 80 – 81. **$18,676.00.**
Photo and description courtesy of Antiquorum Auctioneers, 31 Mar 2001.

Plate 78. Jeremie Gregory, Royal Exchange (London), circa 1665.
Fine silver pair-cased, pre–balance spring, single-hand watch.

Case. Outer: double-body, shagreen covered. Inner: double-body, "bassine," polished, with split bezel and loose ring pendant.
Dial. Silver with radial Roman numerals, the center engraved with a scene depicting a shepherd and his sheep in the foreground, a village in the back. Blued-steel arrow single hand. **Movement.** Hinged gilt brass full plate with early Egyptian pillars, fusee with gut line, short train, verge escapement, circular steel foliot, worm and wheel setup with pierced blued-steel brackets and silver regulator disc, silver florally pierced and engraved cock secured by a screw.
Signed on the back plate.
Diam. 50 mm. **$8,338.00.**
Photo and description courtesy of Antiquorum Auctioneers, 16 Nov 2002.

Plate 79. Henry Crumpe, London, made for the Dutch market, circa 1675.
Exceptionally fine and rare silver, pair-cased, pre–balance spring, single-hand watch with date.

Case. Outer: two-body, green leather-covered, silver studs forming floral and foliate design; inner: two-body, "bassine," polished, split bezel, loose ring pendant. **Dial.** Silver, radial Roman numerals on heart-shaped cartouches, inner quarter-hour ring, blued-steel ring with a pointer outside the hour chapter pointing to the date ring set outermost. Single blued-steel poker hand. **Movement.** 37 mm, gilt metal, full plate, elaborately pierced lyre pillars, fusee and gut, verge escapement, circular steel foliot, pierced and engraved symmetrical cock secured by a screw, worm-gear mainspring setup.
Signed on the back plate.
Diam. 50 mm. **$4,669.00.**
Photo and description courtesy of Antiquorum Auctioneers, 16 Nov 2002.

Plate 80. The Expanding Hand.
Henricus Jones, London, circa 1678.
A unique and highly important silver pair-cased watch with early balance spring with Barrow regulator and expandable minute hand.

Case. Outer: two-body, brass with silver rims, shagreen covered, back and bezel decorated with silver pinwork, square hinge. Inner: two-body, polished shutter for the winding aperture. **Dial.** Silver, central round champlevé radial Roman chapters, hour chapter with quarter-hour divisions, outer oval minute ring with five-minute Arabic numerals. The minute hand changes its length as it travels along the oval ring. **Movement.** 46.5 mm, gilt brass full plate, elaborate tulip pillars, fusee and chain, five-wheel train, verge escapement, three-arm steel balance, short two-coiled blued-steel balance spring with last coil straightened and with Barrow regulator consisting of a worm along which curb pins can move, adjusting the effective length of the straight outer end of the spring, large one-footed gilt brass cock pierced and engraved with scrolling foliage, secured by a screw, worm and wheel setup mounted on the inside of the pillar plate.
Signed on the back plate.
Diam. 60 mm. Published in the Sandberg book, pages 152 – 153. **$206,190.00.**
Photo and description courtesy of Antiquorum Auctioneers, 31 Mar 2001.

Plate 81. Abraham Louis Morant, Berne, circa 1680.
Fine and very rare large, silver, hour and half-hour-striking, pre–balance spring, single-hand coach watch.

Case. Two-body, "bassine," with deep back, band pierced and engraved with inhabited foliage, two shutters for winding apertures. **Dial.** White enamel, large radial Roman numerals, inner half-hour circle. Blued-steel single poker hand. **Movement.** 57 mm, hinged, gilt brass, entirely engraved full plate with baluster pillars, fusee and chain, verge escapement, brass balance with flat balance spring (converted), single-footed cock, count wheel on the back plate, worn gear mainspring setup with engraved tension scale.
Signed on the movement.
Diam. 70 mm. **$8,970.00.**
Photos and descriptions courtesy of Antiquorum Auctioneers, 14 Jun 2003.

Plate 82. The Flight into Egypt.
Gribelin, Paris, circa 1680, painting on enamel attributable to Robert Vauquer, circa 1660.
Very fine and rare 22K gold and enamel single-hand pendant watch without fusee.

Case. Two-body, "bassine," with inward-turned edges, the back very finely painted with the Birth of Christ, showing the Virgin Mary, Saint Joseph, four shepherds, and the Christ child in the manger, the band with four cartouches, each featuring waterside pursuits. Inside the case, a peaceful riverside scene with a boy playing the flute as some cattle drink, polished gold bezel and pendant. **Dial.** Gold, white enamel Roman chapter ring with inner quarter-hour markers, center depicting the flight into Egypt, painted by Robert Vauquer (1625 – 1670) after an engraving by his brother Jacques (1621 – 1686), blued-steel tulip hand. **Movement.** 36.4 mm, hinged, gilt brass full plate, turned vase pillars, going barrel for the four-wheel train, verge escapement, plain three-arm steel balance, blued-steel balance spring, rack and pinion, Tompion-type regulator, typical early single-footed pierced and engraved trefoil cock.
Signed on the movement.
Diam. 45 mm. Published in the Sandberg book, pages 100 – 101. **$46,690.00.**
Photo and description courtesy of Antiquorum Auctioneers, 31 Mar 2001.

Plate 83. Meleager and Atalanta.
Jacobus Garnault, Hague, enamel painting signed by les Freres Huaut, circa 1688.
Magnificent and rare gold and enamel, single-hand pendant watch.

Case. Two-body, "bassine," with curved-in edges, entirely painted on enamel, the main scene on the back, depicting Meleager and Atalanta, taken from an engraving by Cornelis Bloemaert after a painting by Peter Paul Rubens (1577 – 1641). Meleager, the King of Calydon's son, presents Atalanta, the virgin huntress, with a boar's head after the Calydonian boar hunt. The band decorated with four vignettes, each depicting a different house situated close to a lake or a river, linked by a yellow ribbon. The enamel inside the back with a fisherman in a Lakescape, later gold pendant and bow. **Dial.** White enamel radial Roman chapter ring with half-hour markers, the center with a finely painted scene of Diana reposing with a garland of flowers in her hand. Blued-steel hand. **Movement.** 33.5 mm 0, hinged, gilt brass full plate, pierced tulip pillars, fusee and chain for the going train, verge escapement with short balance spring, double-footed early trefoil cock pierced and engraved, worm and wheel setup, rack-and-pinion regulator with silver plate.
Signed on the movement, case signed "Les Freres Huaut."
Diam. 41 mm. Published in the Sandberg book, pages 110 – 111. **$33,350.00.**
Photo and description courtesy of Antiquorum Auctioneers, 31 Mar 2001.

Plate 84. (Jacques) Girod a Copet, Geneva, circa 1690.
Very fine and rare large, silver, single-hand coach watch with alarm.

Case. Double-body, "bassine," polished, the band pierced and engraved with inhabited foliage, back with shutters over winding apertures. **Dial.** Silver champlevé with Roman numerals and inner silver alarm-setting disc with fleur-de-lis steel hour pointer, blued-steel single hand for setting the alarm. **Movement.** 56 mm, hinged gilt brass full plate with Egyptian pillars, fusee and chain, verge escapement, plain steel three-arm balance, flat balance spring, gilt brass cock pierced and engraved with inhabited foliage. Alarm train with fixed barrel pierced and engraved with foliage, striking on a bell. Signed on the back plate.
Diam. 69 mm. **$12,006.00.**
Photo and description courtesy of Antiquorum Auctioneers, 16 Nov 2002.

Plate 85. Dupre a Paris, hallmark for 1692.
Fine silver Louis XIV single-hand "oignon" watch, wound through the center.

Case. Double-body, polished. **Dial.** Enameled, with Roman chapters and quarter-hour divisions. Blued-steel fleur-de-lis hand. **Movement.** 44.8 mm 0, hinged gilt brass full plate with Egyptian pillars, fusee with chain, verge escapement, plain steel three-arm balance, short flat balance spring, fine gilt brass Louis XIV cock pierced and engraved with inhabited foliage, rack and pinion regulator.
Signed on the backplate, inside case stamped with French silver marks, bezel inside stamped "MP."
Diam. 57 mm. Published in the Sandberg book, pages 106 – 107. **$36,685.00.**
Photo and description courtesy of Antiquorum Auctioneers, 31 Mar 2001.

Plate 86. Thomas Tompion, London, No. 73, case by William Sherwood, hallmarked 1696. Very fine, rare, and important 22K gold, pair-cased, two-train, hour-striking clock-watch.

Case. Outer: two-body, gilt metal, leather-covered bezel and back with gold pin and porthole decoration, the center with a pin monogram, a reversed *B* and *MB* conjoined. Tompion is known to have made a watch for a lady with these initials, and probably also one for Marrhew Bent, Alderman of the City of London. Inner: two-body, gold, very finely pierced and engraved with inhabited foliage, a devil's mask at its base, polished center, short pendant, loose ring. **Dial.** Gold, champlevé Roman chapters, inner half-hour ring, outer minute ring and five-minute Arabic numerals in polished carrouches, marred ground, center with Tompion's signature in a cartouche surrounded by garlands of flowers held by two putti. Blued-steel tulip and poker hands. **Movement.** 36.1 mm 0, gilt brass full plate, pierced tulip pillars, fusee and chain for the going train, verge escapement, plain steel three-arm faceted balance, blued-steel balance spring, single-footed gilt cock with streamers, pierced and engraved with asymmetrical scrolling foliage, worm and wheel set-up, rack and pinion regulator with silver plate, striking from a fixed barrel with the visible part pierced and engraved, five-wheel train, the last pinion set in eccentric, adjustable bushing for speed regulation, silver count wheel on the back plate.

Signed on the dial and the backplate, numbered on the backplate, on the outside of the inner case behind the pendant, and inside behind the bell.

Diam. 53.7 mm. Published in the Sandberg book, pages 112 – 113. **$28,014.00.**

Photo and description courtesy of Antiquorum Auctioneers, 31 Mar 2001.

Chapter III
THE PROGRESSIVE YEARS
THE EIGHTEENTH CENTURY

In the seventeenth century, the stage had been set for fairly accurate timekeeping. Some watches could keep time within five minutes a day. It had only been in the last few years of the century that this accuracy could be achieved. Watches had indeed come a long way! They were able to indicate the hours and minutes. They not only could be set for an alarm and strike the hour, but some of them were repeaters that could strike the hours whenever the owners desired.

It would be understandable if watchmakers had just sat back on their laurels and congratulated each other. But thankfully, that was not in their natures. If they had been satisfied, the title of this chapter would not be "the Progressive Years."

THE STORY OF THE CENTURY

The biggest motivating factors for watchmakers in England in the eighteenth century can be summed up in three words: accuracy, award money, and longitude. The new century saw England as the premier manufacturer of watches and clocks, but the country, and indeed the world, was missing one important element in timekeeping — a dependable, accurate sea-going timepiece. Seafarers needed some type of device to gauge longitude. Latitude measurements were fairly easy to gauge by the height of the sun. But to master the seas, an accurate way of calculating longitude was sorely needed. For every four minutes of time difference, a ship could be off one degree east or west in longitude at the equator. On a long journey, a miscalculation could take a ship miles off course and put many lives at risk. In 1704, one of the worst shipwrecks in history happened off the coast adjacent to England and the Scilly Isles. Four ships were pig-tailing together. Because of a miscalculation of longitude by the lead ship's navigator, all the ships were lost and 2,000 men died. Something had to be done!

Finally, in 1714, the Board of Longitude was appointed by an act of Parliament. An award of £20,000, which was a large fortune in that time period, was promised to the person who could make a timepiece that would keep time (within certain limits) accurately enough to determine longitude on a two-months journey from Britain to the West Indies. As you might imagine, many horologists stopped whatever projects they could and devoted their time and creative energy to this lucrative and prestigious goal.

Britain had four rulers in a one-hundred-year span. William III was king from 1689 to 1701. Queen Anne ruled from 1702 until her death in 1714. King George I, the first Hanoverian monarch, took the reign and ruled until 1727, when George II inherited the throne. On George II's death in 1760, he was succeeded by his grandson, George III.

This time period was another century of wars and rumors of war. Many of the areas conquered were conquered by sea. It's not surprising that Britain strove to rule over all the seas. It was Queen Anne who proposed the award for "a suitable and practical solution to the longitude problem." Was it just a coincidence that the previous year Britain had received a contract to supply slaves to Spanish America? Much later, during the reign of George III, and with the king's influence, John Harrison finally received the Board of Longitude award — after years of being denied what was rightfully his. During his wait, his watch and copies of his watch saved many lives that would have otherwise been lost at sea.

Why did this brilliant man have to try so hard and so long to prove himself? The answer to this question can most likely be summed up in two words — pride and politics. John Harrison was a poor country carpenter with no formal training in watchmaking. He had never served as an apprentice in the trade, and this proved to be both an advantage and a disadvantage. The advantage was that he was not tied to any preconceived ideas of what wouldn't work. In today's vernacular, he could "think outside the box." The disadvantage was that some of the members of the committee that chose the winner could not accept the fact that a man with no formal training in horology could solve the "longitude problem" — a mystery that the finest watchmakers in England, and indeed the world, had not been able to solve. Consequently, Harrison had to wait forty-five years after his first trip to London to receive the total sum of the award money.

For an interesting and entertaining story about John Harrison and his efforts to win and collect the award, read the book *A Quest for Longitude* or rent the A&E movie *Longitude*. You will find that either one will make the watchmakers and other characters in this story come alive. To see Harrison's winning watch, #4, you will have to go to the National Maritime Museum in Greenwich, just outside of London. It is definitely worth the trip to see the watch that traveled from Portsmouth to Jamaica from November of 1761 to January of 1762 and met all the requirements for solving the problem of longitude.

THE PROGRESS

The Worshipful Company of Clockmakers had been established in 1631, but when the Swiss mathematician Nicholas Facio immigrated to England in 1687, it didn't take long for the organization to become aware of his talents. He and his friends Peter and Jacob Debaufre applied for a patent for using stones, "natural or artificial," in watches, clocks, or other "engins." They stressed that the stones were not to be used for ornamental purpose only, but as an "internal or useful part of the work."[9] They received the patent, but when the time came for it to be extended, they were refused because of the uproar of the competing watchmakers. One publication stated that the watchmakers didn't mind immigrants coming to live in their country, but that they "didn't want to be deprived of their livelihood by these foreigners."[10]

These "bored jewels" were eagerly accepted and used by the English to further the accuracy of their watches. This accuracy was achieved because the jewels reduced wear and friction. Amazingly, the English watchmakers who demanded that Facio and his partners share the process with them managed to keep the secret of how to bore or pierce jewels from watchmakers in other countries for almost 75 years. This secret played an important part in Britain's position of supremacy in horology during this century.

Another component in the quest to reduce friction was lubrication. This problem was solved to some extent in 1750, by an Englishman, Henry Sully (1680-1720), who designed little cups to go around the bearing holes. These tiny cups, commonly referred to as "oil sinks," were used to keep the oil from running around inside the watch. After Sully's death, the sinks were improved upon by his good friend Julian Le Roy.

John Harrison's amazing abilities to solve accuracy problems lead to a number of progressive strides. He invented the bimetallic (steel and brass) device that, with change in temperature, moved the curb pin with regard to the balance spring, thus accelerating or slowing the balance. For an example of a bimetallic balance, see plate 88 on p. 53.

Because the active length of the balance spring (hairspring) affects the time of rotation of the balance and thus the accuracy of the watch, his device moved the pins closer or further from the spring, giving it less or more play. Colder temperatures caused the strip to move away from the curb pin. Hotter temperatures caused one pin to move closer to the other. This expansion and contraction varied the movement of the spring between the pins and helped to compensate the balance for the changes in temperature.

Harrison also solved the problem of maintaining power while the watch was being wound. Prior to his development, the main spring power was reversed when the watch was being wound, resulting in a loss of time. His mechanism kept the watch going during the winding of the mainspring, and this obviously made the watch more accurate.

Harrison's marine chronometer was also an inspiration to watchmakers. Famous watchmakers such as Pierre Le Roy, John Arnold, Thomas Earnshaw, and Ferdinand Berthoud simplified his complicated movement and developed it into a true chronometer about 1770. These watches used the pivoted detent, an earlier form of the escapement. The spring detent invented by Arnold and Earnshaw in 1780 and improved upon by Earnshaw was favored by the English. The European makers preferred the pivoted detent and continued to use it.

In 1770, a self-winding watch was invented by Abram Louis Perrelet (1729-1826), a very famous watchmaker in Le Locle. Both Louis Recordon and Abraham-Louis Breguet reportedly purchased these watches. Perrelet's invention was patented in Britain by Rocordon in 1780. Obviously, one did not have to invent or even own the rights to an invention in order to patent it in Britain. About a year later, Breguet came out with his "everlasting," or "perpetual" watch; he had greatly improved upon Perrelet's original design.[11]

Jean Antoine Lepine also made some progressive strides in watchmaking. In 1772, he developed a way by which a watch could be hand set from the back of the watch. Four years later, he developed the isochronic hairspring that enabled the balance wheel to oscillate back and forth in equal time whether or not the watch was fully wound. That same year he introduced a thin watch. This was accomplished by doing away with the fusee and replacing it with a going barrel, which has a wheel, with teeth, that interacts directly with first pinion of the train wheel. He then replaced the top plate with a series of bar bridges. When you look at these bridges they appear to be single parts, but actually, some were joined and considered to be a top plate. This "Lepine calibre" was widely accepted in Europe, and thin watches became very popular.

In 1775, a man who was destined to be one of the most famous watchmakers in history started making fine watches. His name was Abraham-Louis Breguet, and it became synonymous with quality and innovative design. In fact, he is known as the "father of modern design" because of his influence. For more information about Breguet, see the Characters section of this chapter.

In 1776, Le Roy improved upon John Harrison's form of temperature compensation by applying the bimetallic strips to the balance wheel. This balance was later adapted by Thomas Earnshaw and John Arnold, and became the cut bimetallic balance. In this form, the balance rim is made of two layers of metal. It consists of an outer layer of brass fused to an inner layer of steel. The balance rim is cut, and can therefore expand and contract with temperature changes.

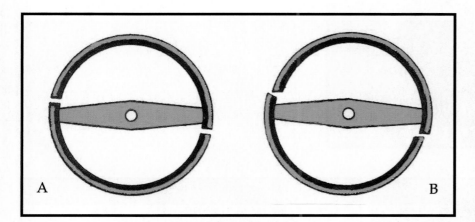

Plate 88. **A.** The balance when not affected by heat or cold. **B.** This illustration shows the effect that heat has on the metals. Notice that the ends on each half that are not attached to the center bar are curved inward. This reduces the diameter of the balance and, consequently, the radius of gyration.

Plate 87. This picture shows a much later version of the Lepine Calibre.

By the end of the century, automated watches complete with figures that appeared to strike bells were being developed. For those who wanted the day and date, a perpetual calendar watch was invented (1792). For those who liked novelty, a musical watch that used a disk instead of bells or gongs was introduced by Antoine Favre in 1796.

Plates 89 and 90. This automaton watch displays men in armor that appear to be striking bells. It is also a repeater, in a 14K case with a display back. $16,500. *Courtesy of Aaron Faber Gallery.*

Plate 91. This musical watch has a comb and a flat circular disk with tiny pins. As the disk revolves, the teeth of the comb passes over the pins on the disk and play a tune. *Courtesy of Dr. Ted Crom.*

Plates 92 and 93. Another musical movement. This one has a round cylinder instead of a disk. The photo on the left shows the back of the movement, with the notes of the song that it plays. The photo on the right is a view of the open center of the dial, which shows the cylinder as it turns to play the tune. *Courtesy of Dr. Ted Crom.*

This is by no means the extent of the progress made in watches during this century. For a more complete look, please refer to the timeline included in this section.

THE ESCAPEMENTS

Because the type of escapement is a major factor in identification, it is important to be able to recognize the different types in order to properly evaluate a watch. As you can see, watchmakers were very busy during the eighteenth century. One of the most important areas of development in this century involved the quest for a better escapement. It was estimated that between 200 and 300 types or versions of escapements were invented. Why was a different type of escapement needed? One of the reasons was to solve the problem that friction in the escapement caused — lack of accuracy.

Since the beginning of watchmaking, the only type of escapement available was the verge and crown wheel that we looked at in the chapter about the sixteenth century. It was a frictional rest escapement in which the escapement is always in contact with the balance or verge staff. Consequently, this hindered the ability of the balance to have the true oscillation needed for accuracy.

THE CYLINDER

A patent was issued in 1695 to Thomas Tompion, William Houghton, and Edward Booth, who also used the last name Barlow. Its description reads like it could have been a concept for the cylinder escapement, but the credit for inventing and making the cylinder escapement was given to "Honest George" Graham in 1726. Graham had worked with Tompion for years and had taken over Tompion's business when he died in 1713. This new escapement was a horizontal escapement that used a smaller balance wheel. This combination allowed for a thinner watch, but like the verge, it was a frictional rest escapement. Unlike the verge, it was a dead beat escapement in which the escape wheel does not recoil. Nevertheless, the cylinder was the first horizontal escapement to achieve acceptance within the industry.

The cylinder did have some disadvantages. One was that it was prone to wear. Consequently, a variety of solutions to cut down on the wear were tried. The most successful was to replace the part of the cylinder that came into contact with the wheel with one made of ruby. This brilliant idea come from the mind of John Arnold in 1764. Unfortunately, this answer to the problem also had some disadvantages. A lapidary, or jewel maker, was needed to cut the ruby stone, and although the stone's hardness made it resistant to scratch, it was breakable. If it broke, it was often replaced with a steel cylinder, because it took so much time and experience to have a ruby one cut. If a dust cover is marked "cylinder ruby," it originally had a ruby cylinder, but further investigation is needed to determine whether or not the original is still there.

Another drawback was that the cylinder escape wheel was more time consuming to make than was the verge crown wheel. One of Graham's contemporaries, Jean Andre Lepaute, complained that it took a skilled man three days to make the escape wheel. That was a slow process, but not too slow when compared to the two to three weeks that it sometimes took for a woman to pierce one of the decorative balance cocks, the function of which was to protect the balance wheel and support the balance staff.

In spite of its imperfections, the cylinder was used by some of the finest watchmakers of the period. But the search for better and more accurate escapements continued.

Let's take a look at the cylinder escapement and determine its most visible, identifiable characteristics.

In the photo below, the cylinder from which the name is derived is shown on the right, but this part is very hard to see without taking the watch apart. The escape wheel on the left is visible, and makes identification of the the escapement possible. To this author, the escape wheel looks as if it has little pointed-toe boots sticking up on a post. Be sure to hold the watch above eye level, and make sure that you can see that they are sticking up. Otherwise, you may not properly identify this escapement.

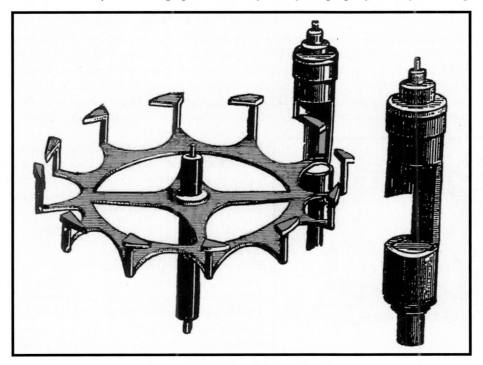

Plate 94. Illustration of the cylinder escapements.

THE DUPLEX

This escapement was conceived by the famous Dr. Hooke. His work was improved upon by Dutreter in 1720 and by Pierre Le Roy in 1750. Thomas Tyrer introduced it to English watchmakers in 1782. Like its predecessor, the cylinder, it was fragile and time consuming to make. But its reputation of being a precision timekeeper was such that it was used in the most expensive quality of watches.

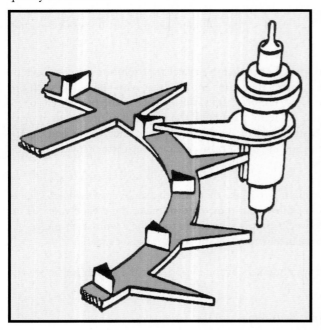 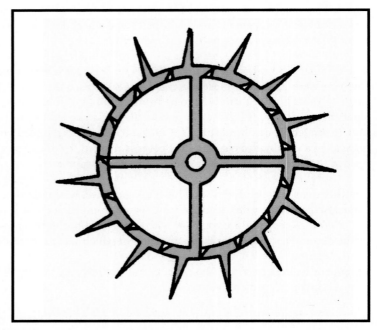

Plates 95 and 96. There were two different versions of the duplex in this time period. Watchmakers on the Continent favored the version with two escape wheels. One wheel has long, pointed teeth and the second wheel, on the top of the first and on the same arbor, has stubby, thumb-like teeth that stand up vertically. The English preferred a wheel with two sets of teeth on the same escape wheel. Like the cylinder, the wheel is the visible, identifying factor. In the nineteenth century, Buck invented a new form of the duplex. We will discuss this when we explore that century.

THE VIRGULE

This funny-looking escapement is also known as the comma escapement, because *vergule* is the French word for "comma." For reasons you will see when we take a closer look at the illustration below, this is an apt name. The virgule was invented in 1750 and as is often the case, this can be attributed to more than one person. References tell us that the credit should go to either Jean Andre Lepaute or Jean Antoine Lepine. The similarity of the names and the fact that both men had the same initials most likely had something to do with the confusion. This escapement was used by French watchmakers in the last twenty years of the eighteenth century. It is not often encountered, but I have included some photos of watches with vergue escapements in this chapter.

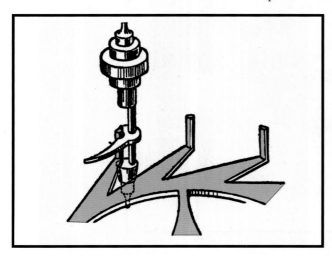

Plate 97. Diagram of the virgule escapement.

As you can see from the picture on the left, this escapement is somewhat similar to the cylinder. The identifying feature of this escapement is slanted, pointed teeth that each have a little upright "neck" on the outer tips. These necks interact with the comma on the balance arbor.

THE DETENT

Harrison's marine chronometer was also an inspiration to watchmakers. Famous watchmakers such as LeRoy, Arnold, Earnshaw, and Berthoud simplified his complicated movement and developed it into a pocket chronometer about 1770. These watches used the pivoted detent that was the earlier form of the escapement. The spring detent invented by John Arnold and Thomas Ernshaw in 1780 was favored by the English. Other European makers preferred the pivoted detent and continued to use it.

During the early years of development and throughout the rest of the century, there were not enough detents available for use by the general public. Making them was a slow, time-consuming process, and all that were made were used for the chronometers needed at sea for deciphering longitude. Chronometers were, and still are, an expensive type of movement.

The spring detent escapement developed by Thomas Earnshaw is the one in use today. It is a detached escapement in which the wheel is locked onto a stone carried in a detent. It is interesting to note that the meaning of the word *detent* is "the end of strained relations." When one of the teeth of the escape wheel is unlocked, an impulse is given to the pallet on the balance staff. This happens with every alternate swing of the balance.

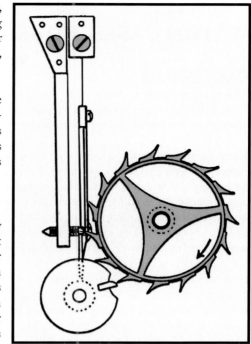

Plate 98. Detent Escapement.

THE LEVER

Thomas Mudge first used his newly invented lever escapement about 1754, in small clocks. His lever escapement is also referred to as an anchor escapement because it looks like a tiny anchor. His first watch using this new detached lever escapement (made in 1759) is housed today at Windsor Castle. It is part of the Royal Collections, because Mudge made the watch for King George III, who gave it to his wife, Queen Charlotte. The watch is only 2½" in diameter. It is cased in 22k gold and bears a 1759 hallmark.[12]

When Mudge retired in 1771, Josiah Emery, a Swiss watchmaker working in London, took up the challenge. From 1795 through 1798, with Mudge's model in hand, he was able to make thirty watches with this escapement.[13]

This escapement, although an improvement on many others, was still not the perfect solution for the accuracy problem. Its one big drawback was that the escapement would tend to be dislodged if the watch was bumped or given a jolt. A solution to this problem was developed by John Leroux in 1785, when he discovered a method by which the escape wheel could have the force of *draw*. This was achieved by making the angles of the escape wheel teeth and the locking faces of the pallet stones at an angle, so that the pressure of a tooth on the locking face of the pallet produced a "drawing" motion of the pallet toward the escape wheel.

With draw, the locking device had developed into a very secure device that was no longer subject to becoming dislodged when jolted. No longer was it dependent on friction alone. Because of this development, we have the detached lever that is used today. It would take until the nineteenth century for Mudge's lever to evolve into the the most popular escapement used for modern mechanical timepieces.

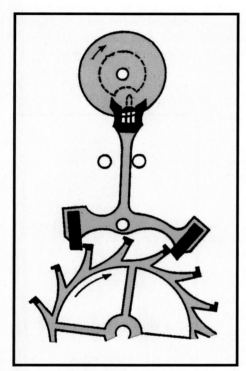

Plate 99. Lever escapement. This is the club foot escapement. Notice how the teeth have evolved into ones that slope. The ends of each of the teeth might be confused at first glance with the "pointed-toe boots" on the cylinder escape wheel. Just remember that the club foot is on the same plane as the tooth, and the cylinder's "boot" stands up on a little post.

THE RACK LEVER

In 1722, Abbe de Hautefeuille wrote a description of what later evolved into the rack lever escapement. As usual, when a breakthrough in knowledge or a new invention comes onto the market, it isn't long before it is improved upon again and again. The new and improved rack lever escapement was patented by Peter Litherland, a watchmaker from Liverpool. The new escapement did not have the advantages of the detached lever, but it lent itself to mass production methods and was used by the makers in Lancaster until about 1840. At that time, they decided to change to the evolved detached lever that was developed by Breguet.

WATCH CASES, EMBELLISHMENTS, AND DIALS

CASE STYLES

This century had two major styles that predominated the decorative arts. The first is known as Louis XV style, or rococo. By 1735, it had become popular in Paris, and with the printing of books or models, as these printed patterns were known, it was not long before the rest of Europe adopted this new fashion.

Rococo was a free and easy style that conveyed a free and easy type of lifestyle. Because goldsmiths and jewelers could beautifully execute the swirling lines, cascades of flowers, and beautiful asymmetrical flowing lines that define this style, it was a popular style for jewelry and watch cases. Consequently, repoussé cases were very much the vogue during this period. Unlike the century before, now repoussé was used for the outer case decoration and the inner case was usually plain. Mythological and Biblical scenes embellished with rococo flourishes were popular subjects. These scenes and figures done in repousse embellished watch cases from about 1725 to about 1750. Two of the more important case makers of the period were Juste-Aurele Meissonnier, a goldsmith who specialized in watch cases, and Francois-Thomas Mondon, a goldsmith jeweler who was known for his chasing, or repoussé work.[14]

Around 1750, the pendulum (or shall we say the balance?) started to swing in the opposite direction. What could have been more of a swing from the asymmetrical curves and fussy designs of Rococo than a style based on the classical periods? Hence, this new style was known as Neoclassical. Later in the century, these sleek, uncluttered designs suited the more sedate and moral social climate. The straight classic lines lent themselves to the engine-turned patterns on the case metal. These patterns were often covered with a colored translucent enamel that tended to show the designs off to their advantage. This type of embellishment, along with enamel paintings done in the classical style, gem stones, paste and pearls continued to be in vogue from about 1770 until the end if the century.

As is the case with any style or period fashion, no one just woke up one morning and said, "Well, it's 1750 and time for the styles to change." The transition between these styles was a gradual and sometimes overlapping process, and just as in the twenty-first century, not everybody adhered to the fashions of the day. As we look at the Watches section this will become evident.

In the 1780s, the chatelaine came back into vague. The chatelaine consisted of a large, decorated central plaque that was either hooked or pinned at the waist. From this extended chains with the watch as the centerpiece and a variety of useful items such as seals and watch keys on either side. Inspiration for this type of accessory may be traced to medieval times, when the keeper of the keys, which were usually worn on a chain around the waist, was the person with authority. The eighteenth century watch version of this assemblage is quite beautiful, and is usually highly embellished with various types of enamel work.

Plate 100. Circa 1760. 18K gold, diamond, red garnet, and tourmaline-set pendant watch, with chatelaine with crank key and two seals. By D. Hubert, #1846 Sandburg Collection. **$24,790.00.** *Photo courtesy of Antiquorum Auctioneers, March 2001.*

Plate 101. Circa 1770. 18K gold and enameled watch with matching chatelaine, key, and seal. By Mathieu Le Jun a Paris #893 *the Little Preacher.* Sandburg Collection. **$9,970.00.** *Photo courtesy of Antiquorum Auctioneers, March 2001.*

MATERIALS
Gold and Silver

Because of the hallmarking system used in England, it is easy to identify the content of gold or silver in English watch cases. Before 1798, all gold cases were made of 22 carat gold. From 1798 to 1854, cases could be made of 18 or 22 carat gold. Please note that the English use *carat* for their gold content whereas Americans use *karat* for gold content and *carat* for the weight of stones. Confusing, isn't it? Whoever said that "We are two nations divided by a single language" was surely right.

Britannia silver was not used much for watch cases in England after 1720, but sterling silver has been used and marked since that year. With a good hallmark book for reference, it is often quite easy to read the hallmark date and find out the town of origin and the maker's mark. With this information one can then look for information about the case maker in *Britten's Old Clocks and Watches and Their Makers* or *Watch Case Makers of England*, both of which you can find listed in the bibliography in the back of book.

Please remember that from 1697 to 1720, the English maker's mark for silver was the the first two letters of the maker's surname but that at the same time, the maker's mark for gold cases consisted of the first letter of his Christian name and the first letter of his surname. This tended to be confusing, and fortunately, in 1720 the makers' marks for both gold and silver cases became the first letters of their first and last names.[15]

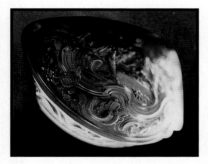

Plate 103. Signature under scalloped pattern on back of case.

Not all cases had to be hallmarked. The repoussé outer cases were exempt from hallmarking because of the obvious risk of damage to the sometimes very thin metal. Makers did manage to press their names into these cases, but don't look for it in only the usual places. The case on thw left has the maker's name worked into the design so beautifully that it takes a skilled observer with a careful eye and a good magnifier to find it. Turn to the Watch section and look at the well-hidden name on the watch case in plate #154 on page 83.

Watch cases incorporating four colors of gold were introduced around 1760 and were made for a number of years. The cases were made of gold and decorated with designs made of colored gold (red or pink, green, blue, and silver) that had been applied to the case. Known by the French as *quatre-couleur*, these multicolored watch cases are highly collectible.

Plate 102. Circa 1785, 18K gold and enamel, diamond and pearl-set dumb quarter repeating watch with chatelaine and matching key and seal. Chatelain a Paris, #155. *Photo cortesy of Antiquorum Auctioneers*, March 2001, **$11,965.00.**

Vermeil

In the chapters covering the last 200 years, we have seen watches made out of several different types of metals, and some made with a combination of metals. One method of watch case embellishment that we have not explored is use of *vermeil* (vair-may). The French definition of vermeil is "silver gilt." Cases made of sterling silver and coated with gold were favored by the French nobility during the reign of Louis XIV and throughout the eighteenth century. In the early nineteenth century, scientist discovered that the mercury used in the vermeil process was causing the metalworkers to go blind. Consequently, the century we are now exploring is the last one in which this mercury process, which provided such a glowing look, was used.

Pinchbeck

Pinchbeck is a metal with which most dealers and collectors of antique jewelry are familiar. What most of them do not know is that the man who invented it, and for whom it was named, was the famous watch and clock maker Christopher Pinchbeck (1670 – 1732). In fact, he was also the inventor of "Astronomico-Musical Clocks." He had a shop in London where he made and sold watches, clocks, and a variety of other

Plate 104. Circa 1785. 18K multicoloured gold, pair-cased, quarter-repeating watch on a bell and a toc, with matching chatelaine and made for the Islamic market. By Geoge Prior, London, #6269. *March 2001. Photo cortesy of Antiquorum Auctioneers.* **$11,303.00.**

items. According to an advertisement in the *Applebee's Weekly Journal* of July 8,1721, "he mends watches and clocks in such sort that they will perform to an exactness which possibly thro' a defect in finishing or other accidents they formerly could not."

The metal he discovered contains no gold; yet looks like gold and wears well. It is not a plate or a coating, but a solid metal made by mixing four parts copper and three parts zinc. This formula was a guarded secret passed down through the family, but other companies developed their own versions. There were so many imitations that Christopher's grandson, Edward Pinchbeck, found it necessary to place this advertisement in the July 11, 1733, edition of the *Daily Post*:

> To prevent for the future the gross imposition that is daily put upon the public by a great number of Shop-Keepers, Hawkers, and Peddlers, in and about this town. Notice is hereby given that the ingenious Mr. Edward Pinchbeck, at the "Musical Clock" on Fleet Street, does not dispose of one grain of his curious metal, which so nearly resembles Gold in Color, Smell and Ductility, to any person whatsoever, nor are the Toys (watches, jewelry and trinkets) made of the said metal sold by any one person in England except himself; therefore gentlemen are desired to beware of impostors, who frequent Coffee Houses, and expose for sale, Toys pretended to be made of this metal, which is a most notorious imposition, upon the public. And Gentlemen and Ladies, may be accommodated by the said Mr. Pinchbeck with the following curious toys: Watch Chains and in particular Watches plain and chased in so curious a manner as not to be distinguished by the nicest eye, from the real gold, and which are highly necessary for Gentleman and Ladies when they travel, with several other fine pieces of workmanship of all sorts made by the best hands. He also makes Repeating and all other sorts of Clocks and Watches particularly Watches of a new invention, the mechanism of which is so simple, and proportion so just, that they come nearer to the truth than others yet made.

The advertisement referred to watches as necessary items for travel. Quite often, copies of favorite pieces, including watches, were made to wear on one's travels. The gold pieces were left safely at home. McKeever Persival, in his book *Chats on Old Jewelry*, states:

> In those days when a journey of even a few miles out of London led through roads infested by thieves and highway robbers, careful folk preferred not to temp the "gentlemen of the road" by wearing expensive ornaments unless traveling with a good escort; so not only would a traveler with a base metal watch and buckles lose less if robbed, by owing to the freemasonry which existed between innkeepers and pestilence and the highwaymen, they were actually less likely to be stopped, as it was not worth while to run risks for such a poor spoil.

With the invention of the electro-gilding process in 1840, and the legalization of nine carat gold in 1854, the used of pinchbeck declined and eventually became passé. When antiquing in England, beware — the dealers there often refer to anything that is not solid gold as pinchbeck, when actually it may be gold filled or gold plated. It is not the same. Most of the watch cases that you find, if they are pinchbeck, were made prior to 1845.[16]

Stones

During the eighteenth century, more stones were used to embellish watch cases. With the discovery, in 1725, of diamonds in Brazil, they became more plentiful and more popular for decorating watch cases and hands. Other stones, such as emeralds, garnets, and banded agate, were also popular. Agate seemed to be especially popular for watches made for the Chinese market.

Plate 105. Circa 1767.

Plate 106. Circa 1770.

Plate 107. Circa 1775.

As you can see, all three cases are very much alike. When watchmakers found a style their Asian customers liked, they kept on using it.
All case photos courtesy of Antiquorum Auctioneers.

A man-made stone also became popular during this century. It was known as paste, and it was not really a stone at all. It was a lead glass made to imitate diamonds and many other types of colored stones. George Ravenscrof had developed flint glass, known as lead glass, in 1675. But the name most associated with paste is Frederick Strauss, who developed a formula of leaded glass that soon became so popular that Louis XV gave his mistress a set of blue paste earrings. Paste stones were also used to embellish watch cases. All stones used for embellishment, whether genuine or man made, were set in closed backs during this time period. In other words, the stones were were completely covered underneath by metal.

ENAMELIST AND ENAMELING

One of the most important discoveries that affected enamel painting during this century happened in 1760, when a new technique for coating enamel work with a glass-like layer of enamel flux was developed. A very pale tint of yellow was used on gold or copper cases, and a very pale tint of blue was used on silver cases. The enamel flux was fired and then machine polished, to add an almost colorless transparent protective glaze. Because of this protection, an outer case was no longer needed.

The enamel paintings of the eighteenth century did not cover the entire case as did the ones in the previous century. The paintings on the back of the case were usually outlined in a border of gold, which was decorated with another form of enamel or was decorated with paste, gem stones, or pearls.

The second generation of the Huaud family was active in this century. After 1700, the sons Jean-Pierre (1665 – 1723) and Ami (1657-1729) used the signatures "les freres Huaut," "Les deux freres Huaut," "Peter et Amicus Huaut," or a Fratres Huaut." To further confuse matters, their last name was spelled three different ways — *Huaud, Huaut,* and *Huault.*[17] Jean Mussard (1681 – 1754) was another popular enamel painter of the period. He began his career as a goldsmith, but later changed to the painting of watch cases. He was an admirer of the Huaud family's work; it was a great influence on his own. His pieces are signed "Mussard," "Jean Mussard pinx," and "Mussard pinx."

Plate 108. These three pictures are of the same watch, and include a close up of the Huaut signature. *Photo courtesy of Antiquorom Auctioneers.*

Plate 109. Another beautifully enameled Huaut watch. From the Sandberg Collection. *Photo courtesy of Antiquorum Auctioneers.*

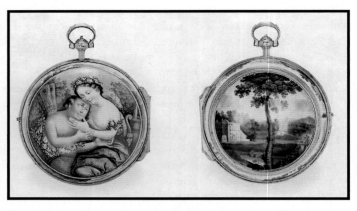

Plate 110. Beautiful enameling by Jean Mussard circa 1720.

Plate 111. Another watch decorated with enamel work of Jean Mussard, Circa 1730.

Photos courtesy of Antiquorum Auctioneers.

Toward the end of the century, it became popular to use transparent colored enamel over a pattern of bright cutting or engine-turned designs. The bright cutting, or *flinique*, was done by hand. *Guilloche* was done by a machine which used a guide called a *rosette* to make the more elaborate patterns. Because of this, this type of embellishment is often referred to as rose engine turning.

CASES AND DIALS

New styles, new metals, and new stones were not the the only changes to the watch case. By 1720, some important identification information could be found on the case; silver watch cases were hallmarked, case makers were putting their initials and marks on cases, and watchmakers began to number their movements. What wonderful information is available for those who want to trace the history of a watch!!

Sherlock Holmes knew that most people looked but that they did not observe. Maybe it was because no one had really shown them what to look for. Let's see if we can train the eye to really see the evolution of watch cases and dials in the eighteenth century. Viewing the cases and dials without the full descriptions of the movements and the prices as distractions will help you to concentrate on the subtle changes in detail that were part of the evolution of the watch. We will see how the changes in style influenced the cases, dials, and even the stems and bows of the eighteenth century watch.

Plate 112. English circa 1700.

Plate 113. French "oignon" alarm watch circa 1710.

Plate 114. French circa 1710.

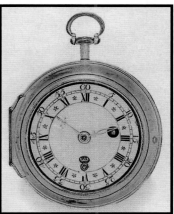

Plate 115. English circa 1720.

Plates 116 and 117. This is the back and front of the same watch. Both sides are glazed. The snake in the painting on the back (at the top) of the case "revolves around the enameled scene pursing and tempting Adam and Eve." Circa 1730.

Plate 118. French silver pair case circa 1740. Outer case is leather with silver studs. Repoussé with scene.

Plates 119 and 120. English circa 1745. The outer case that you can see around the dial is a shagreen on gilt base with gold studs. Note that the red ring in the center of the dial is made of paste stones. The inner case on the right is carnelian.

Plate 121. English circa 1760. The back of this watch is carved from a single piece of bloodstone and so is the bezel.

Plate 122. Circa 1790 Swiss enamel pearl set slim watch. Note the gold Breguet hands.

Plate 123. Swiss circa 1790. The dial has "center seconds and a visible diamond set balance." The back of the case reflects the Neoclassical style of the time period.

Did you really look at the pictures and note how the watch bow and stem changed during the century? What about the hands?

WATCH MANUFACTURING

In the beginning, watches were usually completed by the movement maker, who used his own hand-made tools. As stated before, he occasionally used a case originally used for a musk ball to house his work. This case may have been made and engraved by the same person, or made by one person and engraved by another. Over the years, it became evident that as the demand for watches grew, so must the subdivisions of labor.

Thomas Tompion, to whom we were introduced in the last century, was a master of the subdivision of work. He used his assistants to make the simpler parts, saving his energy and talent for the more difficult and important work. When Dr. Robert Hooke developed the wheel-cutting engine, it became evident that because not everyone could afford this machine and not everyone had the skills necessary for making and finishing the wheels, it was better for one person or a group of people to be responsible for this job. When the balance hairspring was developed, the time, patience, and skill needed to make it proved the job to be a specialty in its own right.

Consequently, the manufacture of diverse parts of watch movements began to be a cottage industry. Large families were common, and often an entire family was involved in the craft. If the father was a watchmaker/finisher, his sons would usually follow in his trade. When a son was ready to serve an apprenticeship, he was usually sent to another watchmaker. One had to be properly trained in order to be a member of the watchmaker's guild. Specialty workers also tended to raise their sons to work in the business.

Women and young girls were were restricted in what they could do in the watch industry, but they were particularly adept at the fine tracery cutout work involved in the making of balance cock covers. The making of watch hands and fusee chains was confined to young women and boys who had the delicate hands and artistic talents needed to work with these tiny pieces.

Other families might be expert balance spring makers or wheel cutters. These skills were interdependent on each other. Notes from the period reveal that a fusee might be swapped by its maker for a spring barrel or for wheels from another maker.

There were several attempts to assemble groups of families who had special skills making watch parts and relocate them to an area that wished to develop a watch industry. In the first quarter of the eighteenth century, Henry Sully, the inventor of the oil sinks and quite a talented watchmaker, moved 60 watch and clock makers and their families from London to Versailles in order to develop a factory. A few years later he established a factory in St. Germain. Unfortunately, it was not successful.

The assembled families usually made partially finished watches that master watchmakers would then complete. The partially finished watches, known as *ebauche* ("in the gray"), were hand made, and each piece of the movement went from one specialist to another until the ebauche was ready.

JAPY'S DO-IT-YOURSELF KIT

Frederick Japy was the first person to successfully produce ebauche by machine. Japy was born in Beaucourt, France, in 1749. When he came of age, he walked to Le Loche, Switzerland, to began an apprenticeship with Perrelet. Perrelet was an excellent watchmaker and had also invented several tools for the watch trade. According to research by Dr. Theodore R. Crom, an internationally-known watch tool historian, "Japy would learn from Perrelet the importance of, and the need to develop, good machine tools, if mass production was the goal."

After his apprenticeship, Japy went to work for Jean-Jacques Jenneret Gris, who also lived in Le Loche. There he worked with a family that designed and built tools.[18] Japy's job provided him with opportunities to work with these new tools and to see how helpful the right tools could be.

In 1777, he walked back to his hometown of Beaucourt. The only piece of land he could afford was in a remote location that had no access to water. On this he built a small watch shop. His dream was to eventually design and build his own watchmaking machines that unskilled workers could operate. Meanwhile, he had Jean-Jacques Jenneret Gris make equipment for him. Keep in mind that the power for these tools had to come from hand cranks, foot treadles, or animals. When Gris was ready to retire, he sold out to Japy.

Japy produced a sort of do-it-yourself kit designed for professional watchmakers. This kit usually consisted of two bridge plates, the barrel bar, the train bridges, the balance cock, the barrel, a brass fusee, and the ratchet, click, and spring. "In the gray" aptly described this collection of unfinished parts.

It is good to remember that Japy did not originate the idea for the ebauche. They had been made for years as a cottage industry. His innovation was to mass produce the parts using machines that were run by unskilled workers. This not only made the finished product more affordable, but it also insured a rise in productivity. According to the records, "one worker in the machine tool factory produced the work of 20 hand workers. At the factory's peak, each ebauche passed through the hands of at least 60 different workmen."[19]

These ebauches were far from finished. Because the parts were not interchangeable, they had to be individually finished and fitted, including the dials and hands. The jobs of making the escapement, putting on the balance spring, and casing the movement were turned over to specialists. After these jobs were completed, the watchmaker/finisher put all the parts together to make sure that they fit properly and would be as accurate as possible. After this task was completed, the watch was then disassembled and sent to polishers, gilters, and screw finishers. Then it went back to the watchmaker/finisher to reassemble and put in a case that he had ordered decorated according to his customer's wishes. The watchmaker's name or that of a retail establishment was usually added to the dial and movement. The Japy name was signed on some movements, but usually in an inconspicuous place; it can only be seen when the watch is taken apart.

By 1793, the firm of Japy supplied at least 40,000 movements to manufacturers in the mountains of Switzerland. Because these manufacturers resented being dependent on foreign suppliers, they started the movement factory of Fontainemelon, in the Val-de-Ruz.[20] This and other competition did not seem to hurt Japy's business.

In 1799, Japy's business had grown to the point that he could afford to make models of, and take patents out on, ten tools. He had probably been using these tools for years, but because Swiss patents were only good for five years, was reluctant to share his drawings or machines before he was well established.

The patent introduction reads: "The following machines execute the principal parts of a watch with speed and precision, employing only workmen of little skill, and even of day laborers or children." This was a dream come true for Japy.

Plate 124. Japy movement from Dr. Ted Crom's collection. Note name on left side of plate.

When he retired in 1806, at the ripe old age of 57, he left his prosperous business to his three sons. The company name was changed to Japy Freres, and the company remained in business until 1910.

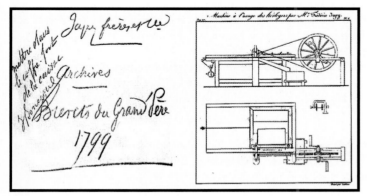

Plate 125. The drawing Japy sent in to apply for his patent. *This illustration used courtesy of Dr. Theodore Crom.*

POLITICS

The French Revolution had an enormous effect on the popularity of the watch. Many beautiful, valuable watches and chains were destroyed during these years. Because any display of wealth was frowned upon, and watches were definitely a sign of wealth or place in society, the industry suffered. The watchmakers that survived did so by exporting their watches to other countries through established contacts.

As stated earlier, styles usually do not change overnight; there is usually an overlapping of the old and the new. After the revolution in France, there was definitely an exception to this rule. Almost overnight, the French government legalized drastic changes. They even changed the side of the road on which carriages could be driven. This is why, to this day, we drive on the opposite side on the road from the English.

Another change was not as lasting. France changed to a decimal system of recording time. Each day had ten hours, and each hour had 100 minutes. The year 1792 was designated as year one. For a while, the change kept watchmakers busy converting movements to fit the new type of dial needed for this new way of measuring time. Eventually the ten hour day proved much too complicated for the average person, and the decimal system was discontinued on January 1, 1806 (year 14). For a look at the dial of a watch that commemorated the Revolution, turn to the Watches section and see plates #198 and #199 on p. 105 and 106.

Throughout most of the eighteenth century, the English were the leaders of the watchmaking industry. They concentrated their efforts on making and developing accurate timepieces. Meanwhile, the French were known for beautifully decorated watches and watch cases. Many watch cases that bear marks from other countries were indeed made and decorated in France. The French were also known for their fine watchmakers, and are credited with bringing thinner watches into fashion. The Swiss concentrated on raising their production of watches during the century, and that soon proved to be their advantage. By the end of the century, the Swiss had became the new leaders in watch production.

THE CHARACTERS

Hopefully, this small section will make some of these important figures in watchmaking seem more real. It seems as if members of the top echelon of any profession seem to know and interact with each other. This was also true in the early years of watchmaking.

HOOKE AND TOMPION

One of the main watchmaking characters of the seventeenth century was Dr. Robert Hooke, born in 1635. According to many reports, he was a genius. Sir Isaac Newton dubbed him "the Considerer." He could assist in astronomical operations or philosophical works. He served as Professor of Mechanics to the Royal Society and at the same time was Professor of Geometry at Gresham College. His other loves were watches and watchmaking tools.

In 1674, Hooke needed a quadrant made and commissioned Thomas Tompion to make it. He was so pleased with Tompion's work that he used him to make his ideas tangible. Hooke was proficent in many areas, and his complicated mind could jump from one project to another. Tompion was quiet and one of the finest watch and clock makers of the century. They were both bachelors and didn't have to report to anyone.

Hooke and Tompion became partners in many projects. With their differences in temperament, they did not always get along. It seems like the glue that held them together was their love for watchmaking and their desire to improve watches and watchmaking tools.

In the book *The History of Clocks and Watches*, Eric Briton describes Tompion as a "model of rectitude." Hooke, on the other hand, is portrayed quite differently. This is a man who, at different times, took in two young girls, one of whom was his niece. When his niece came of age, she became his mistress. When she later married and moved out, he still tried to pursue her. History repeated itself with the second girl. He just couldn't seem to help chasing after them after they left.

There are not any known portraits of Hooke, but Aubrey's *Lives of Eminent Men* contains this word picture: "He is of middling stature, somewhat crooked, pale faced, and his face but little belowed, but his head is lardge; his eie is full and popping, and not quick; a grey eie. He has a delicate head of haire, brown, and of an excellent moiste curle. He is and ever was very temperate and moderate in dyet, &c. As he is of produgious inventive head, so he is a person of great vertue and goodness."

Tompion was four years younger than Hooke. His friendship with Hooke brought him to the attention of many important people. He became one of the most famous, successful watchmakers in English history. When he died in 1713, his body was buried in Westminster Abbey. A look at the timeline for the seventeenth century will give you an idea of his many accomplishments.

TOMPION AND GRAHAM

In 1695, Tompion took George Graham as a journeyman after Graham had served his apprenticeship. Graham was born about 1673. After joining Tompion, he met and married Tompion's niece, Elizabeth. Graham and Tompion's friendship lasted until Tompion died in 1713. Tompion left his business and stock to his dear friend.

Graham carried on the business and became famous in his own right. Graham was the man who met Harrison when he first came to London. Graham was so impressed with Harrison that he loaned him money interest free in order to see Harrison's work continue. They became friends, and Harrison succeeded in winning the prize for solving the longitude problem. A look at the timeline will give you an idea of Graham's many accomplishments.

Prior to Tompion's death, his and Graham's watches were marked "Tompion and Graham." According to *Britten's*, watches with a number greater than 4369 were made after 1713. The highest known number is 6574 and the watch it was found on was made about 1751, the year Graham died. Graham marked his watches in four places so that they would not be as easy to fake as some were.

MUDGE

The next in this line of lives and events was Thomas Mudge (1715 – 1794), who served as an apprentice to Graham. One of Mudge's many accomplishments was the invention of the lever escapement. After Graham died, Mudge set up his own shop and had as a client the king of Spain. Mudge the detached lever escapement, one of his greatest achievements. The queen's watch was the first one that he made using this lever escapement. You may see it at Windsor Castle.

ABRAHAM LOUIS BREGUET

A book on watches would be incomplete without at least a few words about Abraham-Louis Breguet. A popular phrase used to describe architecture in the twentieth century was Louis Sullivan's "form follows function." Breguet seemed to know this instinctively two hundred years earlier. In fact, he is often referred to as the "inventor of modern design."

Breguet was born in Neuchatel, Switzerland, in 1747, but his adopted home became France after his father died. His mother married a watchmaker whose family had a shop in Paris. When Breguet was 15 years old, his stepfather took him to France to serve an apprenticeship. He studied mathematics at College Mazarin. His teacher was Abbe Marie, who also was a tutor to many children from aristocratic families. Consequently, Breguet was introduced to these and to other wealthy people, many of whom later became his clients.

A marriage in 1775 to Cecile Marie-Louise l' Huiller provided him with the money to open a business. In 1781 Breguet developed the perpetual, or self-winding, watch. In 1787 he started using the lever escapement, and two years later he introduced "gong" wires as a substitute for the bells in his repeating watches. These were the years in which the first records of Breguet's business were kept. Between 1787 and 1791, he partnered with a dealer of clocks and watches.

During the French Revolution, Breguet left Paris for Geneva (1793). When he returned to Paris in 1795, he came back full of enthusiam and ideas. He had enjoyed getting to known the watchmakers in Geneva, but he was eager to get back to his adopted home. In this same year, Breguet invented the Tourbillion, for which he received a patent in 1801.

In a workshop notebook begun on December 3, 1797, Breguet expressed his thoughts on taking care of details:

> ...for all sorts of pieces whose plan, determined after long experience has shown what is best, that all the parts have been judged of easy use for the owner, solid, of simple conception and easy to repair anywhere, and that the delicate parts are not liable to be deteriorated by wear or by shocks. The finisher must be informed of the rules guiding its arrangement, the perfectly uniform attention to the careful execution of a given model. The same placement of the balance spring, the same size and number of coils, the same shape of the balance spring stud and the regular index, so that the resemblance strikes the eye. The same is true of the exterior: the dimensions of the case, the dial, the way in which the name is marked either by painting or engraving, must be similar and placed in the same manner as the model. The hands, the crystal dome, the keys, ect. . . . everything must be characteristic of the maker. Once the eye is accustomed to this similitude, the slightest fault, the best counterfeit, will immediately be detected. as a result, the work will be infinitely better in all ways, with advantages for the workmen, who will perfect their efforts and will have more pleasure in accomplishing them, as well as the "establisseur." It is of the highest importance that this procedure be followed for all sorts of pieces.

As you can, see he had definite opinions about how his watches should be made and finished.

In 1790, Breguet invented his "shock proof" or "parachute" watch. Five years later, he invented his unique Tourbillion in which the entire escapement is housed inside a revolving carriage. This arrangement helped the movement remain constant no matter what position the watch was placed in.

From the notebook begun on the December 14, 1801:

> ....that the crystal dome should have the same shape as the case back. That it should not cast any shadows on the dial, that it should touch neither the dial or the hands, nor the central arbor, that it should perfectly penetrate the snap, that it should be more loosely fitting on the bottom of the groove than on the sides: that it should snap when fitted in.[21]

It's evident that Breguet's streamlined look had evolved. His earlier watches had enameled dials and Arabic numbers. He favored pink gold and designed his own "moon hands" which are known today as "Breguet" style. In an article about Breguet, Jean-Claude Sabrier states that on his Breguet-style watches made shortly before the French Revolution, "Arabic numbers were combined with small stars for the division of the minutes and the five minute fractions were marked by a stylized fleur-de-lis."[21] Breguet's early watches were signed "BREGUET." In 1807, his son became a full partner in the company and the signature became "Breguet et Fils."

Because Breguet watches were so highly regarded, there were many fakes on the market. For every genuine Breguet watch exported from Paris between 1790 and 1823, there were 500 fakes. Anyone truly familiar with Breguet's quality and style will probably not be fooled, because fakes were often made as a heavy, chunky pair-case watch.[22] To try and stop of the fraudulent use of his name, Berguet devised a secret signature about 1794. The signature is on a silver dial and is done with a fine engraver, and can only be seen by turning the watch so that reflected light falls on the dial below the number 12. On enameled dials such as the ones on "souscription" watches, you need reflected light plus a magnifier to see the signature. Breguet's souscription watch deserves a book of its own. For this book, Dr. Theodore Crom has allowed us to look at his watch and its secret signature. Breguet had royals and other famous people as patrons and lived to receive numerous awards. Breguet died suddenly in 1823, leaving a legacy of watchmaking excellence that is unsurpassed. He is today considered the greatest horologist of all time. See plates below.

Hopefully, this small glimpse of these five men will help you remember that they were real people. This list could go on, and on but I hope that this gives you an idea of how the chain of men helped the evolution of the pocket watch. Remember that these men also interacted with other eminent watchmakers in other countries. Though these other watchmakers cannot be covered in the confines of this book, there are many books that can give you information about these interesting lives. I recommend *Britten's Old Clocks and Watches and Their Makers*. The National Association of Watch and Clock Collectors has videos about famous watchmakers that are available for loan. That feature alone is worth its small membership fee.

Plate 128. Now you can! Signature under magnification with reflected light. *Courtesy of Dr. Ted Crom.*

Plates 126 and 127. Breguet souscription watch #1498. Can you see the signature on the dial? Just kidding! *Courtesy of Dr. Ted Crom.*

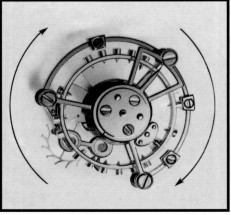

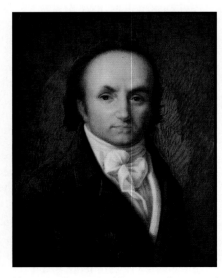

Plates 129 and 130. Two views of the Tourbillon that show the escapement inside a revolving carriage that turns 360 degrees per minute. It is used to solve timekeeping inconsistencies caused by changes in position. *Photos courtesy of Antiquorum Auctioneers.*

Plate 131. Portrait of Breguet. *Courtesy of Antiquorum Auctioneers.*

EIGHTEENTH CENTURY TIMELINE

1704 — Nicolas Facio, along with Peter and Jacob, developed a way to use bored rubies as "seats" to protect pivots, the major wear points in watch movements.

1705 — Beetle- and poker-style hands appeared. They were used for about 100 years.

1714 — Board of Longitude offered a huge award for solving the longitude problem.

1715 – 1774 — Louis VX was King of France.

1715 — Dust-caps started to be used. They were probably introduced by George Graham (1673 – 1751).

1715 — George Graham invented the dead beat escapement used in clocks.

1720 — Christopher Pinchbeck (1670 – 1732) came up with the alloy that bears his name.

1720 — Many case makers started giving themselves credit for their work by putting their initials on the case. Case makers in England had been marking theirs since the seventeenth century.

1722 — Abbe Jean Hautefeuille issued a description of the rack lever escapement. This description was improved and patented in 1791, by Peter Litherland.

1725 – 1750 — Scenes and figures done in repoussé embellished watch cases.

1726 — George Graham, building on the efforts of Thomas Tompion, developed the cylinder escapement.

1727 — George II was King of Great Britain.

1730 – 1773 — Frederick Straus factory operated. It made paste stones (imitation gemstones) used in jewelry and on watch cases.

1734 — John Harrison invented "maintaining power."

1739 — Methodist movement was begun by John Wesley.

1740 — Most watchmakers began to number watch movements.

1740 — Thomas Mudge made the first watch that would repeat the minute. It struck the hours, the quarters, and the minutes.

1749 — Harrison invented the compensation balance.

1750 — The duplex escapement came into use, though it was originally invented in 1720, by Jean Bapiste Dutertre. It was mostly used for high grade watches.

1750 – 1775 — Many watchmakers left Geneva for other countries because of injustices imposed upon them by the class system.

1750 — White enamel watch dials were used.

1750 — Julian Le Roy came out with what was called a "dumb repeater." This watch had a hammer that struck a metal block and therefore did away with bells. The hammer and block also allowed the watch to be thinner. Dumb repeaters made it possible for users to determine the time without disturbing others.

1753 — J. A. Lepaute invented the virgule escapement. It was used in French watches.

1754 – 1759 — Dead beat escapement originally used by George Graham in clocks was modified for use in watches by Thomas Mudge, in England, and Pierre Le Roy, in France.

1755 — Tompion's regulator was improved by Joseph Bosley. It was not used much until near the end of the century.

1756 — Harrison invented the compensation curb.

1759 — Mudge made queen's watch using his lever escapement.

1760 — Watches cases with four different colors of gold were introduced.

1760 — A clear flux enamel was invented for use as a protective coating for enamels.

1760 — The chronometer escapement came onto the scene, but it was not made for a watch.

1760 — George III was King of Great Britain and Ireland.

1761 – 1762 — Harrison's #4 watch was taken on a voyage from Portsmouth to Jamaica (Nov. 1761 to Jan. 1762).

1762 – 1796 — Catherine the Great was Tsarina of Russia.

1764 — The cylinder escapement was improved by using a steel wheel and a ruby cylinder and was introduced by John Arnold. This improvement was used by Arnold, Elliott, and Breguet.

1765 — Center seconds came into use.

1766 — Pierre LeRoy invents pivoted detent escapement for chronometer.

1767 – 1771 — James Cook discovered Australia and named it New South Wales.

1770 — Detached lever escapement invented by Mudge was put into use.

1770 — Self-winding watch was invented by Perrelet.

1770 — Engine-turned decorations were used on watches.

1770 — Pocket chronometer escapement was developed from the marine chronometer.

1770 – 1820 — Development of the lever watch escapement.

1772 — The Lepine watch could be hand set from the back of the watch. It had a cylinder escapement.

1773 — Boston Tea Party.

1774 — British Parliament passed "intolerable acts" against North America.

1775 – 1783 — American war for independence.

1774 – 1792 — Louis XVI was King of France.

1775 — Breguet started making fine watches.

1775 — John Arnold introduced the helical balance spring.

1776 — Declaration of Independence by colonies.

1776 — Lepine developed the isochronic hairspring.

1776 — Thin watches were introduced by Lepine.

1776 — Leroy improved upon John Harrison's compensated balance.

1776 — Fredreick Japy (1749 – 1812) made and assembled machines that a common laborer could operate to make parts.

1776 — Jean Moyse Pouzait (1743 – 1793) invented the center seconds watch.

1780 — The second hand came into use.

1780 — Arabic hour numbers appeared on watches.

1780 — John Arnold and Thomas Earnshaw invented the spring detent escapement.

1781 — Breguet developed the perpetual, or self-winding, watch.

1782 — The duplex was introduced to England by Thomas Tyrer. This escapement was conceived by Dr. Hooke, but modified by Jean Bapiste Dutertre, in 1720, and by Pierre Le Roy, in 1750.

1783 — British recognized the independence of the American colonies.

1785 — Josiah Emery and John Leroux applied draw to the lever watch. It was not used used again until about 20 years later.

1787 — United States Constitution was signed.

1787 — Breguet started making lever watches.

1789 — Washington was elected the first president of the United States.

1789 — Beginning of the French Revolution. The fall of the Bastille. History shows that the leader of the attack was a watchmaker.

1790 – 1820 — Automated watches originated during these years, they had figures on the dial that appeared to strike bells.

1790 — Shock-proof watch was invented by Breguet. He called it a parachute, because it used a form of elastic suspension for the balance shaft pivots.

1791 — Rack lever escapement was patented by Litherland; it was used until about 1840. It was created by Hautefeville in 1722.

1792 — Perpetual calender watch was invented.

1792 — France began the decimal system of timekeeping.

1792 — France declared itself a republic.

1793 – 1794 — Reign of terror in France.

1795 — Breguet made his first perpetual calendar watch.

1795 — Breguet invented the Tourbillion, by which the escapement of the watch revolved. He received his patent in 1801.

1796 — Breguet replaced the bell in a repeating watch with a circular tone spring or gong that coiled around the movement.

1796 — Antoine Favre introduced mechanical music without the use of bells or gongs. His steel comb made miniature musical watches possible because it took up less space.

1798 — Pin pallet escapement was conceived by Louis Perron (1779 – 1836).

EIGHTEENTH CENTURY WATCHES

Photos of watches from the eighteenth century are presented in chronological order.

Plate 132. Fromanteel & Clarke, London, made for a French client, circa 1700.
Extremely rare and very fine 22K gold, pair-cased watch with date, decorated in the French baroque style.

Case. Outer: double-body, engraved with inhabited foliage, a mask at the top, small medallion with a portrait in the center. Inner: double-body, "bassine," polished, loose ring pendant. **Dial.** Gold champlevé, radial Roman numerals, outer minute track with five-minute Arabic markers in polished cartouches, center pierced and chased with inhabited foliage. Blued steel beetle and poker hands. **Movement.** 41 mm, hinged gilt brass full plate with elaborate pierced gilt brass pillars, fusee with chain, verge escapement, plain steel three-arm balance, flat balance spring, gilt brass English cock with streamers pierced and engraved with foliage. Signed on the dial and back plate.
Diam. 57 mm. **$33,350.00.**
Photo and description courtesy of Antiquorum Auctioneers, 16 Nov 2002.

Plate 133. Clock-Watch.
Circa 1700.

A clock-watch basically has two movements inside of it. It is like a clock; it strikes by itself, so it is a self-striking watch. It is not a repeater. This actually strikes, automatically, on the hour and the half, like a clock. Having that kind of movement, it has to be two-trained. There are two winding holes. One winds up the watch and one winds up the striking mechanism. It is made by Windmills, who is a very famous maker. Magnificent and beautiful, the whole family of Windmills were quite famous. They made very expensive, very good quality clocks as well.
$6,000.00.
Description and watch courtesy of Somlo Antiques.

Plate 134. Circa 1700.
Fine early silver pair-case repoussé calendar alarm by J. George Viollier, Geneva.

The **outer case** has a lovely repoussé scene of the Judgment of Paris in particularly fine condition. Fine silver champlevé **dial** has central alarm ring and outer manual calendar. Fine pierced and engraved cock with square foot and streamers. Fancy pierced tulip pillars with fancy capitals. Pierced alarm barrel. The **inner case** has beautiful pierced and engraved inhabited foliage. A fine and handsome early complicated timepiece.
Diam. 57 mm. **$10,250.00.**
Photo and description courtesy of Stephen Bogoff, Antiquarian Horologist.

Plate 135. Vertumnus and Pomona.
Huaud school enamel, circa 1700, movement by De Beaufre, London, circa 1735.
Very fine and rare 20K gold and painted-on enamel-on-copper pair-cased watch.

Case. Outer: two-body, glazed on both sides, the front bezel with scrolls alternating with a posy of flowers, the back bezel with cornucopia, urns, and scrolls. Inner: two-body, "bassine," the back with a very fine enamel painted on copper, showing Vertumnus and Pomona, from an engraving by Cornelis Vermeulen (1644 – 1708/9) after Antoine Coypel (1661 – 1722), the band painted with four cartouches showing countryside landscapes, the enamel inside the back painted with a fisherman beside a peaceful river and a house amongst trees on the far bank, small pendant, gold bow (later). **Dial.** Gold, champlevé Roman chapters with half-hour divisions, outer minute ring with five minute Arabic markers in polished cartouches, blued-steel poker and beetle hands.
Movement. 34.4 mm, hinged gilt brass full plate with round baluster pillars, fusee and chain, verge escapement, plain four-arm brass balance, double-footed gilt cock pierced and engraved with scrolling foliage, wheel and click set-up, pierced and engraved silver bracket for fusee stop lever.
Signed on the movement.
Diam. 42.4 mm, 48 mm with outer case.
Published in the Sandberg book, pages 104 – 105. **$8,252.00.**
Photo and description courtesy of Antiquorum Auctioneers, 14 Jun 2003.

Plate 136. Circa 1700.
Fine and very scarce English jumping-hour sector antique pocket watch by Antram, London.

Handsome engraved gilt **dial** with silver engraved sector section, blued-steel beetle hand, and aperature for the jump hours, with two charming enamel miniatures below. Lovely shagreen outer **case** with typical cracks and some losses to the edge. The masked balance cock with streamers is pierced and engraved with inhabited foliage. Pierced Egyptian pillars with silver capitals. English sector watches are much rarer than those made on the Continent, and this is a particularly attractive and early example.
Diam. 56 mm. **$18,000.00.**
Photo and description courtesy of Stephen Bogoff, Antiquarian Horologist.

Plate 137. Circa 1700.
Fine large and extremely rare Dutch silver pair-case, jump portrait verge and fusee antique pocket watch by Paulus Bramer, Amsterdam.

Fine silver champlevé **dial** with fine blued-steel beetle and poker hands and an aperature disclosing a series of five portraits that can be changed by depressing the pendant. The portraits appear to be of one family, as there are an adult man and woman and three children. Fine fat **movement** with pierced Egyptian pillars and large pierced and engraved balance cock with streamers, the foot and regulator plate also pierced and engraved. The back of the outer **case** mounted with a fine enamel portrait. A wonderful watch in particularly fine condition throughout. Diam. 60 mm. **$12,500.00.**
Photo and description courtesy of Stephen Bogoff, Antiquarian Horologist.

Plate 138. Circa 1700.
Fine large early English silver gilt bell quarter-repeater pair-case antique pocket watch by Joseph Williamson, London.

Champlevé **dial** with blued beetle and poker hands. Fine large pierced and engraved masked balance cock with diamond cap jewel, streamers, the foot and regulator plate also pierced and engraved. The **movement** has dust cover. The **cases** have lovely piercing and engraving.
Very attractive and loud, clear tone.
Diam. 59 mm. **$6,800.00.**
Photo and description courtesy of Stephen Bogoff, Antiquarian Horologist.

Plate 139. Circa 1700. Triple-case watch made by Joseph Windmill of London, one of the top few watchmakers in the history of time.

Inside case, plain, polished. Next **case** is 20K gold. Circa 1700 because it says "& Sons." Prior to 1700, it would have said only "Joseph Windmill." Mint condition.
$20,000.00.
Courtesy of Jeff Rosen, Collector/Dealer, Solvang Antique Center.

**Plate 140. Arman a Collonge, Geneva, circa 1700.
Rare and fine silver single-hand "oignon" watch.**

Case. Two-body, polished. **Dial.** White enamel, radial Roman numerals on raised enamel cartouches, inner quarter-hour ring, center with very small rosette. Gilt beetle hand. **Movement.** 44 mm, hinged, gilt full plate with Egyptian pillars, fusee and chain, verge escapement with brass balance and short balance spring, Louis XIV cock pierced and engraved with scrolling foliage pattern. Signed on the movement.
Diam. 56 mm. **$2,649.00.**
Photo and description courtesy of Antiquorum Auctioneers, 16 Nov 2002.

Plate 141. Thomas Gorsuch, No. 323, Salop, circa 1700. Fine silver pair-cased watch.

Case. Outer: two-body, polished; inner: two-body, "bassine," with deep back, polished. **Dial.** Silver, champlevé radial Roman numerals, outer minute ring with five-minute Arabic markers on polished cartouches, repoussé center with British coat-of arms. Blued-steel beetle and poker hands. **Movement.** 41 mm, hinged, gilt brass full plate with Egyptian pillars, fusee and chain, verge escapement, plain steel three-arm balance, flat balance spring, single-footed cock with straight line base and streamers, neck engraved with a mask.
Signed on the movement.
Diam. 54 mm. **$3,324.00.**
Photo and description courtesy of Antiquorum Auctioneers, 16 Nov 2003.

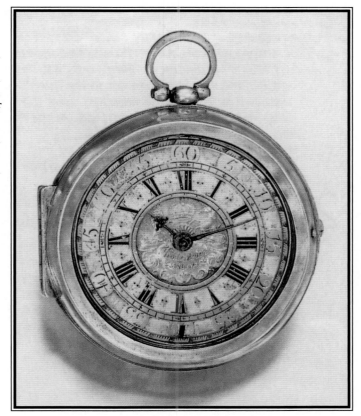

Plate 142. Vertumnus and Pomona. Huaut school enamel, circa 1700, movement by De Beaufre, London, circa 1735. Very fine and rare 20K gold and enamelled copper pair-cased watch.

Case. Outer: two-body, glazed on both sides, the front bezel with scrolls alternating with a posy of flowers, the back bezel with cornucopia, urns, and scrolls. Inner: two-body, "bassine," the back with a very fine enamel painted on copper showing Vertumnus and Pomona, from an engraving by Cornelis Vermeulen (1644 – 1708/9) after Antoine Coypel (1661 – 1722), the band painted with four cartouches showing countryside landscapes, the enamel inside the back painted with a fisherman beside a peaceful river and a house amongst trees on the far bank, small pendant, gold bow (later). **Dial.** Gold champlevé Roman chapters with half-hour divisions, outer minute ring with five-minute Arabic numerals in polished cartouches. Blue-steel poker and beetle hands. **Movement.** 34.4 mm, hinged gilt brass full plate with round baluster pillars, fusee and chain, verge escapement, plain Four-arm brass balance, double-footed cock pierced and engraved with scrolling foliage, pierced and engraved silver bracket for fusee stop lever.
Signed on the movement.
Diam. 42.4 mm, 48 mm with outer case. Published in the Sandberg book, pages 104 – 105. **$13,294.00.**
Photo and description courtesy of Antiquorum Auctioneers, 17 Nov 2002.

Plate 143. Brouncker Watts, London, No. 715, hallmarked 1709 – 1710. Very fine and rare 22K gold pair-cased watch.

Case. Outer: two-body, polished, box-hinged; inner: two-body, "bassine," with deep back, polished. **Dial.** Gold, matte, champlevé radial Roman numerals, inner half-hour divisions, outer minute divisions with five-minute Arabic figures on polished cartouches, chased center with mask and scrolling. Blued-steel beetle and poker hands. **Movement.** 41 mm, gilt brass full plate with Egyptian pillars, fusee and chain, verge escapement, plain steel three-arm balance, flat balance spring, single-footed English cock with streamers. Signed on dial and movement.
Diam. 56 mm. **$9,306.00.**
Photo and description courtesy of Antiquorum Auctioneers, 16 Nov 2002.

Plate 144. (Aniel) Quare, London, No. 3354, circa 1710.
Fine silver pair-cased watch with date.

Case. Outer: double body, polished. Inner: double body "bassine," with deep back part, polished, swivel pendant, loose ring. **Dial.** Silver champlevé with Roman numerals and outer Arabic minute ring, center with pierced cartouche and aperture for date. Blued-steel poker and beetle hands. **Movement.** 41 mm, hinged gilt brass full plate with Egyptian pillars, fusee with chain, verge escapement, plain steel three-arm balance, flat balance spring with 1.5 coils, gilt brass English cock with streamers pierced and engraved with a shell and foliage. Signed on the dial and back plate.
Diam. 55 mm. **$4,485.00.**
Photo and description courtesy of Antiquorum Auctioneers, 14 Jun 2003.

Plate 145. Jupiter en Pluie d'Or.
Jean Mussard, Geneva, circa 1710, movement by George Richards, London, No. 16011.
Very fine and very rare 18K gold and enamel watch.

Case. Two-body, "bassine," the back very finely painted with Danae being visited by Jupiter disguised as a shower of golden rain, band painted with a continuous rural landscape and a traveler with his donkey against a river landscape background. **Dial.** White enamel, Roman hour chapter, outer minute divisions with five-minute Arabic numerals. Gold Louis XV hands. **Movement.** 35mm (15¼"), full plate, square baluster pillars, fusee and chain, verge escapement, steel, three-arm balance with flat spring, one-footed cock pierced and engraved in asymmetrical scrolls and foliage with a flower blossom in the center, rack and pinion regulator with a silver plate calibrated from 1 to 6 in Arabic numerals.
Signed on the movement, the enameller's signature on the case.
Diam. 42 mm. **$16,618.00.**
Photo and description courtesy of Antiquorum Auctioneers, 16 Nov 2002.

Plate 146. George Graham, London, No. 416, casemaker William Sherwood, hallmarked 1716.
Very fine and rare 22K pair-cased quarter-repeating watch.

Case. Outer: two-body, square hinge, back with inhabited foliage centered by a monogram, mask, and exotic birds, hand with four engraved cartouches with four scenes, separated by pierced and engraved masks with dragons. Inner: two-body, band entirely pierced and engraved with exotic birds, dragon heads, mask, all intertwined with foliage, with polished back, gilded dust cap. **Dial.** Gold, champlevé, Roman chapters, outer minute ring arched every five minutes in the Dutch manner with five-minute Arabic numerals, gold beetle and poker hands. **Movement.** 35.3 mm, hinged gilt brass full plate with round baluster pillars, fusee and escapement. Plain steel three-arm balance, single-footed cock, pierced and engraved with asymmetrical foliage and a child's head at the base. Diamond stone. Stogden-type repeating system, repeating on bell by depressing the pendant.
Signed on the movement and dust cap.
Diam. 51 mm. Published in the Sandberg book, pages 130 – 131.
$8,309.00.
Photo and description courtesy of Antiquorum Auctioneers, 31 Mar 2001.

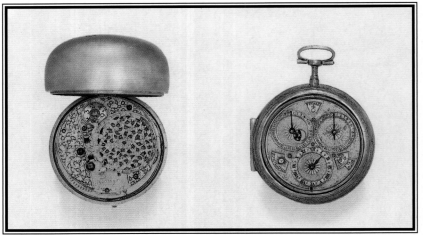

Plate 147. Louys Prevost, Geneva, case by L. Arpin fecit, circa 1710.
Very fine and rare silver, pair-cased, astronomical, single-hand watch with manual perpetual calendar and moon phases.

Case. Outer: "bassine," back engraved with a town scene, surrounded by a strap with foliage and fleur-de-lis pattern. Inner: "bassine," polished. **Dial.** Marred gilt brass plate, entirely chased, the three applied silver subsidiary dial rings showing the date, the hours with Roman chapters, and the age of the moon. A circular aperture within the last indicates the phases of the moon. A sector below the pendant shows the day and its astrological sign, and at four o'clock, the month and the corresponding zodiac sign, at eight o'clock, the four periods of the day. Blued-steel hands.
Movement. 39.4 mm 0, gilt brass full plate, tulip pillars, five-wheel train, verge escapement, plain steel three-arm balance, blued-steel balance spring, large English type cock pierced and engraved with a fruit vase in the centre surrounded by symmetrical foliage, large foot decorated with matching foliage, worm-wheel set-up, rack-and-pinion regulator with silver plate.
Signed "Louys Prevost" on the movement, outer case signed "LARPIN FECIT," inner case stamped inside "IC," under a coronet.
Diam. 51 mm. Published in the Sandberg book, pages 126 – 127. **$38,336.00.**
Photo and description courtesy of Antiquorum Auctioneers, 31 Mar 2001.

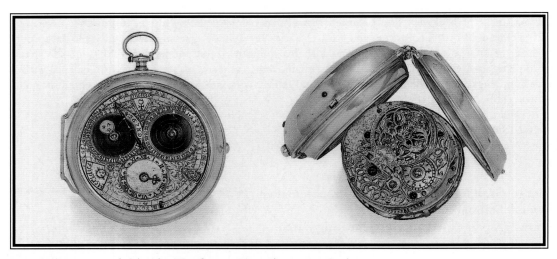

Plate 148. Owen Robinson and Charles Fredman, Napoli, circa 1715.
Very fine and rare astronomical gold watch with manual perpetual calendar, phases of the moon, and regulator-type dial.

Case. Two-body, "oignon" type, box-hinged, polished, engraved on the back "Manuel Godoy Principe De La Paz," slide in the edge opens a winding shutter. **Dial.** Marred gilt brass plate, entirely engraved. The three applied silver subsidiary dials show: on the right, the date with a gilt arrow mounted on a blued-steel revolving disc; on the left, the age of the moon in the same way, and the phases of the moon inset in the disc; below, the hours. Aperture below the pendant for the day and its astrological sign, at four o'clock the month and the corresponding Zodiac sign, and at eight o'clock the four pans of the day. Blued-steel beetle hand and central minute hand with heart tip. **Movement.** 40 mm 0, gilt brass full plate, square baluster pillars, fusee and chain, verge escapement, plain steel three-arm balance, blued-steel balance spring, single-footed gilt brass cock, pierced and engraved with symmetrical inhabited foliage, worm and wheel set-up, rack-and-pinion regulator with silver plate.
Signed on the movement.
Diam. 55 mm. Published in the Sandberg book, pages 126 – 127. **$38,336.00.**
Photo and description courtesy of Antiquorum Auctioneers, 31 Mar 2001.

**Plate 149. Circa 1720.
John Ellicott, London, England,
one of the top three most famous
watchmakers.**

Gold repoussé **case**, mint condition.
Case signed on the back "John Manly
case maker, 1675 – 1730."
$10,000.00.
*Courtesy of Jeff Rosen, Collector,
Solvang Antique Center.*

**Plate 150. Johann Christoph Erhardt, Augsburg,
circa 1720.
Fine and rare gilt brass wandering hour watch
with painted-on enamel portrait.**

Case. Three-body, glazed on both sides, Consular
type, polished and gilt. **Dial.** Silver, Roman champlevé
"wandering" numerals appear in a circular window of a
gilt engraved segment set at the top, surmounted by
silver Arabic minute chapter segment. The window,
with the correct hour inside, points to the correct minutes, below the Roman numeral quarter-hour segment.
The bottom has an applied miniature enamel portrait
of a lady surrounded by two trumpeting cherubs.
Movement. 46 mm, hinged, gilt full plate with elaborate Egyptian pillars, fusee and chain, verge escapement, plain steel balance with flat balance spring,
double-footed glass cock.
Signed on the movement.
Diam. 64 mm. **$5,113.00.**
*Photo and description courtesy of Antiquorum Auctioneers,
14 Jun 2003.*

Plate 151. Circa 1730.
Fine, early, and scarce French gilt and enamel Adam and Eve automaton antique pocket watch by Gille De Beefe a Liege.

Faded gilt consular **case** with glazed back exposing a large enameled scene of Adam and Eve in the garden, with a silver snake revolving around the edge, all within a gilt ring engraved with the name of the maker. The **movement** fancy architectural pillars, the balance is under the dial. White enamel **dial** with gold hands has repairs to the winding and regulator holes.

This is a scarce and very early Adam and Eve watch with a large scene and hour duration snake automaton. Later examples typically have much smaller scenes and faster moving snakes.

Diam. 52 mm. **$10,000.00.**

Photo and description courtesy of Stephen Bogoff, Antiquarian Horologist.

Plate 152. The Temptation.
Gille de Beefe a Liege, circa 1730. Very fine and unusual double-sided gilt metal and enamel Adam and Eve animated watch.

Case. Two-body, glazed on both sides, polished bezels. On the back, framed by an engraved gilt band, there is a circular enamel plaque with a painted scene depicting Adam and Eve in the Garden of Eden, surrounded by animals, with the Tree of Knowledge in the center. The silver snake revolves around the enameled scene, pursuing and tempting Adam and Eve, and making one revolution of the dial per hour. **Dial.** White enamel, Roman chapters, outer minute ring with five-minute Arabic numerals. Aperture for the regulator at 6 o'clock. Gold poker and beetle hands. **Movement.** 39.2 mm, hinged gilt brass full

plate with baluster pillars, square at the bottom and circular at the top, fusee and chain, verge escapement, plain three-arm balance with flat balance spring, mounted under the dial plate, plain bar-type double-footed cock, motion train driven directly from the fusee arbor. The snake is mounted on a gear driven by the main train.

Signed on the frame of the painting.

Diam. 50 mm. Published in the Sandberg book, pages 132 – 133. **$4,934.00.**

Photo and description courtesy of Antiquorum Auctioneers, 14 Jun 2003.

Plate 153. Circa 1733.
Fine, large, and impressive English silver pair-case verge and fusee antique pocket watch by Markham, London.

Fine silver champlevé **dial** with gilt decorations between the numerals and fancy gilt hands. Fine large pierced and engraved silver masked balance cock with streamers, the foot and regulator plate also pierced and engraved. The tapered square pillars have fancy fluted bases.
Very attractive and in excellent condition throughout.
Diam. 57 mm. **$5,000.00.**
Photo and description courtesy of Stephen Bogoff, Antiquarian Horologist.

Plate 154. Circa 1746.
Fine Scottish 20K gold repoussé pair case verge and fusee antique pocket watch by Andrew Dickie, Edinburgh.

The **outer case** has a classical scene (typical wear) of three figures against a landscape within scrolling borders. The **movement** has beautiful masked cock with diamond cap and fancy square pillars.
Good example.
Diam. 49 mm. **$5,000.00.**
Photo and description courtesy of Stephen Bogoff, Antiquarian Horologist.

Plate 155. Circa 1750.
Fine 20K gold English repoussé pair-case verge and fusee bell quarter-repeater antique pocket watch by John Archambo, London.

The **outer case** has a classical scene within rococo borders, which are pierced to let the sound out. The **inner case** pierced and engraved with inhabited folliage. Fine **movement** with dust cover, pierced and engraved masked cock with pierced and engraved foot and regulator plate, formerly with pulse piece. Fully restored **dial** with gold beetle and poker hands.
Loud clear tone.
Diam. 47 mm. **$7,500.00.**
Photo and description courtesy of Stephen Bogoff, Antiquarian Horologist.

Plate 156. Circa 1750.
Pierre LeRoy, a famous French watch maker.
Went up against Harrison for an award. Also had a famous father.
Enameled, 20K gold quarter-hour repeater, #1165 Paris.

$8,500.00.
Courtesy of Jeff Rosen, Collector, Solvang Antique Center.

Plate 157. Hallmarked 1752.
20K yellow gold, pair case, quarter-hour repeater, pierced work. Signed "Thomas Calley." He was one of George Grahams successors.
$7,500.00.
Courtesy of Jeff Rosen, Collector, Solvang Antique Center.

Plate 158. Circa 1755.
Good English 20K gold pair case, verge fusee, with gilt shagreen outer, by John Ellicott, London.

The outer **case** is covered with shagreen (shark skin) decorated with brass pins, with small repair. White enamel **dial** has repaired edge chips and gold hands. The masked balance cock has pierced and engraved table and foot, the regulator plate, similarly pierced and engraved.
Very attractive.
Diam. 50 mm. **$3,500.00.**
Photo and description courtesy of Stephen Bogoff, Antiquarian Horologist.

Plate 159. Circa 1760.
Attractive English gilt and horn pair-case, verge and fusee antique pocket watch, by David Rivers, London.

Typical wear to the gilt **cases,** the outer covered with pinned horn underpainted to simulate tortoise shell. (Chips, cracks, and some of the holding pins missing.) Bold white enamel **dial** has blued-steel beetle and poker hands. Fine large pierced and engraved balance cock, the foot and regulator plate also pierced and engraved.
Diam. 50 mm. **$3,000.00.**
Photo and description courtesy of Stephen Bogoff, Antiquarian Horologist.

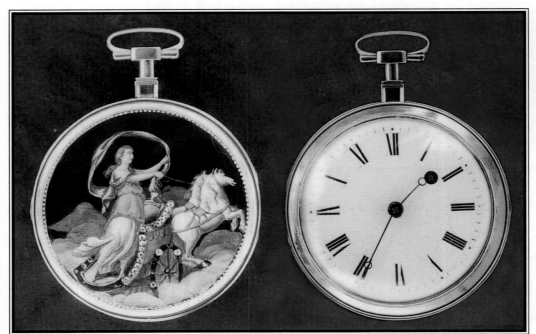

Plate 160. Circa 1760. French, 20K gold, enamelled, verge fusee with beautiful enamelled scene on the back. F. Berthoud, Paris. He was a famous maker and contemporary of LeRoy.

$9,500.00.
Courtesy of Jeff Rosen, Collector, Solvang Antique Center.

Plate 161. Circa 1770.
18K multicolored gold,
verge fusee.
Terrot and Fazy, watchmak-
ers to the Russian Count.

$3,500.00.
Courtesy of Jeff Rosen, Collector,
Solvang Antique Center.

Plate 162. Hallmarked 1770. Eng-
land.
Verge fusee, 20K gold, champlevé
enamel case.
Wm. Sterck.

$3,000.00.
Courtesy of Jeff Rosen, Collector, Solvang
Antique Center.

Plate 163. Crawford, London, No. 1012, made for the Chinese market, circa 1770.
Rare and very fine 22K gold, pair-cased, hard-stone, diamond- and gem-set, hour-striking clock-watch with quarter repeating on a bell.

Case. Outer: gold frame inset with panels of gray striated agate bordered with emeralds and divided by pierced rose-cut diamond-set motifs. Inner: double-body, "bassine," polished, band chased with a scallop shell pierced and engraved with foliate decoration. **Dial.** White enamel with radial Chinese numerals, outer minute track with five-minute Chinese markers. Rose-cut diamond-set Louis XV hands. **Movement.** 32 mm, hinged gilt brass full plate, two train with cylindrical pillars. Going-train with fusee and chain, verge escapement with plain three-arm brass balance and flat spring, gilt brass English cock with diamond endstone, fixed barrel for the striking train. Repeating on a bell by depressing the pendant. Gilt brass dust cap.
Signed on the dust cap and movement.
Diam. 50 mm. **$18,280.00.**
Photo and description courtesy of Antiquorum Auctioneers, 16 Nov 2002.

Plate 164. L'Epine, Hger du Roy, a Paris, circa 1770.
Fine 18K varicolored gold lady's pendant watch.

Case. Two-body, Louis XVI, back centered with an applied varicolored gold flower basket behind a dog, within a green-gold laurel leaf frame, engine-turned ring separating the outer applied green-gold floral decoration, bezels with applied gold repeated pattern. **Dial.** White enamel, radial Roman numerals, outer minute divisions with five-minute Arabic markers, winding aperture between 1 and 2 o'clock. Gold Louis XV hands. **Movement.** Hinged, 24 mm, gilt brass full plate with cylindrical pillars, fusee and chain, verge escapement, plain brass three-arm balance, flat balance spring, continental cock.
Signed on dial and movement.
Diam. 30 mm. **$1,256.00.**
Photo and description courtesy of Antiquorum Auctioneers, 14 Jun 2003.

Plate 165. Circa 1771.
Good English, silver, pair-case, verge and fusee antique pocket watch by William Bayless, London.

Fine white enamel **dial** with blued-steel beetle and poker hands. The **movement** has pierced and engraved cock, foot and regulator plate.
A very nice example.
Diam. 50 mm. **$1,050.00.**
Photo and description courtesy of Stephen Bogoff, Antiquarian Horologist.

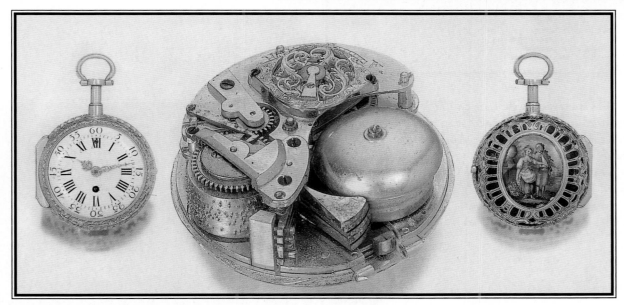

Plate 166. Lovers' Promenade.
Attributed to Jaquet Droz, Geneva, circa 1775.
Exceptionally fine and extremely rare 20K gold and painted-on enamel musical carillon watch playing three tunes.

Case. Two-body, Louis XV, back painted-on enamel without over-glaze, with a scene in oval depicting a young woman strolling with her suitor in a park, border with translucent imperial blue enamel cartouches over flinque, pierced for sound, bezel en suite, extended hinge. **Dial.** White enamel, secured by a single screw at 12, Roman numerals, outer minute divisions with large five-minute Arabic markers. Gold Louis XV hands. **Movement.** 37.5 mm, gilt brass, half-plate, two-tier, cylindrical pillars, cylinder escapement, brass escape wheel, three-arm steel balance with flat balance spring controlled by Joseph Bosley–type regulator, Continental pierced and engraved cock, musical movement activated by depressing the pendant, which winds the spring via fusee-like chain, pinned drum cylinder designed for three tunes, changed automatically after each play, carillon of five bells and five hammers with adjustable stop levers for fine music tuning, most of the musical train set in the lower tier, fly governor with two adjustable wings for regulating the tempo.
Case punched "20K" and "T.F/O."
Diam. 46 mm. **$99,684.00.**
Photo and description courtesy of Antiquorum Auctioneers, 14 Jun 2003.

Plate 167. Romilly a Paris, circa 1775.
Fine and extremely rare 20K gold and "Vernis Martin" watch.

Case. Two-body, "bassine fermee," the front with a portrait of a knight in armour wearing a green sash, a red curtain and a classical column behind him. The insides with a portraits of ladies in period dress, the back cover with a portrait of prince or king wearing ermine over armour and a coronet on his head. **Dial.** White enamel, radial Roman chapters, outer minute ring with five-minute Arabic numerals. Gold heart hands. **Movement.** 31.2 mm. Hinged, gilt brass full plate, cylindrical pillars, fusee and chain, verge escapement, plain three-arm steel balance, blued-steel balance spring, Continental cock pierced and engraved with four scrolls.
Signed on the edge of the dial plate and on the movement.
Diam. 38 mm. Published in the Sandberg book, pages 152 – 153.
$2,332.00.
Photo and description courtesy of Antiquorum Auctioneers, 14 Jun 2003.

Plate 168. Open face watch, circa 1775.
18K multicolored gold, verge escapement, gilt movement #39715, paste stones surrounding porcelain dial.
Maker, Esquivillon Fress and de Choudens of Paris.

$3,000.00.
Courtesy of Jeff Rosen, Collector, Solvang Antique Center.

Plate 169. Circa 1775.
22K gold, small chip out of crystal verge fusee escapement. Beautiful repoussé case. English watchmaker, Walker of London. Case is in mint condition.

$3,500.00.
Courtesy of Jeff Rosen, Collector, Solvang Antique Center.

Plate 170. Circa 1780.
Good French 18K multicolor gold, diamond, and painted enamel antique verge and fusee lady's pendant watch by Theo Melly, Paris.

The **case** back has a beautifully restored painted enamel miniature within a diamond border against a floral multicolor gold background. Fine white enamel **dial** has the typical chips at the winding and fancy gold hands. Gilt **movement** with large balance cock pierced and engraved with scrolling folliage. Quite delicate and lovely.
Diam. 41 mm. **$2,400.00.**
Photo and description courtesy of Stephen Bogoff, Antiquarian Horologist.

Plate 171. Circa 1780.

Early Swiss calendar watch with one dial for the time and two subsidiary dials, one for the month and one for the day of the month.
$1,600.00.
Courtesy of David Strudler.

Plate 172. Blanc Pere & Fils a Geneve, No. 12265, circa 1780.
Extremely rare and fine 18K gold and painted-on enamel, pearl- and diamond-set lady's watch with matching chatelaine in fitted leather box.

Case. Two-body, back very finely painted-on enamel with doves, a lamb and flowers in white and gray enamel over translucent purple enamel on an engine - turned ground, paillon border with green fleur-de-lis, translucent gray enamel frame with irregular black pattern finished with diamond-set ring, pearl-set bezels. Chatelaine, gold and enamel, set with pearls and diamonds, three links, the top similarly painted with two doves, a flower vase and a lamb, diamond-set oval frame, translucent gray borders with similar pattern, lower link en suite with painted dove and dog, two gold and enamel pearl-set chains terminating with matching key and seal. **Dial.** White enamel, radial Roman numerals, outer minute track with five-minute Arabic markers, winding aperture at 2 o'clock. Gold beetle and poker hands. **Movement.** 25 mm, hinged, frosted gilt full plate with cylindrical pillars, fusee and chain, verge escapement, plain brass balance with flat balance spring, Continental cock.
Signed on the movement.
Diam. 33 mm, length with chatelaine 170 mm.
$25,259.00.
Photo and description courtesy of Antiquorum Auctioneers, 16 Nov 2002.

Plate 173. Circa 1780s.
18K verge fusee, quarter-hour repeater, enameled scene on back. Des Arts Geneva.

$9,000.00.
Courtesy of Jeff Rosen, Dealer, Solvang Antiques Center.

Plate 174. Circa 1780.
Fine and unusual 18K gold, pearl and painted enamel verge and fusee antique pocket watch by Duchene, Paris, circa 1780.

The **case** back has a painted enamel scene of a woman in classical garb in a landscape, the enamel let into the case in champlevé style. The bezels set with pearls, with glazed outer protective case. Fine white enamel **dial** has bold signature and fancy gilt hands. Gilt **movement** has pierced and engraved balance cock.
Particularly attractive, very unusual technique, and in lovely condition.
Diam. 51 mm. **$6,000.00.**
Photo and description courtesy of Stephen Bogoff, Antiquarian Horologist.

**Plate 175. Truitte & Mourier 11 Geneve, circa 1782.
Very fine 22K varicolored gold, quarter-repeating watch.**

Case. Double-body, Louis XV, the bezel chased with floral decoration, the back chased with ruins in a landscape in three-colored gold. **Dial.** White enamel with Roman numerals and outer Arabic minute ring. Gold Louis XV hands. **Movement.** Hinged gilt brass full plate with conical pillars, fusee with chain, verge escapement, plain steel three-arm balance, flat balance spring, gilt brass Continental cock with polished steel end piece. Repeating on a bell with optional dumb repeating lever and in tact thumbpiece. Signed on the dial and back plate.
Diam. 43 mm. **$9,867.00.**
Photo and description courtesy of Antiquorum Auctioneers, 14 Jun 2003.

Plate 176. Circa 1784.

English, Wm. Wilson Kidcudbright, verge fusee, 36mm, key wind/key set, sterling silver pair case, porcelain dial, Roman numerals, beautiful full-plate fusee pin plate movement.
This is a very nice pre-1800 pocket watch.
$850.00.
Photo and description courtesy of OldWatch.com.

Plate 177. Circa 1785.
18K yellow gold, special movement, spiral mount, Jean Lepine.

$5,500.00.
Courtesy of Jeff Rosen, Collector, Solvang Antique Center.

Plate 178. The Pearl Star.
Moricand & Compagnie, Geneva, circa 1785.
Fine and elegant 18K gold and enamel pearl-set watch.

Case. Double-body, "Directoire," split pearl-set bezels, the blue enameled back panel centered with a split pearl-inlaid rosette. **Dial.** White enamel with Arabic numerals. Elaborate gold pierced hands. **Movement.** 43.6 mm, hinged gilt brass, Hessen flat caliber with going barrel, cylinder escapement with plain brass three-arm balance, flat balance spring.
Signed on the dial and back plate.
Diam. 54 mm. **$10,925.00.**
Photo and description courtesy of Antiquorum Auctioneers, 14 Jun 2003.

Plate 179. Circa 1785.
18 ct. gold, cylinder fusee, Mvt. #1096.
quarter-hour repeater. Pair case with
engine-turned enamel. Alexander Cum-
ming, London.

$9,000.00.
Courtesy of Jeff Rosen, Collector, Solvang Antique Center.

Plate 180. Lepine a Paris, circa 1785.
Fine and interesting 18K gold and diamond-set double-glazed watch with visible movement.

Case. Two-body, Louis XVI, glazed on both sides, the bezels set with diamonds, band engraved. **Dial.** White enamel. Roman numerals, outer minute ring with five-minute Arabic markers, winding aperture at 2 o'clock. Gold Louis XV hands. **Movement.** 24 mm, hinged, gilt, skeletonized top plate, cylindrical pillars, fusee and chain, verge escapement, plain three-arm steel balance with blued-steel spring, small triangular cock, applied silver ornament pierced and engraved with foliage, surmounted by a crown and set with rose-cut diamonds.
Signed on the dial.
Diam. 31 mm. **$1,346.00.**
Photo and description courtesy of Antiquorum Auctioneers, 14 Jun 2003.

Plate 181. Circa 1786.
English Gould London, verge fusee, 41 mm, key wind/key set, sterling silver pair case, with rare right-facing duty mark.

Fancy porcelain dial marked "Gould London," Roman numerals, beautiful full plate fusee pin plate movement, Egyptian pillars.
This is a very nice pre-1800 pocket watch. A real beauty!
$1,800.00.
Photo and description courtesy of OldWatch.com.

Plate 182. Circa 1788.
Breguet, No. 23/647, entered into the register on March 10, 1788, sold to an unknown person, bought back from Madame Sanze, refinished and sold on June 3, 1850, to Monsieur Brocot, horologer, on behalf of His Imperial Highness, Grand Duc Constantin Nicolaevitch of Russia. Very important and rare 18K gold, quarter-repeating, a tact self-winding small perpetuelle with 60-hour power reserve.

Case. Two-body, "forme collier," the whole engine-turned in a *grains d'orge* pattern with polished circle on the back cover. **Dial.** Enamel, Roman numerals, outer minute track, sunk subsidiary seconds, up and down sector at 10 o'clock. Mounted to gilt brass a bate levee ring. Blued-steel Breguet hands. **Movement.** 41.20 mm, gilt brass 3/4 plate, two going barrels, tandem winding with brass wolf-tooth winding gears, four-wheel train, straight-line lever escapement, four-arm steel and platinum jeweled and capped compensation balance with two screwed quarter-turn lamina segments terminated with a threaded pin at the free end for platinum temperature nuts, two platinum mean time screws, blued-steel helical balance spring with both terminal curves lift on the pallets, convex entry pallet, concave the exit one to equalize both lifts, draw, oil retention slots on the escape wheel, single trapezoidal roller table with inserted trapezoidal jewel working between two upright steel pins mounted at the end of the fork, long fork with banking over the escape wheel arbor with U-shaped end, parachute on top pivot, micrometric screw regulator. Half-ogival platinum weight swinging between two spring-loaded ruby rollers mounted to the case with a stop mechanism triggered when fully wound, Breguet-type repeating mechanism with lifted gathering pallet, all-or-nothing and fixed star wheel, fusee-chain winding, repeating with a single hammer on a short gold in fixed to the case by pull-and-twist piston in the pendant, tone adjustment screw in the bate levee ring.
Signed "Breguet," with the serial number on the dial ring and on the dial.
Diam. 47 mm. **$108,570.00.**
Photo and description courtesy of Antiquorum Auctioneers, 2002.

Plate 183. Circa 1790.
Rare watch, 22K gold, pill case, with miniature verge fusee, surrounded by seed pearls. All hand made.

$8,000.00.
Courtesy of Jeff Rosen, Collector, Solvang Antique Center.

Plate 184. Circa 1790.
Fine and rare early, Swiss, silver, self-winding antique pocket watch by J. Ruegger, circa 1790.

Gilt four-jewel cylinder **movement** with pierced and engraved cock and large crescent weight pivoted across the movement. Good white enamel center seconds **dial** with gold hands. Plain-polish **case** with some light signs of use. An identical watch is in *The Self-Winding Watch* by Chapuis.
Diam. 53 mm. **$6,750.00.**
Photo and description courtesy of Stephen Bogoff, Antiquarian Horologist.

Plate 185. Circa 1790.
Fine French 18K gold, diamond, and enamel verge and fusee antique pocket watch by Lechet, Paris.

The bezels have enamel decoration, the back has cobalt blue enamel over engine turning within a fancy border and centered with a sunburst set with 30 diamonds. White enamel **dial** with blued-steel Breguet hands. The balance cock is pierced and engraved with the maker's name.
A most attractive classic watch, in particularly fine condition.
Diam. 45 mm. **$3,650.00.**
Photo and description courtesy of Stephen Bogoff, Antiquarian Horologist.

Plate 186. Circa 1790.
Fine and very unusual 18K gold, enamel, and pearl antique verge and fusee watch with chatelaine by Green and Ward, London.

Bezels with gold and light blue enamel (with insignificant loss to the front), the back with cobalt blue enamel over engine turning centered with a braid of hair under an oval glass surrounded with pearls. Matching chatelaine with blue enamel white-dot bordered panels, fancy chain, fancy key, and two seals. Fine white enamel **dial** with gold arrowhead hands. The **movement** with beautifully pierced and engraved cock. I have seen lockets and pins with locks of hair, but this is the first time I have seen hair mounted on a watch. Most attractive.
Diam. 54 mm. **$4,750.00.**
Photo and description courtesy of Stephen Bogoff, Antiquarian Horologist.

Plate 187. Circa 1790.
Joseph Starling, verge, fusee, pierced gold hands, with cobalt blue case, enamel.

$4,500.00.
Courtesy of Jeff Rosen, Collector, Solvang Antique Center.

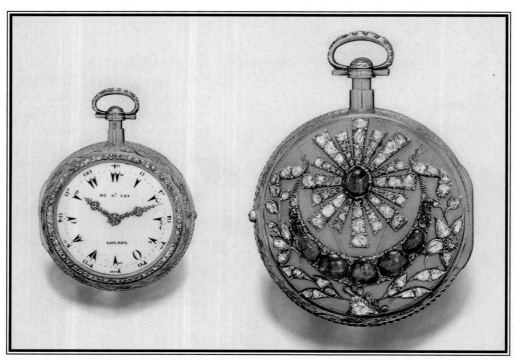

Plate 188. Emerald Crescent and Star.
Daniel de St. Leu, Watchmaker to her Majesty, London, case stamped with the maker's mark of John Penny, made for the Islamic market, circa 1790. Highly important 18K gold pair-cased diamond-, emerald-, and ruby-set quarter-striking clock-watch.

Case. Outer: double-body, the diamond-set bezels chased with varicolored gold floral decoration, the back applied with a diamond-set pattern of flowers and foliage, a crescent set with large emerald cabochons and a star set with large diamonds and centered with a large emerald cabochon over a matte ground. Inner: double-body, "bassine," the back pierced and engraved with scrolling foliage and flowers, a ruby cabochon set on the pendant. **Dial.** White enamel with radial Islamic numerals. Diamond-set "fancy" hands. **Movement.** 42 mm, gilt brass full plate with cylindrical pillars, fusee and chain, verge escapement, plain gold three-arm balance, gilt brass cock pierced and engraved with scrolling foliage. Striking on a bell, strike-silent selection lever on the bezel, gilt brass dust cap.
Signed on the dial, the dust cap, and the back plate.
Diam. 60 mm. **$49,708.00.**
Photo and description courtesy of Antiquorum Auctioneers, 16 Nov 2002.

Plate 189. Bordier, Geneva, No. 52806, circa 1790.
Fine 18K varicolored gold and painted-on enamel pearl-set pair-cased watch with silver cock.

Case. Outer: two-body, Louis XVI back, painted-on enamel with two muses, champleve enamel laurel leaf frame, bezel decorated with repeated pattern; inner: two-body, bassine with deep back, polished. **Dial.** White enamel, Roman numerals. outer minute ring with five-minute Arabic markers. Diamond-set Louis XV hands. **Movement.** 38 mm, gilt brass full plate with pentagonal baluster pillars, fusee and chain, verge escapement, plain brass three-arm balance, flat balance spring, Continental silver cock pierced and engraved with the letters "FB."
Signed on dial and movement and cock.
Diam. 38 mm. **$4,485.00.**
Photo and description courtesy of Antiquorum Auctioneers, 16 Nov 2002.

Plate 190. Circa 1790.
First quality, extremely scarce, large automaton, two-tune musical clock-watch.

Case with pierced bezels set with stones and pearls, with a button in the pendant to activate the musical automaton. Fine white enamel **dial** (hairline) with gold beetle and poker hands, sweep center seconds, fancy exposed balance cock incorporating the regulator, and stone-set rosettes, one to turn the automatic musical on and off, the other to select one of the two tunes. Back with a river scene with automaton water wheel and procession moving across a bridge. The original oil paint has been conserved and stabilized. Extraordinary verge and fusee **movement** plays the two tunes on a nest of five bells.
This wonderful watch is high enough in quality to have been a gift to the emperor.
Diam. 95 mm. **$30,000.00.**
Photo and description courtesy of Stephen Bogoff, Antiquarian Horologist.

Plate 191. Unsigned, Swiss, circa 1790.
Very rare and fine gold diamond-set miniature watch, entire movement weighing 3.1 grams.

Case. Two-body. Louis XVI. entirely diamond-set. **Dial.** White enamel. Breguet numerals, outer minute track. Winding aperture at 2 o'clock. Blued-steel spade hands. **Movement.** 14 mm (6½"), frosted, gilt full plate with cylindrical pillars, fusee and chain, verge escapement, plain brass balance with flat balance spring, Continental cock with unusual piercing.
Diam. 18 mm. **$11,300.00.**
Photo and description courtesy of Antiquorum Auctioneers, 16 Nov 2002.

Plate 192. Circa 1790s.
Verge, fusee.
Chavaller and Company.

Beautifully enameled on the back, mint condition, original crystal. It does open up from the side. The movement swings up from 6 o'clock.
$4,892.00.
Courtesy of Launder Antiques.

Plate 193. Circa 1793.

English Jones, London, verge fusee, 40 mm, key wind/key set, sterling silver pair **case**, with rare right-facing duty mark, porcelain **dial**, Roman numerals, beautiful full plate fusee pin plate **movement**.
This is a very nice pre-1800 pocket watch.
$1,050.00.
Photo and description courtesy of OldWatch.com.

Plate 194. The Revolutionary Watch.
Unsigned, Swiss, case maker "F.P.," No. 1447, circa 1795.
Fine and rare silver watch with decimal Revolutionary dial and traditional duo-decimal dial.

Case. Two-body, polished. **Dial.** White enamel inner fin I vertical Roman chapters from I to X for the Revolutionary hours, on the outer. Arabic numerals from 1 to 12 repeated twice, next Arabic numerals from 1 to 100 for the Revolutionary minutes, and at the edge, Arabic numerals for the traditional 60 minutes. **Movement.** 45 mm 0, hinged, gilt brass full plate, cylindrical pillars, fusee and chain for the going train, verge escapement plain brass balance. Continental cock pierced and engraved, rack and pinion regulator with silver orate.
Diam. 56.5 mm. Published in the Sandberg book, pages 178 – 179. **$6,647.00.**
Photo and description courtesy of Anitquorum Auctioneers, 31 Mar 2001.

Plate 195. Hommage to Rousseau.
Unsigned, Swiss, circa 1795.
Fine and rare 18K gold watch with enameled decimal revolutionary dial, duo-decimal dial and Revolutionary calendar.

Case. Two-body polished. **Dial.** White enamel eccentric dial for the Revolutionary 10-hour indication at the top with Arabic numerals, Revolutionary minute divisions with 25-minute Arabic numerals; on the bottom, duo-decimal dial with Arabic numerals and 15-minute markers; to the right, Revolutionary days of the decade; and to the left, 30-day month indication. Gilt metal hands. The

painting depicts France personified by a young woman breastfeeding her baby, on the other side a tall mast surmounted by a Phrygian cap, symbols of the Revolution, in the background a couple on a riverbank point towards "Rousseau Island," the island in the Geneva bay which is dedicated to the memory of the Genevan philosopher, champion of liberty. **Movement.** 46.8 mm 0, hinged, gilt brass full plate, cylindrical pillars, fusee and chain for the going train, verge escapement, plain brass balance, rack and pinion regulator with silver plate, blued-steel balance spring, Continental cock pierced and engraved with four tulips.
Diam. 57 mm. Published in the Sandberg book, pages 178 – 179. **$11,965.00.**
Photo and description courtesy of Antiquorum Auctioneers, 31 Mar 2001.

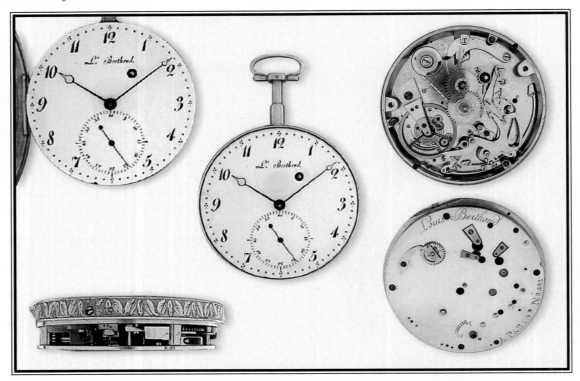

Plate 196. Circa 1795.
Very fine and rare French, 18K gold, repeating chronometer antique pocket watch by Louis Berthoud, Paris.

Very fine gilt fusee **movement** #2521 with Ernshaw-type spring detent escapement with compensation curb, capped escapement, the balance under the dial. Quarter repeating against the plain-polish consular **case**. White enamel **dial** with chips at the winding hole, edge chip at 6:00, and a crack at 9:00. A very fine example of French precision watchmaking in the late eighteenth century by a member of an eminent family of watchmakers.
Diam. 53 mm. **$15,500.00.**
Photo and description courtesy of Stephen Bogoff, Antiquarian Horologist.

Plate 197. Circa late 1700s – early 1800s.
Musical watch, French-Swiss, all hand made, hour and quarter repeater.

$9,500.00.
Description and watch courtesy of Aaron Faber Gallery.

Chapter IV
YANKEE INGENUITY
THE NINETEENTH CENTURY

In the early years of watchmaking, there was a free flow and exchange of knowledge between watchmakers. Inventors and makers were enthusiastic, and more than happy to share with those who traveled from far and near to learn the new trade.

By the the second quarter of the seventeenth century, this had begun to change. The Worshipful Company of Clockmakers was founded in Britain in 1631. This type of guild was formed to ensure quality and to set the rules and regulations concerning apprenticeships. Strict rules also governed who came into the guild and what jobs they were allowed to do. This control over newcomers was meant to control market share by reducing competition.

The nineteenth century saw the guild system fully entrenched in Britain. The class system in Switzerland kept many migrating watchmakers from joining the trade. Meanwhile, in the United States there were no restrictions to prohibit the trade, and many skilled watchmakers had migrated to the new country. Unfortunately, many towns were so sparsely populated that it did not pay to be a full-time watchmaker. Consequently, the ones who did practice the trade usually did so in conjunction with their farming duties or their jobs in repair shops. In order to make their work profitable, they imported ebauche, finished them, and engraved their names or their company names on the movements.

Luther Goddard (1762 – 1842), a watchmaker in Shrewsbury, Massachusetts, had this type of operation. In 1809, when his supply of ebauche was cut off by the Jefferson embargo of imports, he had to seek another way of keeping his watch trade. The parts that needed special skills, such as hairsprings, hands, and dials, were ordered from Boston. One of his apprentices, William H. Keith, later wrote about the equipment that Goddard used: "His tools consisted mainly of a tooth-cutting engine, a common foot lathe, brass pivot turns, and upright tool and sinking, depthing, grooving, and hairspring tools; and the usual variety of pliers, tweezers, files, and other appliances in use by watch repairers, all of which were of English manufacture."[23] With these tools and the help his apprentices, his sons, and those with watchmaking skills in the surrounding areas, he managed to produce some of the first watches made on American soil.

His first watches were marked "L. Goddard," and after his son came into the business they were signed "L. Goddard and Son."

Because of this, he is known as one of the first, and is certainly one of the most written about, watchmakers in this country. Remember, his watches were not machine made, and they were still made in the English style that his customers favored. When the embargo was lifted, after the War of 1812, the flow of imported watches came back into the country. Swiss watches in particular were priced too low for him to stay in competition. He closed his business in 1819.

Plate 198. A Goddard watch. For a description and price, see plate #265 on p. 161. *Photo courtesy of oldWatches.com.*

MACHINE-MADE WATCHES

America's first machine-made watch was produced in East Hartford, Connecticut about 1839. The Pitkin brothers, James (1812 – 1870) and Henry (1811 – 1846), made their own tools and machinery for making some parts, but they still had to import dials, hands, jewels, and hairsprings. They used trial and error to determine the exact type of movement that would work best, and are credited with what Henry named the "American Lever Watch."

Because their family owned a jewelry store, the brothers had a ready outlet for their watch production. Not content to have a small market, they set out to expand their operation to the big city of New York. Unfortunately, the retailers in New York did not greet their product with open arms. The store owners could not rationalize stocking watches that would cost more than the ones that were imported from Switzerland. The Pitkin brothers stopped production in 1842. Even though their movements were machine made, and the parts were somewhat interchangeable, the brothers' business failed. They had tried to expand too soon.[24]

Because they were in business for only a short time (1838 – 1842), authentic watches bearing the name "Henry Pitkin" or the firm name "H. & J. F. Pitkin" are very collectible.

Plate 199. This is one of Pitkin's watches. See plate #296.

Aaron Dennison (1812 – 1895) was destined to be the one to take the next step in the evolution of the American factory-made watch. Early in his career he had worked with Jubal Howe at a jewelry store in Boston. Howe was a foreman at that store, but he had earlier worked as an apprentice to Luther Goddard. Howe gave Dennison his early training in watchmaking. Later, when Dennison went into the watch materials and tools business, he developed the Dennison Standard Gauge to measure main springs.[25]

Dennison was a true entrepreneur. His inventive mind kept him busy with with a large number of projects. His contagious enthusiasm seemed to encourage investors to join him. But because his early training was in watchmaking, he kept thinking of mass producing watches. After all, guns and gun-making machinery were being massed produced in America at prices that lured customers from as far away as England, France, and other countries. Why couldn't mass-produced watches be made and priced to compete with Swiss watches?

In 1849, Dennison approached Edward Howard (1813-1904), a man who was already successful in business and was of like mind. He too was an inventor of various machines and was trained in clock making. It didn't take much persuasion to convince Howard and his partner, David Porter Davis, a clock manufacturer, to join Dennison in this new venture. They raised money and, in 1850, started their company.

That same year Dennison wrote:

> It is now about ten years since I first began to entertain the notion that the manufacture of watches might be introduced into this country with advantage, but I had supposed that in order to compete with the cheap labors of the old countries, Yankee ingenuity would have to be taxed to a considerable extent to produce a favorable result.
> For the first five or seven years of the above period, I contented myself with simply entertaining the opinion. . . . Once I recollected. . . . to Mr. Willard in Congress St. that I believed that ten or twenty years would not elapse before American made watches of a medium quality could be afforded for one-half the price of English manufacture, to, which, as I expected, he expressed dissent. . . . Of course, whether this is correct remains to be proved, but after a still further consideration of the subject I am of the opinion that the final result will be as likely to produce the articles at one-quarter the price of importing as it is to exceed the first estimate by any degree.[26]

The new venture was not easy. The men wanted to make their watches from start to finish with parts made in America. They were smart enough to go to England to learn methods of doing things such as making dials. They even went so far as to hire people from other countries to work for them in the United States factory. If Dennison found that he could not design what was needed, he did not hesitate to find and hire someone who could. Nelson Stratton and Charles Moseley were two of those people. It took much longer than the partners had anticipated to build machines and get things going the way that they wanted. This was an unexpected drain on their capital. Finally, in 1852, some watches were ready to be presented to investors. These watches were marked "Howard Davis & Dennison."

When watches began to leave the factory (about 1853), the company name was changed to the Boston Watch Company The company produced models with names such as "Warren," another name that the three had earlier used for the company, and "Samuel Curtis," in honor of their biggest investor. In 1854, the partners moved their operation to Waltham, Massachusetts.

The great expenditures to start production, along with other factors (such a sales slump in 1856), marked the end of the company. In 1857, the Boston Watch Company was sold at auction. The Waltham plant was purchased by Royal Robbins for $56,000.

Aaron Dennison, the acknowledged father of the American factory-made watch, eventually went on to form the Tremont Watch Company, and Edward Howard formed the E. Howard Watch Company.

Thus began American watch manufacturing. Because this interesting subject demands a book of its own, please do yourself a favor and read the interesting and informative "American Watchmaking — A Technical History of the American Watch Industry 1850-1930," written by Michael C. Harrold as a supplement to the *NAWCC Bulletin* and listed in the bibliography.

CHRONOLOGICAL LISTING

Most books list American watch companies in alphabetical order because they are usually listed with the movement serial numbers and it makes these numbers easier to find. Company serial number information is also included further on in this chapter. First let's look at the companies in chronological order.

Originally, I had intended to give the watch companies and their successors in the business a color code, but there are so many companies that are related by reorganization that there were not enough colors to assign all of them. It is also amazing that watch-making machinery was so frequently moved around the country and even overseas to places such as England, Russia, and Japan. Almost all the watch companies that sprang up in the nineteenth century were either linked by machinery, employee migration, or ownership. Hopefully, seeing the companies in chronological order will give you some quick circa-dating clues as you learn about them.

APPLETON, TRACY & CO.
Waltham, Massachusetts
1857 – 1859
The investors who purchased the Waltham plant of the Boston Watch Co. formed this company. Most of the machine tools that they needed were already in place, and trained personnel were already in the area. The two important ingredients that the new owners had that the original owners did not were working capital and a distribution network. As a result, it didn't take long for watch production to begin. In 1859, the company changed its name to the American Waltham Watch Company.

E. HOWARD & CO.
Roxbury, Massachusetts
1858 – 1903
When the Boston Watch company was auctioned off in 1857, it didn't take long for Edward Howard to be back in the watch business. In fact, he went to work for a man who had loaned the former company some money. Since some of the machinery was used as collateral, Charles Rice took it back to the factory in Roxbury. Howard and a number of other former Boston Watch Company employees went with him and managed the company. A year later, Howard purchased the company, and he and his nephew formed E. Howard & Company.

With his own company, Howard finally had a chance to make watches the way he believed they needed to be made. He made many changes in the movements, including using his own series of sizes. But one of his most costly changes, and the most foreign to mass production, was to add some hand finishing. His watches could be depended on to be of the highest quality and workmanship.

Howard retired in 1882, but the business continued until 1903. At that time, the Keystone Watch Case Company purchased the rights to use the Edward Howard name on watches. The "&" was left off, and the new movements were signed "E. Howard Watch Co."

Plate 200. F. Howard and Co. stamps. If the Howard movement was stamped with a hound, it was unadjusted. A horse meant the movement was adjusted for temperature and isochronism; a deer meant adjusted for temperature, isochronism, and position.

AMERICAN WALTHAM WATCH CO.
1859 – 1957

In 1859, the Appleton Tracy Watch Company changed its name to the American Waltham Watch Company, which was later (1885) was shortened to the Waltham Watch Company. This became one of the most successful watch companies in the country.

NASHUA WATCH CO.
Nashua, New Hampshire
1859 – 1862

This was another company that produced high grade watches. It also suffered the same problem as many other early companies — cash flow. Within three year, it had managed to spend fifty-three thousand dollars, a fortune in those days. Fortunately, the company was purchased by the American Watch Company, which used Nashua equipment to create a division to produce high grade watches.

NATIONAL WATCH CO. (ELGIN WATCH CO.)
Elgin, Illinois
1864 – 1964

This was the first of five watch companies that were started in 1864 by businessmen who wanted to make watches for the railroads. The Elgin location was chosen because it was the hometown of one of the company owners. One of the company's backers, B. W. Raymond, was the former mayor of Chicago.

The company was founded in 1864, but it did not produce watches until three years later. Fortunately, it had good financial backing and hired experienced men, many of whom were lured away from the American Waltham Watch Company. Good management by men experienced in the mass production of watches, combined with half a million dollars of working capital and the right equipment, proved to be the formula for success. National eventually produced more watches than any other factory in America.

NEWARK WATCH CO.
Newark, New Jersey
1864 – 1867

Most of the watches made by this company had the retail jeweler's name on the dial and case. Its watch production was short lived because of a shortage of working capital. In 1867, the company was sold to the Cornell Watch Company.

U.S. WATCH CO.
Marion, New Jersey
1864 – 1872

Plate 201. An Elgin Boy trade card.

This is another company with beginnings in 1864. Because it had to build and equip a factory, its first watches were not produced until 1867. It concentrated on making fine, stem-wind watches with damaskeened nickel movements. It was also plagued with money problems. In 1872, it was reorganized as the Marion Watch Company.

TREMONT WATCH CO.
Boston, Massachusetts
1864 – 1866

Aaron Dennison was one of the driving forces behind the formation of this company. He reasoned that by combining Swiss- and American-made components, this new company could make a good watch at a very competitive price. The escapements, balance, and trains were made in Switzerland, and the other parts were made in Boston.[27] Dennison went to Switzerland to manage that part of production, leaving Belding D. Bingham in charge of the Boston plant.

In 1865, this company's watches were ready for the marketplace. Tremont's initial production took only one year, whereas all the other companies that started in 1864 took three years to produce their first watches. It looked as if Tremont was going to be a successful company. Inspired by the initial success but not smart enough to leave well-enough alone, Dennison's partners decided that they wanted to move the company to Melrose, which was closer to where they lived. They also wanted to make the entire watch at that location. Dennison knew that the company could not compete with all-American-made watch companies. After all, it would be in price competition with well-established companies. For this reason, he left the company. The company was renamed the Melrose Watch Company.

NEW YORK WATCH CO.

Providence, Rhode Island	Springfield, Massachusetts
1864 – 1867	1867 – 1875

This idea for this company was conceived by Don Mozart, who had migrated to the U.S. from Italy. In 1864, he designed the details of a watch with a unique escapement. Not only was he a mechanical genius, but he must have also been a pretty good salesman, because he managed to sell a group of investors on the idea of setting up a factory to produce his watches.

The factory was set up in Providence in 1864, and although Mozart was great with machines, he was evidently not so great at estimating the job. His backers brought in experts from other companies to reorganize the factory in order to make a more conventional style movement. Needless to say, Mr. Mozart left the company. About that same time (1867), the company had a chance to buy a vacant factory in Springfield, Massachusetts. When it was finally ready to open the new plant (1870), fire destroyed part of the building and caused a delay. The first watches did not reach the market until 1871. This company certainly proved that it had a lot of persistence as well as a lot of Yankee ingenuity.

In 1873, a panic struck the country, and the resulting slump in sales caused financial stress for the company. It decided to reorganize. The new company was named the New York Manufacturing Company.

MELROSE WATCH CO.
Melrose, Massachusetts
1867 – 1868

When the Tremont Watch Company owners decided to move the factory to Melrose and produce all parts there, they changed the name of the company to reflect the new location. Although they were able to produce watches within a year of the move, it proved to be a costly mistake. The new setup absorbed all their available funds. The investors hired Dennison to find a buyer for the machinery. In 1868, it was sold to a company in Birmingham, England, to set up the English Watch Company. This is a good example of how many times machinery changed hands and traveled a long distance from its original location. It also shows how much value was placed on not having to start from scratch to set up a watch factory, and what lengths people were willing to go to in order to gain this advantage.

PHILADELPHIA WATCH CO.
1868 – 1886

There are not any records to show that this company ever had a factory in America. In fact, it is likely that all of its watch parts were imported from Switzerland. In America, the watches were finished, signed, and sold as American made. Some people believe that the parts were made at the International Watch Company in Switzerland, which had been founded in 1868 by an ex-employee of E. Howard & Co., Mr. Florentine A. Jones. Mr. Jones used American-made machinery and Swiss labor, which was much less expensive than American.

ILLINOIS WATCH CO.
This company operated under the following three names:
1869 – 1879 — Illinois Springfield Watch Co.
1879 – 1885 — Springfield Illinois Watch Co.
1885 – 1927 — Illinois Watch Co.

This company produced fine conventionally-jeweled watches and railroad grade watches. In spite of its quality products, it remained number three in production, behind Waltham and Elgin. In 1927, the company was sold to Hamilton Watch Company.

Plate 202. One of the Illinois Watch Co. trademarks.

CORNELL WATCH CO.
Newark, New Jersey
1871 – 1876
Paul Cornell purchased the Newark Watch Co. in 1876, with high hopes of being successful. By 1870, the leader in the industry was the American Waltham Company and Elgin was a close second. It was difficult to compete with these more established companies. In 1870, Cornell moved the Newark factory to Grand Crossings, Illinois. The new location was not any more profitable than the old. A new partner, W. C. Ralston, was brought in and the equipment was moved to California; it was hoped that the cheap Chinese labor there would bring the cost of production down. The new company was named the Cornell Watch Company of San Francisco. As you can see, much watchmaking equipment traveled more that most people during these years. But in those days, just as it does today, poor machinery made for a poor quality watch, and the Cornell Watch Co. used poor machinery. The company closed in 1876, when Ralston committed suicide. It was later discovered that the company had a huge amount of debt that Ralston had kept hidden.[28]

MARION WATCH CO.
Marion, New Jersey
1872 – 1874
The reorganization of the company from the U.S. Watch Company of Marion brought with it reductions in the quality of its watches. By lowering its standards in order to make less expensive watches, the Marion Watch Company hoped to gain a better share of the market, but the economy was working against them. Watch prices continued to be lowered to meet the competition, and it was certainly a case of the survival of the fittest. In 1874, reorganization was again a necessity.

EMPIRE CITY WATCH CO.
Marion, New Jersey
1874 – 1877
The Marion Watch Company reorganized as the Empire City Watch Company. Although it made an effort and displayed its watches at the Philadelphia Centennial Exposition, this was not enough to resuscitate the languishing company.

DIETRICH GRUEN (GRUEN WATCH CO.)
1874 – 1879
This company used ebauche made in Switzerland from Gruen's specifications. The ebauche were then finished in Gruen's plant in Columbus, Ohio. By 1879, the company had grown so much that Gruen was ready to expand. This meant taking on a partner. He and his new partner, W. J. Savage, were known as Gruen and Savage until 1882, when they became the Columbus Watch Company.

LANCASTER WATCH CO.
This name was used by a series of companies from 1874 to 1890. They are as follows:
1874 – 1876 — Adams & Perry
1876 – 1878 — Lancaster Watch Co.
1878 – 1879 — Lancaster Penn. Watch Co.
1879 – 1884 — Lancaster Watch Co.
1886 – 1890 — Keystone Standard Watch Co.
All of these companies used this name and made medium grade watches. They also used their predecessors machinery. When the competition got tough, the companies who made the high grade watches and those who made the cheapest watches survived. Companies that made average grade watches, such as Lancaster Watch Company, were soon squeezed out of the race.

FREEPORT WATCH CO.
Freeport, Illinois
1874 – 1875
This company was started when Eber Ward, of Detroit, purchased machinery made by C. H. Hoyt. Hoyt had been making watches with this machinery for a jewelry store in Detroit. Freeport's factory was destroyed by fire before the company really had a chance to start production. Only a few watches were made using this name.

THE ROCKFORD WATCH COMPANY
Rockford, Illinois
1874 – 1901

A former Cornell Watch employee enticed some of the investors of the Cornell Watch Company to join him in forming a new watch company, to be headquartered in Rockford, Illinois. He chose this location because three railroads came through the town. He planned to make watches that would appeal to railroad employees. By buying equipment instead of building its own, and by hiring some of the Cornell Company's former employees, the Rockford Watch Co. was ready to produce its first watches in only one month.

The next year it built a new factory, and by 1876, watches were ready for the marketplace. Rockford watches had a train on the dial as the company's trademark. After twenty successful years, the company fell on hard times. Beginning in 1896, it was managed by a receivership until 1901. At that time, the company was reorganized as the Rockford Watch Company Ltd. It continued producing watches until 1915.

THE FITCHBURG WATCH COMPANY
Fitchburg, Massachusetts
1875 – 1878

This company was started by Sylvanus Sawyer. He had been a stockholder in U.S. Watch Co. and when the company failed, he decided to have a try at making his own watches. He was wise enough to hire some of the former employees of the bankrupt company. He also purchased used machinery. He decided to close the factory only three years after forming the company. According to Mike Harrold, there is only one known prototype watch. As of today, there are no known production watches. Who knows what might be out there, yet to be discovered?

Plate 203. Rockford Watch Co. advertising card.

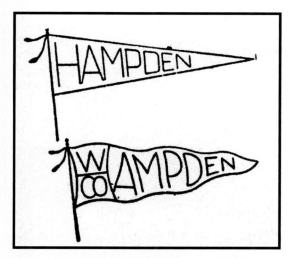

Plate 204. Two of Hampden's trademarks.

NEW YORK MFG. CO.
1875 – 1876

The reorganization of the New York Watch company did little to solve the company's problems. Therefore, the stockholders decided to reorganize once again. Charles Rood come with new money, new plans, and new leadership. This new company was the Hampden Watch Co.

HAMPDEN WATCH CO.
1876 – 1930

The timing of this business venture was better than that of the New York Manufacturing Company, because the recession was beginning to pass and the business was reflecting this positive note. The company's finances improved with the economy and again when it merged with the Dueber Watchcase Company. The company then moved its operations to Canton, Ohio. It was the first American company to produce a 23-jewel watch, and it was a leader of promoting highly-jeweled watches and watches in a wide range of sizes.

AUBURNDALE WATCH CO.
1876 – 1883
Auburndale, Massachusetts

In 1876, Willen B. Fowle founded this company to produce a watch whose design he had purchased from Jason Hopkins. The design was unique in that the watch had a rotary movement, which meant that the movement rotated with the barrel. The watch made use of a lever escapement. The rotary design wasn't a bad concept, but the watch company was plagued with problems. It had purchased secondhand machines from the defunct United States Watch Company, and it just wasn't capable of producing the details necessary for quality construction. Consequently, only about 1,000 rotary movement watches were made. The company continued in business by producing the Auburndale timer (1876 – 1883), which used a simplified pin wheel escapement. It also made and sold thermometers. Lack of capital forced the company to cease business in 1883.

BENEDICT & BURNHAM MFG. CO.
Waterbury, Connecticut
1877 – 1879

Benedict and Burnham were originally in the brass business. Because watch and clock manufacturing made use of so much brass, it was natural for them to think along the lines of going into the clock and watch business. The Waterbury Clock Company was started in 1857, but it took much longer for them to find just the right watch to produce. They wanted to make an inexpensive watch, one that was cheaper than any on the market, one that every man could afford. History had already proven that this was not an easy task. Although the leading manufacturers of the day had developed less expensive lines of watches, most of these still sold for more than the average man could make in a week.

These businessmen realized that to make a cheaper watch, it must have fewer parts and an escapement that was easily stamped out of a sheet of brass. An inexpensive case and dial made by their company would also be necessary.

One of the brightest minds of the century came up with the answer. Mr. Daniel Azro Ashley Buck, who seemed to be able to make anything, came up with the solution. His model had a rotary movement. This meant that the entire movement moved around once each hour. More importantly, his model used a duplex escapement unlike any other. Whereas the original duplex had a wheel with teeth on two planes of elevation, his had two differently shaped teeth alternating with each other on the same plane. This made it very easily mass produced. To minimize the cost of materials, his model had about half the number of parts used in a regular watch movement. It didn't have any jewels, but the spring was so long that it wrapped around the entire back of the case and it took 150 half turns of the stem to wind.

Plate 205. Photo of Dr. Crom's stamped Buck's-style wheel.

It didn't take long for the watches to be on the market. Within a year of making the model (1877), they were selling briskly for $3.50 each. They had the novelty of an open dial that showed the working parts, and this proved to be a good selling point. These early watches only had 54 parts, and were marked with the Benedict & Burnham Manufacturing Company name, until the Waterbury Watch Company was formed in 1880.

BALL WATCH CO.
Cleveland, Ohio
1879 – 1969

Web C. Ball had an advantage over some of the other watch companies, although he never had a factory or made a watch. Because his name was associated with advocating the standards for railroad watches, he was able to capitalize on this by having companies make watches to his specifications and with his name on the dial.

He used Hampden, Hamilton, E. Howard & Company, Keystone Howard, Seth Thomas, Waltham, and Illinois, and he even had some watches made in Switzerland. Most of Ball's railroad watches were marked "Official Standard." Watches marked "Commercial Standard" are not railroad grade.

BOWMAN WATCH CO.
Lancaster, Pennsylvania
1879 – 1882

E. F. Bowman was a jewelry and watch retailer who had previously worked for one of the watch companies in Lancaster. He decided to produce his own watches and formed the Bowman Watch Company. His watches made use of an escape wheel with a star tooth design. Only about 50 watches were made. Ezera Bowman later sold some of his equipment to J. P. Stephens.

WATERBURY WATCH COMPANY
Waterbury, Connecticut
1880 – 1898

This company was formed in 1880, but it took a year for the first watches to be produced because the company first wanted to build a beautiful brick building. Because it had a successful parent company (Benedict & Burnham), it started with about four times the working capital of most start-up watch companies. The company used letters of the alphabet to designate series. In the 1880s, the series G was produced, and it was a rotating model. Its nine-foot-long spring had 24 coils, and it ran for 24 hours. In 1891, a short-wind non-

Plate 206. Waterbury trade card with old man.

rotating version of the watch replaced the long-wind model.

Many Waterbury watches were used for advertising purposes or as premiums for selling other products. If the company purchasing the watches placed a large enough order, it could have its name and advertisement on the watch.

Although Waterbury was known for inexpensive watches, it was never able to produce a watch that could be sold for a dollar. In 1898, the company reorganized to form the New England Watch Company.

NEW HAVEN CLOCK CO.
New Haven, Connecticut
watches, 1880 – 1956
This clock company started business in 1853. In 1880, it decided to try its luck at producing cheap watches. Over the years its watches evolved from ones that wound in the back like a clock to a standard stem wind watch. New Haven became one of the top three producers of this type of watch.

INDEPENDENT WATCH CO.
Fredonia, New York
This company operated under the following three names:
1880 – 1883 — Independent Watch Co. N.Y.
1883 – 1885 — Fredonia Watch Co. N.Y.
1885 – 1895 — Peoria Watch Co. (Peoria, Illinois)

This company was started by the Howard brothers of Fredonia. They had a catalog company that also sold watches made in America and Switzerland. In 1883, these two bought used equipment and decided to make their own watches to sell through their catalog. They marketed and signed their watches with the name "Mark Twain," hoping to associate their product with the famous writer's reputation of excellence. Even though the new watch division was called the Fredonia Watch Company, retail jewelers were reluctant to buy watches from a company that was in competition with them in the mail order business.

By 1885, it seemed wise for the brothers to sell their watches in another state under a different name, so they sold their machinery, which wasn't that good anyway, and formed a company in Peoria, Illinois. This new company was Peoria Watch Company. The new company produced moderately-priced watches and also ones that it hoped would appeal to the railroads. The Peoria Watch Company remained in business until 1895.

COLUMBUS WATCH CO.
Columbus, Ohio
1882 – 1903
The main difference between this newly-named operation and the one from which it evolved (Greun and Savage) is that its watches were now made entirely at the plant in Ohio. The company made watches for some of the railroads before standards were set. In 1894, finances dictated that it go into receivership. With new management, it continued in business until 1903, when it was sold to a new company named South Bend Watch Company. The machinery was then moved to South Bend, Indiana.

J. P. STEVENS & CO.
Atlanta, Georgia
1882 – 1887
Josiah Percy Stevens was a successful Atlanta jeweler who was fascinated with watches. After he invented his Stevens Patent Regulator, he purchased some of the Bowman Watch Company equipment, unfinished movements, and parts, and began making watches that included his regulator. In 1882, the J. P. Stevens Watch Company was formed with the help of J. C. Freman, a major investor in both companies.

When Freman died, Stevens sold his interest in the company to Freman's estate. The company closed and the machinery was sold.

MANHATTAN WATCH CO.
New York, New York
1883 – 1892
This company sold inexpensive watches that were cased at the factory. According to Harrold's book, this company's movements were "unique with unusual escapements and setting mechanisms." Manhattan is also known for making timers.

TRENTON WATCH CO.

This company operated under the following three names:
1883 – 1887 — New Haven Watch Co., New Haven, Connecticut
1887 – 1908 — Trenton Watch Co., Trenton, New Jersey
1908 – 1922 — Ingersoll Trenton, Trenton, New Jersey
This company started business as the New Haven Watch Company. When it decided to move its operations to New Jersey, it was evident that the company had to change its name. Trenton Watch Company concentrated on making inexpensive, jeweled watches. It was in business under the name Trenton for twenty years before it were bought out by Ingersoll. The new owners wisely kept the Trenton Watch Company name for the watch division, but renamed the company Ingersoll Trenton.

Plate 207. Trenton trademark.

CHESHIRE WATCH CO.

Cheshire, Connecticut
1883 – 1894

This company specialized in inexpensive, jeweled watches. Their superintendent was D. A. A. Buck, one of the great minds of the watch industry. A selling agent in New York was the company's sole representative. The company had the cash flow problems that seemed to affect most of the newly-formed watch companies. In 1890 it went into receivership, and the new owners continued to finish another 3,000 movements. Cheshire's old machinery was purchased by Remington Watch Company and moved to Appleton, Wisconsin, about 1901.

AURORA WATCH CO.

Aurora, Illinois
1883 – 1892

This company started before the railroad standards were set, but it had making watches that would be used by the railroad as a goal. Another goal was to have a jeweler in every town selling its watches. When these goals were not achieved, it had to close (1892). Its machinery was sold to the investors who founded the Hamilton Watch Company and was used there.

Plate 208. Seth Thomas trademark.

SETH THOMAS CLOCK CO.

Thomaston, Connecticut
Watches, 1884 – 1915
The clock manufacturer Seth Thomas was so successful that the town he lived in (Plymouth Hollow) renamed itself after his name. In 1883, his company decided that it would like to get its share of the lucrative watch business. It took about two years for the company to get its watches on the market, but this old, established clock company had known what to expect and had had an adequate budget.

The company evolved from making mostly inexpensive watches to also including higher grade models around 1886. Competition from Ingersoll's low-priced watches, combined with the growing popularity of wristwatches, led its decision, in 1915, to cease doing business.

UNITED STATES WATCH CO. OF WALTHAM

Waltham, Massachusets.
1884 – 1896

Charles Vander Woerd formed this company in 1884. It was never able to produce enough watches per day to keep up with the competition. It absorbed the Suffolk Watch Company, originally the Columbia Watch Company. The buying out and absorbing of watch companies was very common throughout this century. The U.S. Watch Company of Waltham also suffered this fate and in 1896 was purchased by Keystone Watchcase Company.

NEW YORK STANDARD WATCH CO.

Jersey City, New Jersey
1885 – 1929

It took this company three years to get its product ready for the marketplace. It wanted something novel enough to set itself apart from the competition. Its gimmick was a "worm drive" escapement. The "worm" was visible through a star-shaped cutout in the back plate of the watch. This company made a name for itself by selling inexpensive, jeweled watches. In 1903, it became one of the many companies purchased by Keystone.

Plate 209. Worm drive watch. Look through the star-shaped hole to see the worm.

NON-MAGNETIC WATCH CO. OF AMERICA

Geneva, Switzerland and America
1887 – 1905
This was basically a sales company that purchased American and Swiss watches and sold them under its own name. Its main supplier of American watches was the Peoria Watch Company. The company name was derived from the fact that it primarily specialized in watches that had Paillard's patented non-magnetic balances and balance springs.

NON-MAGNETIC WATCH CO. CHICAGO

The watches of this company were made by the Illinois Watch Company. Because they used Paillard's non-magnetic balances and balance springs, they were marketed under this name.

OTAY WATCH CO.

Otay, California
1889 – 1894
This company didn't last long, so its production was limited. In 1894, its machinery was sold and shipped to San Jose, California, to be used by the newly formed San Jose Watch Company. This company produced even fewer watches before the machinery was shipped out again. This time it went to Osaka, Japan. Though the few watches made there had the Osaka name, they looked liked the Otay Watches.

WATERBURY CLOCK CO.

Waterbury, Connecticut
watches, 1890 – 1922
This company began in 1857 and, like the Waterbury Watch Company, was an offspring of the Benedict & Burnham Manufacturing Company. It decided to produce watches in 1890, and concentrated on cheap watches. By 1894, it was supplying watches to the Ingersoll Brothers. Later (1922), it was able to buy the company to which it had been supplying watches.

Waterbury Clock Company was wise enough to continue to use the Ingersoll name on its watches. In 1944, the clock company was absorbed by the U.S. Time Corporation.

KNICKERBOCKER WATCH CO.

New York, New York
1890 – 1930
This company made use of Buck's duplex. Harrold, in his book about American watch companies, suggests that Knickerbocker may have been a sales company and not a manufacturer. It sold duplex watches that had the Knickerbocker name but were made by the New England Watch Company.

HAMILTON WATCH CO.

Lancaster, Pennsylvania
1892 – 1970s
The company was started in 1892, and the owners hoped to have watches ready for the 400th anniversary of Columbus's discovery of America. The new company was to be named Columbian Watch Company, but that name was already protected. Because the company's first model was to be the Hamilton, the owners decided to make that the name of the company. A few of its earlier movements were confined to less than 15 jewels, but virtually all Hamilton's production was highly jeweled watches of very good quality. Hamilton is known for its fine grade railroad watches.[29]

Plates 210 and 211. This shows the Hamilton watch company building in Lancaster, Pennsylvania.

ROBERT INGERSOLL & BROS.

New York, New York
1892 – 1922

The brothers Robert and Charles had a mail order business that sold many items for one dollar. Their catalogs also included some watches that they imported from Switzerland and sold for less than $4.00.

The first Ingersoll watches were sold to dealers for a dollar, and were probably retailed for about $2.00. These watches were made for them by the Waterbury Clock Company. Ingersoll became the sole distributor of watches for this clock company in 1894.

By 1896. the company was finally able to retail a watch called "The Yankee" for the unbelievably low price of $1.00. Ingersoll's new slogan became "The watch that made the dollar famous." Even at a dollar, the watch still cost what an average laborer was paid for a day's work.

In 1908, Ingersoll purchased Trenton Watch Company. Six years later, Ingersoll was purchased the New England Watch Company.

When the assets of the company were purchased by the Waterbury Clock Company, in March of 1922, Waterbury proudly announced that "the Ingersolls are now marketed directly by the manufacturers, who have made Ingersolls from the beginning." As you can see from the *Saturday Evening Post* advertisement on page 248, by June 3rd, 1922, the price of The Yankee had been raised to $1.50. Please remember that the Ingersoll watches were made by the Waterbury Clock Company and not the Waterbury Watch Co. To make matters even more confusing, the clock company, started in 1857, and the watch company, started in1880, were both founded by Benedict & Burnham Manufacturing Company.

Plate 212. D. Gruen & Son trademark.

D. GRUEN & SON

1894 – 1903

When new management took over the Columbus Watch Company, Mr. Gruen knew it was time to leave. He started a new company with his son, Fred. This venture went back to the importing and finishing system that had originally made Gruen successful. After importing watches for a while, Gruen eventually invested in a manufacturing company in Switzerland that made watch parts and sent them to his plant in Cincinnati, Ohio. Gruen used Dennison's dream for the Tremont Watch Company and created a very successful company. Fortunately, Dennison lived to see that his idea did work.

CHICAGO WATCH CO.

Chicago, Illinois
1895 – 1903

This was not a watch company, but a sales company that sold many types of watches manufactured by other companies.

COLUMBIA WATCH CO.

1896 – 1899

Waltham, Massachusetts

This firm made small, inexpensive, jeweled watches. In 1901, it evolved into the Suffolk Watch Company, which was later absorbed by the U.S. Watch Company of Waltham (1901) and later still by the Keystone Watch Case Company.[30]

NEW ENGLAND WATCH COMPANY

Waterbury, Connecticut
1898 – 1914

This company also used Buck's duplex escapement and it is known for its 16 size skeletonized-movement watches and its beautiful ladies' watches. Both types are highly collectible.

Later the company made ladies' watches that had either four jewels or seven jewels. For a while, this company was very successful. It got into financial difficulty when it began producing a seven-jewel chronograph. By 1912, the company was in receivership. It was sold to R. H. Ingersoll & Brothers of New York.

Plate 213. Three of the New England Watch Company's trademarks.

WESTERN CLOCK CO. (WESTCLOX)

Athens, Georgia

watches, 1899 – present

This company, founded in 1887, was the last of the clock companies to join in the production of watches. The name Westclox did not appear on its watches until 1906. It was really the better name for fitting on a watch dial. This company was a big producer of dollar-type watches. It remains in business today.

Plate 214. *The Cautauquan*, Dec. 1887.

U.S. WATCHES COMPANIES AND SERIAL NUMBERS

The information listed in this section is the result of research done by my friend Roy Ehrhardt. He is well known in the industry for his wealth of information and his willingness to share it. I highly recommend any and all of his books, listed in the bibliography. Roy has selected and compiled this information from all sources, including all of his books and the three books by Col. George E. Townsend. With this list, he has tried only to show you (if possible) when your watch was made. A name in parentheses is at least one of the actual makers.

Abbott Sure Time, Chicago (Howard) 1910
Adams & Perry; Lancaster, PA . . . . .1874 – 1876
Lancaster W. Co.; Lancaster, PA . . . . .1877 – 1878
    Lancaster Penn. W. Co.; Lancaster, PA . . . . .1878 – 1879
    Lancaster W. Co.; Lancaster, PA . . . . .1879 – 1886
    Keystone Standard W. Co.; Lancaster, PA . . . . .1886 – 1890
Advance-USA, by Trenton W. Co.
American Leader-N. Games (Waltham)
America-Philadelphia USA (Elgin Export)
American General, Chicago (New England)
American Repeating W. Co.; Elizabeth, NJ . . . . .1885 – 1892
American Star-N. Games (Illinois)
American W. Co. (Waltham)
Ansonia W. Co.; Ansonia, CT . . . . .1873 – 1930
                         227 to 203,624. Total production, 10,000,000
Appleton Tracy & Co. (Waltham)
Appleton W. Co.; Appleton, WI. . . . . .80,000 to 95,000, 1887 (Cheshire)
Aristocrat RR STD (Ingersoll)
Ariston W. Co., Chicago (Illinois)
Atlas W. Co., Chicago (Elgin)
Auburndale Watch Co., Auburndale, MA . . . . .1876 – 1883
                                       2 to 3,230
Aurora Watch Co.; Aurora, IL . . . . .1883 – 1886
                                15,100 to 231,000
Bailey, Banks & Biddle; Philadelphia, PA
    (Waltham, Elgin, Hamilton, Swiss, and others)
Bannatine W. Co.; Waterbury, CT . . . . .1905 – 1911
                 50,000, 1906; 150,000, 1908; 350,000, 1911
Bartlett, P. S. (Waltham)
Belmont-USA (Rockford)
Benedict & Burnham Co.; Waterbury, CT . . . . .1855 – 1880
Benjamin Franklin-USA (Illinois)
Bingham, B.D.; Nashua, NH . . . . .1838 – 1862
B & M Special (Illinois)

WEBB C. BALL
Cleveland, Ohio
Chicago, Illinois
Serial Numbers and Production Dates

Waltham	Hamilton	Elgin	Approx. Prod. Date
7B 777,001	13,001	————	1898
9B 060,701	90,101	————	1899
10B 056,501	170,001	————	1901
11B 004,501	284,001	————	1902
12B 037,001	284,901	————	1903
13B 202,001	458,001	11,853,001	1904
13B 204,301	462,001	12,282,000	1905
15B 225,001	497,001	————	1906
————	503,001		1907
————	585,001		1909
————	B 600,001		1910
18B 240,001	B 601,801		1912

(Elgin Balls that Roy has seen have the full serial number on them and are all size 18.)
(Illinois used "B" prefix and left off the millions numbers.)

Illinois	Waltham	Hamilton	Approx. Prod. Date
————	20B 225,001	B 603,001	1914
————	————		1916
————			1917
————	22B 260,001		1918
————	23B 265,001		1919
————	————	————	1920
————	————	————	1921
————	24B 270,001	B 607,001	1922
800,000	————	————	1923
————	————	B 616,501	1925
————	————	B 624,001	1927
————	————	B 636,001	1929
801,000	————	B 639,001	1930
803,000	————	B 640,001	1935
————	————	B 650,001	1942
————	————	2B 001	1942

Hamilton used the "B" or "2B" prefix after the 600,000 numbers.
Waltham left off the millions and prefixed the last six numbers with "B".
Hamilton probably sold watches to Ball, maybe as late as the 60s. All of the "16 S" Illinois movements I have seen have the serial numbers in the 800,000 range and the "12 S" in the 400,000 range, with the prefix "B."
Hampden "18 S," 759, 657 – 759,760 and 761, 660 – 866, 975.
Howard "18 S," 226,201 – 307,456 and 308,146 – 308,449.
Seth Thomas "18 S," serial number 95,509.
The Time Ball Special is a Swiss fake. No Swiss Ball watches are listed here.

BORRENSON RAILWAY STANDARD — C. E. DELONG

B & O Standard (Illinois, Hamilton)

Boston W. Co., Roxbury & Waltham, MA . . . . .1853 – 1857
1,001 to 5,000 +

Bowman, E. F.; Lancaster, PA. . . . . .1879 – 82
1 to 50

Brown, J. R. & SHARPE; Providence, RI . . . . .1856 +

Brown, Robert & Sons; Providence, RI . . . . .1833 – 1856

Bulova W. Co. (Swiss)

Burlington W. Co., Chicago (Illinois)

California W. Co.; Berkeley, CA 1876-1877
25,105 to 30,174

Calumet-USA (Trenton)

Canadian Northern SPL (South Bend)

Canadian Pacific Railway (Waltham)

Canadian Railway Time Service (Waltham)

Carthage Electric Railway (Illinois)

Century W. Co. (Seth Thomas) . . . . .1,200 to 1,275,610

Chesapeke & Ohio SPL (Illinois)

Cheshire W. Co. Cheshire, CT . . . . .1883 – 1894
282 to 89,505

Chicago (Columbus)

Climax-USA (Howard)

Club W. Co. (South Bend)

Colonial W. Co. (Seth Thomas)

Colorado & Eastern W. Co. (Lancaster)

Columbia-USA (N. Y. Std.)

Columbia W. Co.; Waltham, MA . . . . .1896 – 1901

COLUMBUS WATCH COMPANY
1883 – 1903

Serial#	Date	Serial#	Date	Serial#	Date
20,000	1883	190,000	1890	400,000	1897
40,000	1884	220,000	1891	420,000	1898
65,000	1885	250,000	1892	440,000	1899
90,000	1886	275,000	1893	460,000	1900
115,000	1887	310,000	1894	480,000	1901
138,000	1888	350,000	1895	490,000	1902
163,000	1889	375,000	1896	500,000	1903

Cornell W. Co.; San Francisco, CA . . . . .1874 – 1876
25,105 to 31,000

Cornell W. Co.; Chicago, IL . . . . .1870 – 1874
6,900 to 25,000

Connecticut W. Co. (Ingersoll)

Corona W. Co., N.Y. (Seth Thomas)

Cosmopolitan W. Co.-USA (Illinois)

Crown W, Co., (N,Y. Std.)

Custer, J. D.; Norristown, PA . . . . .1840 – 1945
1 to 15

Delaware W. Co. Phila. (Ingersoll)

Des Moines W. Co. (Illinois)

Diamond W. Co. (Seth Thomas)

Dominion Railway (Waltham)

D. & R. G. Special (Waltham)
Duber-Hampden W. Co., Canton, Ohio (Hampden)
Dudley W. Co., Lancaster, PA . . . . .1918 – 1925
P. W. Baker Co. . . . . .1925 – 1935
XL Watch Co. . . . . .1935 – 1976

Series 1, 1 – 2,000;   Series II, 2,000 – 4,800;
Series III, 4,800 to 6,600

ELGIN NATIONAL WATCH CO.
1874 – Mid 1900s

Serial#	Date	Serial#	Date	Serial#	Date	Serial#	Date
101	1867	3,000,000	1888	14,000,000	1909	26,000,000	1923
100,000	1870	4,000,000	1890	15,000,000	1910	29,000,000	1926
200,000	1874	5,000,000	1893	16,000,000	1911	33,000,000	1929
400,000	1875	6,000,000	1895	17,000,000	1912	34,000,000	1933
500,000	1877	7,000,000	1897	18,000,000	1914	36,000,000	1936
600,000	1879	8,000,000	1899	19,000,000	1916	38,000,000	1939
700,000	1880	9,000,000	1900	20,000,000	1917	41,000,000	1942
800,000	1881	10,000,000	1903	21,000,000	1918	43,000,000	1945
1,000,000	1882	11,000,000	1904	22,000,000	1919	45,000,000	1948
2,000,000	1886	13,000,000	1907	23,000,000	1920	50,000,000	1953

Eagle, Picture of (Seth Thomas)
Eastern W. Co.-Nevada (Lancaster)
Edgemere W. Co., Chicago (Made for Sears, Roebuck by Seth Thomas)
Ellery, WM. (Waltham)
Empire City W. Co. (U.S. W. Co.; Marion, NJ)
Engle National W. Co. (Illinois)
Equity W. CO., Boston (Waltham)
Excel SPR-USA (N.Y. Std.)
Fasoldt, Charles, Rome & Albany, NY . . . . .1850 – 1878
1 to 524 (Some Swiss)

Federal W. Co., NY (Aurora & Swiss)
Ferguson Dial Co; Monroe, LA . . . . .Ca. 1913
Fitchburg W. Co.; Fitchburg, MA . . . . .1875 – 1878
Few.

Flint, E. H.; Cincinnati, OH 1877
Freeport W. CO.; Freeport, IL 1875
1,2,4,7, & 11 seen

Frederick Atherton & CO. (U.S. W. Co.; Marion, NJ)
Fredonia W. CO.; Fredonia, NY (Independent W. Co.) . . . . .1883 – 1885
French, S. D.; Wabash, Indiana 1866
Garden City W. CO., Chicago (Seth Thomas)
Globe W. CO. (Illinois & Swiss)
Goddard, Luther, P & D, etc.; Worcester, MA . . . . .1817 – 1872
20 to 3,673 (English)

Granger W. Co.; San Francisco, CA (Elgin)
Grant-USA (Illinois)
Greenwich (Made for Montgomery Ward, by Illinois)
Gruen W. CO.; Cincinnati, OH (Swiss)
Hanson, W.-the Atlanta
Harvard W. CO.-USA (N.Y. Std.)
Herald Square (Illinois)
Hi-Grade-USA (N.Y. Std.)
Hollers W. Brooklyn (Columbus)

Home Watch Co.; Boston, MA (Waltham)
Howard, Davis & Dennison (Waltham)
Howard & Rice (Howard)
Ideal-USA (N.Y. Std.)
Illinois Watch Case Co. (Trenton)

HAMILTON WATCH COMPANY
1893 – 1948

Serial#	Grade	Date	Serial#	Grade	Date	Serial#	Grade	Date
1	936	1893	1,648,001	992L	1924	H1001	980	1934 – 51
2,000	7J	1894	1,831,001	920	1918	H50001	400	1929 – 32
6,801	932	1894	1,882,901	900	1921 – 22	J1001	401	1930 – 33
14,001	999	1895	2,000,001	988	1913 – 17	L 101	982	1935 – 51
15,701	939	1900	1,989,001	194	1923	M001	997	1936 – 41
20,501	999E	1896	2,035,001	981	1923	N001	982M	1941 – 51
23,301	11J	1903	2,327,001	992L	1925	001	721	1939 – 49
25,001	11J	1896 – 99	2,538,001	974L	1929	R001	987	1937 – 48
30,001	11J	1896	2,567,001	992L	1930	5001	923	1937 – 49
50,001	962	1896	2,611,001	950	1936	55001	950B	1941 – 53
55,601	969	1898	2,581,001	992E	1930 – 40	T001	9875	1940 – 48
70,001	976	1901	2,611,401	950E	1937	V001	911	1938 – 50
80,001	972	1902	3,000,001	922	1924 – 36	X001	911 M	1941 – 50
104,001	940	1899	3,056,001	902	1926 – 28	HWR001	917	1936 – 54
150,001	924	1901	3,100,001	916	1923 – 28	Y001	H917	1938
200,001	926	1902	3,135,001	918	1928 – 36	CY001	747	1947 – 54
400,001	924	1904	3,200,001	912	1924 – 36	001A	748	1948 – 54
501,001	926	1906	4,025,301	987E	1928 – 37	001C	750	1949 – 54
601,001	926	1908	A001	9808	1937 – 46	001E	751	1950 – 54
710,001	993	1908	1B-001	999	1943 – 54	001F	752	1951 – 54
900,001	940	1911	2B-701	9998	1943	001H	753	1951 – 54
1,000,001	972	1913	C001	9508	1943	001K	754	1952 – 54
1,079,001	992L	1914	E001	9928	1940-54	HW001	756	1954
1,156,001	996L	1915	F101	989	1928-36	W1001	H98O	1942 – 49
1,305,001	956P	1918	G101	995	1931-39		9801	1942 – 48

HAMPDEN WATCH CO.
Springfield, Massachusetts
Canton, Ohio

Serial#	Date	Serial#	Date	Serial#	Date
52,000	1877	1,258,000	1889	2,600,000	1903
156,000	1878	1,358,000	1890	2,850,000	1905
260,000	1879	1,458,000	1891	3,050,000	1907
364,000	1880	1,558,000	1892	3,200,000	1909
368,000	1881	1,658,000	1893	3,400,000	1911
472,000	1882	1,758,000	1894	3,600,000	1913
576,000	1883	1,859,000	1895	3,800,000	1915
690,000	1884	1,958,000	1896	4,000,000	1917
854,000	1885	2,150,000	1889	4,200,000	1919
958,000	1886	2,250,000	1899	4,400,000	1921
1,058,000	1887	2,350,000	1900	4,500,000	1923
1,058,000	1888	2,450,000	1901	4,600,000	1925

HOWARD WATCH COMPANY
Boston, Massachusetts, 1857 – 1930

Serial#	Descrip.	Date	Serial#	Descrip.	Date	Serial#	Descrip.	Date
1	Series I	1857	100,000	Series VI	1870	309,069	Gr. 8&10	1903
1,984	Keywind	1860	105,197	6S HC	1899	309,958	18S OF	1895
2,017	Series II	1859	200,001	Series VII	1880	600,001	Gr. 8&10	1896
2,985	Keywind	1860	230,000	18S HC	1899	601,091	16S HC	1903
			300,001	Series VIII	1884	700,001	Gr. 8&10	1896
Experimental — 3,000 to 3,500			310,000	18S OF	1899	701,253	16S HC	1903
			400,001	Series IX	1890			
3,543	Series III	1861	404,947	185 HC	1895	**Keystone Howards**		
27,483	Keywind	1879	500,001	Series X	1890	854,001		1905
			501,506	12S OF	1899	970,001		1908
30,001	Series IV	1868				1,100,000		1915
Key & Stem			**Pat. 1893 – 1894 Nickel Split Plate, Grade 8 & 10**			1,100,000		1920
49,840	18S HC	1882				1,200,000		1925
50,001	Series V	1869				1,396,000		1930
Key & Stem			228,080	Gr. 8&10	1895			
70,300	16S HC	1899	229,966	18S HC	1895			

ILLINIOS WATCH COMPANY
Illinois Springfield Watch Co., 1869 – 1879
Springfield Illinois Watch Co., 1879 – 1885
Illinois Watch Co., 1885 – 1927

Serial#	Date	Serial#	Date	Serial#	Date	Serial#	Date
1 – 2,000	1872	2,881 – 2,900		61,001 – 61,300	1880	1,600,000	1902
2,411 – 2,550		2,201 – 2,210	1877	65,001 – 66,000		1,700,000	1904
3,001 – 3,700		2,231 – 2,250		69,401 – 88,100		1,844,000	1906
4,401 – 4,360		2,261 – 2,270		102,801 – 102,900		2,032,000	1908
4,401 – 4,470		2,901 – 3,000		133,901 – 150,000		2,220,000	1910
5,001 – 5,500		51,401 – 51,650	1878	154,901 – 162,000		2,408,000	1912
2,301 – 2,410	1873	58,001 – 59,000		162,001	1881	2,596,000	1914
2,551 – 2,720		96,401 – 102,400		235,000	1882	2,873,000	1916
3,701 – 4,000		112,101 – 118,600		310,000	1883	3,241,000	1918
4,361 – 4,400		50,601 – 50,700	1879	390,000	1884	3,609,000	1920
4,471 – 5,000		51,651 – 51,700		470,000	1885	3,977,000	1922
5,501 – 6,840		54,901 – 55,200		552,001	1886	4,492,501	1924
7,001 – 10,000		57,001 – 57,800		672,000	1887	4,700,000	1926
2,001 – 2,100	1874	118,601 – 133,900		792,000	1888	5,000,000	1928
2,721 – 2,830		150,301 – 154,900		912,000	1889	5,300,000	1930
6,841 – 7,000		46,001 – 48,000	1880	1,030,001	1890	5,488,301	1932
2,101 – 2,160	1875	50,701 – 51,000		1,300,001	1896	Moved to Hamilton	1933
2,831 – 2,880		55,201 – 57,000		1,400,000	1898	5,610,586	1948
2,211 – 2,230	1876	57,801 – 58,000		1,500,000	1900	5,698,800	Last

Imperial W. Co. (Illinois)
Independent W. Co.; Fredonia, NY (Also made by other companies.) . . . . .1880 – 1883
1 to 350,000
Ingersoll, Robert H. & Bros.; Trenton, NJ and Waterbury, CT . . . . .1881 – 1944

Serial#	Date	Serial#	Date	Serial#	Date
100,000	1892	54,000,000	1920	92,000,000	1940
6,000,000	1900	74,000,000	1930	96,000,000	1944
25,000,000	1910				

Ingraham; Bristol, Conn. (Dollar, 1884 – 1958)
International W. Co.; Jersey C ....1902 – 1907
Dollar.

Interstate Chronometer-Sears (Illinois)

J. P. Stevens W. Co.; Atlanta, GA (Hampden, Aurora, Waltham, Swiss) ....1882 – 1885
1 to 600.

Karr, Jacob; Washington, DC ....1864 – 1885
Kelly W. Co., Chicago (aluminum) ....Ca. 1900
Keystone Watch Case Co. (watches); Riverside, NJ ....1885 – 1929
Few watches with this name.

Knickerbocker W Co.; New York ....1890 – 1930
made Dollar and imported Swiss.

La Salle-USA (N.Y. Std.)
Lake Shore W. Co.; Fredonia, NY (Fredonia)
Landis W. Co.; Chicago (Illinois)
Leland W. Co.; Minneapolis, MN (Rockford)
Leonard W. Co. (New Haven C. Co.)
Lincoln Park-USA (Illinois)
Locomotive SPL, Chicago (Trenton)

McIntyre W. Co.; Kankakee, IL 1915
Few watches — no numbers.

Maiden Lane (Seth Thomas)
Main Line W. Co.; Minneapolis, MN (Hamilton)
Manhattan W. Co.; New York ....1883 – 1892
5,000 to 140,000; low grade and stop.

Manistee W. Co.; Manistee, MI ....ca 1909.
Up to 40,000

Marion W. Co.; Marion, NJ ....1872 – 1874
(See U.S. W. Co., Marion)

Marvel W. Co. (Trenton)
Melrose W. Co.; Melrose, MA ....1866 – 1868
About 30,000 to 33,200

Mermod, Jaccard, King; St. Louis, MO (Hampden, Hamilton, Elgin, Rockford, and Swiss)
Metropolitan Watch. Co., New York (Manhattan W. Co.) ....Ca. 1890

Miner, the (Elgin)
Monarch W. Co., Chicago (Illionois, Seth Thomas)
Montgomery Ward & Co. (Illinois, Seth Thomas, Swiss)

Mozart W. Co.; Providence, RI ....1864 – 1870.
1 to 165

Muscatine W. Co. (Illinois)

Nashua W. Co.; Nashua, NH ....1859 – 1862
1,036 – 1,215

National W. Co. (Elgin)
Newark W. Co.; Newark, NJ ....1864 – 1870
3,650 – 19,585

New England W. Co.; Waterbury, CT ....1898 – 1912
Not many numbered.

New ERA-USA (N.Y. Std)
New Haven Clock Co.; New Haven, CT . . . . .1853 – 1956
New Haven Watch Co.; New Haven, CT . . . . .1883 – 1887
Low grade.

New Jersey W. Co. (Swiss & Trenton)
New York Chronograph W. Co., New York . . . . .1890 – 1897
Dollar.
New York Standard W. Co.; Jersey City, NJ . . . . .1885 – 1929
1+ to 10,000 used prefix and no numbers.

New York W. Co.; Springfield, MA . . . . .1866 – 1875
1 to 44,000
Non-Magnetic W. Co. of America by Peoria, Elgin, Illinois, and Swiss . . . . .1880 – 1930

O'hara Waltham Dial Co. (Waltham) . . . . .1890 – 1923
Orleans W. Co. (Seth Thomas)
Otay W. Co. (Otay) . . . . .Ca. 1889 – 1890
1,000 to 1,500 and 30,000 to 31,000
Oska W. Co.; Oska, Japan . . . . .Ca. 1892

Pailliard Non-Magnetic W. Co. . . . .(See Non-Magnetic W. Co.)
Palmer, D.O., W. Co.; Waltham, MA . . . . .1864 – 1875
1 – 1,100

Pan-American (Seth Thomas)
Patch, Dan (N.Y. Std., New England)

Pastor Stop Watch Sterling W. Co., New York
Peerless (Trenton) . . . . .Ca. 1900
Pennsylvania Special (Illinois, Waltham, Elgin)
Peoria W. Co. (made some Pailliard Non-Magnetic); Peoria, IL . . . . .1885 – 1895
1 to 47,000
Perfection-USA (N.Y. Std)
Philadelphia W. Co.; Philadelphia, PA . . . . .Now believed to be Swiss.
Pitkin, James & Henry; East Howard, CT . . . . .1838 – 1841
Up to 400, others Swiss.
Plymouth W. Co., Sears-Roebuck (Illinois, Rockford, Seth Thomas)
Potter, Albert H., W. Co., N.Y.; New York and Chicago . . . . .1855 – 1875, Swiss after 1876
Potter Bros. (W. C. Potter), Chicago, IL . . . . .After 1875
Progress-USA (N.Y Std.)
Providence W. Co. (Seth Thomas)

Railroad Reliance (Trenton)
Railroad W. Co.; Cleveland, OH (Hamilton)
Reed, Goerge P.; Boston, MA . . . . .1868+
Up to about 800.
Regent-USA (N.Y. Std.)
Reliance W. Co., Chicago (Trenton)
Remington W. Co. (N.Y. Std.)
Republican-USA (Seth Thomas)
Ross, Betsy (U.S Watch Co., Waltham)
Royal Gold American W. Co., New York . . . .(See U.S. W. Co.; Marion, NJ)
Rugby-USA (New England)

ROCKFORD WATCH COMPANY
1876 – 1915

Serial#	Date	Serial#	Date	Serial#	Date
8,000	1876	128,000	1887	414,000	1900
18,000	1877	140,000	1888	448,000	1901
30,000	1878	152,000	1889	482,000	1902
40,000	1879	164,000	1890	550,000	1904
50,000	1880	176,000	1891	655,000	1907
60,000	1881	198,000	1892	730,000	1909
70,000	1882	234,000	1894	815,000	1911
80,000	1883	294,000	1896	850,000	1912
90,000	1884	324,000	1897	880,000	1913
140,000	1885	354,000	1898	930,000	1914
116,000	1886	384,000	1889	936,000	1915

San Jose W. Co., San Jose, CA...1891+

Few watches.

Santa Fe Special (Illinois)
Santa Fe Route (Waltham)
Santa Fe W. Co.; Topeka, KS (Illinois)
Sears Roebuck & Co. (Rockford, Illinois, Seth Thomas, Swiss)

SETH THOMAS WATCH CO.
Thomaston, Connecticut, made watches 1884 – 1914

Serial#	Date	Serial#	Date	Serial#	Date
4,000	1885	288,000	1895	763,000	1905
9,000	1886	817,000	1896	817,000	1906
20,000	1887	376,000	1897	937,000	1907
50,000	1888	418,000	1898	1,057,000	1908
80,000	1889	460,000	1899	1,177,000	1909
110,000	1890	500,000	1900	1,325,000	1910
150,000	1891	552,000	1901	1,835,000	1911
176,000	1892	604,000	1902	2,355,000	1912
204,000	1893	657,000	1903	3,000,333	1913
246,000	1894	710,000	1904	3,600,000	1914

Shell Watch (Swiss)
Smith, M.S.; Detroit, MI ....Ca. 1874

50 to 76

SOUTH BEND
South Bend, Arizona, 1904 – 1928

Serial#	Date	Serial#	Date
336,000	1904	912,000	1920
480,000	1908	1,056,000	1924
768,000	1916	1,239,000	1928

Springfield Illinois W. Co. (Illinois)
Standard American W. Co.; Pittsburg, PA (Lancaster)
Standard-USA (N.Y. Std.)
Standard W. Co.; Minneapolis, MN (Swiss)
Standard W. Co.; Pittsburgh, PA (Illinois)
Standard W. Co.; Syracuse, NY (Swiss)
Stewart W. Co. (Illinois)
Studebaker W. Co. (South Bend)
Suffolk W. Co.; Waltham, MA ....1901+
Sun-Dial USA (Elgin)
Tiffany, New York (Waltham, Elgin, Swiss)
Trainmen's Special, Chicago (Seth Thomas)
Tremont W. Co., Tremont and Boston, MA...1864 – 1866
about 40,000 to 42,000.

Trenton W. Co., Trenton, NJ ....1887 – 1907
1,200 to 3,192,784.

20th Century (Montgomery Ward by Seth Thomas)
United States W. Co.; Marion, NJ ....1864 – 1872. 1,000 to 287,000.
United States W. Co.; Waltham, MA ....1884 – 1896
100 to 802,000

Von Der Heydt, Herman, Chicago. ....1883 – 1890
1 to 40.

WALTHAM WATCH COMPANY
Waltham, Massachusetts, 1850 – mid-1900s

Serial#	Date	Serial#	Date	Serial#	Date
1,000	1857	900,000	1876	15,000,000	1907
14,000	1858	1,000,000	1877	17,000,000	1908
17,000	1859	1,160,000	1878	18,000,000	1910
20,000	1860	1,351,000	1879	19,000,000	1913
23,000	1861	1,499,000	1880	20,000,000	1914
34,000	1862	1,675,000	1881	21,000,000	1917
46,000	1863	1,837,000	1882	22,000,000	1918
118,000	1864	2,000,000	1883	23,000,000	1919
190,000	1865	2,356,000	1884	24,000,000	1921
262,000	1866	2,650,000	1885	25,00,000	1927
335,000	1867	3,300,000	1887	27,000,000	1929
410,000	1868	4,000,000	1889	28,000,000	1934
470,000	1869	6,000,000	1892	29,000,000	1936
500,000	1870	7,000,000	1895	30,000,000	1939
550,000	1871	9,000,000	1899	31,000,000	1942
600,000	1872	10,000,000	1901	32,000,000	1945
691,000	1873	12,000,000	1903	33,600,000	1951
720,000	1874	13,000,000	1904	33,830,000	1953
80,000	1875	14,000,000	1905	35,000,000	1957

Washington W. Co. (Illinois)
Waterbury W. Co.; Waterbury, CT 1898
Series and dollar, no numbers.
Welch Mfg. Co., E.N.; Bristol, CT ....1864 – 1903
Western Clock Co.; Peru, IL
    United Clock Co. ....1884 – 1887
    Westlox...to present
Western Watch Co., Chicago. ....1877 – 1880
Up to 31, 299. Three seen, 21, 23, and 364.
Zahm, G.M.; Lancaster, PA..1865

THE TIMES IN THE UNITED STATES

The dawn of the nineteenth century found the United States awakening to its potential. It had won its independence from Great Britain and felt ripe with possibilities. Changes were taking place at a rapid pace. The fruits of the Industrial Revolution were bringing about new social and economic conditions.

The American spirit of creativity was boundless. These were the years in which Luther Goddard made some of the first watches made in America (1809), Horace Breeley founded the *New York Tribune* (1841), Elias Howe invented the sewing machine (1846),Charles Lewis Tiffany opened his first store (1849), Aaron Dennison pursued his dream of making machine-made watches with interchangeable parts (1850), and Gail Borden patented his process for condensing milk (1856).

The country was vast, and in that time period, land equaled wealth. On January 24, 1848 gold was discovered in California. As the eyes of the world turned toward Sutter's mill, many people headed that direction. They went by wagon, by horse, and by foot, seeking their fortunes. This migration led to new towns all across the country. California's population increased 2,500% in just one year.[31]

Because of both this migration and the earlier expansion of the Northwest Territory, railroads were expanding. As the country grew, so did the need for transporting goods and people. In 1840, there were 3,000 miles of railroad track. By 1860, the total had grown to 30,000 miles. Railroads were definitely on the move, bringing economic success with them.

As in most centuries, the economy did have its ups and downs. A business recession in 1856 was partly responsible for the demise of the Boston Watch Company. The Civil War and the railroads helped boost the economy. The country suffered a short lived panic in 1873 and business in general experienced in downfall. This didn't keep four new watch companies from forming in 1874. Fortunately, this country has always had a good supply of optimists.

Most new watch companies were formed with one hundred thousand dollars or less of capital. The exception to this was Elgin, which was formed with a half million dollars, and Waterbury, which started with three hundred thousand dollars. In spite of how much or how little capital they had to work with, most founders of watch companies were unprepared for the length of time it took to make the machinery needed and to get watches into the marketplace. This is why so many companies continued to reorganize with new investors, and under a new name, whenever they ran short of funds.

Insofar as the American watch industry was concerned, some of the most significant events of the century were the beginning of the machine-made watch with interchangeable parts, the Civil War, the changes in the living patterns of the country, the expansion of the railroads, and the Centennial Exposition.

Even though Dennison's first attempt at producing machine-made watches with interchangeable parts was not a financial success, it paved the way for the development of factory production. As evidence of this, when the Boston Watch Co. was sold at auction, it brought considerably more money than had been expected. Evidently, some bidders believed that Dennison's dream was still viable.

THE CIVIL WAR AND RAILROAD EXPANSION

The first shots of the Civil War were fired in April 1861. Neither side expected the war to last long. The mood was almost jovial as the men rushed off to battle, but this changed as the days and weeks turned into years. There was much bloodshed, and the country experienced pain and suffering. People came to realize that a country at war with itself could never have a true victory. Both sides were relieved when the fighting finally came to an end.

The war created significant changes in the watch industry. The American Watch Company, which produced a line of lower-priced watches, thrived. In 1861/62 it came out with the William Ellery, a big seller during the Civil War. Any soldier that could afford a watch wanted one to take into battle, where 15 minutes sometimes seemed like hours. Officers also needed to know the time in order to accurately synchronize their attacks. The war made some industrialists very rich. The watch, being the traditional symbol of wealth, was a necessity for this new class of wealthy people.

Even before the war ended, many businessmen saw the watch business as a lucrative investment. Consequently, five new watch companies sprang up in 1864. After the war, other new watch companies continued to be formed, but many were short lived.

Railroads played an important role in the war. Ammunition and supplies had to be moved from one area to another and this form of transportation was needed. The Civil War was the first war to rely on the railroads. After the war, soldiers coming home were acutely aware of the changes. Railroads and industries such as iron and steel were booming. The reconstruction of the South depended upon the railroads to bring in goods, and business was brisk.

At the same time, the railroads desperately needed the returning soldiers in order to expand track into the west and populate the land. The Pacific Railroad developed a postwar employment project for returning veterans. It was most successful. An 1865 advertisement for the Illinois Central Railroad Company, offered "1,200,000 acres of rich farming lands for sale." They were willing to sell "tracts of 40 acres and upward on long credit and at low prices." Many veterans decided to use their bonus money for land and equipment.

In 1869, a golden spike was driven at Promontory Point, Utah, to celebrate the fact that railroad tracks now spanned the continent. While this was a great accomplishment, this vast span of track from east to west came with a unique problem. As trains moved across the country to the west, there was a shift in time. These differences in time precipitated problems in scheduling. Some companies used their own time standards, and this sometimes caused more problems than it solved.

THE CENTENNIAL EXPOSITION

An unlikely event ultimately had a lasting effect on the watch industry. In 1876, America celebrated her one hundredth birthday with a huge exposition in Philadelphia. It drew exhibitors from all over the world and offered Americans who had had very little, if any, opportunity to travel outside of the country a chance to see new and exciting things from strange and wonderful places.

Each country tended to display the very best of its products. This was the perfect setting to show off what Yankee ingenuity could accomplish. New products, such as Alexander Graham Bell's telephone, the new electric light, and the typewriter, were only briefly noted because most visitors could not see a real need for these things. The attention grabbers were the huge machines that were displayed and demonstrated. President Grant and Emperor Dom Pedro were there to start the huge Corliss Steam Engine. It is noted that when they opened the throttle "they felt that they had indeed witnessed the wonder of the age."[32]

This attention to machines was exactly what the American watch factories were hoping for when they not only brought examples of their finest machine-made watches, but also pieces of machinery to show the parts being made. Any watch factory that could possibly afford it wanted to show at this exhibition. Doing so would not only add prestige to its product, but would be a perfect opportunity to acquaint people with its name and product. For the first time, the visitors would see beautiful machine-made parts that were as good or better than hand-made ones. Seeing is believing, and many people would realize that machine-made products were no longer to be considered inferior.

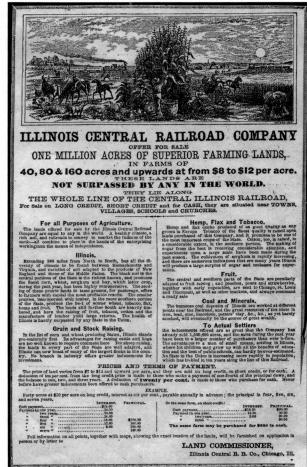

Plate 215. Advertisement from *Godey's Lady's Book*, 1865.

Unfortunately, for the American companies the displays also gave the biggest competitors of these companies a chance to see and compare the American-made watches to their Swiss-made ones. Edouard Favre-Perret, a Swiss member of the International Jury on Watches, was impressed with the American watches. He not only took one home with him, but made it his mission to give a wake-up call to the Swiss watchmakers that it was time for them to embrace the machine-made watch. If not, he stressed, Swiss watches would run a poor second to American-made watches. He displayed the watch that he brought back from the show and said, "One can understand by this example how it is that an American watch should be preferred to a Swiss watch."

$ TYPE WATCHES

As the century progressed, the country slowly but surely went from an exclusively agricultural country to one primarily industrial. The lure of the city and the opportunities it might offer drew the younger generation from the farms to the factories. With work schedules to be met, offices to be opened on time, and trains to be caught, the need for an inexpensive watch that the average man or woman could afford became evident.

The Benedict & Burnham Company had been in the brass business since 1833. Some of its best customers were clock companies that used brass to make movements. In 1857, it went into the clock making business itself by forming the Waterbury Clock Company. It diversified again in 1880 by forming the Waterbury Watch Company. The company believed that it could make inexpensive watches for the masses.

The businessmen of Waterbury Watch realized that a cheaper watch must have fewer parts and an escapement that could easily be stamped out of a sheet of brass. An inexpensive case and dial made by their own company would also be necessary.

One of the brightest minds of the century came up with the answer. Mr. Daniel Azro Ashley Buck, who seemed to be able to make anything, came up with the solution. His watch model had a rotary movement; the entire movement moved around once each hour. More importantly, his model used a duplex escapement unlike any other. Whereas the original duplex had a wheel with one of a kind teeth repeated on two different planes of elevation, his had two differently-shaped teeth that alternated with each other on the same plane. This made it very easy to be mass-produced. To minimize the cost of materials, his model had about half the number of parts used in a regular watch movement. It didn't have any jewels, but the spring was so long that it wrapped around the entire back of the case and took 150 half turns of the stem to wind. This model was called the Waterbury Long Wind. But no matter how hard the company tried, its watches never retailed for less than $3.00.

The same year that Waterbury Watch Company was formed, the New Haven Clock Company decided to try its luck producing cheap watches. The inexpensive punch-press manufacturing method was making it possible for almost every household to own a small clock. The company reasoned that it could produce a watch by adapting a small clock movement to fit into a watch case. In the early years, New Haven's watches wound in the back like an alarm clock.

In 1890, The Waterbury Clock Company also decided to get involved making inexpensive watches. It also decided that the easiest and least expensive way was to modify a small clock movement to fit a watch case. This branch of Benedict & Burnham had the necessary machinery to produce the punch-pressed parts, and it was soon in the watch business.

These early companies that were trying to make inexpensive watches for the average working man or woman had one big hurdle — distribution. They needed to find a new way to distribute the large volumes of watches they would need to sell in order to be profitable. Traditional watch companies had relied on retail jewelers to sell their products. In fact, many watch companies had investors or owners who were in the jewelry business. Jewelry stores would see no reason to sell a $3.00 watch. They sold to a higher income level of the marketplace.

Also, over the years, a chain of distribution had been established for watch companies. The manufacturer sold to wholesalers, and they in turn sold to retail jewelers, who then sold to the public. With every turnover of the watch, that link in the chain made a nice profit. This type of distribution was too expensive for inexpensive watches. They needed to be sold as directly to the public as possible.

The Waterbury Clock Company happened to be in the right place at the right time, and the Ingersoll Company chose Waterbury watches to sell in its stores and catalogs. Ingersoll's six retail stores were the original dollar stores. The company had started by selling rubber stamps and then expanded to selling almost anything that it could sell for a few dollars or less and still make a profit. It also had a big catalogue business. Before it took on the Waterbury Clock Company watches, it was selling watches from Switzerland that were priced at less than $4.00. The first Waterbury-made watches it sold were sold to Ingersoll dealers for $1.00 and probably retailed for about $2.00. Ingersoll was so pleased with the watch sales that soon it was buying Waterbury Clock's entire yearly production.

Plate 216. "Sweet Home Soap — buy 120 cakes and get a free watch."

As with most manufacturing methods, and especially those of making inexpensive items, the larger the production and the less the cost of distribution, the cheaper the product can be sold and still be profitable. For Waterbury, this was a perfect setup. It had only one customer for its entire year's production. By 1896, Ingersoll was finally able to retail a watch for a dollar. Its new slogan was "the watch that made the dollar famous." Most laborers were happy to trade a day's pay for a watch. For the first time in the history of the watch, the average man could afford the pleasure of owning a watch — a privilege that had formerly been reserved for the wealthy.

RAILROAD WATCHES

In 1872, the first scheduling meeting involving superintendents of the railroads was held. By 1883, these meetings had grown large enough to convene the General Time Convention, where the attendees adopted a system of five standard time zones for the United States and Canada.

As the railroads continued to expand, it became increasing important to have accurate timekeepers. Engineers and other railroad employees desperately needed watches they could depend on.

As traffic on the tracks increased, it was most important that trains run on schedule. Often, trains going in opposite directions shared the same track. At a specific time, one train had to pull to a side track so that the oncoming train could pass. If an engineer's watch was not keeping accurate time, this could lead to a head-on collusion. Knowing that this could happen, many of the railroads took action to set standards for the watches used by their employees. In 1867, Waltham came out with the first watch made specifically for railroads. This was followed the next year by the B. W. Raymond, a railroad model made by Elgin. Not to be outdone, the following year (1869) Waltham came out with the Model 70 railroad watch. By 1870, Elgin advertisements proudly featured letters of endorsement from the general superintendents of the Union Pacific Railroad, the Hudson River Railroad, and the Pennsylvania Central Railroad.

Some companies had specifications for the watches used by their employees, but there were not any uniform standards in the industry. In 1886, the Standard Code of Railroad Operating Rules was developed. It required that watches be inspected and certified every six months. A watch was allowed no more than a 30-second error in time during the period of a week.[33] Needless to say, there were many watches in service that did not meet those standards.

Plate 217. 1870 advertisement for Elgin, endorsements from railroad superintendents.

The need for standards in timekeeping was brought to the public's attention when a tragic train accident occurred in 1891. It was never really proven that a faulty timepiece contributed to the accident, but it was a fact that a mail train had crashed head-on with a Lakeshore and Michigan Southern Railroad train and eleven employees had been killed.

The accident called attention to the dangers of the railroad, and this was not good for business. In 1892, a commission was formed to set standards and guidelines for all watches used by the railroad employees responsible for schedules. The General Railroad Timekeeping Standards were adopted in 1893. With typical Yankee ingenuity, the watch industry set out to meet or exceed these standards.

Webb C. Ball played a part in implementing these standards. He was hired by the Lakeshore and Michigan Southern Railroad to put together a system for checking timepieces to insure that they were in good working order. He realized that there needed to be certain standards, not for just checking watches, but also to ensure that the watches used were reliable timepieces.

131

After an employee had the right kind of watch, it was important to make sure it was serviced on a regular basis. Ball set up a system for making sure this was done. He enlisted jewelers in each town to be designated Railroad Watch Inspectors. The railroads paid Ball, and the jewelers received their compensation by having this prestigious title and the increase in repair business that it produced. Because railroad standards required that watches were to be inspected every two weeks, railroad workers tended to get to know the store owners and would naturally turn to them when they wanted to make a purchase. These jewelers were also required to keep an inventory of spare parts, and to make sure that a watch card, which each trainman was required to carry, was filled out properly after each servicing. They also keep loaners in stock, so that if a watch needed to be left at the store, the railroad employee would still have an accurate timepiece. This ingenuous plan earned Ball the title of General Time Inspector for a number of railroads.

Because it was impossible for Ball to cover all railroad cities, many railroads hired their own people, but even these railroads generally used the standards set up by the 1886 Standard Code of Railroad Rules and the 1893 General Railroad Standards. The Ball name became associated with these railroad standards, and it certainly helped his watch business. He had been selling watches bearing his name since 1879. Look under the Chronological Listing and the U.S. Watch Companies and Serial Numbers headings in this chapter for more about his company.

RAILROAD WATCH STANDARDS

Watch Requirements

1. Open face.
2. Wind stem at 12 o'clock.
3. 16 or 18 size.
4. Minimum of 17 jewels.
5. Adjusted to at least 5 positions, plus isochronism.
6. Adjusted to temperatures of 34 and 100 degrees Fahrenheit.
7. Double roller with lever escapement.
8. Steel escapement wheel.
9. Lever set.
10. Micrometric regulator and overcoil hairspring.
11. Arabic numbers in bold black on white dial with minute division.
12. Bold black hands and a second hand.
13. Accurate to within 30 seconds a week (gain or loss).
14. Dust-tight case.

The Railroad Standards Act made sure that watches made for the railroads included all of these features. Some of them are self-explanatory and others are a little harder to understand. Let's explore what these terms mean.

1. An open face was just what the name implies, a watch without a cover on the face.
2. The watch had to be wound at the stem and the dial had to be placed at the top of the watch, with the number 12 under the stem.
3. Size 16 and 18 watches were larger and easier to handle, and it was easier to see the time on them.
4. The movement must have at least 17 jewels to reduce friction and wear on the pivots.
5. The movement had to be adjusted so that it kept the correct time whether the watch was held with the stem up or down, whether it was lying on its face or back, and whether it was turned so that the stem up positioned to the left or the right. If the balance spring was adjusted for isochronism, the long and the short arcs of its swing were performed in the same time, whether the spring was fully wound or almost wound down.
6. This ensured that a watch would keep the correct time under hot or cold conditions. In this time period, the watches were exposed for several weeks to cold refrigeration and hot oven temperatures on an alternating basis. If a movement's timekeeping ability was affected during these tests, changes were required.
7. If you don't remember what a lever escapement looks like, please go back to chapter 3 for a memory refresher. The double roller is something that we haven't explored. Mike Harrold has this easy to understand description:

> The balance had to carry a roller jewel to interact with the lever, in addition to having a safety mechanism that prevented the lever from being jarred out of position. Both functions could be incorporated into a single roller on the the balance staff, or a different roller table used for each, i.e., a double roller. The English almost always used a single roller and so did the Swiss. American companies followed along avoiding double rollers until they were written into railroad watch standards in the 1890s.[34]

Obviously, the railroad felt that if one was good, a double must be twice as good.

8. Steel escape wheels were more durable.
9. Setting the hands with a lever instead of with the stem was a safety precaution. To set the lever, the bezel containing the crystal had to be screwed off, the lever pulled out to set the hands, the lever pushed back into place, and the bezel rescrewed onto the case. This action was very deliberate, and there wasn't any chance the watch might be set accidently. With a stem-set movement, there was a chance that the stem might accidently be pulled while taking the watch out of the pocket.
10. The Micrometric regulator is a very precise type of regulator used to adjust a watch for gain or loss of time. The overcoil hairspring is also known as the Breguet hairspring. Instead of the outer end of the spring being attached to the outside, the spring swung around in a three-quarter circle until its end was directly over the center of the spring. The end was fastened there. This allowed the center to expand evenly all around, and kept the outer coil from being caught in the regulator pins. Regular hairsprings that were fastened at one side expanded to the opposite side instead of evenly around.
11. Bold black numbers and minute divisions against a white background were easier to read.
12. Black hands against a white dial made it easier to see and read the time, and second hands provided extra accuracy.
13. In order to be sure that watches met this 30 second loss or gain in a week, a system of checking watches on a regular basis had been instigated before these standards were set.
14. The cover had to keep out all dust and dirt.

THE COLUMBIAN EXPOSITION

In 1893, the World's Columbian Exposition was held in Chicago. Throughout the nineteenth century, expositions and exhibitions played a unique role in the development of art and industry. The event was planned to celebrate the 400th anniversary of the discovery of America. Countries from all over the world were represented. A visitor was given a mini-tour of the world past and present.

With a fifty cent admission ticket, a visitor could tour the buildings, view the exhibitions, and marvel at the canals, complete with gondolas, from Venice. The midway was an exciting place where everyday people could mingle with visitors from all over the world. Belly dancers from Egypt, Dahomeyans from Africa, jugglers from East India, and natives from Java were just a few of the human attractions. The Egyptian dancers received an unusual amount of attention. James William, who wrote *The Magic City*, described the dance as "a suggestively lascivious contorting of the abdominal muscles, which is extremely ungraceful and almost shockingly disgusting."

The different departments and buildings included women's departments, the fine arts department, foreign departments, mining departments, the manufacturer's and liberal arts department, the machinery department, the electricity department, and the transportation department.

THE LOCOMOTIVE PIONEER AT THE WORLD'S FAIR

It is interesting to note that the transportation department included two original locomotives. The first was the locomotive Pioneer. *The World's Columbian Exposition Illustrated* had this to say about the Pioneer:

We are able to present to our readers in the accompanying illustration a view of the Pioneer, which was the first locomotive to run out of the city of Chicago. A complete history of this engine is not obtainable, but it is gathered from the information the company has been able to secure, that it was built at Philadelphia by M. W. Baldwin, for the Utica & Schenectady Railroad in June 1836, and was purchased from that company by the Chicago & Galena Union Railroad Company, by whom it was removed to Chicago in October, 1848. The weight of the engine is about ten tons, and it was the thirty-seventh locomotive turned out by the establishment now known as the Baldwin Locomotive Works. The cylinders are 11 x 18 inches, and the original cost of the engine to the Chicago & Galena Union Railroad Company was $3,500. This engine was the first ever run out of Chicago and was in service about thirty-five years.

Plate 218. The locomotive Pioneer.

The construction of the track upon which the locomotive was run is quite interesting. Cross-ties were laid three feet apart, and grooved to receive two longitudinal stringers, made of pine. On top of these stringers an oak strip about one inch thick was laid, and on the top of the strip an iron band three-quarters of an inch, which was fastened. A great deal of trouble was experienced on account of the ends of the iron strips coming loose, turning up and catching in the pilot. To remedy this, the iron pilot on the engine was removed as a matter of safety. If the old statements can be relied on, the Pioneer was off the track more than it was on.

Mr. John Ebbert, an experienced steamboat engineer, superintended the removal of the locomotive from the deck of the vessel which brought it from Buffalo to the railway company's docks. Subsequently, he became master mechanic and assistant superintendent of the road. The latter position he held for four years. Mr. Ebbert was born in Johnstown, Pa., in 1816, and since 1843 has been a resident of Chicago. The Pioneer is now in the Transportation building at the World's Fair, and will be in the charge of Mr. Ebbert during the Exposition, in connection with the display of the Chicago & Northwestern road.

The comparison between the Pioneer and the Lord of the Isles shows the strides in locomotive building.

According to Dr. Ted Crom, the M. W. Baldwin that this article refers to as having made the locomotive started his carreer as a watch repairman.

The Lord of the Isles, the broad gauge English locomotive this article refers to, was also shown in the magazine.

Plate 219. Lord of the Isles.

The following is an article from the same publication, written about the Lord of the Isles:

One of the most interesting exhibits in the Railway department of Transportation building will be the great broad gauge engine Lord of the Isles. The engine is a part of the exhibit of the Great Western Railway of England. This engine was made in Swindon in 1851, and was in service continually until 1881. During that period it traveled about 800,000 miles.

The gauge of the engine is seven feet. This gauge was used by the Great Western until last year, when they changed their system to the same gauge as all roads in this country — 4 feet 8½ inches. The diameter of the cylinders is 18 inches; length of stroke, 24 inches; diameter of driving-wheels, 8 feet; diameter of leading and trailing wheels, 4 feet 6 inches. It weighs about 42 tons, and is capable of carrying a load of 120 tons at an average speed of 60 miles an hour, and has reached a speed of 80 miles.

They have a space 11 x 120 feet in the Transportation building, and besides the Lord of the Isles will have a complete exhibit of their railway facilities. This company's railway system extends from London to Liverpool, passing through such historical places as Oxford, Stratford-on-Avon, and Coventry.

THE TIMES WORLDWIDE

The new century found the British making the same type of watch they had been. Since the Lepine calibre had appeared on the scene, the Swiss and the French had made slimmer, more fashionable watches. The English still preferred a chunky, solid feel to their timepieces. The British also continued to believe that any watch made by machines was inferior to their craftsmanship.

It has often been said that the British made the type of watch they wanted, and the Swiss made what other people wanted. That was certainly true in the nineteenth century. It was also one of the main factors in both the decline of British watch production and the ascent of Swiss watch production.

The ebauche continued to be favored. The Swiss could tailor them to suit their customers. They made ebauche in the English style that most Americans preferred in the first half of the century. Even though the colonies had fought hard to win their political independence from England, it was hard for them to give up looking across "the pond" for the fashions in clothing and watches. The English-style movement had a verge fusee and a round cock, with a half-moon-shaped bridge with one screw. On the movements the Swiss made for their Continental customers, the cock covers were referred to as "bridges," and their pierced circular centers were secured on two sides with brackets attached by screws. These movements usually had a cylinder or Swiss lever escapement.

The Swiss were also great merchandisers. As Eugene Jaquet and Alfred Chapuis stated in their book *The Swiss Watch*, the watchmakers in the Jura valley knew the "taste of the Sweeds, the Danes, or the Russians, as well as the daily caprice of French fashion." They made it their business to know what people wanted, and their vast assortment of watches reflected this.

As usual, the Swiss were not satisfied with the status quo and were still actively working on improving their reputation in the industry. Realizing what a motivator prize money could be, The Society of Arts of Geneva organized competitions for watchmaking and jewelry in 1817. The winner had to write the best treatise of "the watchmaking and jewelry trades of Geneva" and explain how these could be improved.[35] In 1822, the School of Geneva Watchmaking opened and in 1823, Switzerland's first jewel making factory was started.

In the first quarter of the century, the form watch was revived. But the forms that the nineteenth century watch took were much different ones than those of the seventeenth century. Instead of reflecting the sober wisdom of the watch owners, the new shapes took the form of butterflies, flowers, fruits, nuts, seashells, and musical instruments. A combined watch and perfume sprinkler was even created in the shape of dueling pistols. These watches were definitely made to amuse and delight, not to reflect one's spirituality.

Mechanical inventions were also being developed. A mechanism that allowed a watch to be hand set and wound at the pendant was invented by Louis Audemars and Sons, of Le Brassus, in 1838. About four years later, another method of winding and setting was invented by Adrain Philippe. This form allowed the watch to be wound by turning the crown to the right. By turning the crown to the left, the hands could be set. When Phillippe joined forces with Patek, a manufacturer, Patek Phillippe & Company was born. Philippe's system was improved upon, and today the company is one of the leading makers of quality watches.

Another inventive mind in this time period was that of George-Auguste Leschot (1800 – 1884). Although he had served as a watchmaking apprentice, and had also made jewels, his real love was designing machines and improving watchmaking methods. He made a name for himself in the industry as the person who improved the Swiss lever escapement by developing draw, so that this mechanism rapidly entered into current manufacture, and soon assumed very great importance in the industry. Leschot encouraged one of the young men (Antoione Lechaud) who worked with him to help produce these lever escapements. From about 1842, Lechaud and his associates were able to supply many of their well-made lever escapements to Genevese watchmakers.

Remember that Leschot developed the lever escapement for Swiss watches almost 60 years after the English had adapted it.

From 1839 to 1843 Leschot, working as a contract laborer for Vacheron and Constantin, designed a pantograph machine to make identical watch plates. The pattern for the plates included an apparatus allowed the screw holes in a watch plate to be drilled directly. Later, Leschot made machines that made parts for movements. While this allowed a more uniform product and much faster production, the parts were not interchangeable. For their efforts in the advancement of watchmaking, Leschot and the firm of Vacheron and Constantin were awarded a gold medal and 600 francs by the Society of Arts in 1848.

THE GREAT EXHIBITION

In 1851, the eyes of the world turned to England and the Great Exhibition of the Industry of All Nations. The purpose of this exhibition was to provide an arena for the celebration of the arts and industry of man. Each country displayed its newest and best, in four divisions: raw materials, machinery and mechanical inventions, manufacture, and sculpture and plastic art. Prizes were awarded in each category.

The exhibition was housed in a building designed by Joseph Paxton and built by the firm of Fax and Henderson. The building's glass and iron construction made it look like a gigantic greenhouse. Dubbed the "Crystal Palace," it was truly a wonder to behold! Built in the shape of a parallelogram, it had an enclosed area of 772,284 square feet (about 19 acres). The construction used 9,000,000 feet of glass, 550 tons of wrought iron, and 3,500 tons of cast iron. The building had such a light and airy look that people were initially concerned about its safety. After several tests proved the strength and safety of the design, the public could hardly contain its excitement until opening day.

The queen and her husband presided at the official opening on May 1, 1851. An estimated 25,000 special guests attended. After opening day, the general public came. Using England's excellent railroads, people flocked from all over to see the Crystal Palace and its contents. Many days were required to view the contents properly. There were literally miles of things to see. For a small fee, the average working man or woman could see sights normally reserved for royalty.

The largest section in the building housed machinery. Machines for making rope, lace, silk, flax, and furniture could be seen in operation. Steam hammers, hydraulic presses, and fire engines were on display. Power for the machinery was furnished by an engine house built one hundred and fifty-five feet from the main building. Its five boilers produced enough steam power to serve the entire exhibition.[36]

Each country had a section in which to show the best of its machinery, inventions, art, and products. The English took pride in their beautifully crafted watches. A good example of the quality of the watches shown was one made by Alexander Watkins of London. It was a quarter-hour repeater clock-watch with an eight-day movement, and was housed in a beautiful four-colored gold case. This was obviously not a machine-made watch. In spite of the great show of steam power at the exhibition, there was only one English firm at the exhibition that used steam-powered machinery to make the watches it exhibited. That company was Rotherham & Sons, of Coventry, and it certainly seemed to be ahead of its time in England. By 1880, it had purchased and installed American machine tools in its factory.

The Swiss had a good showing of their many styles of watches. They took advantage of this opportunity to show off the beauty of watches made with the help of machinery, but their exhibits also included watch parts. Jean-Celanis Lutz (1800 – 1863) invented a process for making balance springs of hardened steel. He had been given an award by the Society of Arts in Geneva, and when his springs were displayed at the Crystal Palace, he received the highest award, the Council Medal. With the help of the machines designed by Leschot, Vacheron and Constentin demonstrated the interchangeability of some of its watch parts. The Swiss had fifty exhibitors and won four medals. A brilliant showing!

The Great Exhibition was a success from every point of view. It was estimated that over six million people visited the exhibition. This success instigated a series of exhibitions. The United States had a Crystal Palace Exposition in 1853. It was promoted by P. T. Barnum and yes, it was called the Crystal Palace Exposition. An International Exhibition was staged in Paris in 1855, London had another in 1862, Paris had a second one in 1867, and this was followed by an exhibition in Vienna in 1873 and the Philadelphia Centennial in 1876. The list goes on and on. Clearly everyone could see the advantages of these exhibitions.

ROSKOPF WATCHES

Trained as a watchmaker, George-Frederic Roskopf (1813 – 1889) had been in business as an establisseur (one who finishes and merchandises watches), and he exported watches to Belgium and North America. His dream was to make a "proletarian" watch that the average man could afford. He believed it could be done for twenty francs. Although he wanted his watch to be very inexpensive, he did not want it to be a "cheap and shoddy" timepiece.

In 1860, Roskopf decided to make his dream tangible. First, he laid out his "moral principles." These were to make a good dependable watch that almost anyone could afford, to eliminate "all luxurious and unnecessary work," to use good materials, and to pay his workers a decent wage.

This he meant that he had to reduce the number of parts in the movement, simplify the escapement, and use a simple case. He used a large barrel, a pin pallet escapement which he made as one unit, strong hands on the dial so that they could be set with a finger, and a "thick white metal German silver case without a joint on the back."[37]

It was six years before his watches were ready to go on the market. In 1867, he decided to show his plain, "un-showy" watch at the Universal Exhibition of Paris. To his surprise, it was awarded the bronze medal. The prestige and recognition that came with the award was exactly what he needed. His watch became an instant seller.

Because Switzerland did not have a patent system at that time, Roskopf couldn't apply for a patent there, but he did receive patents in other countries. This meant that his watches were safe from duplication everywhere except the country in which he lived, and this was one place where imitations of the work of others ran rampant.

Roskopf's had been the first successful attempt to make affordable watches. It would be another thirteen years before the Waterbury Watch Company made its first watches, and twenty-eight years before Ingersoll was able to make a watch that would sell for a dollar.

SWISS WAKE-UP CALL

The Swiss watch industry was working well using a craft system of subdivision of labor. Watchmakers became experts at making the part or parts assigned to them. Year by year, the Swiss list of foreign clients grew. After Switzerland's fine showing at the Crystal Palace exhibition in 1851, its exports to great Britain increased tremendously. Trade with Russia, Turkey, Italy, Flanders, Pursia, the Indies, China, Japan, and Holland had been going on for 150 years and continued to thrive.

Exportation to the United States had been good even before the colonies won their independence. Of course, the watches came to the new country by way of England, and "London" was added to the names of the Swiss watchmaker. After the American Revolution, Swiss watch companies had agents in all major American cities. Watches made by Breguet and Jurgensen were so well known that they were mentioned in popular American novels of the time. Business was indeed good!

Swiss watchmakers were aware of what was happening in the United States, and of America's growing watch industry. But it wasn't until the Philadelphia Exhibition in 1876 that the Swiss began to see the U.S. as a possible competitor. This was the first time that the Swiss had exhibited in the U.S., and they expected to impress the Americans. Instead, they were the ones to be impressed. Edouard Favre-Perret, a Swiss member of the International Jury on Watches, was so impressed with American machine-made watches that he borrowed one from Waltham to take back home. When he returned to Switzerland, he made it his business to speak to as many watchmaking groups as possible and to warn them of the dangers of not going forward into mass-produced machine-made watch production. In 1870, Switzerland's exports to the United States had numbered 330,000, and by 1876, this amount had fallen to 75,000.[38] This was definitely a wake-up call.

The Swiss heeded the call, and machinery was set up for the production of not only pocket watches, but also for watches that were to be worn on the wrist. Max Cutmore states, in his book *Watches 1850 – 1980*, that by 1880, "the Atlas watch factory in the Jura had a 30-horsepower steam engine, gas lighting, a winter heating boiler, and 30 machines producing 60,000 watches a year." The Swiss were finally beginning to catch up to American mass-produced watch production.

Having machinery that would produce small watches to be worn on the wrist proved to be an advantage for Swiss factories, even though U.S. watchmakers dismissed such watches as a product the American people would not buy. The Swiss had the last laugh when, years later, the wristwatch replaced the pocket watch.

Although a multitude of watches were being produced in the U.S., the Swiss continued to export. They were good at making watches that commemorated what was happening in the U.S. and appealed to the American spirit. Watches with dials that portrayed subjects such as Kit Carson, Wild West mountain men, and Civil War soldiers and nurses were reverse painted on glass in the center of the dials. (See plate #301 on page 179.) Whatever subject a customer desired could be put into place in the center of a dial. These center sections were interchangeable, making it easy to customize a watch.

Some of the 19th Century Swiss Watch Companies

Audemars, Piguet & Cie.	1875 – present	
Henry Capt.	1802 – 1880	Geneva
Ditisheim, Paul	1892 – 1920	
Dubois et Fils	1785 – present	Geneva
Dunard	1890 – 1930	
Farve-Leube	1851- present	
Girard-Perregaux	1856- present	
Golaya, Leresche & Fils	1844 – 1900	
Huguenin & Co.	1880 – 1959	
International Watch Co.	1869 – present	
Invicta	1837	
Jules Jurgenson	Circa 1830	
Koehn, Edward	1891 – 1930	
Le Coultre & Co.	1833 – present	
Le Phare	1890 – 1940	
Longines	1866	
Massey Tissot	1886	
Nardin, Ulysse	1846	
Patek Philippe & Cie.	1851 – present	
Omega Watch Co.	1848 – present	
Tavannes Circa	1895	
Tissot, Charles	1853	
Vacheron & Constantin	1819 – present	
Zeneth	1865 – 1920	La Locle

THE ENGLISH MAKE AN EFFORT
ANGLO-AMERICAN WATCH COMPANY
1871 – 1874

During this century, the English watchmakers held to their belief that their watches would never really have to compete with what they believed were the inferior mass-produced machine-made ones.

The few watchmakers who did see some advantage in the new machines suffered because their ideas went against general consensus. Nevertheless, some watchmakers attempted to sell machine-made watches. Some even succeeded, in spite of the staid opposition of the majority.

One of the first in England to make use of machinery was none other then Aaron Dennison, who many considered the initiator of mass-produced watchmaking in America. In 1863, his job as an agent for a U.S. machine-making company kept him in Europe, and he decided to make England his home. A year later, he returned to America for a visit that culminated in the formation of the Tremont Watch Company.

When the owners of Tremont moved the company to Melrose and the Tremont Watch Company became the Melrose Watch Company, the company failed. Dennison was commissioned to find a buyer for the machinery. He found one in England. In 1871, with this old Tremont equipment, the Anglo-American Watch Company was formed. It tried exporting watches to the United States, but was not successful. In 1874, it was forced to sell.

THE ENGLISH WATCH COMPANY
1874 – 1916

The machinery and tools from the Anglo-American Company were purchased to form the English Watch Company. The owner, William Bragge, managed the company until 1883, when his son, Robert, took over the reins. The Tremont Watch Company business was originally dependent upon some imported parts from Switzerland. So was the new company, which used machines originally used by Tremont. Very slowly the new company began to introduce new features to its watches. By 1881, it was making chronographs with three push buttons. In 1885, it took it a step further and combined a minute repeater with the chronograph. This new *chrono-micrometer* was shown that year at the Inventors Exhibition in England. Reports state that the company failed in 1897, and was taken over by Williamson. He used the English Watch Company name and continued in business until at least 1916.

WILLIAM EHRHARDT
1874 – 1924
William Ehrhardt (1831 – 1897) was another transplant. He moved to England from his homeland in Germany in 1851. He decided to settle in Birmingham in 1856. His dream was to have his own watch factory using his own ideas. From 1856 to 1863 he wholesaled watches. By 1872, he was able to advertise that he had "constructed machinery to make the Patent Keyless Movement on the interchangeable system." His factory was finally built in 1874. The company survived until about 1924.[39]

Plate 220. William Ehrhardt mark.

P & A GUYE
1867 – 1932
This company was formed by Augusti Guye (1835 – 1893), a watchmaker who had come to England from Switzerland in 1856. His brother Fritz was a part of the new company. His brother Phillippi stayed in Geneva and formed Ph. Guye & Cie. Phillippi also became a partner in the English company.

Augusti designed his own machinery. The company advertised in 1872, "all pieces being so adjusted that they can be forwarded to be replaced..... on receipt of the number of the watch."[40]

Plate 221. P & A Guye mark.

J. W. BENSON (James William Benson)
1892 – 1941
This company's history dates back to 1749. Sometime after 1840, the name of the company was changed from S. S. & J. W. Benson to J. W. Benson.

Benson's early watches were made in the traditional way, and they were expensive. They must have been of fine quality workmanship, because beginning in 1879, the company was patronized by the royal family. This fact was proudly inscribed on J. W. Benson watch movements.

It wasn't until 1892 that the company joined the machine age and opened a steam-powered factory. This venture was successful, but unfortunately, J. W. Benson went out of business after the factory was bombed in 1941.

ROTHERHAM & SONS
1888 – 1934
The Rotherham family had been involved in watchmaking since 1790. In 1867, Rotherham tried making ebauche with interchangeable parts, using the traditional English system of labor without machinery. In the 1880s, with machinery probably based on or inspired by the American Watch Tool Company's, his first machine-made mass-produced watches were made. Cases were made in Switzerland by a company owned by Rotherham. His company stayed in business until the 1960s, but making watches was not its main interest by that time.

Plate 222. Rotherham & Sons mark.

NICOLE, NIELSON & COMPANY
1876 – 1888
Adolphe Nicole had been in the watchmaking business with other partners since his arrival from Switzerland in 1840. When his sister-in-law, Emil Nielson, joined the company in 1876, it officially became Nicole, Nielson & Company. In 1888, the firm's name was changed to Nicole, Nielson & Co., Ltd., after the company was purchased by a Mr. North. Watches made after 1888 might bear that name.

According to Max Cutmore's *Watches 1850 – 1890*, it is almost impossible to identify a Nicole, Nielson movement, because the company made so many different models specifically for certain retailers, such as Benson and Frodsham.

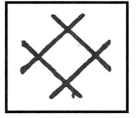

Plate 223. Nicole, Nielson & Company mark.

THE LANCASHIRE WATCH COMPANY
1888 – 1910
The Lancashire Watch Company was formed in 1890, in Prescott, to make machine-made watches. To insure that it had committed employees, the company purchased the watchmakers' tools when it hired them. Lancashire also ordered some machine tools from America. It then set out to make complete watches, including the cases, at its new factory. Prescott was traditionally a watchmaking center, and this proved to be both an advantage and a disadvantage. It was an advantage because there were skilled workers available to work in the factory; the disadvantage was that these workers did not really like to produce machine-made watches.

To do so seemed beneath them and against the ideals of their profession.

Nevertheless, by 1893, the company was producing about 50,000 watches a year.[41] Obviously, it knew how to make watches. Its failure came as a result of poor marketing techniques. Lancashire closed in 1910.

Plate 224. Coventry mark.

COVENTRY WATCH COMPANY
1892 – 1917

In 1889, this company was formed by members of the Coventry Cooperative Watch Manufacturing Society, Ltd., with S. Yeomans as chairman. Its goal was to supply makers with movements. With only a small amount of money to buy machinery and tools, it set out to make fusee watches. This early attempt failed, and the company had to be reorganized. This time, it hired engineers to design machinery that would be cost-effective. This approach increased production, but the company still had to supplement its supply by buying from the Lancaster Watch Company. It struggled along until 1907. Then it was forced to manufacture items other than watches. Cutmore states that it probably stopped producing watches about 1895. It kept the company name until about 1917.

H. WILLIAMSON LTD.
1896 – 1931

In 1896, Williamson purchased a small watch factory. He kept the former owner as manager. This was a good start for the expansion Williamson envisioned. He already owned a successful clock manufacturing company, and after going into watches, also purchased a factory in Buren to make parts in Switzerland. Later, all the parts were made and assembled in England. The watches that were still made in the factory in Buren were marked "Swiss Made." H. Williamson Ltd. was forced to go out of business in 1931.

Some Other English Watchmakers		
Barraud & Lunds	1750 – 1929	London
Cole, James Ferguson	1799 – 1880	
Cooper, T. F.	1850 – 1890	Liverpool
Earnshaw, Thomas	1749 – 1829	London
Johnson, Joseph Circa	1800 – 1850	Liverpool
Marwick Markham	1725 – 1825	London
Roskell, Robert	1798 – 1830	Liverpool
Tobias & Co.	1805 – 1868	Liverpool
Thomas Russell & Sons	circa 1870 – 1910	London
Prior, Edward	circa 1820 – 1868	London
Joseph Johnson	1810 – 1850	Liverpool
E. J. Dent	1830 – 1968	London

FRENCH WATCHMAKERS

Although the French were no longer in their heyday as far as production numbers were concerned, they certainly had some of the world's finest watchmakers. Abraham-Louis Breguet is by far the best known.

Breguet, Abraham-Louis	1775 – present	Paris
Oudin, Charles	1807 – 1830	Paris
Bovet, Edouard (Also in Switzerland)	1818 – 1918	

ART NOUVEAU

Art Nouveau was the only decorating style to develop in the nineteenth century. Because Art Nouveau was a decorative period style, its influence was felt in all areas of design. Henride Toulouse-Lautrec painted posters in this style. Antonio Gaudi (Spain) and Victor Horta (Belgium), designers, and even watch case makers were using the new motifs.

The social climate and mood of the late 1880s was perfect for the style to emerge. *The fin de siecle* ("end of the century") had put the world on edge psychologically. There was an almost unreal feeling, perhaps from being between the end of one century and the beginning of another — a "one foot in the boat and the other on the shore" sort of sensation. Art Nouveau designers portrayed things as they would like for them to be instead of how they really were. This idealism was expressed by the impressionist artists of the day. If the mood of the country could have been painted, it would have definitely been a soft and hazy pastel. At the same time, people were more daring. Maybe it was because of all the progress that had been made in the nineteenth century and the promise of what the new century might bring. People were confident and ready for anything.

Art Nouveau provided a form of expression that seemed to be unlimited. All the forces of nature could be captured in the free-flowing asymmetrical lines. Characteristic motifs of Art Nouveau designs are exotic flowers, plants, sinister-looking reptiles, and women with mystical faces and long, flowing hair.

WATCH CASES, DIALS, AND EMBELLISHMENTS

CASES

Mass-produced machine-made watches were made to certain standards, and that lead to the standardization of watch case sizes. Aaron Dennison set up the system based on thirtieths of an inch. Using this method, a 0 size movement equals $^{35}/_{30}$". A 1 size is a thirtieth larger, making it $^{36}/_{30}$". By 1880, the standard sizes of 0, 6, 8, 10, 12, 14, 16, and 18 enabled the customer to not only pick out a movement that suited their needs and budget, but to also select the style of case. Howard Watch Company chose not to go with the Dennison system. Instead, it used letters. The letter *G* in their system is actually $1^{6}/_{16}$", a size 6 in the Dennison system. Their letter *L* is Dennison's size 16.[42] The Swiss measured their movements in *lignes*. One ligne is equal to 2.26 mm, or $^{1}/_{11}$". Remember that these are movement sizes.

During the nineteenth century, some of the cases available were the open face, hunting case, demi-hunter, and for a while, even a convertible case that could be changed from an open face to a hunting case. Cases could be boxed hinged, plain, or even have scalloped ("pie crust") edges.

Plate 225. Open-face case.

Plate 226. Hunting case. This case has a scalloped, or pie crust, edge. *Courtesy of Jewelry Box Antiques.*

Plate 227. Demi-hunter. Case is embellished with chiseling and taille 'eperne enamel. *Courtesy of Aaron Faber Galleries.*

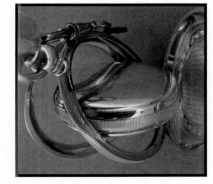

Plates 228 – 230. Convertible watch. The first photo shows the open-face watch with the bezel opened, the second shows the case in the process of of converting, and the third shows how the glass-covered dial (at the bottom) will turn toward the back of the case (on the right) to make it a hunting case. The covered back will swing into the open bezel, forming the back of the watch. *Courtesy of Dr. Ted Crom.*

CASE MATERIALS

In Europe during this time period, 18k gold was the standard. In England, 9k and 15k were legalized in 1854, so watches made after this year could be 9, 15, or 18k. American cases could be as high as 18k or as low as 8k. Before the Metals Stamping Act of 1906, some case manufactors used trademark-type symbols to designate gold content.

For those whose budget did not include a gold watch, there many alternatives. For the look of a gold watch, one could choose pinchbeck (in the first half of the century), gold plated (after 1840), or gold filled. All of these were sold under the heading of imitation gold.

For gold plating, the case was made of a base metal and then electroplated with a thin coat of gold. Obviously, the gold look was not long-lasting, because the coating did not hold up under daily wear.

For gold-filled watch cases, a sandwich was made using a sheet of gold, a sheet of base metal, and another sheet of gold. A case was guaranteed to wear a number of years according to the thickness of the top and bottom sheets of gold.

These distinctions cause confusion for the general public today. Of course, they were probably meant to confuse the original buyer. Often, people think that they have a 14k gold case when in fact it is gold filled. A "14K" mark on the back lid of a case is misleading if under this mark are the words "guaranteed twenty-five years." This means that the case is 14k gold filled. It could be guaranteed for five, ten, fifteen, twenty, twenty-five, or thirty years, according to how thick the layers of gold were. Such watches were priced accordingly.

Plate 231. A celluloid bookmark give-away advertisement.

Plates 232 and 233. Advertising card for crown cases.

Customers who liked the look or the price of silver also had an array of choices. American silver watch cases were usually marked "coin," "silver," or in the later years of the century, "sterling." Those who wanted a more economical case could have their choice of "silverode," "silverore," or "silverine." These names alluded to silver, but these metals did not have any silver content. Instead they were alloys of nickel, copper, or magnesium. Keystone Watch Case Company made "silveroid," Fays used the name "silverore,"

Plate 234. Swiss Silverex mark.

Duber named their alloy "silverine," and the Philadelphia Watchcase Company had "silvrode." Some Swiss cases made of this alloy are marked "silverex."

Some cases that looked like silver were also marked "nickel silver" or "German silver." They may look like silver, but these metals are both the same alloy of copper, nickel, and zinc. They have no silver content. The nineteenth century was filled with false advertising and misleading names.

DIALS

A cursory look through the Watches section of this century will show the many different types of dials that were available. Until the 1880s, American watch factories imported dials. Still later in the century, a process was developed by which a dial could be transfer printed by machine. Paper dials were often used for dollar watches.

For a few dollars extra, watch companies would put a person's name on a dial. Retailers often had the name of their company put on the dial. The watch factories also proudly displayed their own names on the dial, but often, initials in fancy script style were substituted for the complete name of a company. Some watch companies that had a reputation for quality watches, such as Waltham, used other names on their cheap watches.

In the late 1800s, fancy dials were popular. These were used for multicolored gold watches, ladies' enameled watches, and even silver watches. Fancy dials were popular then (just as they are now) because of the beauty they added to the watch.

Railroad watches also had a variety of dials. In fact, the variety is surprising since all conformed to railroad standards. Today, the dials on some railroad watches bring more money than some movements. This is especially the case with those watches made after the turn of the twentieth century.

Below are a few examples of the many styles of dials.

Plate 235. Name dial. The name on this dial is probably that of the watch owner, Nathan Ayers. Note that the first letters of the first and last names are black and the others are red. *Courtesy of Jewelry Box Antiques.*

Plate 236. Another name dial; this one has the first letter of the first name in red and the others in black. *Courtesy of Aaron Faber Gallery.*

Plate 237. Railroad dial. This Bunn Gothic dial can sell for $175.00 – 200.00. *Courtesy of Dan Dollof.*

Plate 238. Beautifully fired enamel porcelain fancy dial. *Courtesy of Laura Green.*

EMBELLISHMENTS

Watches made in the first quarter of the nineteenth century kept many of the characteristics of the watches made in the last decade of the eighteenth century. Dials surrounded by half pearls and cases decorated with rose-engine-turned designs covered with translucent enamel were still in vogue, but the watch stem became a bit flatter and stubbier. Automation watches with figures (*jaquemarts*) that appeared to ring bells were still highly sought after. To these, scenes were added that included automations such as windmills that turned, revolving spinning wheels, knife grinders at work, and even horses drinking out of fountains.[43] In the first quarter of the century, form watches came into vouge again. As in the last century, they took the shape of amusing and whimsical items.

By the mid-nineteenth century, many watches were were engraved with scenes and other decorative motifs. *Taille d' epergne* (TAH-ye de A-purn), an ancient form of enameling, was also revived during these years. For this type of enamel work, a design was deeply engraved or cut into the metal and filled with powered opaque enamel. The piece was then fired and polished. Although any color could be used in taille d' epergne, the Victorian era favored black or blue.

Toward the end of the century, multicolored gold embellishments were again used to decorate all types of watch cases. These solid gold designs were used on karat gold, gold-filled, and silver cases of all sizes. By the late 1880s, many women's watches became lavishly decorated with enameled Art Nouveau motifs such as flowers and sensuous women with flowing hair. Watches with multicolored gold embellishments or Art Nouveau motifs are highly sought after today.

It is not surprising that the Art Nouveau case designers made use of ancient enameling techniques. The scope and range of enameling produced an endless variety of effects. One enamel could be applied on top of another to create the varied, flowing colors that were so indicative of the period. Colors could be opaque or transparent. The possibilities were unlimited, and enamel's durability made it suitable for everyday use.

Enamel is a glass-like mixture made of silica, quartz, borax, feldspar, and lead. Metallic oxides are added to produce a desired color. All of these materials are ground into a fine powder and applied to the article being embellished.

The mixture must be fired at a temperature of about 1700 degrees Fahrenheit in order to bond to the article. Care must be taken, since the melting point of the article should be higher than that of the enameling mixture. Each color is fired separately. The color with the highest melting point is fired first. Those colors requiring less heat are fired in descendant order. Methods of enameling are named according to the the method used to prepare the article being decorated. The most popular forms of enameling used during this period on watches were champlevé, basse taille, and niello.

Champlevé (Shomp-leh-VAY, meaning "to cut out") is an enamel technique in which designs are cut out of a metal background. The metal between the cut out areas becomes an intricate part of the design. The hollowed areas are filled with enamel and then fired. Polishing is required to finish the piece once the firing is complete.

For *basse taille* (Bahs-TAH-ye, meaning "shallow cut"), designs are cut and engraved into the metal. But instead of just filling these depressions, the enameler covers the entire piece with a transparent enamel. Many beautiful designs can be achieved using this method because the color varies with design depth.

Niello (nye-EL-oh) is considered a form of enameling, even though the mixture used is not a true enamel. A mixture of sulfur, lead, copper, or silver is used instead of the powdered glass enamel. After a design is engraved into the metal, the niello mixture is applied and the piece is fired. The piece is then polished to such a degree that the niello mixture is removed from all but the incised portion of the design. Black niello is easy to distinguish from black enameling because it lacks sheen. Instead, it has a metallic look.

The metals used with enamel were as varied as the different enameling methods. For champlevé, copper and bronze were often used. Gold and silver provided an excellent base for all enameling techniques. Although the metal that was used is a consideration when determining value, the execution of design and the clarity of colors are of the utmost importance. A case that is beautifully done in copper using several enameling techniques can sometimes be more valuable than one in gold using one color and technique.

During the gay nineties, many women's watches were made in the shape of a ball. Women were wearing less clothing than they had worn in hundreds of years. The delicate look of a small ball watch encrusted with pearls and gemstones complimented the new, more delicate styles.

Plate 239. Taille d' epergne and painted enamel embellish this watch. *Courtesy of Jack Harvey.*

Plate 240. Inspired by the Art Nouveau movement, the watch and pin show the beauty of nature. *Courtesy of Somlo Antiques.*

Plate 241. Niello. *Courtesy of Jewelry Box Antiques.*

Plate 242. Niello case and chain. *Courtesy of Doug Webster.*

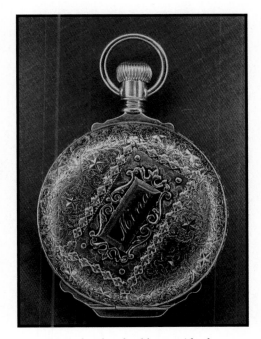

Plate 243. Multicolored gold case with a box hinge. *Courtesy of Jewelry Box Antiques.*

145

MOVEMENTS

At the end of the eighteenth century, everything that the nineteenth century watchmakers needed, insofar as the basic parts of the movement were concerned, had already been invented. The job of watchmakers in the new century was to improve upon past creations. That they did.

The first changes in movements were made as part of the effort to mass produce watches. As a result, developments such as a different type of escape wheel (see plate #209 on p. 114) for the duplex and more uses of the lever evolved. In 1893, the standards for railroad watches were set. Some new parts of a watch are discussed in the Railroad Watch Standards section.

The only "new" escapement used in the nineteenth century had actually been invented by Louis Perron in 1798. It was perfected by G. F. Roskopf and used in his watches.

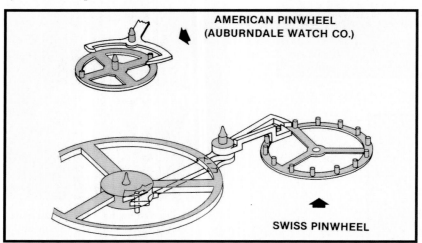

Plate 244. Pin-pallet or pin-lever escapement. The pin pallet or pin lever was used in many cheap watches made at the end of the century, because it had been designed to be stamped out very inexpensively. *Courtesy of Michael C. Harrold.*

A better way to wind the watch was also a challenge for the nineteenth century. Between 1842 and 1845, Adrain Philippe invented a pendant winding mechanism. A watch was now wound by turning the winding crown to the right. The hands were set by turning the crown to the left. This was later improved upon by Philippe when he joined with Patek, a manufacturer, to form Patek Philippe & Company in about 1851. The system used by these two men is the one we use today. Four years later, a pin-set watch was patented in England. Many pin-set and lever-set movements were made before button winding began to be used between 1867 and 1868.

In the 1840s watches were accurate enough to warrant a bi-metallic balance. Prior to that time, they had been reserved, to a large extent, for English chronometers.

About 1844, Adolphi Nicole designed a chronograph that would allow the center seconds hand to stop, rest, and restart without interfering with the mean time. In the 1880s, a split-second chronograph began to appear on the market. It was made to act as a double chronograph. It is interesting to note that these were also the years in which Edward VII was heavily immersed in his passion for horse racing. He was quoted as saying that it was the happiest day in his life when his racehorse Persimmon won the Royal Derby. The publicity caused by his indulgences not only made horse racing a popular social activity, but motifs such as horseshoes, riding crops, and racehorses started to be used in jewelry and watch fobs.

The American factory better grade watches were temperature compensated by the 1850s. In the 1880s, most grades of jeweled movements had bi-metallic balances.

By the 1880s, most watch repair shops were expected to stock spare parts. This tended to movtivate customers to buy major watch company brands.

Plate 245. H. C. watch with the lever (between Roman numeral III and V) pulled out to set the hands.

Plate 246. Silver hunting case watch (rear view.) Note the small pin on the top right-hand side. This pin had to be pushed down with a fingernail in order to set the hands.

DAMASKEENING

Damaskeening is a form of embellishment that watch factories devised to make watch plates or bars look beautiful. The Swiss started buffing patterns on their bars, and Americans followed suite by expanding the patterns and using machines.

Remember that this was a period in which a customer would often select a movement and then a case. Movements were on display in stores, and beautiful damaskeening certainly appealed to the eye.

The name of this decoration comes from the ancient city of Damascus, which was known for its ornamental metal work. This technique is not at all like the damascening in which metal is inlaid into steel, although some damascene patterns were used by American companies.

At first glance, one might assume that the patterns were done by a rose engine machine. Not so! These patterns were not made using a cutting tool. Instead, they were accomplished using a small rotating dowel (buffing tool) that was attached to a swing arm over the watch plate, which was placed on a stand that allowed it to be turned. This simple machine could make very complex patterns that were buffed onto the metal. Damaskeening is actually a fine polishing. The patterns it mechanically produces can be quite beautiful.

By using a standard setup, the tool could duplicate the same pattern over and over. It could also easily make one-of-a-kind patterns. Waltham's Model 72 used damaskeening as a sales tool. The company advertised that no two were alike. This claim certainly appealed to the man who wanted to have a one-of-a-kind watch.[44]

THE BUTTERFLY

Although this sounds more like an embellishment than something that is a part of a watch movement, it really does belong under this heading. This was the unique design that The United States Watch Company of Marion came up with to enable its early escapements to be easily adjusted. The company put a butterfly cutout in the top plate. This was not only decorative, but it also allowed the escapement to be adjusted without the removal of the full top plate.

CRYSTAL PLATE WATCHES

Another decorative innovation was the crystal plate movement by Waltham. Made in the 1880s and 90s, its only purpose was to make the movement more beautiful, and it certainly achieved this goal. The transparent rock crystal plates made the gold train and ruby jewels appear to be floating inside the case. Most of these watches were size 6 and had crystal backplates only. Waltham also used its size 16 Model 72 and embellished it in several ways. According to Harrold, one model was made "having a crystal back with ruby jewels, non-magnetic balance, skeleton dial, having rubies at the minutes hand and sapphires at the hours, and an 18k display case." Another model had front and back plates of crystal, and the same dial as the one Harrold described, but didn't have the non-magnetic balance. A small size 4 version was also made. It included a crystal backplate and display case that was carved out of one piece of rock crystal.

Plate 247. Look closely and you can see the butterfly cutout near the top left side of the movement.

Plate 248. Two views of a Waltham Crystal Plate. *Courtesy of Dr. Ted Crom.*

Plate 249. "Mamma's TICK TICK."

NINETEENTH CENTURY TIMELINE, U.S.

1812 – 1814 — U.S. and Britain were at war over shipping and territory disputes.

1809 – 1812 — Trade restrictions against importing ebauche into the U.S. were implemented.

1809 — First watches were made in America, by Luther Goddard.

1838 — Pitkin Brothers started business. First American machine-made watches.

1840 — Aaron Dennison invented the Dennison standard gauge.

1841 — Slavery was abolished in New York.

1848 — Gold was discovered in California.

1853 — Crystal Palace Exposition was held in New York.

1852 — Watches were made by Howard, Davis and Dennison.

1853 — Aaron Dennison, Edward Howard, and D. P. Davis joined together to form Warren Manufacturing Co. When watch production started, the name of the company was changed to the Boston Watch Company.

1854 — U.S. made trade treaty with Japan.

1857 – 1859 — Appleton, Tracy & Co. operated.

1857 – 1859 — American Waltham Watch Co. operated.

1858 – 1903 — E. Howard & Co. produced watches.

1861 — Abraham Lincoln became president of the United States.

1861 – 1865 — Civil War.

1863 — Lincoln abolished slavery in the United States.

1864 – 1964 — National Watch Co. (Elgin Watch Co.) was founded in Elgin, Illinois.

1864 – 1867 — Newark Watch Co. operated in Newark, New Jersey.

1864 – 1872 — U.S. Watch Co. operated in Marion, New Jersey.

1864 – 1866 — The Tremont Watch Co. was formed in Boston, Massachusetts.

1864 – 1875 — New York Watch Co. operated, in Providence, Rhode Island (until 1867), and Springfield, Massachusetts (until 1875).

1865 — President Lincoln was assassinated.

1865 — The Civil War ended.

1866 — Waltham made the first watch made especially for the railroad.

1867 – 1868 — Melrose Watch Co. operated in Melrose, Massachusetts. It was formerly the Tremont Watch Co., but the move to Melrose necessitated a name change.

1867 — B. W. Raymond, a railroad watch model, was made by Elgin.

1867 – 1876 — Cornell Watch Co. purchased the Newark Watch Co.

1868 – 1886 — Philadelphia Watch Co. operated.

1869 — Waltham made its Model 70 railroad watch.

1870 — A year of recession.

1872 – 1874 — U.S. Watch Co. was reorganized in Marion, New Jersey, as the of Marion Watch Co.

1872 — First meeting of railroad superintendents to discuss schedules for trains was held.

1874 – 1879 — Dietrich Gruen madewatches.

1874 – 1877 — Empire City Watch Co. was formed from a reorganization of the Marion Watch Co.

1874 – 1875 — Freeport Watch Co. operated.

1875 – 1876 — New York Mfg. Co. became the new name of the reorganized New York Watch Co.

1876 — Philadelphia was the site of America's Centennial Exhibition.

1876 – 1930 — Hampden Watch Co. was the new name chosen for the reorganized New York Mfg. Co.

1876 – 1883 — Auburndale Watch Co. operated.

1877 – 1879 — E. F. Flint Watch Co. operated.

1878 — Benedict and Burnham started the Waterbury Watch Co. that was to later become The New England Watch Co. and, later still, the Ingersoll Watch Co.

1879 – 1882 — Gruen and Savage watch company operated. It was formed from the partnership of Dietrich Gruen and W. J. Savage.

1879 – 1969 — Ball Watch Co. operated.

1879 – 1882 — Bowman Watch Co. operated.

1880 – 1889 — Waterbury Watch Co. operated.

1880 — New Haven Clock Company started making watches.

1881 – 1885 — Fredonia Watch Co. operated.

1881 — President James A. Garfield was assassinated.

1882 – 1903 — Columbus Watch Co. became the new name of Gruen and Savage.

1882 – 1903 — The E. Howard name was used on watches made by the Keystone Watch Case Co.

1883 — John C. Adams designed the Adams System of Time Records to help the railroad keep time.

1883 — General Time Convention adopted five time zones in the U.S. for use by railroads.

1883 – 1892 — Aurora Watch Co. operated.

1884 – 1914 — Seth Thomas Clock Company made watches.

1886 — Stand and Code of Railroad Operating Rules went into effect.

1890 – 1930 — Knickerbocker Watch Co. operated.

1890 — Waterbury Clock Co. started making watches.

1890 — Colored and fancy dials came into vogue.

1890 — Multicolored gold watch cases became popular again.

1892 — Hamilton Watch Co. was formed. It is still in business.

1892 – 1922 — Ingersoll Watch Co. operated.

1895 – 1903 — Chicago Watch Co. operated.

1898 – 1914 — New England Watch Co. operated.

1894 – 1903 — D. Gruen & Son operated.

1885 — American Waltham Watch Co. name was shortened to Waltham Watch Co.

1892 — Railroad Watch Standards were set.

1896 — Ingsersoll has a one-dollar watch.

1898 — United States and Spain were at war.

1899 — Western Clock Company made its first watches.

NINETEENTH CENTURY TIMELINE, WORLDWIDE

1800 — Electric battery was invented by Volta.

1800 — By this time, repeaters were being made for the general public.

1800 — Pearls continued to be a popular embellishment for watch cases.

1801 — Britain and Ireland united to become the United Kingdom.

1802 — Napoleon Bonaparte was created first consul.

1804 — Legion d'Honneur was given by Napoleon I to Frederic Japy.

1804 — Machines were imported into Geneva for making watch parts.

1804 — Napoleon crowned himself emperor.

1805 — Henry Maudslay improved the micrometer.

1807 — Slave trade was abolished in the British Empire.

1807 — Richard Trevithick (English) built the first successful steam locomotive.

1812 — Patent for the dead beat escapement design was issued to Samuel Smith.

1814 — Napoleon was exiled to Elba.

1814 — Edward Massey developed a version of the detached lever escapement that later evolved into the English lever.

1814 — Geneva joined the Swiss Confederation.

1820 – 1830 — George IV was King of Britain.

1820 — Nineteenth century style of form watches was popular.

1822 — Geneva watchmaking school opened.

1823 — Jewel-making factory was set up in Switzerland by P. F. Ingold.

1825 — The table roller was introduced. The table roller was not a roller at all, but a flat disc mounted on a staff.

1827 — Breguet finished the Marie Antoinette watch.

1828 — The Industry class of the Geneva Society of Arts held the first national exhibition in Switzerland.

1830 – 1837 — William IV was King of Britain.

1830 — First passenger steam railways opened in England.

1830 — George Auguste Leschot introduced draw in early Swiss levers.

1832 — In Great Britain, the right to vote extended to the middle class by the Reform Act.

1833 — England's Factory Act forbade factories to employ children under the age of nine.

1835 — Chinese form of the duplex created.

1837 — Victoria became Queen of England.

1838 — A mechanism that allowed a watch to be hand set and wound at the pendant was invented by Audemans.

1839 — The Patek Philippe Watch Co. was established.

1839 – 1843 — Leschot, working as a contract laborer for Vacheron and Constantin, designed a pantograph machine that would make identical watch plates.

1840 — The electro-gilding process was invented.

1840 — Thin metal dials became popular for the thinner flatter watches.

1843 — Pierre Frederic Ingold (1787 – 1878) designed a machine for manufacturing top and bottom watch plates.

1842 – 1845 — Adrain Philippe invented a pendant-winding mechanism. It was wound by turning the winding crown to the right. The hands were set by turning the crown to the left. This was improved upon when Philippe joined with Patek, a manufacturer, and formed Patek Phillippe & Co. This winding system is still used today.

1842 — China ceded Hong Kong to Britain.

1844 — Adolphi Nicole designed a chronograph that could stop, rest, and restart without interfering with the mean time.

1846 — Rocker winding was developed by Nicole of the firm Nicole and Capt. It is still used today in some very expensive wristwatches.

1848 — Year of revolution in Europe.

1850 — The lever watch was popular on the Continent and in England.

1851 — Gold rush in Australia.

1851 — Crystal Palace exhibition took place in London.

1852 – 1870 — Second Empire was set up by Louis Napoleon (Napoleon III), Emperor of France .

1853 — Crystal Palace exposition in New York.

1854 – 1856 — Crimean War.

1854 — Nine and fifteen karat (carat) gold was legalized in England.

1855 — Paris exhibition.

1855 — The pin-set watch was patented in England.

1858 — British Horological Institute was founded.

1861 — Queen Victoria's beloved Albert died.

1861 — Gold rush in New Zealand.

1862 — The push system for the stop watch, still used today, was introduced.

1862 — London exhibition.

1867 — Paris exhibition.

1867 — Inexpensive watches (by the standards of the day) were made by G. F. Roskopf (1813 – 1899) of Switzerland. His products were not machine made. Not a lot were produced in his day. His watches used a pin-lever escapement that had been developed by him.

1862 — First chronograph with hands capable of returning to the zero position at the will of the watch owner appeared.

1867 – 1868 — Button winding began to be used.

1868 — Universal Exhibition of Paris. A Roskopf watch won a bronze metal.

1869 — International Watch Co. was founded in Geneva.

1871 — Britain legalized trade unions.

1873 — Waltham Watch Company opened an office in London.

1876 — Centennial Exposition was held in Philadelphia.

1877 — Queen Victoria was proclaimed Empress of India.

1880 — Verge escapement was finally phased out in England.

1880 — Split-second chronograph appeared on the market. It acted as a double chronograph.

1880 — Greenwich time was established by the Definition of Time Act in the U.K.

1882 – 1885 — Woerd patented a screw-making machine.

1883 — National Exhibition was held in Zurich.

1883 — An international conference about Greenwich time was held in Rome. From this meeting, the notion of Universal time appeared.

1884 — Kew Observatory issued ratings certificates (A, B, C grades) for watches.

1884 — International time zone was established.

1886 — Gold was discovered in South Africa.

1888 — Patents were introduced in Switzerland.

1890 — The Chambre Suisse d'horolgerie was formed to act as a consultative body for the industry.

1890 — Lancashire Watch Co. was formed in Prescott, England.

1892 — Karrusel watch was patented by Bonniksen.

1895 — Grenthot invented a machine process to transfer print dials.

1896 — National Exhibition was held in Geneva.

1897 — The Invar alloy was invented by Charles-Edouard Guillaume.

NINETEENTH CENTURY WATCHES

Plate 250. Circa early 1800s.

18K yellow gold **case** with engine turning on the rear. Jump second hand. Silver **dial**, engine turned with hours and minutes on an off. set chapter. It is a two train cylinder watch, not signed. It could have been made by an apprentice.
$3,000.00.
Description and watch courtesy of David Strudler, Dealer.

Plate 251. Circa 1800. Lovely French gilt brass, enamel and brilliant set verge and fusee antique pocket watch.

Very colorful back with a painted enamel scene of a woman spinning within a border of flowers (minor edge restoration) within a bezel set with brilliants. Beautifully restored **dial** with a painted enamel river scene. Gilt **movement** with pierced and engraved balance cock. Diam. 53 mm. **$2,150.00.**
Photo and description courtesy of Stephen Bogoff, Antiquarian Horologist.

**Plate 252. London,
gilt enamel, pair-cased pocket watch,
circa 1800.**

Case. Outer: gilt metal. Inner case: gilt silver, set with red and white paste, circular. **Dial.** White enamel, black Arabic numerals, yellow lance hands. **Movement.** Key wind and set fusee, gilt, verge escapement, monometallic balance wheel, flat balance spring.
Signed "Y. M. Smith" on movement.
Diam. 56 mm. **$822.50.**
Photo and description courtesy of Bonhams and Butterfields, San Francisco, 24 Mar 2003.

**Plate 253. Circa 1800.
Fine and lovely 18K gold, pearl and painted enamel verge and fusee antique lady's pendant watch for the Asian market.**

Pearl bezels front and rear, the back with a fine painted bouquet against a light blue background. Fine gold **dial** with enamel chapter and bluedsteel hands. Verge and fusee **movement** with pierced and engraved cock. Chinese market watches are more typically from a later period with bar movements; an early verge example like this is scarce. In particularly fine condition throughout.
Diam. 31 mm. **$2,000.00.**
Photo and description courtesy of Stephen Bogoff, Antiquarian Horologist.

Plate 254. Circa 1805.
Breguet, No. 1348, sold to Messieurs Meyer et Tues for 2,160 francs on 3 fructidor an 13 (21 Aug 1805).
Exceptionally fine and highly important large, 20K gold watch with annual Gregorian calendar and additional gold index for the Julian calendar, signs of the Zodiac, special disengaging equation of time and days of the week.
In original Breguet Morocco fitted box, with original gold Breguet key on short gold chain, accompanied by two Breguet certificates.

Case. Four-body, No. 427 by master casemaker Mermillot, Empire, polished, gilt-hinged cuvette with winding and setting apertures, one for the mean time, one for equation. **Dial.** White enamel, by Borel, secret signature below, 12 o'clock, Breguet numerals, outer minute track, outermost annual calendar scale with months and corresponding Zodiac signs, and days of the month, subsidiary days of the week dial (reprinted) below 12 o'clock. Blued steel Breguet hands, Julian calendar indicated by a gold pointer fixed to the annual calendar spear hand, equation of time with serpentine Breguet hand. **Movement.** 54 mm, (24"), gilt brass, very elegant and rare caliber based on the famous "three bridge caliber," hanging barrel, Breguet hanging ruby cylinder, three-arm plain brass balance, blued-steel flat balance spring with compensation curb and parachute on the top pivot, the annual calendar driven from the hour wheel meshing with an intermediate wheel with a very small, ingeniously arranged two-leaf lantern pinion which drives the days of the week wheel, which in turn, through a worm gear, drives the annual wheel, the equation cam set at the center of the annual wheel with an ingenious system of power transmission from the mean time motion work to the solar time motion work via a special double wheel/double rack-and-pinion mechanism.
Signed on dial, cuvette, and movement, case punched with the movement serial number, case maker trademark and his number and French 20k guarantee marks, dial signed on the reverse "Borel, fructidor an. 11."
Diam. 62 mm. **$934,395.00.**
Photo and Description courtesy of Antiquorum Auctioneers, 2002.

Plate 255. Circa 1810.
Fine 18K gold and enamel ultra flat virguile antique pocket watch.

Back with a finely painted landscape with shepherdesses and a lamb. Gilt **movement** of unusual calibre single plate design with pierced and engraved single-footed balance cock. Fine white enamel **dial** with open-work gold hands. A fine, lovely, and rare watch.
Diam. 54 mm. **$6,500.00.**
Photo and description courtesy of Stephen Bogoff, Antiquarian Horologist.

Plate 256. Dubois et Fils. Le Lode, Swiss.
Circa 1810.
Fine, rare, and slim 18K gold, skeletonized, early minute-repeating watch.

Case. Double-body, "directoire," with sunburst engine-turned back. Hinged glazed gilt brass cuvette. **Dial.** White enamel chapter ring with Breguet numerals. Blued-steel Breguet hands. **Movement.** 45 mm, gilt brass, engraved and skeletonized with gold wheel train, the barrel with gilt brass cap engraved with foliage, cylinder escapement, plain steel three-arm balance, flat balance spring with regulator, polished steel balance cock with ruby ends tone. Repeating on blued steel and polished serpent-shaped gongs by depressing the pendant, visible repeating work set on backplate.
Signed on the dial and the cuvette.
Diam. 62 mm. **$13,455.00.**
Photo and description courtesy of Antiquorum Auctioneers, 14 Jun 2003.

Plate 257. Ma plus Belle.
Amalric Freres, Geneva, No. 18399, circa 1810.
Fine 18K gold and enamel savonette form watch designed as a sphere.

Case. Spring-loaded two-body, black background, front with white enamel lettering "Ma plus Belle," back with gold and pink enamel roses, dragonfly, flowers, band with azure enamel with repeated gold pattern. **Dial.** White enamel. Breguet numerals, outer minute divisions, winding aperture at 2 o'clock. Gold skeletonized spade hands. **Movement.** 21.5 mm, hinged, gilt full plate with cylindrical pillars, fusee and chain, verge escapement, plain brass balance, Continental cock pierced and engraved with six symmetrical lilies.
Signed on the dial and movement.
Diam. 25 mm. **$2,834.00.**
Photo and description courtesy of Antiquorum Auctioneers.

Plate 258. Circa 1811. Good English, silver, pair-case, rack lever and fusee by S. I. Tobias, Liverpool.

Gilt seven-jewel **movement** with dust cover and diamond cap, engraved "Patent" on the cock. Bold enamel **dial** with minor hairline. Later plastic crystal. Diam. 58 mm. **$950.00.**
Photo and description courtesy of Stephen Bogoff, Antiquarian Horologist.

Plate 259. Piguet et Meylan, Geneva, No. 1185, case by Georges Reymond, made for the Chinese market circa 1815. Very fine and very rare 18K gold and enamel musical box fitted with a watch, in the shape of an exotic butterfly.

Case. Four-body, hinged wings, one revealing the watch, the other a compartment, finely painted on enamel in an exotic pattern, gold thorax and head over translucent dark blue enamel, white enamel edges, sides with dark blue translucent enamel over a flinque pattern partially painted in black, the bottom in dark blue translucent enamel over wavy engine turning painted in a black geometrical pattern. **Dial.** White enamel, Roman numerals, outer minute track, blued-steel unusual skeleton hands. **Movement.** Following the shape of the case, brass, fixed barrel, cylinder escapement, three-arm plain brass balance with flat balance spring. Musical movement: fixed barrel, pinned disc with pins on both sides, 22 tuned teeth, eight-wheel train, the last pinion set in adjustable eccentric bushing as governor.
Punched and numbered with the maker's mark on the movement, case maker's mark.
Diam. 72 x 43 x 16 mm. **$79,950.00.**
Photo and description courtesy of Antiquorum Auctioneers, 14 Jun 2003.

Plate 260. Petit Medaillon d'or
Abraham-Louis Breguet, No. 2919, "Petit Medaillon d'or a deux aiguilles,"
shipped to Le Roy in Constantinople on September 2, 1816, for 2,000 francs.
Very fine and extremely rare 20K gold and enamel cabriolet pendant watch made for the Islamic market.

Case. Outer: two-body, by Joly, No. 2052, scarlet champlevé enamel over flinque, central star. Inner: three-body, back and bezel on the same hinge, light blue champlevé star, gold laurel leaf wreath, bezels en suite. **Dial.** White enamel, by Lucard, No. 1919, radial Islamic numerals, outer minute divisions with fifteen-minute Islamic markers, secret signature below 12 o'clock, secured by a single screw. Blued-steel Breguet hands. **Movement.** 31.2 mm (14"), gilt brass, Lepine-type caliber, ruby cylinder escapement. Three-arm gold balance, flat balance spring, parachute on the top pivot.
Signed on the dial, case, and movement with the same number, case punched with Joly's master mark.
Diam. 39 mm. **$52,026.00.**
Photo and description courtesy of Anitquorum Auctioneers, 14 Jun 2002.

Plate 261. Circa 1815.
LeSien, Paris.
18K yellow gold lady's miniature enamel watch
— verge, museum condition.

Intricately enameled inside and out.
$7,500.00.
Courtesy of Jeff Rosen, Dealer, Solvang Antique Center.

Plate 262. Circa 1817.

L. Goddard and Son verge fusee, 45mm, L. "Goddard," key wind/key set, correct silver-marked pair **case** with eagle, porcelain **dial**, Roman numerals, blue hands, beautiful full plate fusee pin-plate **movement** marked "L. Goddard & Son Shewsbury." Included is a watch paper marked "D. Goddard & Co. Watchmaker 19 Main St. Worcester Ma. (464) - 1825." You might never see one of these again.
$22,000.00.
Photo and description courtesy of OldWatch.com.

Plate 263. Circa 1819.
Abraham-Louis Breguet, No. 3322.
Sold to Lord John Campbell on September 30, 1819, for 1,062 francs.
Very fine and interesting 18K gold pocket watch.

Case. Four-body, Empire, engine-turned, gilt hinged cuvette. **Dial.** Silver, painted radial Roman numerals, outer minute dot divisions, subsidiary sunk seconds between 4 and 5 o'clock, engine-turned center. Blued-steel spade hands. **Movement.** 51.5 mm (23"), gilt brass, Lepine caliber, ruby cylinder escapement, 3-arm brass balance, blued-steel flat balance spring, compensation curb, parachute on top balance pivot. Signed on dial, case, and movement.
Diam. 56 mm. **$28,704.00.**
Photo and Description courtesy of Antiquorum Auctioneers, 14 Jun 2003.

Plate 264. Circa 1820.

Repoussé **outer case**. **Inner case** with English **movement** by Charles Kirby. Painted **dial** with boy fishing; made by Charles Kirby.
$1,275.00.
Courtesy of a private collector.

Plate 265. Circa 1820.
18K Swiss.

Silver **dial** — great enameling; cylinder escapement — thin **movement**.
$2,500.00.
Courtesy of Jeff Rosen, Dealer, Solvang Antique Center.

Plate 266. Circa 1820.

Coin silver hunting case with small dial for hour and minute hands is set off to the left side and it has a jump second. Early jump second watches were made with two separate trains. One ran the jump second and one to run the watch regular time, so that when you stopped the jump second you didn't stop the time. This was not designed to start and stop, just to be a jump second with a single train. This maker used a scrap tooth duplex escapement, one escapement designed just like a duplex with a double stock (a standard lever working on a duplex wheel). It halts, drops into the slot, stops again (double stop). Releases in one second. Has holding actions. Most duplex escapements are built like a spiked wheel. A spike slaps against the side of the balance staff (stops). Staff turns, the tip of the tooth

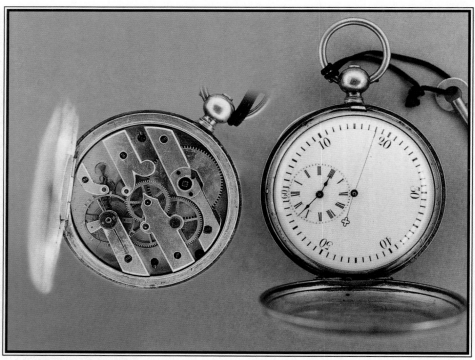

falls into the slot and is captured by it and then is released by the other side. When released the thumb sticking up whacks a jewel and keeps the action going. In this one it is done as simple lever. The escapement is on one plane instead of two planes - one horizontal plane. The only difference between watches other than quality and complication is how it starts and stops. That's all a watch is, a mainspring that starts and stops at a set rate. The difference is the escapement, the way the maker decides to make the watch stop and start.

NAWCC Club Price **$3,200.00.**

Courtesy of Joseph Conway, Dealer/Collector.

Plate 267. Louis Moricand. Geneva, circa 1820.
Fine and unusual 18K gold skeletonized watch with movement in the shape of a vase.

Case. Three-body, Empire, reeded band, glazed on both sides. **Dial.** Small white enamel. Arabic numerals, outer minute divisions. Blued-steel Breguet hands. **Movement.** Vase-shaped, gilt brass, full plate fully decorated on both sides with engraved foliate and repeated pattern, cylindrical pillars, fusee and chain, verge escapement, plain brass three-arm balance, flat balance spring, small two-footed steel cock.

Signed "Ls. M." on the dial, pendant punched with the Montibeliard Assay Office mark (bull) used between 1819 and 1838. Diam. 47 mm. **$16,100.00.**

Photo and description courtesy of Antiquorum Auctioneers, 14 Jun 2003.

**Plate 268. Unsigned, Swiss, circa 1820.
Fine and interesting 18K gold skeletonized quarter-repeating watch.**

Case. Four-body, Empire, the back engraved with a house under a tree, engine-turned border, reeded band, gilt hinged cuvette. **Dial.** White enamel chapter ring with Breguet numerals, glazed center for viewing the movement, polished steel Breguet hands. **Movement.** 47 mm, gilt skeletonized and engraved brass, cylindrical pillars, fusee and chain, verge escapement brass balance with flat balance spring, double-footed steel cock.
Case punched "C&LL."
Diam. 55 mm. **$3,588.00.**
Photo and description courtesy of Antiquorum Auctioneers, 14 Jun 2003.

Plate 269. Circa 1820.

Very high quality watch with a round offset dial, great condition.
$7,085.00.
Description and watch courtesy of Somlo Antiques.

Plate 270. Circa 1820.

Enameled silver gilt made for the Chinese market, with center seconds, Swiss, cylinder **movement**. **$10,122.00.**
Description and watch courtesy of Somlo Antiques.

Plate 271. Harbor Scene.
Edward Prior, London, No. 43802, made for the Islamic market, circa 1820.
Fine 18K gold and enamel diamond-set quarter-repeating watch.

Case. Outer: double-body, glazed, with scalloped edge, the bezels with champlevé enamel decoration, diamond-set thumb piece. Middle: double-body with scalloped edge, bezels with champlevé floral decoration, the back with a finely painted seaside landscape, a castle to the right, a ship in the foreground. Inner: double-body, "bassine," back painted with a flower bouquet on a translucent scarlet ground over engine turning, the band pierced and engraved with foliage, diamond-set pendant. **Dial.** White enamel with radial Islamic numerals. Gold poker and beetle hands. **Movement.** 28 mm, hinged gilt brass full plate with cylindrical pillars, fusee with chain, verge escapement, plain steel three-arm balance, flat balance spring, gilt brass English cock with ruby endstone. Repeating on a bell by depressing the pendant.
Signed on the dial and backplate, case with London prestige marks.
Diam. 50 mm. **$10,316.00.**
Photo and description courtesy of Antiquorum Auctioneers, 14 Jun 2003.

**Plate 272. Cupid in Flowers.
Unsigned, Geneva, circa 1820.
Very fine and rare 18K gold and enamel pearl-set skeletonized medallion pendant watch.**

Case. Circular thin medallion pierced and engraved with Cupid with his bow and arrows among gold, enamel and paillon flowers and foliage, azure enamel pearl-set frame, gold scalloped edge, ring pendant, the movement set in the upper portion, bezel decorated with blue and white enamel in a repeated pattern, back cover with azure enamel and gold roses within a blue and white enamel frame, small steel pin to open the bezel. **Dial.** White enamel, Arabic numerals, outer minute track with fifteen-minute Arabic markers, winding aperture between 3 and 4 o'clock. Gold arrow hands. **Movement.** 21.5 mm (9½"), rare gilt brass full plate caliber with three apertures for the fixed barrel. Balance and train, each with its own plate, cylinder escapement, three-arm plain brass balance with flat balance spring.
Diam. 61 mm. **$20,367.00.**
Photo and description courtesy of Antiquorum Auctioneers, Nov 2002.

**Plate 273. The French Horn.
Unsigned, Geneva, circa 1820.
Unusual gold and enamel pearl-set form watch designed as a French horn.**

Case. Three-body, translucent imperial blue enamel on the back, bezels set with double rows of pearls, encircled by gold and champlevé enamel French horn with champlevé enamel embouchure end, three gold suspension chains. **Dial.** White enamel. Roman numerals, outer minute divisions, winding aperture at 2 o'clock. Brass Breguet hands. **Movement.** 25 mm, hinged, frosted gilt full plate with cylindrical pillars, fusee and chain, verge escapement brass balance with flat balance spring, Continental cock.
The suspension ring punched "ET."
Diam. 63 x 43 mm. **$8,073.00.**
Photo and description courtesy of Antiquorum Auctioneers.

Plate 274. Scarlet Tulip.
Unsigned, Geneva, circa 1820.
Very fine 18K gold and enamel form watch designed as a tulip.

Case. Three-body, two spring-loaded petals very realistically painted on enamel, hinged to the base of the flower of translucent red enamel over flinque with green leaves stemming from a gold stalk, suspended by four chains joined by a single ring. **Dial.** White enamel, Breguet numerals, outer minute divisions, Arabic 15 minutes, winding aperture at 1 o'clock. Blued-steel lozenge hands. **Movement.** 19.5 mm (8¾"), hinged, gilt full plate with cylindrical pillars, fusee and chain, verge escapement, plain brass balance, Continental cock.
Case stamped with an "A" superimposed with an inverted "A."
Diam. length 37 mm, width 25mm. **$4,428.00.**
Photo and description courtesy of Antiquorum Auctioneers, Nov 2002.

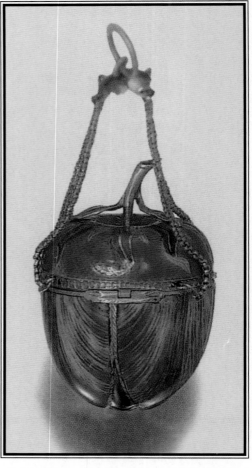

Plate 275. Breguet a Paris, Swiss, circa 1820.
Fine and interesting 18K gold skeletonized quarter-repeating watch with visible repeating works.

Case. Four-body, Empire, polished back, reeded band, gilt hinged cuvette. **Dial.** White enamel chapter ring with Breguet numerals, glazed center for viewing the movement. Blued-steel Breguet hands. **Movement.** 47 mm, gilt skeletonized and engraved brass, cylindrical pillars, fusee and chain, verge escapement brass balance with flat balance spring, double-footed steel cock.
Signed on dial and cuvette.
Diam. 54 mm. **$3,588.00.**
Photo and description courtesy of Antiquorum Auctioneers, 14 Jun 2003.

Plate 276. Circa 1823.

Breguet, Horloger de la Marine Royale, No. 4270, entered in the register on October 31, 1823, finished on July 9, 1825, and sold on the same day to Monsieur Suzanne de Breaute, pere, for 3,500 francs.

Exceptionally fine and highly important large, 18K gold Grande Sonnerie clock-watch with quarter-repeating and special escapement, built on the principles of the Garde Temps, with a gold Breguet key on a short gold chain, in a Desoutter-fitted Morocco box. Accompanied by Breguet certificate.

Case. Four-body, "forme quatre baguettes," No. 288 by master casemaker Joly, engine turned, gilt hinged cuvette, bolt at 6 o'clock for striking/silent and at 1 o'clock for repeating. **Dial.** Silver, radial Roman numerals on bright finished ring with outer minute dot track, engine-turned and whitened center. Blued-steel Breguet hands. **Movement.** 53 mm (24"), gilt brass, bridge and standing barrel system for the going train, full plate sonnerie mechanism, 40 jewels, entire train jeweled with endstones, Robin-type chronometer escapement, cut bimetallic compensation balance with copper-silver outer lamina and the inner ones of blued steel, Breguet balance spring, repeating and striking on two large rectangular gongs.

Signed on dial and case, case also punched with the casemaker's mark and French gold guarantee marks.

Diam. 62 mm, total weight 200 grams. **$157,500.00.**

Photo and description courtesy of Antiquorum Auctioneers, 14 Jun 2003.

Plate 277. Circa 1825.

P & D Goddard verge fusee 47mm, P & D Goddard key wind/key set, correct silver "DG"-marked hunting **case** with eagle, porcelain **dial**, Roman numerals, gold hands, beautiful full plate fusee pin-plate **movement** marked "P & D Goddard WORCESTER (3676) - 1842."
$11,500.00.

Photo and description courtesy of OldWatch.com.

Plate 136. Circa 1828.
Plate 278. Breguet, No. 4461, sold to Monsieur Bidaux, on August 2, 1828, for 840 francs.
Very fine 8K gold, large souscription watch.

Case. Three-body, Empire, engine-turned back and band, short pendant. **Dial.** White enamel, Breguet numerals, by Droz, outer Five-minute divisions, secured by a screw below 12 o'clock. Blued-steel hand. **Movement.** 57mm (25"), gilt brass, souscription caliber with center barrel wound from either side, four-wheel train, ruby cylinder escapement, three-arm plain brass balance, blued-steel flat balance spring, compensation curb, parachute on top pivot. Signed on dial and movement, case punched with the number, case maker's mark and French guarantee marks.
Diam. 62 mm. **$24,794.00.**
Photo and description courtesy of Antiquorum Auctioneers, 2002.

Plate 279. Circa 1830.
Fine and beautiful 18K gold and champlevé polychrome enamel quarter repeater ladies antique pendant watch by Lepine.

Case with cast and chased bezels, the back with a rich and dense floral design and very small edge repair. Silver engine-turned **dial** with faded numerals and gold Breguet hands. Fine gilt Lepine calibre eight-jewel cylinder **movement** with parachute and compensation curb. The repeat, which is activated by withdrawing, turning, and depressing a plunger in the pendant, has clear tone. A particularly attractive repeater by a famous maker.
Diam. 35 mm. **$4,000.00.**
Photo and description courtesy of Stephen Bogoff, Antiquarian Horologist.

Plate 280. Circa 1830.
14K hunting case watch lever fusee, made in Liverpool.

It did not really need a fusee, but the conservative nature of the English maker led him to put one in. The **case** opens from 3 to 9, zip lock–type dust cover. The **movement** has Liverpool windows (i.e., big jewels that you can almost see through). The watch is jeweled all the way through to the fusee itself. It has 19 jewels. When you purchased the watch you paid extra for every set of jewels and every adjustment. This was one of the most expensive movements that you could buy at this time. Signed "Joseph Johnson, Liverpool." Probably used in railroad service because of the quality of the watch.
NAWCC Club Price **$2,500.00.**
Courtesy of Joseph Conway, Collector/Dealer.

Plate 281. Circa 1830.
Fine and unusual French 18K gold champlevé enamel digital antique pocket watch circa 1830.

Case and dial of this very attractive watch completely covered with beautifully executed inhabited folloage against a black enamel background. The **dial** with aperatures for jump hours and running minutes. Gilt six-jewel keywind cylinder **movement**. I do not recall ever having seen another digital watch from this period with champlevé dial. Numerous small restorations to the enamel on the dial and case.
Diam. 41 mm. **$3,500.00.**
Photo and description courtesy of Stephen Bogoff, Antiquarian Horologist.

Plate 282. Jumping Hour.
Louis Duchene et Fils, Geneva, No. 29542, circa 1830.
Fine and rare 18K gold and enamel jump-hour digital pocket watch.

Case. Four-body. "bassine," entirely decorated with black champlevé enamel forming an elaborate foliate and floral design, spring-loaded back cover, gold hinged cuvette. **Dial.** Silver, engine-turned, jump-hour aperture at the top, minute aperture at 6 o'clock **Movement.** 40.5 mm. (18"). Gilt, early bar caliber, jeweled cylinder escapement, three-arm gold balance with flat balance spring.
Signed on dial and cuvette.
Diam. 49 mm. **$3,542.00.**
Photo and description courtesy of Antiquorum Auctioneers, Nov 2002.

Plate 283. Circa 1830.
Fine and unusual Swiss 18K gold and enamel jump-hour quarter-repeater antique pocket watch by Moynier & Fils, Geneva.

Silver engine-turned **dial** with jump-hour aperture above eccentric minute chapter with later minute hand. The **case**, pendant, and bow beautifully engraved and enameled, with restorations to the back. Lepine calibre six-jewel cylinder **movement** chimes the time when the pendant is depressed.
Diam. 40 mm. **$3,750.00.**
Photo and description courtesy of Stephen Bogoff, Antiquarian Horologist.

Plate 284. Circa 1830.
Good English, 18K gold, hunting-cased, Massey III, lever and fusee, antique key wind pocketwatch with multicolored gold dial by George Forrester, Liverpool.

Dial with attractive oxidation. The **movement** with engraved cock and barrel bridge, diamond cap, and uncut bimetallic balance. Substantial engine-turned **case** with cast bezels, pendant and bow.
Diam. 55 mm. **$2,500.00.**
Photo and description courtesy of Stephen Bogoff, Antiquarian Horologist.

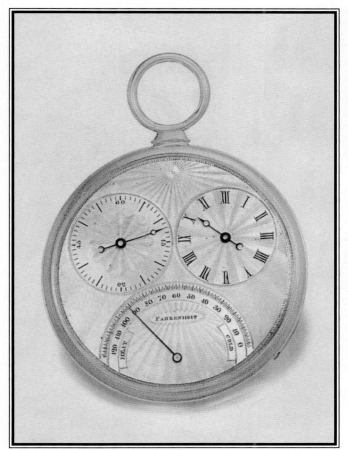

Plate 285. Sylvain Mairet, No. 63, made for J. E. Cooper, London, circa 1835.
Very fine and elegant extra-slim 18K gold watch with ruby cylinder escapement, Reaumur thermometer and regulator dial.

Case. Three-body, coin-edge, engine-turned back, gold hinged cuvette with winding and setting apertures, elegant bow smoothly extending from the pendant. **Dial.** Silver, by "GC," engine-turned in a sunburst pattern, eccentric Roman chapter at 2 o'clock, Arabic minute chapter symmetrically to the left, thermometer sector with Fahrenheit scale at the bottom. Blued-steel Breguet hands. **Movement.** 42 mm. (19"), frosted gilt, ruby cylinder escapement, three-arm gilt balance with flat balance spring, compensation curb, steel and brass bimetallic thermometer curb acing on spring-loaded rack-and-pinion transmission. Punched with Mairet's master mark on the pillar plate.
Diam. 47 mm. **$12,558.00.**
Photo and description courtesy of Antiquorum Auctioneers, 14 Jun 2003.

Plate 286. Circa 1836. English silver pair case verge and fusee.

White enamel **dial** with bold numerals and gilt hands. The **movement** with masked cock pierced and engraved in a lovely floral design.
Diam. 55 mm. **$500.00.**
Photo and description courtesy of Stephen Bogoff, Antiquarian Horologist.

**Plate 287. Circa 1840.
Good English 18K gold key wind lever and fusee antique pocket watch with engraved multicolor dial.**

Case with cast and chased bezels, pendant and bow; the engine turned back with the usual wear at the edge and small ding. The **dial** with a fine engraving of a castle and a multicolor floral border. Lever and fusee movement by F. T. Renaud, Liverpool, with diamond-cap jewel and dust cover.
Diam. 52 mm. **$1,500.00.**
Photo and description courtesy of Stephen Bogoff, Antiquarian Horologist.

**Plate 288. Circa 1840.
Beautifully scalloped and enameled hunting case lady's or man's watch.**

$7,085.00.
Description and watch courtesy of Somlo Antiques.

**Plate 289. Pan, Geneva, circa 1840.
Fine 18K gold and enamel, pearl-set watch for the Chinese market.**

Case. Four-body, Empire, the back with finely painted flowers against translucent scarlet enamel over engine turning, the band pendant and bow in black and white geometrical pattern champlevé enamel, spring-loaded back, brass hinged cuvette, bezel set with half pearls. **Dial.** White enamel, Roman numerals, outer minute divisions. Gilt Breguet hands. **Movement.** 25 mm, gilt full plate with cylindrical pillars, fusee and chain, verge escapement, plain brass balance, Continental cock pierced and engraved in symmetrical scrolling pattern.
Signed on dial and movement.
Diam. 30 mm. **$2,870.00.**
Photo and description courtesy of Antiquorum Auctioneers, 14 Jun 2003.

Plate 290. Unsigned, Geneva, No. 3115, made for the Chinese market circa 1840.
Very fine 18K gold and painted-on enamel pearl-set pendant watch.

Case. Four-body, Empire, spring-loaded back finely painted-on enamel with a flower bouquet on green background, half pearl-set bezels, pendant and bow, gold hinged glazed cuvette. **Dial.** White enamel, radial Roman numerals, outer minute track, subsidiary sunk seconds. Blued-steel Breguet hands. **Movement.** 34 mm, gilt and silvered brass, entirely engraved bar caliber, 15 jewels, lateral counterpoised lever escapement, monometallic balance with flat balance spring.
Punched inside the case with Geneva guarantee marks, and case maker's trademark, "CB," in oval.
Diam. 39 mm. **$4,126.00.**
Photo and description courtesy of Antiquorum Auctioneers, 14 Jun 2003.

Plate 291. Just & Son, London, No. 3461, made for the market, circa 1840.
Very fine 18K gold and painted-on enamel center seconds watch.

Case. Two-body form, "collier," back finely painted-on enamel with bouquet of flowers on translucent dark blue enamel over engine turning, translucent scarlet border with gold scrolling, pearl-set bezels, pendant and bow, gilt cuvette hinged to the movement ring. **Dial.** White enamel, radial Roman numerals, outer minute/seconds track with 15-minute Arabic markers. Gold spoon hands. **Movement.** 44 mm. (19½"), gilt brass, typical Chinese caliber with standing barrel, 13 jewels, lateral counterpoised lever escapement with the lift on the pallets, plain steel three-arm balance with blued-steel flat balance spring.
Signed on the movement, cuvette punched with Cyrillic characters.
Diam. 55 mm. **$21,252.00.**
Photo and description courtesy of Antiquorum Auctioneers, Nov 2003.

Plate 292. Ami Sandoz & Fils, Geneva, No. 25765, circa 1840.
Fine 18K gold, small, extra-slim pendant watch with bagnolet caliber.

Case. Three-body, "bassine pincee," back cover engine-turned and centered with flowers, coin-edge band with gold Breguet-type key. **Dial.** Silver, Roman numerals, outer minute track. Gold Breguet hands. **Movement.** 22 mm, (9¾"), gilt brass, ten jewels, Bagnolet inverted caliber, freestanding barrel and the train of wheel sunk in the single plate engraved on the reverse with floral decoration, cylinder escapement, gilt three-arm balance, flat balance spring with regulator, female winding.
Signed on the movement, case punched with Sandoz's trademark.
Diam. 25 mm. **$3,050.00.**
Photo and description courtesy of Antiquorum Auctioneers, 14 Jun 2003.

Plate 293. Circa 1847.
Fine and rare Breguet No. 569 very early stem-wind 18K gold and enamel quarter-repeating antique pocket watch.

Cobalt blue enamel **case** back mounted with the crest of Count Allegro, to whom this watch was sold for 3,500 francs. Coin-milled bezels front and rear; repeat slide in the band. Breguet's special lever escapement with parachute shock-proofing, platinum timing screws, 21 jewels, and provision for regulating the watch from the band without opening the back. Fine white enamel **dial** with gold Breguet hands and tiny secret signature at 6:00. Typical Breguet case stamped with serial number over "B," French 18K gold guarantee stamp, case maker's stamp and a case number 75 over "P." With a letter from Emanuel Breguet confirming their manufacture of this watch. This is just the sort of aesthetically pleasing technically advanced complicated watch for which the firm is justly famous.
NOTE: This watch has a keyless winding and setting system that was apparently designed by Breguet. His earlier keyless designs had two separate arbors for winding and setting. In this elegant design, a double pinion on the winding stem disengages from the winding and engages the setting when the crown is pulled. Breguet only used this system for about three years.
Diam. 47 mm. **$26,250.00.**
Photo and description courtesy of Stephen Bogoff, Antiquarian Horologist.

Plate 294. Circa 1850.
Fine and scarce miniature lady's 18K gold, enamel, pearl, and diamond antique watch with pin and tassels by Rosselet, Geneva.

Suite all in gold with cobalt blue enamel. The tiny watch with diamonds on the back, white enamel **dial**, and gilt ten-jewel cylinder **movement**. Insignificant repairs to the enamel on the tassels.
Diam. 21 mm. **$2,975.00.**
Photo and description courtesy of Stephen Bogoff, Antiquarian Horologist.

Plate 295. Circa 1850.
Early Patek Philippe 18K gold midsize antique pocket watch made for Tiffany.

Engine-turned case #3884 signed "Patek & Co." and also "T Y & E" (for Tiffany Young & Ellis) on the dust cover. Gilt jeweled cylinder movement numbered 3884 and signed "Patek & Co." under the dial. White enamel dial (hairlines and glaze chip) with eccentric subsidiary seconds and fancy gold hands. This is one of the first movements completely made by Patek; prior to this time they purchased ebauches from other makers. This is also one of the earliest Patek watches sold to Tiffany.
Diam. 40 mm. **$2,200.00.**
Photo and description courtesy of Stephen Bogoff, Antiquarian Horologist.

Plate 296. Circa 1840s – 1850s

Pitkin W. Pitkin 44 mm, 15 jewels, key wind/key set, sterling silver hallmarked swingout **case**, single sunk porcelain **dial**, Roman numerals, blue spade hands, full plate gilt lever fusee **movement**, screwed-down jewel settings, "(41918)." **$3,200.00.**
Photo and description courtesy of OldWatch.com.

Plate 297. Dimier & Cie., Geneve, made for the Chinese market circa 1850.
Very fine, small, 18K gold and painted-on enamel, pearl-set pendant watch.

Case. Four-body, Empire, spring-loaded back finely painted-on enamel with a pair of doves and a flower bouquet, blue background, half pearl-set bezels, pendant and bow, gold glazed cuvette. **Dial.** White enamel. Roman numerals, outer minute divisions. Blued-steel spade hands. **Movement.** 23 mm, entirely engraved brass bar caliber with polished steel pillar plate, cylinder escapement, three-arm gilt balance with flat balance spring.
Signed on dial and movement.
Diam. 27 mm. **$3,409.00.**
Photo and description courtesy of Antiquorum Auctioneers, 14 Jun 2003.

Statue of Mieszko I and Mieczyslaw Chrobry made by Christian Rauch in 1837/38 and set up in Gold Chapel in Poznan Cathedral in 1841. The pedestal was made by O. Sokolowski.

Plate 298. Two Monarchs.
Patek Philippe & Co. a Geneve, No. 8190, made for the Polish market in 1850, sold on April 15, 1852.
Extremely rare and very fine 18K gold and enamel keyless dress watch with early Philippe winding/setting system, accompanied by the Extract from the Archives.

Case. Four-body, "bassine et filets," back finely engraved and filled with champleve black enamel, representing the statue of the two first rulers of Poland — Duke Mieczyslaw I and his son King Boleslaw Chrobry, after Christian Rauch's sculpture created circa 1840 for the Poznan Cathedral, scrolling and floral border, reeded band, gold hinged cuvette. **Dial.** White enamel, radial Roman numerals, outer minute divisions, secured by two small screws. Blued-steel Breguet hands. **Movement.** 40 mm (18"). Cal 9, frosted gilt, hanging barrel with Geneva stop work, cylinder escapement, three-arm gilt balance with flat balance spring. third Philippe winding/setting system.

Signed on dial, case, and movement, movement in addition punched with the maker's trademark under the dial.
Diam. 45 mm. **$13,455.00.**
Photo and description courtesy of Antiquorum Auctioneers, 14 Jun 2003.

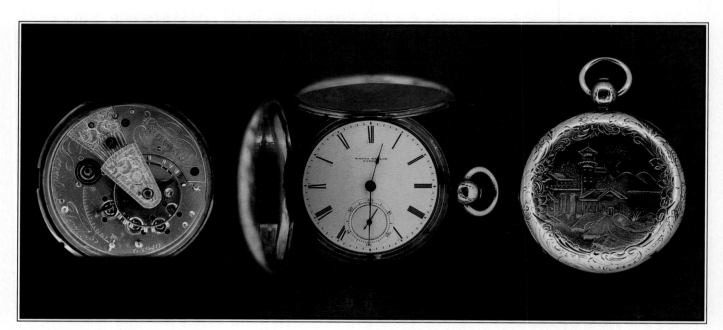

Plate 299. Circa 1850s – 1860s.

Lever fusee, no English hallmark, note Liverpool windows (big sapphire-type jewels) on the **movement**, engraved scene on case (lockets were made with the same scene); movement signed "David Taylor, Liverpool."
$600.00.
Watch and description courtesy of David Strudler.

Plate 300. Circa 1860s.

18K Swiss — silver **dial**, cylinder escapement, thin **movement**, nice enameling.
$900.00.
Courtesy of Jeff Rosen, Dealer, Solvang Antique Center.

Plate 301. Circa 1860s.

Sterling silver, Swiss made, with a reverse painting on glass of Civil War soldiers and a nurse. This watch comes complete with a book about Civil War nurses.
$3,500.00.
Description and watch courtesy of Dan Doloff.

Plate 302. Circa 1860.
Silver gilt and painted enamel antique lady's pendant watch for the Chinese market by Juvet.

Front with a painted enamel portrait against a cobalt blue enamel background, over engine turning, within an enamel border. White enamel **dial** with gold signature and fancy blued-steel hands. Gilt ¾-plate key wind ten-jewel cylinder **movement** also with Chinese signature.
Diam. 34 mm. **$1,350.00.**
Photo and description courtesy of Stephen Bogoff, Antiquarian Horologist.

Plate 303. Circa 1860.
Fine, very scarce, and very fancy Girrard Perrigaux pivoted detent pocket chronometer for the South American market with thermometer dial.

Silver **dial** with applied gold decorations, two-tone hands, large thermometer section, and faded Roman numerals. Gilt ¾-plate **movement** with the jewels in screwed gold settings, diamond cap jewel, spherical hairspring, the balance with oval gold weights. Fancy 18K gold **case** engraved overall, with typical wear at the edges. There is an interesting contrast between the austere precision movement and the extravigant decoration of the dial and case.
Diam. 53 mm. **$13,000.00.**
Photo and description courtesy of Stephen Bogoff, Antiquarian Horologist.

Plate 304. Joseph Geiss in Wien, circa 1860.
Interesting painted on enamel oval silver lady's pendant watch.

Case. Two-body, "bassine," with curved-in edge, back painted with a shepherdess and her suitor in the countryside, band with scrolling on white background, inside painted with a shepherdess weaving a flower wreath, surrounded by her sheep; silver hinged bezel. **Dial.** Gilt silver, white champlevé radial Roman numerals in translucent imperial blue enamel frame, stylized champlevé foliage on edges. Blued-steel Breguet hands **Movement.** 29 mm, frosted gilt full plate with cylindrical pillars, fusee and chain, verge escapement brass balance with flat balance spring, Continental cock.
Signed on the movement.
Diam. 55 x 38 mm. **$1,435.00.**
Photo and description courtesy of Antiquorum Auctioneers, 14 Jun 2003.

Plate 305. Circa 1860.
Fine and unusual lady's key wind 18K gold and enamel pendant watch, chain, and pin.

All of the pieces decorated with a star design against cobalt blue backgrounds. One of the watch covers with a monogram matching the monogram on the pin. White enamel **dial** with blued-steel Breguet hands. Fancy dust cover engraved with details of the movement and the name of the maker, "L. A. Counis, Geneva." Gilt ten-jewel keywind cylinder **movement.** Small repairs to the enamel on the watch, pin, and chain. Chain length 15.5 inches.
Diam. 35 mm. **$3,300.00.**
Photo and description courtesy of Stephen Bogoff, Antiquarian Horologist.

Plate 306. Charles Oudin, Horloger de la Marine, Palais Royal 52, Paris, Nos. 25249 and 11389, sold to Casimir-Perier, French Minister of the Interior, executed by Louis Audemars, Brassus, circa 1865.

Exceptionally fine and rare 18K gold keyless early minute-repeating double train keyless watch with independent dead seconds.

Case. Four-body, all hinged, "bassine et filets," engine-turned back with elaborate initials "CP," repeated in mirror image, gold hinged cuvette, early round pendant. **Dial.** White enamel, Roman numerals, outer minute divisions with five-minute/seconds Arabic markers. Blued-steel spade" hands. **Movement.** 43 mm, frosted gilt, tandem winding, gold trains, nickel motion work, 38 jewels, straight line calibrated lever escapement, cut bimetallic compensation balance with Breguet balance spring, independent train engaged via gold flirt meshing with escape wheel pinion, repeating on gongs through activating slide in the band.

Case punched with Audemar's master mark, cuvette and dial signed by the retailer, owner's name and address engraved inside back cover and cuvette, case and movement with the same serial number.

Diam. 52 mm. **$23,322.00.**

Photo and description courtesy of Antiquorum Auctioneers, 14 Jun 2003.

Plate 307. Mikhail Semyonovitch Bronnikov, circa 1865.

Very rare and fine watch entirely made of birchwood and bone, in its original fitted case, accompanied by its original carved wood chain and key.

Case. Double-body, hinged back cover, polished, bezels with turned ribs at the edges, small circles in the center. Chain: single, carved from birchwood, 10 mm ring-links, hinged folding walnut box. **Dial.** Wooden with Arabic numerals on bone cartouches and subsidiary seconds. Wooden hands. **Movement.** Entirely made of wood with pinned wooden bridges, excluding the mainspring, balance spring, and pivots; with going barrel, cylinder escapement with bone staff, plain wood three-arm balance.

Signed inside back cover.

Diam. 50 mm. **$23,023.00.**

Photo and description courtesy of Antiquorum Auctioneers, Nov 2003.

**Plate 308. Circa 1866.
Attractive, very small, 18K gold verge and fusee hunting case antique lady's pendant watch with matching chain and key.**

Plain polish drum-shape **case**. White enamel **dial** (minor repair at winding hole) with gold spade hands. The gilt **movement** with pierced and engraved balance cock, 32-inch chain, the key set with a moonstone.
Diam. 24 mm. **$1,900.00.**
Photo and description courtesy of Stephen Bogoff, Antiquarian Horologist.

Plate 309. Circa 1866.

Waltham 20 size Appleton Tracy, 20K, 15 jewels, key wind/key set from the rear, very nice correct 18K solid gold **case**, single sunk porcelain **dial**, Roman numerals, blue spade hands, ¾-plate gilt **movement**, internal Maltese stop works, micrometric regulator (200398).
$8,850.00.
Photo and description courtesy of OldWatch.com.

Plate 310. Circa 1868.

Hunting case, 18k; 6 size lady's scalloped case; 18 ruby jewels, lever escapement, J. Huguenin of Copenhagen; enameled — yellow, white, and deep blue; accented by rose-cut diamond.
$2,900.00.
Courtesy of Jeff Rosen, Dealer, Solvang Antique Center.

Plate 311. Circa 1869.
Scarce Howard Type III antique pocket watch with Cole's escapement.

Typical faded gilt **movement** with curious empty holes on the balance cock. Nicely recased in a somewhat worn period spring-hinged coin silver **case**. **Dial** with clean hairlines and Howard umbrella hands.
Diam. 58 mm. **$2,000.00.**
Photo and description courtesy of Stephen Bogoff, Antiquarian Horologist.

Plate 312. Circa late 1860s.

Cornell Watch Company **movement**. This watch survived the October 1871 Chicago fire. Cornell Watch Company put an advertisement in the paper saying, "If anyone has a Cornell watch that survived the Chicago fire, we will rebuild the watch for free, just so we can advertise that the Cornell watch can survive even the Chicago fire." This is the only one found at that time, and none have been found in the last 30 years. This one was found in the Republic Life Insurance vault.
$25,000.00 – 30,000.00.
Description and watch courtesy of Dan Doloff.

Plate 313. Circa 1870s.

United States Watch Co. 18 size Edwin Rollo, 15 jewels, key wind/key set, excellent silveroid triple-hinged open-face **case**, single sunk porcelain **dial**, Roman numerals, blue spade hands, full plate gilt **movement** with butterfly cutout, gold jewel settings, micrometric regulator (6274). **$750.00.**
Photo and description courtesy of OldWatch.com.

Plate 314. Circa 1870s.

Philadelphia Watch Co. 16 size, 19 jewels, key wind/key set from the rear, excellent two-tone sterling silver triple-hinged open-face **case** with gold accents, single sunk porcelain **dial**, Roman numerals, blue spade hands, beautiful ¾-plate gilt **movement**. Paulus Patents 1868, micrometric regulator (6337). **$950.00.**
Photo and description courtesy of OldWatch.com.

Plate 315. Circa 1870.

18k hunting **case**; key wind, key set; green enamel with diamond on cover; 13-jewel nickel-grade **movement** with side lever escapement; by J. M. Sandoz; movement number 13384; blue spade hands on porcelain **dial**.
Diam. 41 mm. **$1,750.00.**
Courtesy of Jeff Rosen, Dealer, Solvang Antique Center.

Plate 316. Circa 1870s.

Independent Watch Co. 18 size, 11 jewels, key wind/key set, nice coin silver triple-hinged open-face **case**, single sunk porcelain **dial** marked "Howard Bros. Fredonia NY," Roman numerals, blue spade hands, full-plate gilt **movement** marked "Fredonia NY, Improved April 10th 1879," silver balance cock micrometric regulator (180476).
$750.00.
Photo and description courtesy of OldWatch.com.

Plate 317. Circa 1871.

Elgin 18 size, C. Z. Culver, 15 jewels, key wind/key set, outstanding yellow-gold-filled, box hinged hunter **case**, single sunk porcelain **dial**, Roman numerals, blue morning glory hands, full plate gilt **movement**, gold jewel settings, marked adjusted micrometric regulator (173718).
$850.00.
Photo and description courtesy of OldWatch.com.

Photo and description courtesy of Antiquorum Auctioneers, 21 May 2003.

Plate 318. Joseph Penlington, Liverpool, No. 13455, London case hallmarked 1871 – 1872.
Fine, 18K gold, half-hunting, keyless freesprung watch with 30-hour power reserve indicator.

Case. Five-body, "bassine," with double bezels, polished, front cover with blue champleve Roman hour chapter around the center aperture, gold hinged cuvette. **Dial.** White enamel, Roman numerals, outer minute track, up and down indicator at 3 o'clock, subsidiary sunk seconds at 9 o'clock. Double spade and Poker blued-steel hands. **Movement.** 43 mm, half-plate, frosted gilt, lateral calibrated lever escapement, cut bimetallic compensation balance with gold screws, freesprung Breguet balance spring.
Dial and movement signed.
Diam. 50 mm. **$2,990.00.**

Plate 319. Dent, Maker to the Queen, 33 Cockspur St., Chafing Cross, London, No. 27214, hallmarked 1871 – 1872.
Very fine and very rare, 18K gold, keyless, double-train independent dead seconds watch with split-seconds chronograph and two time zones.

Case. Four-body, "bassine et filets," polished, gold hinged cuvette, chronograph activation pushpiece at 9 o'clock.
Dial. White enamel (attributed to Willis), two small Roman chapters for two time zones, outer minute track, sunk centers, outer seconds track with five-minute Arabic markers, subsidiary sunk seconds. Spade blued-steel hands. **Movement.** 43 mm, ¾ plate, frosted gilt, two going barrels, 29 jewels, lateral counterpoised lever escapement, cut bimetallic compensation balance with gold and platinum screws, blued-steel Breguet balance spring, diamond endstone, dead seconds mechanism via gold dart engaging the escape wheel, unusual split-seconds mechanism as well as concentric setting mechanism with double-clutch wheel.
Dial and movement signed. Case punched by the casemaker, "JTW."
Diam. 49 mm. **$8,625.00.**
Photo and description courtesy of Antiquorum Auctioneers, 21 May 2003.

Plate 320. Circa 1872.
Good English key wind lever and fusee antique pocket watch with winding indicator by Wm. McFerran, Manchester.

Bold white enamel **dial** with gold and blued-steel hands. Plain polish substantial **case** engraved with a coat-of-arms. Gilt ¾-plate 17-jewel **movement** with engraved balance cock.
Diam. 54 mm. **$2,200.00.**
Photo and description courtesy of Stephen Bogoff, Antiquarian Horologist.

Plate 321. Circa 1874.

Corrnell 18 size, John Evan, key wind/key set, 15 jewels, excellent 4 oz. Waltham coin silver hunting **case**, single sunk porcelain dial, blue spade hands, full-plate gilt **movement**, micrometric regulator (22157).
$1,200.00.
Photo and description courtesy of OldWatch.com.

Plate 322. Circa 1874.

Elgin 18 size, G. M. Wheeler, 15 jewels, key wind/key set, nice coin silver triple-hinged open-face **case**, single sunk porcelain **dial**, Roman numerals, blue spade hands, full-plate gilt **movement**, gold jewel settings, micrometric regulator (293570). **$255.00.**
Photo and description courtesy of OldWatch.com.

Plate 323. Swiss gold, diamond, enamel hunting cased pocketwatch, circa 1875.

Case. 18K yellow gold, circular, hinged, four-bodied, front and back with blue enamel, set with diamonds. **Dial.** White enamel, black Roman numerals, sunk auxiliary seconds dial, blued-steel Breguet hands. **Movement.** Key wind and set, nickeled, 15 jewels, lever escapement, monometallic balance wheel, flat balance spring.
Signed "DuBois & Co. Geneva" on case, dial.
Diam. 39 mm.
Accompanied by 18K yellow gold chain set with blue and white enamel. **$1,292.50.**
Photo and description courtesy of Bonhams and Butterfields, San Francisco, 24 Mar 2003.

Plate 324. Circa 1875.

Elgin, size 18, model 2, H. H. Taylor. Number of jewels, 15; serial number 355384. Transitional, lever set, stem and key wind. Gold gilt plates.
$250.00.
Photos and description courtesy of Edward Ueberall, Collector/Dealer.

Plate 325. Circa 1878.

Lancaster 18 size West End, 10 jewels, very nice silverine open-face **case**, single sunk porcelain **dial**, Roman numerals, blue spade hands, gilt **movement**, key wind/key set from the rear, micrometric regulator (47323). An early Lancaster.
$255.00.
Photo and description courtesy of OldWatch.com.

Plate 326. Circa 1878.

Tiffany, size 16; number of jewels, 20; serial number, 8704. **Movement** made by (not for) Tiffany in Geneva, has gold helical hairspring.
$2,500.00.
Photo and description courtesy of Edward Ueberall, Collector/Dealer.

Plate 327. Circa 1879.

Elgin 16 size, grade 84, doctor's watch, 15 jewels, excellent 14k solid gold box end hunting **case**, porcelain **dial** with outer numeral chapter, Roman numerals, blue Breguet hands, sweep second hand, lever set, ¾-plate nickel **movement**, gold jewel settings, marked adjusted, micrometric regulator (632329).
$3,500.00.
Photo and description courtesy of OldWatch.com.

Plate 328. Circa 1879.

Waltham 18 size, George Washington, model 77, Quick Train, key wind/key set, 11 jewels, nice Waltham sterling silver hunting **case**, single sunk porcelain **dial**, blue spade hands, full-plate gilt **movement**, micrometric regulator (1466538). A very rare George Washington model 77. Very few of these were made. This is a very collectible watch. **$1,800.00.**

Photo and description courtesy of OldWatch.com.

Plate 329. Circa 1879.
Good American Waltham 14K gold 8/S hunting case lady's antique pendant watch.

Both covers engraved with an urn amidst scrolling folliage. Fine white enamel **dial** with blued-steel hands. Gilt ¾-plate seven-jewel key wind William Ellery **movement**. Diam. 42 mm. **$550.00.**
Photo and description courtesy of Stephen Bogoff, Antiquarian Horologist.

Plate 330. 1879.

Illinois 18 size, 11 jewels, key wind/key set, very nice nickel silver open-face **case**, single sunk porcelain **dial**, Roman numerals, blue spade hands, full plate gilt **movement**, micrometric regulator (128234). **$255.00.**
Photo and description courtesy of OldWatch.com.

Plate 331. Circa 1870 – 1880s.

Sterling silver **case** with Swiss **movement**, porcelain **dial** has a reverse painting of a mountain man hunting in the mountains. If this dial had a painting of a house, it would be a $400 watch. If it were more interesting, it could be a $1,500 watch. With a Civil War painting, $2,000.00 – 3,500.00.
$3,500.00 – 5,000.00.
Description and watch courtesy of Dan Doloff, Collector.

Plate 332. Circa 1800s.

Sterling silver hunting case watch, with a picture of Edward VII on the cover. Both covers enameled with sterling.
$1,200.00.
Description and watch courtesy of Dan Doloff, Collector.

Plate 333. Circa 1880.

Illinois 18 size, model 2, grade 5-S, Rail Road King, 15 jewels, railroad grade, yellow-gold-filled hunting case, double sunk porcelain **dial** marked special for railway service, Roman numerals, blue hands, lever set, full plate gilt Rail Road King **movement**, marked adjusted, screw down jewel settings, Chalmers patent micrometric regulator (311858). A very hard-to-find watch. Only 225 of these were made.
$1,950.00.
Photo and description courtesy of OldWatch.com.

Plate 334. Circa 1880s.

Cheshire 18 size, 3rd model, seven jewels, very nice triple-hinged coin silver open-face **case**, single sunk porcelain **dial**, blue hands, Roman numerals, lever set, gilt **movement**, micrometric regulator (66226). **$550.00.**
Photo and description courtesy of OldWatch.com.

Plate 335. Circa 1880s.

Manhattan 16 size two-button stopwatch, gold-filled open-face screw-back **case**, porcelain **dial**, Roman numerals, blue spade hands, full-plate gilt **movement**, micrometric regulator (125654). **$850.00.**
Photo and description courtesy of OldWatch.com.

Plate 336. Circa late 1870s – early 1880s.

Auburndale timer 18 size, ten-minute ¼-jump seconds timer, five jewels, Auburndale marked nickel **case**, porcelain **dial**, Arabic numerals, blue spade hands, sweep second, fly back, ¼-jump seconds, ¾-plate nickel **movement**, micrometric regulator (2551). **$850.00.**
Photo and description courtesy of OldWatch.com.

Plate 337. Circa 1880s.

Manhattan 16 size two-button stopwatch, gold-filled open-face screw-back **case**, porcelain **dial**, Roman numerals, blue spade hands, full-plate gilt **movement**, micrometric regulator (125654). **$850.00.**
Photo and description courtesy of OldWatch.com.

Plate 338. Tiffany & Co., attributed to Patek Philippe & Cie., Geneva, No. 76786, circa 1880.
Very fine and rare, 18K gold, keyless miniature pendant watch.

Case. Four-body, "bassine, carrure ronde," polished, gold hinged cuvette, swivel pendant. **Dial.** white enamel, Roman numerals, outer minute divisions. Blued-steel spade hands. **Movement.** 6", nickel, "fausses cotes" decoration, 18 jewels, straight-line lever escapement, cut bimetallic compensation balance with blued-steel flat balance spring. Dial and movement signed by the retailer.
Diam. 21 mm. **$4,836.00.**
Photo and description courtesy of Antiquorum Auctioneers, 21 May 2003.

Plate 339. Tiffany & Co., Geneva and New York, No. 15089, circa 1880.
Very fine 18K gold, keyless, five-minute repeating watch with split-seconds chronograph, presented to J. H. Bradford.

Case. Four-body, "bassine et filets," with concave bezels and reeded edges, back engraved with coat-of-arms with motto "Esse Quam Videri," gold hinged cuvette. **Dial.** White enamel, Roman numerals, outer minute ring, outermost chronograph divisions with five-minute/seconds red Arabic markers, subsidiary sunk seconds. Spade blued-steel hands. **Movement.** 45 mm (20"), nickel, half-plate, 35 jewels, straight line calibrated lever escapement, cut bimetallic compensation balance with Breguet balance spring, split-seconds mechanism under the dial, repeating on gongs through activating slide in the band.
Dial, case, and movement signed by the retailer.
Diam. 55 mm. **$5,750.00.**
Photo and description courtesy of Antiquorum Auctioneers, 19 Mar 2003.

Plate 340. Circa 1880.
14K yellow gold, hunting case, automaton,
striking watch.

$10,628.00.
Description and watch courtesy of Somlo Antiques.

Plate 341. Circa 1880.
Attractive 18k gold and enamel lady's hunting case antique pendant watch.

Case engraved overall, the edges with enameled flowers, the front centered with a monogram within a shield, the back with a bouquet. Gold **dial** with fancy hands. Gilt ten-jewel cylinder **movement**.
Diam. 37 mm. **$1,250.00.**
Photo and description courtesy of Stephen Bogoff, Antiquarian Horologist.

Plate 342. LeCoultre, Swiss enamel pocket watch, circa 1880.

Case. 18k yellow gold, circular, open face, bezel with blue enamel guilloche, back of case with multicolored enamel scene of birds. **Dial.** white enamel, black Roman numerals, blued-steel spade hands. **Movement.** Gilt, jeweled, cylinder escapement, monometallic balance wheel, flat balance spring.
Signed "LeCoultre" on movement.
Diam. 24 mm. **$2,643.75.**
Photo and description courtesy of Bonhams and Butterfields, San Francisco, 24 Mar 2003.

Plate 343. Circa 1881.

Fredonia 18 size, special anti-magnetic spring 15 jewels, Robert Gressler, Strawberry Point IA, raiload grade, aged, 3 oz. coin silver hunting **case**, double sunk porcelain **dial**, Roman numerals, blue spade hands, lever set, full-plate nickel **movemen**t, Fredonia regulator disc gold jewel settings, marked adjusted, marked special anti-magnetic spring (432).
$1,100.00.
Photo and description courtesy of OldWatch.com.

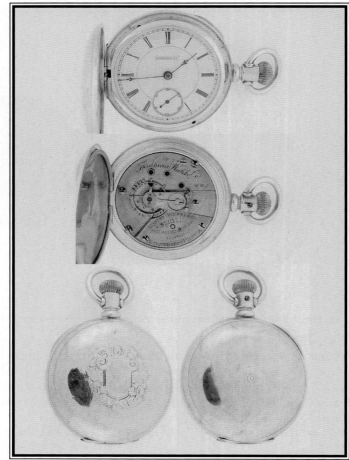

Plate 344. Circa 1883.

Rockford, size 18, model 6; number of jewels, 15; serial number, 199383. High-grade Rockford with cut-out plates exposing the escapement, marked "15 RJ" (ruby jewels).
$675.00.
Photo and description courtesy of Edward Ueberall, Collector/Dealer.

Plate 345. Circa 1883.

18 size Waltham, open-face, silver case, with a pink-gold train and a gold bolt inlayed in the back of the case. 83-model Railroad King. The number of pieces of gold on the back determined part of the value.
$850.00 (because of damage on dial — without dial damage, the watch would be priced at $1,000.00).
Description and watch courtesy of Dan Doloff, Collector.

Plate 346. Louis Audemars, Brassus & Geneva, No. 14607, circa 1885. Fine and unusual keyless movement with perpetual calendar and split-seconds chronograph.

Case. Nickel, later. **Dial.** White enamel, Roman numerals, outer minute/seconds track with five-minute/seconds red Arabic markers, four subsidiary sunk dials for days of the week, date, months of the four-year leap cycle, and subsidiary seconds concentric with phases of the moon aperture. Blued-steel spade hands. **Movement.** 42 mm, nickel. 27 jewels, straight-line calibrated lever escapement, cut bimetallic compensation balance with Breguet balance spring, rack-and-pinion micrometric regulator.
Signed on dial and movement.
Diam. 53 mm. **$12,558.00.**
Photo and description courtesy of Antiquorum Auctioneers, 14 Jun 2003.

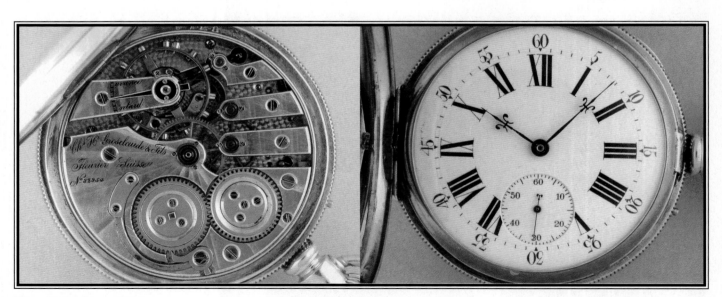

Plate 347. Circa 1885.

Grosclaude, size 18; number of jewels, 20; serial number, 32954. Pivoted detent chronometer **movement**.
$2,200.00.
Photos and description courtesy of Edward Ueberall, Collector/Dealer.

Plate 348. Tiffany & Co., New York, No. 15127, circa 1885. Very fine and very rare 18K gold five-minute repeating watch with split-seconds chronograph and black dial.

Case. Four-body, all hinged, "bassine et filets," polished with monogrammed back, gold hinged cuvette.
Dial. Black enamel, radial white Arabic numerals, outer white minute track, outermost seconds divided into fifths, five-minute/seconds white Arabic markers, subsidiary sunk seconds. Steel spade hands. **Movement.** 44 mm (19½"), maillechort, half plate, 34 jewels, straight-line calibrated lever escapement, cut bimetallic compensation balance with Breguet balance spring, repeating on gongs through activating slide in the band.
Signed on dial, case, and movement. Diam. 55 mm. **$8,522.00.**
Photo and description courtesy of Antiquorum, Auctioneers 14 Jun 2003.

Plate 349. Circa 1886.

Elgin, size 6, model 3, grade 94; number of jewels, 11; serial number, 2173620. Lady's 14k gold hunting-case watch. **$575.00.**
Photo and description courtesy of Edward Ueberall, Collector/Dealer.

Plate 350. Circa 1887.

Peoria, size 18; number of jewels, 15; serial number, 35638. Made for Non-Magnetic Watch Co. of America. Micrometer regulator is missing.
$425.00.
Photos and description courtesy of Edward Ueberall, Collector/Dealer.

Plate 351. Circa 1887.

Illinois 18 size, No. 4 Railroader, 11 jewels, railroad grade, very nice and unusual Fahy's open-face pair **case**, correct single sunk porcelain 24-hour **dial**, with Roman/Arabic numerals, blue spade hands, lever set, full-plate gilt **movement**, with locomotive and coal car engraved on it, Chalmers patent regulator (704113). The only watch movement Illinois ever put a locomotive on!
$1,100.00.
Photo and description courtesy of OldWatch.com.

Plate 352. Montre Geographique Callier, Horloger de l'Observatoire, Fournisseur de la Marine de l'Etat, Paris, dated 1887. Very fine and rare 18K gold, keyless, double-face 24-hour world time watch.

Case. Four-body, massive, "bassine," polished.
Dial. White enamel with radial Roman numerals, days in red, nights in black, outer dot minute divisions with five-minute Arabic markers. Blued-steel Breguet hands. Center with revolving enamel disc painted with the northern hemisphere. Gilt index hand to be set for designated longitude. Back dial for minutes only: white enamel with minute track with five-minute red Arabic markers, subsidiary sunk seconds, sub-dial for regulating at 1 o'clock. Gold lozenge hand. Both minute and seconds hands going counterclockwise. **Movement.** 48 mm (21"), frosted gilt, 19 jewels, straight line calibrated lever escapement, cut bimetallic compensation balance with Breguet balance spring, rack-and-pinion regulator. Signed on the dial.
Diam. 59 mm. **$37,674.00.**
Photo and description courtesy of Antiquorum Auctioneers, 14 Jun 2003.

Plate 353. Circa 1888.

Paillard, size 16, grade 72; number of jewels, 20; serial number, 57689. Non-Magnetic Watch Co. of America probably made by Baddollet (Swiss).
$550.00.
Photos and description courtesy of Edward Ueberall, Collector/Dealer.

Plate 354. Circa 1888.

American Waltham Watch Co. 17 size, model 72, crystal plate or stone movement, 17 jewels, plain polish solid gold screw-back and bezel **case** #1773, double sunk porcelain **dial** marked "A.W. Co. Waltham" in gothic-style script, radial Arabic numerals, blue Breguet hands, lever set, stunning agate plates with free sprung balance, gold escape wheel, gold pallet fork, gold fork bridge, and banking pins; flat balance cock.[12] The only 17 size free sprung stone **movement** known to exist. It adorned the cover of the *NAWCC Bulletin* in October of 1999 and has been the subject of great debate ever since. The watch has been examined by some of the most learned gentleman in the watch collecting world, and verified.
$500,000.00.
Photo and description courtesy of OldWatch.com.

Plate 355. Patek Philippe, Geneve rare gold chronograph pocket watch, circa 1888.

Case. Heavy repoussé, 18k yellow gold, circular, open face, hinged, four-bodied. **Dial.** Engraved dial with enamel cartouches with blue Roman numerals, enamelled circle for chronograph with center seconds counter, blued-steel Louis XVI hands. **Movement.** Rhodiumed, highly jeweled, lever escapement, cut bimetallic screwed balance wheel, Breguet balance spring.
Signed "Patek Philippe" on case, movement.
Diam. 44 mm. **$8,812.50.**
Photo and description courtesy of Bonhams and Butterfields, San Francisco, 25 Jun 2002.

**Plate 356. Circa 1890.
18K yellow gold, hunting case watch with center seconds, made for the Oriental market.**

Dial has painting of a jockey made to look like he is striking a bell.
$2,279.00.
Courtesy of Somlo Antiques.

Plate 357. Circa 1889.

This watch was made to com-
memorate the Spanish-American
War; the dial has Dewey, American flag, and the words "I hope it
will fly there forever." The real
Dewey watches will have the word
"Maine" stamped inside the back
lid. All of them do not have the
flag, etc. on the dial, but they will
all have "Maine" on the inside of
the back lid.

$1,200.00 (if perfect, $9,000.00).
*Description and watch courtesy of
Dan Doloff, Collector.*

Plate 358. Circa 1889.

Another Dewey watch. These
watches marked "Maine" (see back
cover) were made from a two-ton
iron gun, raised up from the
Havanah Harbor that was on the
Maine. Dial says, "Dewey, May 1,
98. American Watch Special."
$500.00.
*Description and watch courtesy of Dan
Doloff, Collector.*

Plate 359. Circa 1880 – 1889.

14K multicolored gold, boxed hinge, hunting **case** with horse head and diamonds; E. Howard & Company, **movement** number 223422, series 7, size N; owned by Joseph A. Keaton, First Battalion Chicago Fire Department.
$7,800.00.
Description and watch courtesy of Jack Harvey, Dealer.

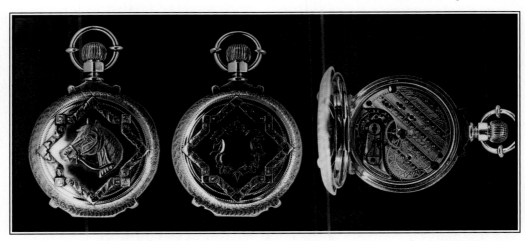

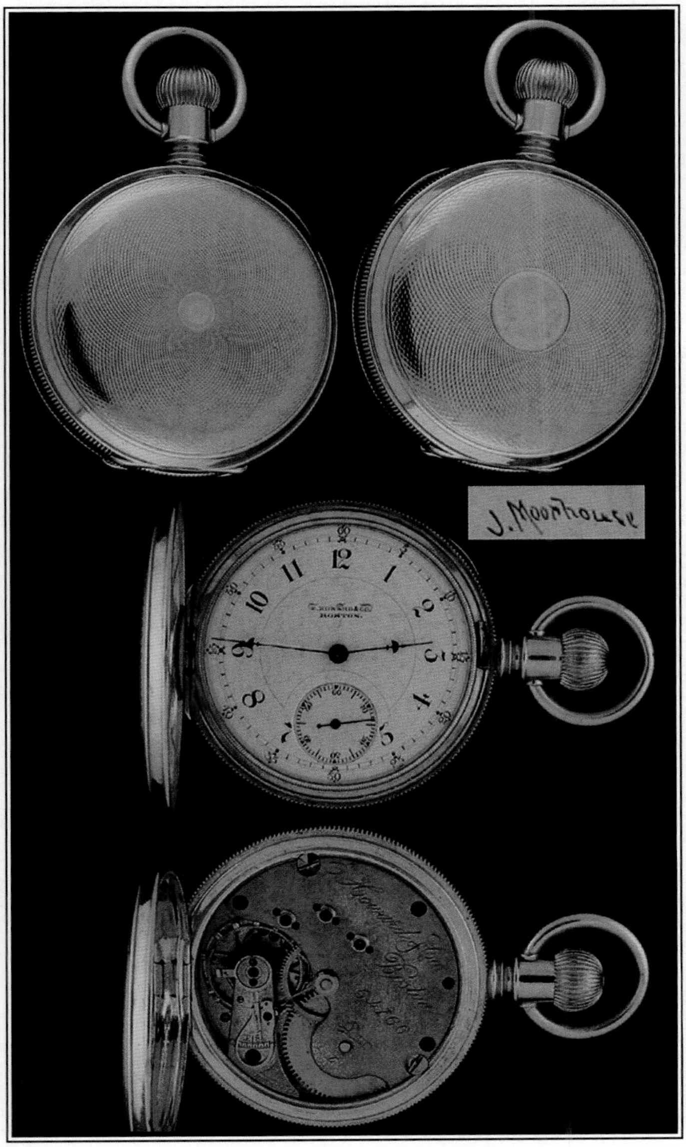

Plate 360. Circa 1889.

Howard 16 size series V, 15 jewels, nice correct 14K solid gold W. P. & H. hunting **case**, single sunk porcelain Moorhouse-signed **dial**, Arabic numerals, blue correct Howard hands, ¾-plate gilt **movement**, marked heat and cold, and a horse, raised gold jewel settings, micrometric regulator (64166).
$4,600.00.
Photo and description courtesy of OldWatch.com.

Plate 361. 1880s – 1890s.

Lady's enamel ball watch studded with diamonds, suspended from a black cord.
$6,400.00.
Description and watch courtesy of Somlo Antiques.

Plate 362. Circa 1890.

Lady's pendant watch, Patek Philippe, case and broach studded with pave-set diamonds, original watch pin.
$17,700.00.
Description and watch courtesy of Somlo Antiques.

Plate 363. Circa 1890.

Hampden 18 size, New Railway, 17 jewels, railroad grade, excellent nickel open-face **case** with town scene on the back, double sunk porcelain **dial**, Arabic numerals, blue spade hands, lever set, beautifully damaskeened full-plate nickel **movement**, marked "New Railway," gold jewel settings, marked adjusted, micrometric regulator (626680). **$425.00.**
Photo and description courtesy of OldWatch.com.

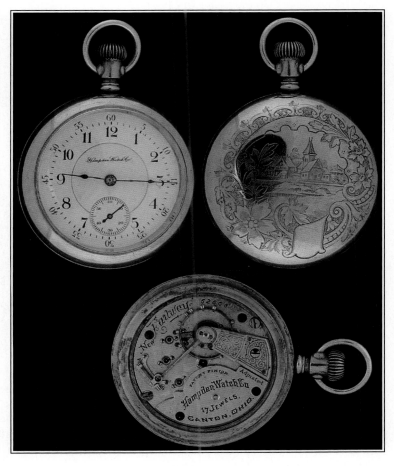

Plate 364. Circa 1890.

Seth Thomas 18 size, 15 jewels, railroad grade, swing-out nickel **case**, double sunk porcelain **dial**, Arabic numerals, blue spade hands, lever set, full-plate two-tone nickel **movement**, gold screw-down jewel settings, micrometric regulator (280455). **$550.00.**
Photo and description courtesy of OldWatch.com.

Plate 365. Louis Audemars, Brassus & Geneva, No. 1049, circa 1890.
Very fine and very rare 18K gold, hunting-cased, astronomical, minute-repeating, perpetual calendar, phases and age of the moon and special patented split-seconds chronograph in original mahogany fitted box, accompanied by original certificate and spare crystal.

Case. Six-body, "bassine et filets," polished, gold hinged cuvette over glazed gold bezel for viewing the movement. **Dial.** White enamel, radial Roman numerals, outer minute track, outermost seconds divided into fifths, five-minute/seconds Arabic markers, four subsidiary sunk dials for days of the week, date, months of the four-year leap cycle, and subsidiary seconds concentric with phases of the moon aperture, blued-steel spade hands. **Movement.** 43 mm (19"), frosted gilt, 35 jewels, straight-line calibrated lever escapement, cut bimetallic compensation balance with Breguet balance spring, chronograph activated by patented vertical coupling via pushbutton to the right of the pendant, repeating on gongs through activating slide in the band.
Signed on dial, case, movement, and box.
Diam. 55 mm. **$48,438.00.**
Photo and description courtesy of Antiquorum Auctioneers, 14 Jun 2003.

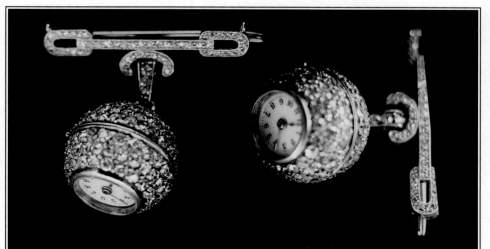

Plate 366. Circa 1890s.

Small ball watch on lapel pin set with diamonds.
$1,200.00.
Description and watch courtesy of Somlo Antiques.

Plate 367. Circa 1890s.

Potter Charmilles 16 size, 7 jewels, excellent original Potter nickel **case**, single sunk porcelain **dial** marked "Charmilles Geneve," blue spade hands, Roman numerals, pendant set, ¾-plate **movement**, marked "Charmilles Potters Patents," non-magnetic hairspring, micrometric regulator (150685). **$975.00.**
Photo and description courtesy of OldWatch.com.

Plate 368. Circa 1880s – 1890s.

American Waltham Watch Co. 4 size, crystal plate or stone **movement**, 16 jewels, coin silver snap back open-face **case**, porcelain **dial** marked "A.W. Co. Waltham," Arabic numerals, blue spade hands, stunning clear quartz plate with metal balance, gold escape wheel, full gold train. There can only be one number one and this is the number one 4 size crystal plate! **$45,000.00.**
Photo and description courtesy of OldWatch.com.

Plate 369. Dent, Watchmaker to the Queen, 61 Strand & 4 Royal Exchange, London, No. 45421, hallmarked 1890 – 1891. Very fine keyless, minute-repeating watch.

Case. Four-body, "bassine et filets." Polished, gold hinged cuvette. **Dial.** White enamel, by Willis. Roman numerals, outer minute track, subsidiary sunk seconds. Spade blued-steel hands. **Movement.** 44 mm, ¾-plate, frosted gilt, 21 jewels, lateral counterpoised lever escapement, cut bimetallic compensation balance with blued-steel Breguet balance spring, diamond endstone, repeating on gongs through activating slide in the band.
Dial and movement signed.
Diam. 52 mm. **$6,900.00.**
Photo and description courtesy of Antiquorum Auctioneers, 21 May 2003.

Plate 370. Haas Jne, Geneva, No. 15527, circa 1890.
Very fine, 18K gold, hunting-cased, keyless, astronomical, minute-repeating watch with perpetual calendar and phases of the moon.

Case. Five-body, "bassine," polished, gold hinged cuvette. **Dial.** White enamel, Roman numerals, outer minute track with gold five-minute markers, four subsidiary dials for days of the week, date, months of the four-year leap cycle, and phases of the moon aperture concentric with subsidiary seconds, spade gold hands. **Movement.** 43 mm (19"), nickel, 31 jewels, straight-line calibrated lever escapement, cut bimetallic compensation balance, Breguet balance spring, punched twice with "Geneva Quality Hallmark," repeating on gongs through a slide on the band.
Case signed.
Diam. 58 mm. **$8,050.00.**
Photo and description courtesy of Antiquorum Auctioneers, 21 May 2003.

Plate 371. Patek Philippe & Cie., Geneve, No. 75322, circa 1890.
Very fine and exceptionally rare t 8K gold and enamel, pearl set, keyless, "Boule de Geneve" watch, suspended from a matching brooch.

Case. Spherical, three-body, entirely set with split pearls, revolving pearl-set bezel winding the watch. Pearl-set brooch with five graduated links, each link in the form of a star, double pin. **Dial.** By Pierre Reymond, white enamel with upright black Arabic numerals, the figure "12" in red, outer minute track, secured by two small screws at 2 and 8 o'clock. Blued-steel spade hands. **Movement.** 17.6 mm (8"), cal. 7L, frost gilt, cylinder escapement, three-arm brass balance with flat balance spring, wound by means of the revolving bezel.
Diam. 21 mm; length with the brooch, 53 mm. **$43,056.00.**
Photo and description courtesy of Antiquorum Auctioneers, 14 Jun 2003.

Plate 372. Circa 1890s.

Ball watch embellished with pearls, suspended from bar pen set with pearls; revival style.
$3,800.00.
Watch and description courtesy of Somlo Antiques.

Plate 373. Unsigned, Swiss, enamel painting signed by Amedee Champod, circa 1890.
Very fine 18K gold and enamel, diamond-set, hunting-cased, keyless, two-train, Grande et petite Sonnerie, quarter-repeating clock-watch made for the Indian market.

Case. Four-body, solid, "bassine et filets," the back cover with a finely painted-on enamel portrait of Nawab Bahadur Khanji. signed "A. C.," the monogram of Champod, the front with the diamond-set monogram "H B," the band and bezels engraved with a repeated pattern, the gold hinged cuvette with a second portrait, a glazed gold bezel below the cuvette to view the movement. **Dial.** White enamel. Roman chapters, subsidiary sunk seconds dial. Blued-steel Breguet hands. **Movement.** IS, nickel, "fausses cotes" decoration, 31 jewels, tandem winding, straight-line lever escapement, cut bimetallic compensation balance, Breguet balance spring, lever set, strikes and repeats on two gongs by a slide in the case band, silence/striking lever at 12 o'clock, changing lever from grande to petite sonnerie at 6 o'clock.
Diam. 52 mm. **$23,000.00.**
Photo and description courtesy of Antiquorum Auctioneers, 19 Mar 2003.

Plate 374. Circa 1890.

LeCoultre, size 16; number of jewels, 32. 14K hunting case minute repeater/chronograph, signed "LeCoultre" under hammer. **$6,200.00.**
Photos and description courtesy of Edward Ueberall, Collector/Dealer.

Plate 375. Henry Capt, Geneve gold minute-repeating, hunting-cased pocket watch, circa 1890.

Case. 18k yellow gold, circular, hinged, four-bodied. **Dial.** White enamel, black Roman numerals, sunk auxiliary seconds dial, blued-steel Lance hands. **Movement.** Rhodiumed, 31 jewels, lever escapement, cut bi-metallic screwed balance wheel, Breguet balance spring.
Signed "Henry Capt" on case, dial, movement.
Diam. 50 mm. **$4,993.75.**
Photo and description courtesy of Bonhams and Butterfields, 21 Mar 2003.

Plate 376. Patek Philippe & Cie., No. 80951, made for Tiffany & Co., circa 1890.
Very fine and rare 18K gold, keyless, split-seconds chronograph watch. Accompanied by an Extract from the Archives.

Case. Four-body, "bassine," with unusual double-bezel construction, chronograph safety bolt at II o'clock, gold hinged cuvette. **Dial.** White enamel, radial Arabic numerals, outer minute ring, outermost chronograph ring with red five-minute/seconds Arabic markers. Spade blued-steel hands. **Movement.** 35 mm (15½"), nickel, half-plate, 25 jewels, straight-line calibrated lever escapement, cut bimetallic compensation balance with Breguet balance spring, split mechanism under the dial. "8s" winding/setting Patek Philippe system.
Dial, case, and movement signed by the retailer.
Diam. 45 mm. **$6,900.00.**
Photo and description courtesy of Antiquorum Auctioneers, 19 Mar 2003.

Plate 377. Hope and Faith, Tiffany & Co., New York, No. 17708, Swiss-made, circa 1890. Very fine 18K gold keyless minute-repeating watch with chronograph.

Case. Four-body, "bassine," with concealed hinge, polished, with engraved coat-of-arms on the back with motto "Speset Fides" (Hope and Faith), gold hinged cuvette. **Dial.** White enamel, radial Arabic numerals, outer minute track, outermost chronograph track divided into fifths, five-minute/seconds red Arabic markers, subsidiary sunk seconds. Blued-steel spade hands. **Movement.** 43 mm, nickel, "fausses cotes" decoration, 35 jewels, straight-line calibrated lever escapement, cut bimetallic compensation balance with Breguet balance spring, repeating on gongs through activating slide in the band.
Signed on dial, case, and movement.
Diam. 54 mm. **$6,279.00.**
Photo and description courtesy of Antiquorum Auctioneers, 19 Mar 2003.

Plate 378. Le Roy & Fils, Horlogers de la Marine, Palais-Royal, 13 & 15, Gallerie Montpensier, Paris, 211 Regent Street, London, No. 54198, circa 1890.
Fine 18K gold, keyless, minute-repeating watch in original fitted box.

Case. Four-body, "bassine et filets," engine-turned back with engraved initials, gold hinged cuvette. **Dial.** White enamel, Roman numerals, outer minute track with five-minute Arabic markers, subsidiary sunk seconds. Gold spade hands. **Movement.** 43 mm, frosted gilt, 31 jewels, straight line calibrated lever escapement, cut bimetallic compensation balance with Breguet balance spring, wolf-tooth winding wheels, repeating on gongs through activating slide in the band.
Signed on the cuvette.
Diam. 51 mm. **$7,176.00.**
Photo and description courtesy of Antiquorum Auctioneers, 14 Jun 2003.

Plate 379. Circa 1890.

Vacheron, size 18; number of jewels, 20; serial number, 265985. Large-size **movement** marketed for the U. S. and Canada railroad market.
$1,100.00.
Photos and description courtesy of Edward Ueberall, Collector/Dealer.

Plate 380. Circa 1890.
Fine Swiss Dent, 18K gold, demi-hunter, quarter-repeater antique pocket watch.

Attractive **case** with elaborate monogram and traces of engine turning. Fine white enamel **dial** with blued-steel hands. Good quality gilt 19-jewel lever **movement** with wolf's-tooth winding. Dust cover inscribed "Examined by Dent, watchmaker to her Majesty and H.R.H. the Prince of Wales..." Dent was the maker of Big Ben. A handsome watch with loud, clear tone.
Diam. 47 mm. **$2,500.00.**
Photo and description courtesy of Stephen Bogoff, Antiquarian Horologist.

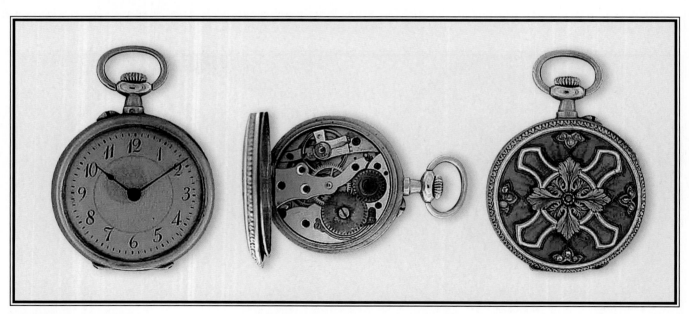

Plate 381. Circa 1890.
Lovely LeCoultre 18K gold, enamel, and diamond antique lady's pendant watch.

Very decorative chased **case** with three colors of enamel and 12 diamonds. Gilt **dial** with blued-steel hands. Gilt 10-jewel oxidized cylinder **movement**.
Diam. 30 mm. **$1,300.00.**
Photo and description courtesy of Stephen Bogoff, Antiquarian Horologist.

Plate 382. Circa 1890.
Fine and lovely Swiss LeCoultre 18K gold and enamel lady's Art Nouveau antique pendant watch.

Fabulous **case** with high relief applied enamel and diamond flowers wrapping around from the back across the band and onto the front, the floral motif continued on the bow. Fine enamel **dial** with gold and silver minute marks and fancy gilt hands. Gilt 10-jewel cylinder **movement**. An exceptional watch in superb condition.
Diam. 24 mm. **$2,750.00.**
Photo and description courtesy of Stephen Bogoff, Antiquarian Horologist.

Plate 383. Circa 1892.

Patek Philippe, size 16; number of jewels, 20; serial number, 92403. Made as private label for Spaulding & Co. Fits standard 16 size case.
$1,850.00.
Photo and description courtesy of Edward Ueberall, Collector/Dealer.

Plate 384. Circa 1892.

Hampden size 16, model 2, grade D; number of jewels, 17; serial number, 815757. Micrometer regulator is missing.
$185.00.
Photos and description courtesy of Edward Ueberall, Collector/Dealer.

Plate 385. Patek Philippe & Cie., Geneve, No. 92747, case No. 209011, circa 1892.
Very fine, massive, 18K gold, hunting-cased keyless pocket watch.

Case. Five-body, "bassine," engine turned, gold hinged cuvette. **Dial.** White enamel, Breguet numerals, outer minute track, subsidiary sunk seconds. Gold Louis XV hands. **Movement.** 42 mm (19"), cal. 180, frosted gilt, 20 jewels, straight-line calibrated lever escapement, cut bimetallic compensation balance with Breguet balance spring, Wilmot patented micrometric cam regulator. Signed on dial, case, and movement.
Diam. 53 mm. **$3,409.00.**
Photo and description courtesy of Antiquorum Auctioneers.

Plate 386. Circa 1893.

Hamilton 18 size, 7 jewels, nice silverode open-face screw-back **case**, single sunk porcelain **dial**, Roman numerals, blue morning glory hands, lever set, beautiful full-plate gilt **movement**, micrometric regulator (2756). A first year watch! A first-run watch! One of only 1,300 ever made!
$2,700.00.
Photo and description courtesy of OldWatch.com.

Plate 387. Circa 1895.

Elgin 18 size, grade 149, 21 jewels, railroad grade, 14k solid gold boxed hinged hunting **case**, double sunk porcelain Canadian railroad **dial**, Roman/Arabic numerals, blue spade hands, lever set, full-plate nickel **movement**, with red inlay, marked adjusted, gold jewel settings, micrometric regulator (6348014). This is a first-run watch. It is in the first run of 18 size, 21-jewel Elgin watches ever made! Canadian railroad dial.
$4,500.00.
Photo and description courtesy of OldWatch.com.

Plate 388. Circa 1895.
Good Swiss 18K gold and diamond antique lady's pendant watch.

Cover set with 25 good-size diamonds in the design of a star surrounded by comets. Good white enamel **dial** with gold minute markers and gold hands. Gilt ten-jewel cylinder **movement**.
Diam. 25 mm. **$1,650.00.**
Photo and description courtesy of Stephen Bogoff, Antiquarian Horologist.

Plate 389. Circa 1895.
Good Swiss LeCoultre 18K gold minute-repeater antique pocket watch.

Substantial plain polish **case**. White enamel **dial** with decal for 13 – 24 (which, if you like, can be easily removed). Gile 29-jewel lever **movement** jeweled to the center and the hammers and signed "LeCoultre" under one of the hammers. A solid watch from a well-respected maker in particularly fine condition with loud, clear tone.
Diam. 53 mm. **$4,250.00.**
Photo and description courtesy of Stephen Bogoff, Antiquarian Horologist.

Plate 390. Circa 1895.

Elgin, size 18, model 2, grade 149; number of jewels, 21; serial number, 6360522. Early 21-jewel RR-approved hunting **movement**. **$520.00.**
Photos and description courtesy of Edward Ueberall, Collector/Dealer.

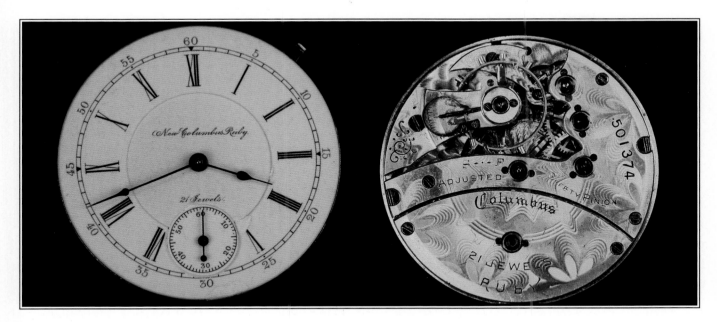

Plate 391. Circa 1895.

Size 16, model 1, 21 jewels; serial number, 501374. Only 16 size, 21-jewel watch made by Columbus. **$1,100.00.**
Photos and description courtesy of Edward Ueberall, Collector/Dealer.

Plate 392. Circa 1895.
Fine, rare, and beautiful Patek Philippe 18K gold, diamond, and enamel repoussé pair-case lady's antique pendant watch.

This watch is in the style of watches made 100 – 200 years earlier. **Outer case** repoussé with a classical scene. White enamel **dial** with blue and red numbers and fancy gold hands. The **inner case** covered with cobalt blue enamel and 47 diamonds, the back with a cartouche of painted enamel flowers. The **movement** in a **third, inner, case** with crystal over the nickel 18-jewel movement #107,961 with wolf's-tooth winding. The dial with hairlines and two minor cobalt enamel repairs. Spectacular watch by the maker of the very best watches.
Diam. 32 mm. **$20,000.00.**
Photo and description courtesy of Stephen Bogoff, Antiquarian Horologist.

Plate 393. Circa 1896.

Waltham, size 16; number of jewels, 21; serial number, 7000605. Uses four diamond endstones. Special **dial** with "Waltham" in script.
$2,150.00.
Photo and description courtesy of Edward Ueberall, Collector/Dealer.

Plate 394. Circa 1897.

Waltham, size 18, model 1892, grade Special; number of jewels, 21; serial number, 7902813. Made for use on Canadian Pacific Railway.
$2,700.00.
Photos and description courtesy of Edward Ueberall, Collector/Dealer.

Plate 395. Circa 1897.

Gruen, size 16, grade Precision; number of jewels, 20; serial number, 63414. Made by Assman in Dresden Germany for Gruen. Accepted for RR service.

$1,300.00.

Photos and description courtesy of Edward Ueberall, Collector/Dealer.

Plate 396. Circa 1897. Fine lady's Patek 18K gold Philippe antique hunting case pendant watch.

Fine white enamel **dial** signed by the retailer, with fancy gold hands. Nickel 18-jewel **movement** marked "Special," with wolf's-tooth winding. Diam. 30 mm. **$1,650.00.**
Photo and description courtesy of Stephen Bogoff, Antiquarian Horologist.

Plate 397. Circa 1898.

Elgin 6 size, seven jewels, excellent coin silver hunting **case**, single sunk porcelain **dial**, Roman numerals, blue spade hands, lever set, ¾-plate gilt **movement**, micrometric regulator (783501).
$325.00.
Photo and description courtesy of OldWatch.com.

Plate 398. Circa 1898.

Hampden Watch Company, open face, engraved inside "Captain A. L. Potter, Co F, Second Mass, USV, Lakeland, Fla, Tampa, Fla, Santiago, Cuba 1898," sterling silver carried by Rough Riders. Went up San Juan Hill with Rough Riders.
$8,000.00.
Description and watch courtesy of Dan Doloff, Collector.

Plate 399. Circa 1898.

Hampden, size 16, model 2; serial number, 1040615. TuTone **movement**, very early high-grade 23-jewel movement. Detail of hunting case engraving.

$1,025.00.

Photos and description courtesy of Edward Ueberall, Collector/Dealer.

Plate 400. Circa 1898.

Hamilton, size 16, H. W. Wheeler, number of jewels, 21; serial number, 175111. Special grade made for Wheeler, a major NYC wholesaler.

$1,900.00.

Photos and description courtesy of Edward Ueberall, Collector/Dealer.

Plate 401. Circa 1898.

Columbus 18 size, the President, 17 jewels, railroad grade, nice yellow-gold-filled hunting **case**, double sunk porcelain **dial**. Marked "The President," 17 jewels, Arabic numerals, blue spade hands, lever set, full-plate nickel two-tone **movement**, raised gold screw-down jewel settings, marked adjusted, micrometric regulator (335848). The 17-jewel the President hunter is a hard watch to find. The President 17-jewels marked dial is even harder to find!

$1,750.00.

Photo and description courtesy of OldWatch.com.

Plate 402. Circa 1899.

Seth Thomas, size 18, model 5, grade Maiden Lane; number of jewels, 24; serial number, 208875. Multicolor gold-filled **case**, radial numeral 24-hour **dial**.

$3,350.00.

Photos and description courtesy of Edward Ueberall, Collector/Dealer.

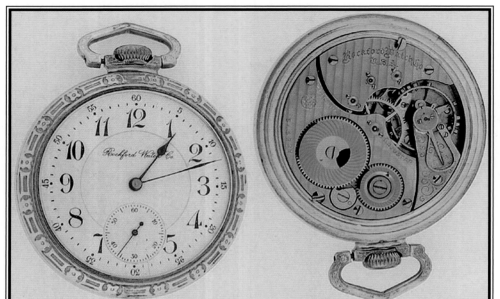

Plate 403. Circa 1899.

Rockford 16 size, 535 RG, 21 jewels, railroad grade, nice yellow gold open-face **case**, double sunk porcelain **dial**, Arabic numerals, blue spade hands, lever set, beautifully damaskeened ¾-plate nickel **movement** with gold inlay, marked "RG," gold jewel settings, marked adjusted, double roller, full gold train, micrometric regulator (545229).

$1,250.00.
Photo and description courtesy of OldWatch.com.

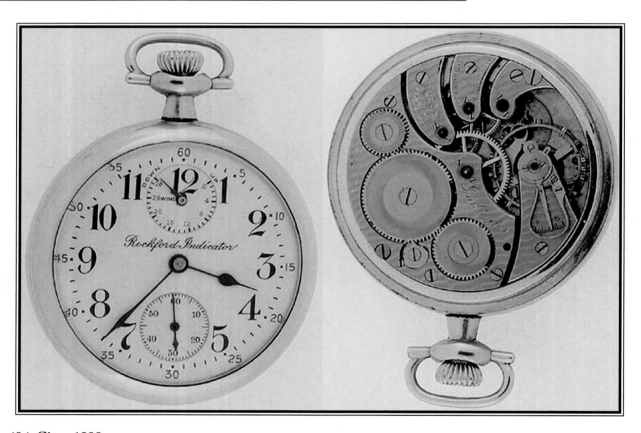

Plate 404. Circa 1899.

Rockford 16 size, indicator, wind indicator, 17 jewels, railroad grade, excellent yellow-gold-filled open-face screw-back **case**, nice single sunk porcelain wind indicator **dial**, Arabic numerals, blue spade hands, three-finger bridge nickel **movement** with gold inlay, marked indicator gold jewel settings, gold center wheel, marked adjusted, micrometric regulator (833334) circa 1910.

$2,500.00.
Photo and description courtesy of OldWatch.com.

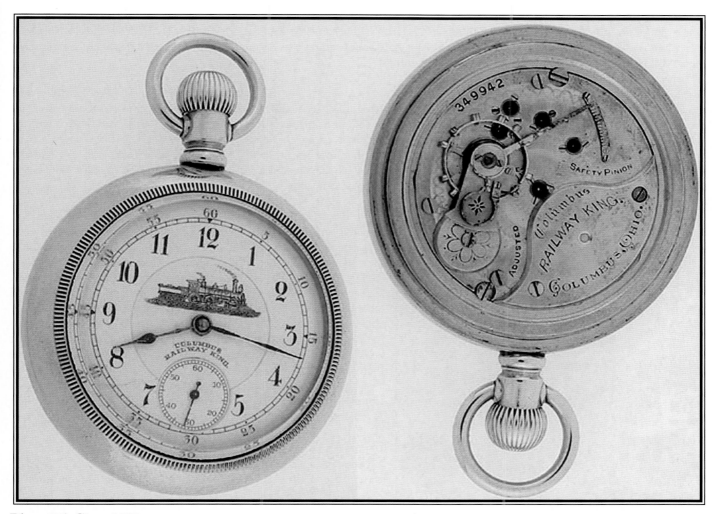

Plate 405. Circa 1899.

Columbus 18 size Columbus Railway King, 17 jewels, railroad grade, nice silverode screw-back open-face **case**, double sunk porcelain **dial** marked "Columbus Railway King with CHOO CHOO," Arabic numerals, blue spade hands, lever set, full plate nickel two-tone **movement**, screw-down jewel settings, marked adjusted, micrometric regulator (349942).
$1,400.00.
Photo and description courtesy of OldWatch.com.

Chapter V
FROM RAILROAD WATCHES TO SWISS DOMINANCE THE FIRST HALF OF THE TWENTIETH CENTURY

THE TIMES

The twentieth century began on a note of optimism. America had become the leading industrial nation in the world. In New York society, 400 people could boast of more diamonds than some European royalty. At the same time, other were living in slum tenements. But rich or poor, people still appreciated lovely things.

Art Nouveau had revived the art of enameling. Enameled watches were made in this style in Europe and in America. For those on a more limited budget, the New England Watch Company made beautifully enameled 0 size ladies' watches to provide accurate time for the women now going to work in offices. For those who could not afford the enamel version, New England Watch Company made watches in different finishes and patterns. Until 1904, New England used mostly duplex escapements. In 1904, it introduced a small four-jewel lady's watch. This was the smallest watch made in America at that time. By 1917, other companies, such as Elgin and Waltham, also offered watches in the size. For those with a larger budget, companies like Vacheron, Constantin, Patek Philippe, and Henri Capt made beautifully enameled and jeweled works of art in the same style.

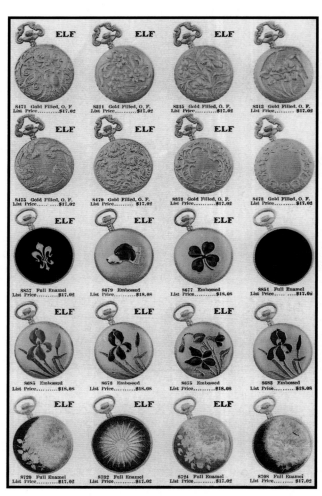

Plate 406. New England Watch Company watches in embossed, gold-filled, and enamel cases circa 1909.

The railroad standards had made many people aware of what was required for a good-quality watch. They might not have known what a bimetallic balance was, but they did know what a jewel was. Or at least they thought they did. To many, jewels equaled value. If a customer wanted more jewels in a movement, the watch cost more. What people didn't realize was that the higher price more reflected labor cost than jewel value. Synthetic sapphires and rubies were available in this time period, and when natural stones were used, they were industrial grade, not gem quality. In spite of this, the stones do look beautiful. Believe it or not, some people are still reluctant to leave their watches to be repaired for fear that the watch repair person will steal the jewels. Believe me, doing so would not be worth the time or trouble. Playing on the public's concept of the value of jewels, the American watch companies tried to "out jewel" each other.

Railroad watches were extremely popular. Railroads required them, but there were others who just wanted the quality of a railroad-grade watch. According to Dan Doloff, a long standing member of N.A.W.C.C., the three Bs of railroad watches are the "Bs, the Balls and the Buns." This represents the 992 B watches made by Hamilton, the Bun Specials produced by Hamilton, and those watches produced by the Ball Watch Company that have the company name on the dial. If the watch was not a railroad grade, but it had a train on the dial or on the case, it was highly prized.

During these same years, the Swiss watch companies were selling wristwatches. As early as 1885, Girard Perregaux and other Swiss watch companies already had orders from Berlin for military wristwatches for German naval officers. When the Swiss had the wake-up call to mechanize, they also developed the machinery necessary for wristwatches. They had tried to introduce them into the U.S. in the latter part of the nineteenth century, but the wholesale buyers had rejected the watches, saying that the American people would never accept a wristwatch. Slowly but surely, the American people proved the wholesalers wrong.

By 1913, wristwatches were already creeping into catalogs. The *Universal Trading Catalog* of 1913 included 21 pages of pocket watches and three ladies' bracelet watches. *The National Coat and Suit Catalog* for spring and summer 1916 featured a bracelet to convert a lady's pendant watch into a wristwatch. In three years, wristwatches had gained more acceptance. That 1916 issue included six pages of men's pocket watches, and only three bracelet watches.

The American Watch Companies were not equiped to make wristwatches. This was a major problem, because gearing up for a new line sometimes took years and a huge amount of capital. Working with what they had, American companies started by using 0 size pendant watches, because they could be easily converted into wristwatches. Some of the ladies' watches were sold in a box that included the pendant watch, a watch pin, and a band to convert it to a wristwatch.

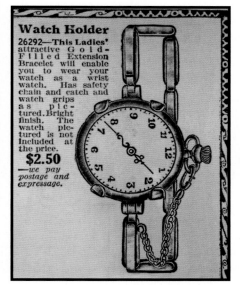

Plate 407. A catalog advertisement showing a watch bracelet, used to convert a pendant watch to a wristwatch.

Plate 408. Sisters, all wearing their watches. One is holding her diploma, and one is most likely a teacher. Their watches are attached with watch pins, but these are attached to a watch slide chain. The watches, chains, and pins are all contemporaneous to the photograph.

THE WAR TO END ALL WARS
On April 6, 1917, a declaration of war was passed by Congress. America was drawn into the "War to End All Wars." Necessary changes were made to the pocket watch during the war years. The pin-set watch had to be replaced by the more convenient one that was set by pulling out the crown and stem. Because it was necessary to be able to tell the time at night, luminescent dials or hands were often added.

During these years, it became increasingly evident that the pocket watch was losing its battle to the wristwatch. Soldiers in fox holes found it difficult to pull watches from their pockets and check the time while being on guard for the enemy. Consequently, the war helped to make men's wristwatches an acceptable, utilitarian accessory. It might be a coincidence, but the same year that we entered the war, the *John V. Farrell Company Catalog*, which had 22 pages of pocket watches, for the first time included one man's wristwatch. The watch was priced at $6.00.

After the war, wristwatches became increasingly popular. The war also put an end to Art Nouveau style. The world had had to face the grim realities of war, and the spirit of fantasy and illusion that had been captured by Art Nouveau designs faded into the past.

THE TWENTIES
The twenties were years of action and reaction. The word used most to describe this decade is "roaring," but "scandalous," "shocking," and "flaming" are also apt adjectives. The world had survived the war, and a feeling of recklessness prevailed.

When the Eighteenth Amendment made alcohol illegal, it became fashionable to break the law. Speakeasies sprang up overnight, and with them came a new devil-may-care society. The forbidden, the sinister, and the shocking had more allure than ever before. It did not take long for organized crime to become involved in bootlegging. Al Capone and his business associates made headlines. Instead of watching this criminal drama with disdain and disgust, many Americans were fascinated and sometimes even envious. The country's values were turned upside down, and money glittered on top of the heap.

This recklessness was also expressed in the popular dances. The loose and uninhibited steps of the Charleston and the Black Bottom were performed across the nations. Dance marathons became the rage. Couples danced for days and sometime weeks to win the prizes these contests offered.

This new age welcomed the new decorative style that is now called Art Deco. The name applied to this decorative style of the 1920s and 1930s was never used during the time period in which the style was popular. Art Deco takes its name from the International Exposition des Arts Decoratifs that was held in Paris in 1925. Nations from all over the world were invited to participate, with the stipulation that they submit only those exhibitions executed in modern designs. Any designs based on styles of the past, or that incorporated those styles, were strictly forbidden. Art Nouveau had been an expression of rejection of machines, but the Art Deco style embraced machines and the things they could produce. The exposition became the focal point for new, modernistic designs. In the years that followed, the new style became more defined.

Through the set designs of the Ballets Russes, which made its 1910 debut performance in Paris, many people were exposed for the first time to modern art. Cubism and its offspring — orphism, neoplastecism, fauvism, and futurism — provided the geometric lines and abstract designs for Art Deco style. The new art expressed a psychology of design for people living in a modern world filled with action and speed.

Automobiles increasingly had an effect on the American way of life. Fifteen million new cars were registered between 1920 and 1929. As production rose, prices declined. By 1924 a Tin Lizzie could be brought for as little as $290.00. (It's interesting to note that a Premier Maximus watch in an 18k case sold for about $400.00 at that time.) With 470,000 people employed by the automobile industry, the car was becoming a way of life. People who did not even own a bathtub took pride owning a new automobile.

All companies were offering merchandise on deferred payment plans. Why wait to own a new car, radio, or even watch, when for only a few dollars down and a few dollars a month, it could be enjoyed now? More and more people adopted this philosophy, even though such plans increased customer costs.

The *C. B. Norton Catalog* for 1924 included a new watch "built by Elgin for railroad service." The movement was a B. W. Raymond with 21 jewels and eight adjustments (five of which were positioned). "A long thin main spring ensured a run of 40 hours on one winding." It was priced at only $55.00 in a 20-year-guaranteed, yellow-gold-filled case. It also included the Corsican, which was a "series of 12 sized, thin model Elgins." These watches had 21 jewels, Lord Elgin movement, eight adjustments, and the finest craftsmanship throughout. They came in a choice of 14k green gold with a white gold back, green gold with a white gold bezel and border, or an all white gold, all green gold, or all yellow gold. The sleek look of the watches reflected some of the elements of Art Deco style. A Corsican watch listed for $207.80.

The descriptive words for 1920s are *sleek* and *chic* and thin was definitely in. Even though the wristwatch was becoming more popular, pocket watches were still highly sought after. American watch companies were making the finest watches of the twentieth century. They were waging a battle against the competition of the wristwatch and they were bringing out their big guns — their premium grades.

If someone wanted a Premier Maximus, it was priced at $620.00 in a 14k gold case. The Howard railroad watch grade number 23 with 21 jewels was listed for $233.50 in 18k gold, and the Howard period watches such as the Tudor, Agustan, Ionic, Doric, and Victorian, sold from $82.50 to $159.00. The Illinois Watch Company came out with The Illini. It was an extremely thin 12 size, with 21 jewels and adjusted to five positions. It also came in five different style choices. The Farrell's 1924 catalog listed Illini watches from $170.00 to $220.00.

For the budget minded, the catalog included Ingersoll watches. The Ingersoll jeweled 12 size Waterbury could be bought for $5.00, the Radiolite for $6.00, the Midget for $3.50, or the Yankee (now referred to as the "New Yankee") for $2.00.

Everybody loves success stories. After hearing how average people had made fortunes in the stock market, the general public was eager to try its luck. Housewives shaved money from their household allowance to invest. Instead of putting the money into savings accounts, people bought stocks, hoping to make their fortunes. But on October 24, 1929, the bubble burst. The market went under, carrying with it the hopes, dreams, and fortunes of thousands of people.

Things were not looking good for the American watch industry. According to Mike Harrold, in 1924 pocket watches had 85% of the market, and wristwatches had 15%. By 1929 the roles had reversed; wristwatches had 85% of the market. Most American watch companies did not have the money or the inclination to spend the huge amount it would take to "tool up" for wristwatches. Ingersoll had closed in 1922, New York Standard in 1925, and Illinois in 1927.

THE THIRTIES

The thirties began on a somber note. After the gaiety of the twenties, the thirties were a nightmare. Alan Jenkins described this decade in his book *The Thirties*: "This was the depression, the slump, deeper than anyone could have imagined, after the twenties bull market and the 1929 crash; the first middle class poverty that America had ever known, the worst years America went through not excluding two world wars."

Then came F. D. Roosevelt and his New Deal. No one really knew what this New Deal was, but almost anything would be better than what they had. Roosevelt won the election by a landslide. True to his word, he immediately began to implement new government programs. These programs became known to the people by their initials. The NRA regulated working hours and wages; the CCC employed young men to work in areas of conservation; the PWA financed the programs of the WPA. People were employed to do everything from building bridges to entertaining. The nation was working its way out of the economic crisis. Roosevelt's New Deal was the right deal.

During this time of uncertainty, radio offered a delightful means of escape. By turning to *Amos n' Andy*, people could forget their troubles and laugh. Movies were more popular than ever. A double feature complete with newsreel was only a dime, a small price to be transported into a make-believe world of glamour, sophistication, and adventure.

In the latter years of the decade, a new sound played to a new beat emerged. The sound was big band; the beat was swing. The new pied pipers were Benny Goodman, Glenn Miller, Jimmy Dorsey, and Artie Shaw. With this new style came jive talk and jitterbugging. A new generation had emerged.

By the end of the decade, America had a new hope — technology. People felt that through science and engineering, the world would become a better place in which to live. DuPont was developing new materials such as nylon and polyethylene. Laboratories were experimenting with sulphur drugs and antibodies. In 1939, the World's Fair opened in New York. It was filled with displays that pointed to a future bright with hope.

Unfortunately, "future bright with hope" was not a phrase that applied to the American watch industry. By the 1930s, pocket watches were becoming passé. The Montgomery Ward Catalog for fall and winter 1931 – 1932 included five full pages of wristwatches and only two full pages of pocket watches. The next year, the Sears catalog still had some pocket watches, but they were mostly railroad grade. The Sears Catalog for 1936 – 1937 contained seven full pages of wristwatches and only two partial pages of pocket watches. It did include the so-called new lapel watch. In that same year, the Swiss, with their wristwatches, surpassed the U.S. in production of watches. By 1939, the Sears catalogue featured seven pages of wristwatches and only 1¾ pages of pocket watches. Wristwatches had definitely won the popularity contest. Consequently, railroad watches were going down, down, down in price.

If the replacement of pocket watches by wristwatches was not a big enough problem, a second blow to America's watch industry came when the the U.S. signed the Reciprocal Trade Treaty. This treaty lowered the duties on Swiss watches by 50%. This, coupled with the inflationary period in the U.S. after WWII, priced American labor out of the watch business. America could no longer compete with Switzerland. Howard and Hampden went out of business in 1930. In that same year, Russia purchased Hampden and Ansonia in order to start a watch industry. By 1936, Switzerland had surpassed America in the production of watches.

ANOTHER WAR

The 1940s dawned on a world filled with "wars and rumors of war." Most Americans did not want to become involved in these foreign entanglements. However, as the European situation changed, people began to think that the United States should give aid to Great Britain. Any indecisiveness about American involvement was in World War II shattered on December 7, 1941, when the Japanese bombed Pearl Harbor. Shocked and indignant, the country united to fight the enemy.

Everyone pulled together to ease the workload created by the war. Ships, planes, guns, shells, and a million other things were needed to win the war. There was work for everyone. Almost 18 million women worked outside the home. My mother worked for Rheem's Manufacturing Company in Birmingham, Alabama. When she brought home ashtrays, vases, and pencil holders, all made from the gun casings that the company produced, I was thrilled to see "real gun shells."

Women discovered that they could do jobs that had traditionally been assigned to men, and do them well. Many women did volunteer work in blood banks and canteens. Others planted gardens and raised a large portion of their food. These activities made them feel like working partners with the men in uniform. These jobs did not lend themselves to wearing a pendant watch. Most women began to wear wristwatches.

People were earning more money than ever before, but there was little to spend it on. The war had caused shortages in everything from gasoline to sugar. Rationing coupons and points became a part of American life. The slogan "use it up — wear it out — make it do" was enacted daily by people who wanted to do their part in the war effort. Money was needed to win the war, and the public responded to this need by putting its money into war bonds.

During the war, Elgin and Waltham not only made watches but also made unusual timers for the government. Waltham's Admiralty #6 pattern stopwatch, circa 1940, was made to measure distances up to 5,000 yards.[45] The war's emphasis on timers made the general public aware of them. Catalogs were filled with timers.

When the war ended on August 14, 1945, people celebrated by ringing church bells, kissing strangers, blowing whistles, and partying. At last their friend and loved ones would be coming home; Congress had prepared for the homecoming by passing the GI Bill of Rights. This program provided funds to make the veterans' assimilation back into society easier. Money was made available to them for going back to school, buying a house, or going into business.

By 1950, Waltham was out of business. Elgin held out until the early 1960s. Ball Watch Company closed in 1969, and Hamilton produced its last American Railroad Watch that same year. Thus ended the American reign of the pocket and railroad watch industry. The Swiss reigned supreme.

Plate 409. A postcard of Waltham Watch Factory.

Plate 410. Elgin watch factory.

Plate 411. South Bend Watch Company.

FIFTY YEARS OF CATALOG WATCHES

Instead of looking at the cases, dials, and embellishments separately, as we did in the last century, we will look at the watches the way many Americans did, through catalogs. Included are catalogs from companies such as Sears Roebuck and Company and Montgomery Ward, along with jewelers' trade catalogs from which many retail stores ordered their stock.

Please take into consideration that even though there are Swiss watches included in these selections, they are not from the high-end Swiss companies. Those watches are well represented in the Watch section.

Plate 412. These three advertisements appeared in the April 1900 issue of *McCall's Magazine*. In the first two, the watch companies seem to be enlisting women to sell watches by forming clubs, in order to get watches at wholesale prices. The third advertisement offers a watch as a premium for selling jewelry.

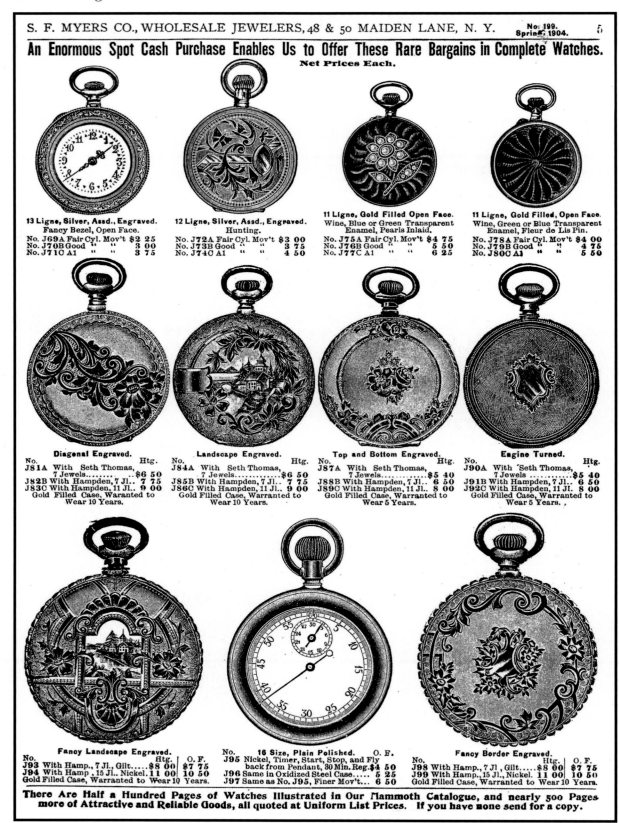

An Enormous Spot Cash Purchase Enables Us to Offer These Rare Bargains in Complete Watches.

Net Prices Each.

13 Ligne, Silver, Assd., Engraved. Fancy Bezel, Open Face.
No. J69A Fair Cyl. Mov't $2 25
No. J70B Good " " 3 00
No. J71C A1 " " 3 75

12 Ligne, Silver, Assd., Engraved. Hunting.
No. J72A Fair Cyl. Mov't $3 00
No. J73B Good " " 3 75
No. J74C A1 " " 4 50

11 Ligne, Gold Filled Open Face. Wine, Blue or Green Transparent Enamel, Pearls Inlaid.
No. J75A Fair Cyl. Mov't $4 75
No. J76B Good " " 5 50
No. J77C A1 " " 6 25

11 Ligne, Gold Filled, Open Face. Wine, Green or Blue Transparent Enamel, Fleur de Lis Pin.
No. J78A Fair Cyl. Mov't $4 00
No. J79B Good " " 4 75
No. J80C A1 " " 5 50

Diagonal Engraved.
No. Htg.
J81A With Seth Thomas, 7 Jewels.........$6 50
J82B With Hampden, 7 Jl.. 7 75
J83C With Hampden, 11 Jl.. 9 00
Gold Filled Case, Warranted to Wear 10 Years.

Landscape Engraved.
No. Htg.
J84A With Seth Thomas, 7 Jewels.........$6 50
J85B With Hampden, 7 Jl.. 7 75
J86C With Hampden, 11 Jl.. 9 00
Gold Filled Case, Warranted to Wear 10 Years.

Top and Bottom Engraved.
No. Htg.
J87A With Seth Thomas, 7 Jewels.........$5 40
J88B With Hampden, 7 Jl.. 6 50
J89C With Hampden, 11 Jl.. 8 00
Gold Filled Case, Warranted to Wear 5 Years.

Engine Turned.
No. Htg.
J90A With Seth Thomas, 7 Jewels.........$5 40
J91B With Hampden, 7 Jl.. 6 50
J92C With Hampden, 11 Jl.. 8 00
Gold Filled Case, Warranted to Wear 5 Years.

Fancy Landscape Engraved.
No. Htg. O. F.
J93 With Hamp., 7 Jl., Gilt.....$8 00 $7 75
J94 With Hamp., 15 Jl.. Nickel. 11 00 10 50
Gold Filled Case, Warranted to Wear 10 Years.

16 Size, Plain Polished. O. F.
No.
J95 Nickel, Timer, Start, Stop, and Fly back from Pendant, 30 Min. Reg.$4 50
J96 Same in Oxidized Steel Case..... 5 25
J97 Same as No. J95, Finer Mov't... 6 50

Fancy Border Engraved.
No. Htg. O. F.
J98 With Hamp., 7 Jl., Gilt.....$8 00 $7 75
J99 With Hamp., 15 Jl., Nickel. 11 00 10 50
Gold Filled Case, Warranted to Wear 10 Years.

There Are Half a Hundred Pages of Watches Illustrated in Our Mammoth Catalogue, and nearly 500 Pages more of Attractive and Reliable Goods, all quoted at Uniform List Prices. If you have none send for a copy.

Plate 413. This page from the *S. F. Meyers Co. Wholesale Jewelers Catalogue*, spring 1904, includes enamel Swiss watches, Seth Thomas watches, and Hampden watches. The middle watch on the bottom row is a timer that could be ordered in a nickel or an oxidized steel case.

A Courageous Bursting of PRICES Among GOOD SELLERS

NET PRICES EACH.

Silver—Top and Bottom Engraved.
6 Size. Stem Wind.   Hunting.
No. J100 With Hampden, 7 Jewel, Gilt $7 25
No. J101 With Hampden, 11 Jewel, Nick. 8 50
No. J102 With Hampden, 15 Jewl., Nic. 9 25

Silver, Fancy Engraved.
12 Size, Stem Wind. Fits 6 Size Movement.
                                    H. C.   O. F.
No. J103 With Hamp. 7 J., Gilt $7 50 $7 00
No. J104 With Hamp. 11 J., N. 8 75   8 25
No. J105 With Hamp. 15 J., N. 9 50   9 00

Silver, Plain Polished.
12 Size, Stem Wind.
                            O. F.   S.B.&B.
No. J106 Walt. or Elg. Hunt.
  7 Jewel, Nickel......$9 25 $9 00 $8 45
No. J107 Walt. or Elg.
  15 Jewel, Nickel......12 00 11 75   11 20

18 Size, 3 Oz., Silverore, Plain Polished or Engraved.
                                        O. F.
No. J108 With Hampden, 7 Jew., Gilt...$4 40
No. J109 With Hampden, 11 Jew., Nick. 5 50
No. J110 With Hampden, 15 Jew., P. R. 6 50
No. J111 With Hampden, 17 Jew., A... 9 50

18 Size, Double Stock, Plain, Gold Inlaid Locomotive or Stag.
                                        O. F.
No. J112 With Hampden, 7 Jew., Gilt. $7 50
No. J113 With Hampden, 11 Jew., Nic.   8 75
No. J114 With Hampden, 15 J., P. R..   9 75
No. J115 With Hampden, 17 Jew., A... 11 25

16 Size, Gold Filled Engine Turned.
Case Warranted 20 Years.
                                     Hunting.
No. J116 With Hampden, 7 Jew., Gilt.$ 8 00
No. J117 With Hampden, 15 Jew., Nic. 10 25
No. J118 With Hampden, 17 Jew., Nic. 13 75

SPECIAL { No. J143 1904 Thin Model. 16 Size, "Ansonia" Watches, Nickel Case, Open Face, Plain, 30 Hours' Time, Stem Wind and Pendent Set, each **$1.00**
No. J144 Ingersoll's "Yankee" Watch, Gents' Size, Nickel Case, Open Face, Jointed Back, Gilt Works, Sets and Regulates with Key Attachment, each **80 cents**

There are Half a Hundred Pages of Watches illustrated in Our Mammoth Catalogue, and nearly 500 Pages more of Attractive and Reliable Goods, all quoted at Uniform List Prices. If you have none send for a copy.

The beautiful "Meloton" Piano has been especially designed to meet the demand for a Superior Instrument at a Moderate Price. In Material Value, Superb Musical Qualities, Perfect Workmanship, Beauty of Finish, Guaranteed Durability and Artistic Excellence it has no superior. Interesting details and prices will be found on back cover of this Bulletin.

Plate 414. Another page from the same 1904 catalog. It's interesting to note that this page contains a thin watch and also one that has three ounces of silverore.

8 No. 199.
Spring, 1904.   S. F. MYERS CO., WHOLESALE JEWELERS, 48 & 50 MAIDEN LANE, N. Y.

LADIES' "OOO" SIZE, Solid Gold and Gold Filled, DUEBER-HAMPDEN HUNTING CASE WATCHES.

The Smallest Reliable American Watch Made. Sold Only as Complete Watches.
Gold Filled Cases, Warranted to Wear 25 Years.   Net Prices Each.

Solid Gold, Fancy Engraved.	Solid Gold, Plain Polished.	Solid Gold, Diagonal Engraved.	Solid Gold, Verm. Borders, Engr.
No. Hunt.	No. Hunt. O. F.	No. Hunt.	No. Hunt.
J150 7 Jewels, Gilt.....$18 50	J153 7 Jewels, Gilt....$18 50 | $18 00	J156 7 Jewels, Gilt....$18 50	J159 7 Jewels, Gilt....$18 50
J151 15 Jewels, Nickel.. 22 00	J154 15 Jewels, Nickel.. 22 00 | 21 50	J157 15 Jewels, Nickel.. 22 00	J160 15 Jewels, Nickel.. 22 00
J152 16 Jls., Nickel, P.R. 24 00	J155 16 Jls., Nickel, P.R. 24 00 |	J158 16 Jls., Nickel, P.R. 24 00	J161 16 Jls., Nickel, P.R. 24 00

Gold Filled, Plain Engraved.	Gold Filled, Plain Polished.	Gold Filled, Fancy Engraved.	Gold Filled, Fancy Engraved.
No. Hunt.	No. Hunt. O. F.	No. Hunt.	No. Hunt.
J162 7 Jewels, Gilt.....$12 50	J165 7 Jewels, Gilt. ...$12 50 | $12 00	J168 7 Jewels, Gilt.....$12 50	J171 7 Jewels, Gilt.....$12 50
J163 15 Jewels, Nickel.. 16 00	J166 15 Jewels, Nickel . 16 00 | 15 50	J169 15 Jewels, Nickel.. 16 00	J172 15 Jewels, Nickel.. 16 00
J164 16 Jewels, Nickel.. 18 00	J167 16 Jls., Nickel, P.R. 18 00 |	J170 16 Jls., Nickel, P.R. 18 00	J173 16 Jls., Nickel, P.R. 18 00

LADIES' (6) SIZE, DUEBER Gold Filled, Hunting Cases, with the Reliable HAMPDEN Movements.

Fancy Engraved.	Fancy Engraved.	Fancy Engraved.	Full Engraved.
No.	No.	No.	No.
J174 With 7 Jls., Gilt...$10 00	J177 With 7 Jewels, Gilt....$10 00	J180 With 7 Jls., Gilt.... $9 50	J183 With 7 Jls., Gilt.. $9 50
J175 With 11 Jls., Nickel 11 50	J178 With 11 Jls., Nickel... 11 50	J181 With 11 Jls., Nickel 11 00	J184 With 11 Jls., Nickel 11 00
J176 With 15 Jls., Nickel 12 00	J179 With 15 Jls , Nickel... 12 00	J182 With 15 Jls., Nickel 12 00	J185 With 15 Jls., Nickel 12 00
Warranted 25 Years.	Warranted 25 Years.	Warranted 20 Years.	Warranted 20 Years.

We are the ONLY house in New York which keeps in stock EVERYTHING PERTAINING TO THE TRADE. We illustrate in our 500-page Big Catalogue a greater variety of goods in our line than any other house in this country. Every dealer can secure a copy on request.

Plate 415. Another page from the same catalog. This one features ladies' 000 size watches.

G-32 **MENS' 12 SIZE 14K SOLID GOLD CASES**

EXTRA HEAVY SOLID 14K AND 18K CASES

On this page we illustrate the finest watches in the world, and as lack of space will not permit showing each individual grade made by the different watch companies, we ask you to write for quotations on the particular grade in which you are interested.

No. G202 and G206 are remarkable values. They have extra heavy solid 14 K. gold cases, and contain absolutely reliable moderate-priced movements. We can, however, furnish you the Lord Elgin movement or any other make of movement that you wish in these cases and quotations will be furnished upon request. Do not on account of the low price imagine that you are obtaining a cheap, flimsy or light-weight case.

The balance of the watches illustrated on this page are sold only as complete watches, and are the finest watches made by the Waltham, Hamilton, Howard and Elgin Watch Companies.

REMEMBER we do not handle any light-weight or cheap gold cases, and we do not advise our customers to buy a cheap gold case because it will not afford sufficient protection for the works.

23 Jewel Lord Elgin

23 extra fine ruby jewels, gold settings, adjusted to temperature, isochronism and five positions. Quick train, gold wheels, straight line escapement, steel escape wheel, exposed pallets, compensating balance, Breguet hairspring, micrometric regulator. Will pass any railroad inspection. Movement, $70.00

17J. Adj. Waltham Royal.

Nickel — 17 Jewels, red gold settings, exposed pallets, compensating balance, adjusted to temperature and three positions, patent Breguet hairspring, hardened and tempered in form, patent micrometric regulator. Movement, $18.00

Solid 18 K, Gold Minute Repeater.
G217. A beautiful extra thin model 12 Size repeater, containing 25 pigeon-blood ruby jewels, steel escape wheel and every known improvement. It is adjusted to 5 positions, and the accuracy of this watch is nothing short of marvelous.

By pressing the projection, the watch strikes a beautiful silver gong, giving you the exact time. It also strikes the quarters, half hours and three-quarters. It has a gold dial and plain polished case. Price, $225.00

Heavy solid 14 K Gold, Open Face.
G202. Plain polished. One of the most serviceable cases made. Thin model. Strong and substantial. Monogram, $2.50 extra.
Waltham or Elgin Movement.
7 Jewel, $23.00
15 Jewel, 25.50
17 Jewel, 27.50
17 Jewel, Adj. 33.00
G203. Hunting or closed case, $4.50 extra.

G206. 14 K. Gold, open face, engine-turned. One of the neatest, most conservative and practical designs ever made. The popularity of this case will always last.
Waltham or Elgin Movement,
7 Jewel, $26.00
15 Jewel, 28.00
17 Jewel, 30.50
17 Jewel, Adj. 35.50
G207. Hunting or closed case, $4.50 extra.

Waltham Premier Maximus.
G204. 16 Size, solid 18 K. gold, extra heavy. The finest watch ever built by the Waltham Watch Co. and the finest ever made in America. It contains 23 ruby and diamond jewels set in gold settings, and is adjusted to 5 positions.

The small dial directly under the figure "12" shows when the watch is wound up, when it needs winding, and the length of time the watch has been running. Science could not produce a more perfect watch or accurate timekeeper. Price, $250.00

No. 822 Howard.
G205. 12 Size, solid 18 K. gold. Open face, plain polished. Extra thin model. 21 Jewel, adjusted to 5 positions, temperature and isochronism. Hand-painted glass enamel dial, red marginal figures. It is the most accurate 12 size watch made, and is the finest 12 Size watch made by the E. Howard Watch Co. It's guaranteed to pass railroad inspection. Price $140.00

WE GUARANTEE TO PLEASE YOU

G208. A Genuine Baird-North value. Gentlemen's solid gold, 16 Size. Engine turned. 17 Jewel adjusted, Hamilton movement, adjusted to five positions, temperature and isochronism, double sunk dial, red marginal figures. We recommend this watch as one of the best values in our catalog. Hamilton watches are preferred by practically all railroads. Price complete, $42.50

Plate 416. Baird North Catalog (Wholesale), 1913. This page features a 23-jewel Elgin, a Waltham, and a Howard, plus a minute repeater.

Universal Trading and Supply Company, Chicago

18 SIZE MOVEMENT WATCHES. Continued.

ELGIN. No. 307 Hunting
No. 308 Open Face.

Nickel, 7 Jewels; exposed pallets; cut expansion balance; Breguet hair-spring; polished oval regulator; sunk second dial; nickel index; dust ring; damaskeened plates.

ELGIN. No. 335 Hunting.
No. 336 Open Face.

Nickel, 17 Jewels; exposed pallets; cut expansion balance; Breguet hair-spring; micrometric regulator; sunk second dial; dust ring; damaskeened plates.

16 Size Movement Watches.

WALTHAM-RIVERSIDE.

Nickel, 17 Jewel, fine Ruby Jewels; raised gold settings; double roller escapement; steel escape wheel; exposed sapphire pallets; compensating balance adjusted to temperature and three positions; patent Breguet hairspring, hardened and tempered in form; patent micrometric regulator; tempered steel safety barrel; exposed winding wheels; red gold center wheel.

ELGIN No. 242. (HUNTING BRIDGE.)

Nickel, 17 jewels (gilded settings); adjusted to temperature; gold center wheel; exposed pallets; compensation balance; Breguet hairspring; micrometric regulator; display winding work; patent recoiling click; patent self-locking setting device; double sunk dial; dust ring; damaskeened plates; thoroughly well finished.

WALTHAM ROYAL.

Nickel movement, 17 jewel, red gold settings; exposed pallets; compensating balance; adjusted to temperature; patent Breguet hair-spring; hardened and tempered in form; patent micrometric regulator; tempered steel safety barrel; exposed winding wheels; red gold centre wheel.

ELGIN.
No. 241—Hunting Bridge.
No. 244—Open Face.

Nickel movement, 17 jewels (gilded settings), adjusted to temperature; gold center wheel; exposed pallets; compensating balance; Breguet hairspring; micrometric regulator; display winding work; patent recoiling click; patent self-locking setting device; sunk second glass enamel dial; dust ring; damaskeened plates.

WALTHAM NO. 625.

Nickel, 17 jewels; red gilded settings; exposed pallets; cut expansion balance; patent Berguet hairspring, hardened and tempered in form; patent micrometric regulator; tempered steel safety barrel; exposed winding wheels; red gilded center wheel.

WALTHAM NO. 620.

Nickel, 15 jewels; red gilded settings; exposed pallets; cut expansion balance; patent Breguet hairspring, hardened and tempered in form; patent micrometric regulator; tempered steel safety barrel; exposed winding wheels; red gilded center wheel.

12 Size Movement Watches.

ROYAL.

Nickel, 17 jewels; red gold settings; exposed pallets; compensating balance, adjusted to temperature; Breguet hairspring, hardened and tempered in form; patent micrometric regulator; tempered safety barrel; exposed winding wheels.

WALTHAM NO. 225.

Nickel, 15 jewel settings; exposed pallets; cut expansion balance; patent Breguet hairspring; hardened and tempered in form; patent micrometric regulator; tempered steel safety barrel; exposed winding wheels.

ELGIN.
No. 321—Hunting.
No. 322—Open Face.

Nickel, 17 jewels (raised gilded setting), adjusted to temperature; gilded center wheel; exposed pallets; compensating balance; Breguet hair-spring; micrometric regulator; display winding works; patent recoiling click; patent self-locking setting device; sunk glass enameled second dial; dust ring; damaskeened plates.

ELGIN.
No. 314—Hunting.
No. 315—Open Face.

Nickel, 15 jewels (setting); exposed pallets; cut expansion balance; Breguet hair-spring; micrometric regulator; display winding work; patent recoiling click; patent self-locking setting device; sunk second dial; dust ring; damaskeened plates.

6 Size Movement Watches.

LADY WALTHAM.

Nickel, 16 ruby jewels (settings); exposed pallets; compensating balance, adjusted; patent Breguet hair-spring, hardened and tempered in form; patent micrometric regulator; tempered steel safety barrel.

0 Size Movement Watches.

LADY WALTHAM.

Nickel, 16 ruby jewels; raised gold settings; exposed pallets; compensating balance; adjusted; patent Breguet hairspring, hardened and tempered in form; patent micrometric regulator; tempered steel safety barrel; exposed winding wheels; red gold center wheel.

ELGIN.
No. 318—Hunting.
No. 319—Open Face.

Nickel, 15 jewels (setting); exposed pallets; cut expansion balance; Breguet hair-spring; polished regulator; display winding work; patent recoiling click; patent self-locking setting device; sunk second dial; dust ring; damaskeened plates.

Plate 417. A page featuring Waltham movements, from the Universal Trading and Supply Company 1913 catalog .

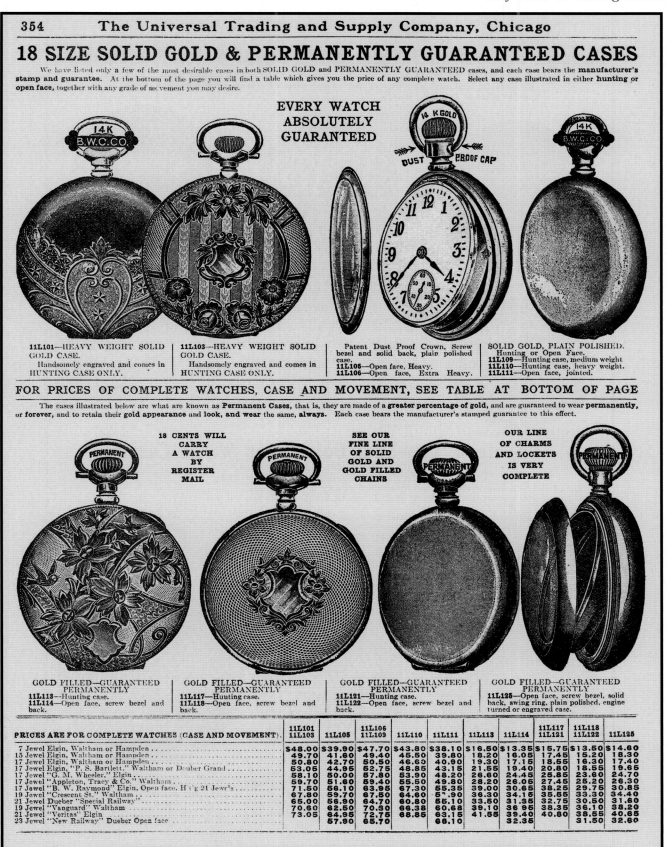

354   The Universal Trading and Supply Company, Chicago

18 SIZE SOLID GOLD & PERMANENTLY GUARANTEED CASES

We have listed only a few of the most desirable cases in both SOLID GOLD and PERMANENTLY GUARANTEED cases, and each case bears the **manufacturer's stamp** and guarantee. At the bottom of the page you will find a table which gives you the price of any complete watch. Select any case illustrated in either **hunting** or **open face**, together with any grade of movement you may desire.

EVERY WATCH
ABSOLUTELY
GUARANTEED

11L101—HEAVY WEIGHT SOLID GOLD CASE.
Handsomely engraved and comes in HUNTING CASE ONLY.

11L103—HEAVY WEIGHT SOLID GOLD CASE.
Handsomely engraved and comes in HUNTING CASE ONLY.

Patent Dust Proof Crown, Screw bezel and solid back, plain polished case.
11L105—Open face, Heavy.
11L106—Open face, Extra Heavy.

SOLID GOLD, PLAIN POLISHED.
Hunting or Open Face.
11L109—Hunting case, medium weight.
11L110—Hunting case, heavy weight.
11L111—Open face, jointed.

FOR PRICES OF COMPLETE WATCHES, CASE AND MOVEMENT, SEE TABLE AT BOTTOM OF PAGE

The cases illustrated below are what are known as **Permanent Cases**, that is, they are made of a **greater percentage of gold**, and are guaranteed to wear **permanently**, or **forever**, and to retain their gold **appearance** and look, and wear the same, **always**. Each case bears the manufacturer's stamped guarantee to this effect.

18 CENTS WILL
CARRY
A WATCH
BY
REGISTER
MAIL

SEE OUR
FINE LINE
OF SOLID
GOLD AND
GOLD FILLED
CHAINS

OUR LINE
OF CHARMS
AND LOCKETS
IS VERY
COMPLETE

GOLD FILLED—GUARANTEED PERMANENTLY
11L113—Hunting case.
11L114—Open face, screw bezel and back.

GOLD FILLED—GUARANTEED PERMANENTLY
11L117—Hunting case.
11L118—Open face, screw bezel and back.

GOLD FILLED—GUARANTEED PERMANENTLY
11L121—Hunting case.
11L122—Open face, screw bezel and back.

GOLD FILLED—GUARANTEED PERMANENTLY
11L125—Open face, screw bezel, solid back, swing ring, plain polished, engine turned or engraved case.

PRICES ARE FOR COMPLETE WATCHES (CASE AND MOVEMENT).	11L101 11L103	11L105	11L106 11L109	11L110	11L111	11L113	11L114	11L117 11L121	11L118 11L122	11L125
7 Jewel Elgin, Waltham or Hampden	$48.00	$39.90	$47.70	$43.80	$38.10	$16.50	$13.35	$15.75	$13.50	$14.60
15 Jewel Elgin, Waltham or Hampden	49.70	41.60	49.40	45.50	39.80	18.20	16.05	17.45	15.20	18.30
17 Jewel Elgin, Waltham or Hampden	50.80	42.70	50.50	46.60	40.90	19.30	17.15	18.55	16.30	17.40
17 Jewel Elgin, "P. S. Bartlett," Waltham or Deuber Grand	53.05	44.95	52.75	48.85	43.15	21.55	19.40	20.80	18.55	19.65
17 Jewel "G. M. Wheeler," Elgin	58.10	50.00	57.80	53.90	48.20	26.60	24.45	25.85	23.60	24.70
17 Jewel "Appleton, Tracy & Co." Waltham	59.70	51.60	59.40	55.50	49.80	28.20	26.05	27.45	25.20	26.30
17 Jewel "B. W. Raymond" Elgin, Open face, H'g 21 Jew'ls	71.50	66.10	63.95	67.30	55.35	39.00	30.65	38.25	29.75	30.85
19 Jewel "Crescent St." Waltham	67.80	59.70	67.50	64.60	5''.90	36.30	34.15	35.55	33.30	34.40
21 Jewel Deuber "Special Railway"	65.00	56.90	64.70	60.80	55.10	33.50	31.35	32.75	30.50	31.60
19 Jewel "Vanguard" Waltham	70.80	62.50	70.50	66.38	60.68	39.10	36.95	38.35	36.10	38.20
21 Jewel "Veritas" Elgin	73.05	64.95	72.75	68.85	63.15	41.55	39.40	40.80	38.55	40.65
23 Jewel "New Railway" Deuber Open face		57.90	65.70		66.10		32.35		31.50	32.60

Plate 418. Another page from the same catalog, showing cases. The bottom of the page shows prices for case and movement.

Popular Price Nickel American & Swiss Watch Movements

THESE MOVEMENTS FIT ANY AMERICAN CASE OF LIKE SIZE.

By selecting grade of case wanted and adding price of movement to price of case you can get price of complete watch.

No. M100. 12 Size, 7 Jewel. Lever nickel Swiss movement, open face, pendant set, French porcelain dial, steel hands, the best movement that can be gotten at present for the price.
Price, each, **$3.50**

No. M103. 16 Size, 7 Jewel. Nickel lever Swiss movement, burnished concave steel, display winding wheels, white enameled French porcelain dial, open face. Price, each, **$3.50**

No. M105. 16 Size, 21 Jewels. Open face, Transpacific high-grade Swiss nickel movement, exposed winding wheels, raised ruby jewels, quick train, stem wind and stem set, white enameled double sunk dial, red marginal figures, 21-jewels.
Each, **$4.75**

ELGIN WATCH MOVEMENTS

16 Size Elgin Movement.

No. E344. 12 size, 17-J. Elgin Htg. movement. Price, each, **$12.60**

No. E345. 12 size, 17-J. Elgin O. F. movement. Price, each, **$12.60**

No. E314. 12 size, 15-J. Elgin Htg. movement. Price, each, **$10.65**

No. E315. 12 size, 15-J. Elgin O. F. movement. Price, each, **$10.65**

No. E301. 12 size, 7-J. Elgin Hunting movement. Price, each, **$7.45**

No. E303. 12 size, 7-J. Elgin O. F. movement. Price, each, **$7.45**

No. E386. 16 size, 17-J. Elgin Htg. movement. Price, each, **$12.60**

No. E312. 16 size, 15-J. Elgin Htg. movement. Price, each, **$10.35**

No. E313. 16 size, 15-J. Elgin O. F. movement. Price, each, **$10.35**

No. E290. 16 size, 7-J. Elgin Hunting movement. Price, each, **$6.45**

No. E291. 16 size, 7-J. Elgin O. F. movement. Price, each, **$6.45**

Napoleon Ten-Year Gold Filled Watch Cases

Manufactured By The
ILLINOIS WATCH CASE CO., ELGIN, ILL.

ILLINOIS Napoleon Brand stands for standard quality in 10-Year Gold Filled Cases, and is recognized the world over as the **LEADER** in this particular grade.

Our illustrations convey an idea of the handsome designs which are reproduced on NAPOLEON Cases by hand-engraving, fancy engine turning, brocading, etc. Workmanship and finish fully warranted. The makers' guarantee stamped in every case.

No. 273. 16 Size Hunting Case. Napoleon, 10 year gold filled, bascine model, elliptical pendant, French bar bow, elaborately engraved. Case only.
Price, each, **$4.20**

No. 274. 16 Size Open Face Case. Screw back and bezel, otherwise as above. Case only. Price, each, **$3.10**

No. 271. 12 Size Hunting Case. Napoleon, 10 year gold filled, bascine model, elliptical pendant, French bar bow, fancy engraved patterns. Case only.
Price, each, **$3.85**

No. 272. 12 Size Open Face Case. Screw back and bezel, otherwise as above. Case only. Price, each, **$3.00**

No. 275. 18 Size Hunting Case. Napoleon, 10 year gold filled, bascine model, elliptical pendant, French bar bow, elaborately engraved. Case only.
Price, each, **$4.60**

No. 276. 18 Size Open Face Case. Screw back and bezel, as above. Case only. Price, each, **$3.25**

Plate 419. A page from the Shryock-Todd Notion Co. catalog, St. Louis, MO, in 1921. Here we have lever-set Swiss movements, a selection of Elgin movements, and watch cases manufactured by the Illinois Watch Case Co. at Elgin.

In Reverence *the Old* Guild Watches
Were Conceived

SO devout, so filled with a love of their art, were the worthy masters of the ancient guilds of watchmakers that they were wont, at the opening of each session, to seek inspiration in a prayer to God, "that He might further the interests of these people and this craft."

To these old-time craftsmen who thus sought in prayer to consecrate their daily toil, the ideals and traditions of the guild were things of paramount importance. Rigidly they guarded the secrets of the craft from lesser artisans who sought to copy. With endless care they labored at their benches 'neath the vaulted arches of the old guildhalls, striving ever for perfection in their masterpieces.

So now, inspired by the ancient ideals of fine craftsmanship, do the modern Gruen artisans labor at their significant task, fashioning for the men of today watches whose rare elegance and accuracy bespeak the highest artistry.

In the Gruen Guild of Watchmakers may be found many of the descendants of the old guild masters. Here live the same ideals, the same love of fine craftsmanship, as obtained in the ancient guildhalls.

Where the old guild spirit dwells today

In the Gruen workshops at Madre-Biel, Switzerland, the Gruen Watches are conceived. There,

with the aid of American machinery, master craftsmen fashion the movements to the exacting standards of the guild. On Time Hill, Cincinnati, is the American workshop. Here the beautiful hand-

No. 91—*Gruen Verithin. Gold filled,* $65.00
14-kt. solid gold, $100.00

THE OLD WAY | VERITHIN WAY

How the Gruen Pat. Wheel Construction made an accurate watch logically thin. It isn't a Verithin unless it is a Gruen

wrought cases are made, the movements fitted into them and then given their final adjustments and tests for accuracy.

In the accompanying panel may be seen the Gruen Verithin — America's first accurate *thin* watch — unsurpassed for elegance, sturdiness and simplicity of line. In it has been solved a watch making problem four centuries old. With a simple rearrangement of wheels that saved half the movement space without reducing the size or strength of parts the Gruen craftsmen set a new standard for precision accuracy in a pocket watch of beautiful form.

At the sign of the Gruen Guild

Gruen Watches are sold only by chartered agencies, among the best jewelry stores in each locality. Look for the Gruen Service Emblem. There you will find this beautiful Gruen model and other Gruen Guild Watches for men and women.

Prices: $25 to $750; with diamonds from $100 to $6000.

A book of Etchings and Photographic Plates showing Gruen Guild Watches for men and women will be sent if you are sincerely interested.

GRUEN WATCHMAKERS GUILD, Time Hill, Cincinnati, U.S.A.
Canadian Branch, Toronto
Masters in the art of watchmaking since 1874

 # GRUEN Guild Watches
Including the original and genuine "VERITHIN" model

Plate 420. The *Saturday Evening Post,* September 17, 1921. Gruen announces its Guild Watches.

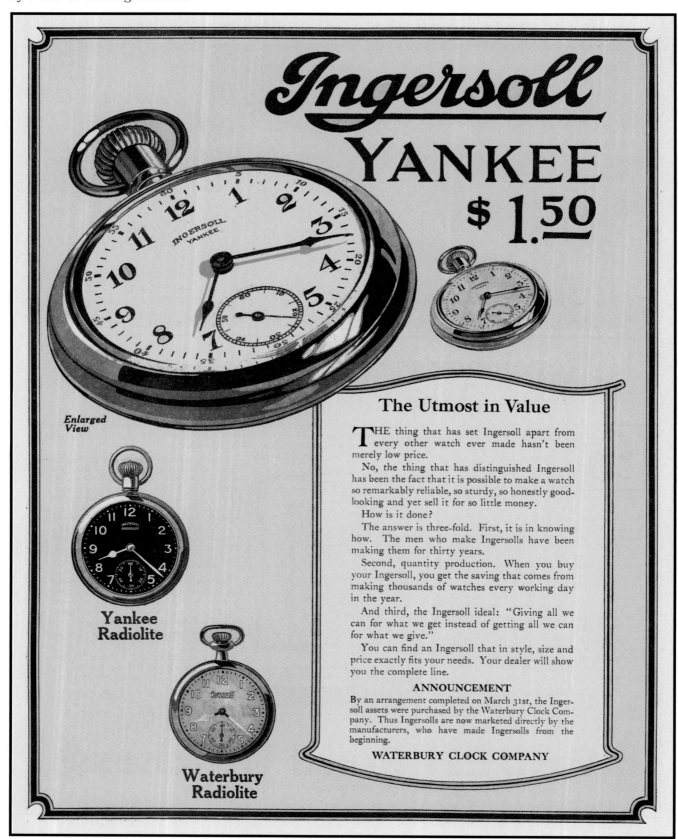

Plate 421. The *Saturday Evening Post*, June 3, 1922. This advertisement came out the same year that the Waterbury Watch Company purchased Ingersoll Brothers, as you can see by the announcement that "the Ingersolls are now marketed directly by the manufacturers, who have made Ingersolls from the beginning." The Yankee was priced at $1.50 instead of the original price of $1.00.

Plate 422. Two years later, Ingersoll watches were advertised in the C. B. Norton trade catalog. The ad features a Radiolite Two-in-One clock, seven pocket watches, and a wrist Radiolite for women, boys, sportsmen, etc.

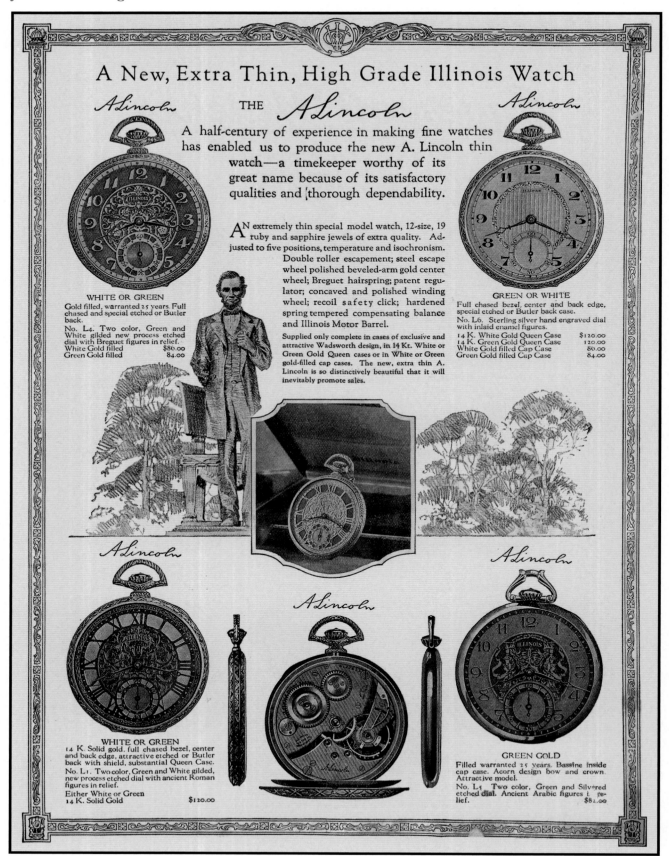

A New, Extra Thin, High Grade Illinois Watch

THE *A Lincoln*

A half-century of experience in making fine watches has enabled us to produce the new A. Lincoln thin watch—a timekeeper worthy of its great name because of its satisfactory qualities and thorough dependability.

AN extremely thin special model watch, 12-size, 19 ruby and sapphire jewels of extra quality. Adjusted to five positions, temperature and isochronism. Double roller escapement; steel escape wheel polished beveled-arm gold center wheel; Breguet hairspring; patent regulator; concaved and polished winding wheel; recoil safety click; hardened spring tempered compensating balance and Illinois Motor Barrel.

Supplied only complete in cases of exclusive and attractive Wadsworth design, in 14 Kt. White or Green Gold Queen cases or in White or Green gold-filled cap cases. The new, extra thin A. Lincoln is so distinctively beautiful that it will inevitably promote sales.

WHITE OR GREEN
Gold filled, warranted 25 years. Full chased and special etched or Butler back.
No. L4. Two color, Green and White gilded new process etched dial with Breguet figures in relief.
White Gold filled $86.00
Green Gold filled   84.00

GREEN OR WHITE
Full chased bezel, center and back edge, special etched or Butler back case.
No. L6. Sterling silver hand engraved dial with inlaid enamel figures.
14 K. White Gold Queen Case $120.00
14 K. Green Gold Queen Case   120.00
White Gold filled Cap Case   80.00
Green Gold filled Cap Case   84.00

WHITE OR GREEN
14 K. Solid gold, full chased bezel, center and back edge, attractive etched or Butler back with shield, substantial Queen Case.
No. L1. Two color, Green and White gilded, new process etched dial with ancient Roman figures in relief.
Either White or Green
14 K. Solid Gold $120.00

GREEN GOLD
Filled warranted 25 years. Bassine inside cap case. Acorn design bow and crown. Attractive model.
No. L5. Two color, Green and Silvered etched dial. Ancient Arabic figures i relief. $82.00

Plate 423. The 1924 C. B. Norton trade catalog was also filled with high-grade watches.

Illinois SPRINGFIELD Watches

The Autocrat

The Autocrat

Plain Marquis
Green Gold Only
Special Luminous Dial
$47.00

The Autocrat

Plain Bassine
Regular Gold Only
Silvered, Gilt or Enamel Dial
$41.00

The Autocrat

Chased Marquis
Green Gold Only
Moire Dial
$49.00

The Autocrat

Chased Marquis
Green Gold Only
No. 36 Engraved Dial
as shown in box above
$49.00

Above Illustration Three-Quarters Size

17 jewels; adjusted to temperature; hardened compensating balance with timing screws; double roller escapement; steel escape wheel; gold center wheel; Breguet hairspring; patent micrometric screw regulator; safety screw center pinion; concaved and polished winding wheels; recoil safety click; rayed pattern damaskeening; gilt lettering.

Fitted in the following cases:

25 year filled Bassine case,	$41.00
25 year filled Green Gold Marquis case,	$42.00
25 year Chased Green Gold Marquis case, Special Radium Luminous Dial or Raised Figure or Engraved Silvered or Gilt Dial,	$49.00
25 year filled 14k white gold Chased Marquis case,	$53.00
14k Bassine Calumet regular gold case,	$71.00
14k Green Gold Bassine Calumet case,	$74.00
14k Bassine, inside cap, regular gold case,	$98.50
14k Green Gold Bassine inside cap case,	$102.50
14k Heavy, Green Gold hand made chased border (special shape) case with cap, Special Luminous ro Fancy Dial,	$132.00

Raised Figure, Luminous or Engraved Dials, extra, $5.00

Plates 424 – 426. The ads shown here and on the next two pages, from the 1924 C. B. Norton trade catalog, feature Illinois watches.

Illinois SPRINGFIELD Watches

No. 410
23 Jewels, Hunting and Open Face
12 Size

23 extra quality ruby and sapphire jewels, gold settings; adjusted to temperature, six positions and isochronism; spring tempered compensating balance, gold screws including timing screws; steel escape wheel; double roller; gold train wheels; Breguet hairspring; patent regulator; safety screw center pinion; safety recoil click; Illinois Superior Motor Barrel; double sunk dial; is accurately constructed and highly finished in every detail.

$75.00

Every Illinois-Springfield Watch is fully guaranteed to be perfect in construction and to be a satisfactory timekeeper.

A. Lincoln
21 Jewels, Hunting and Open Face
12 Size

21 ruby and sapphire jewels, gold settings; adjusted to temperature, five positions and isochronism; special quality hardened and tempered compensating balance, with gold screws including mean time screws; exposed double roller escapement; sapphire roller and pallet jewels; beveled steel escape wheel; entire escapement cap jeweled; conical pivots; beveled and polished gold center wheel; patent micrometric screw regulator; best quality Breguet hairspring; patent safety screw center pinion; concaved and polished visible winding wheels; double sunk dial; damaskeened in bright striped pattern; black enamel lettering.

$53.00

Hunting or Open Face

No. 405
17 Jewels, Hunting and Open Face
12 Size

17 jewels, oreide settings, adjusted to temperature, spring tempered compensating balance with timing screws, double roller escapement, hardened and polished steel escape wheel, sapphire pallets, sapphire jewel pins, gold, beveled and polished center wheel, Breguet hairspring, patent micrometric screw regulator, safety screw center pinion, perfect self-locking setting device, concaved and polished winding wheels, safety recoil click, damaskeened in bright striped pattern.

A very attractive, well finished and thoroughly dependable movement.

$27.00

If better watches could be made, grade for grade, the Illinois Watch Co. would make them.

No. 305
17 Jewels, Hunting and Open Face
16 Size

17 jewels, polished settings, adjusted to temperature, hardened compensating balance with timing screws, double roller escapement, steel escape wheel, rounded arm train wheels, gold top center wheel, Breguet hairspring, patent micrometric screw regulator, safety screw center pinion, concaved and polished winding wheels, recoil safety click, double sunk dial, striped rayed pattern damaskeening, black enamel lettering.

A watch that can be conscientiously recommended.

$26.50

Special
19 Jewels, Adjusted 3 Positions
Lever or Pendant Setting

19 Jewels; adjusted to temperature and three positions; spring tempered compensating balance with timing screws; double roller escapement; sapphire pallets and roller jewel; steel escape wheel; rounded arm train wheels; gold center wheel; Breguet hairspring; patent regulator; recoil click; double sunk dial.

16 Size - - $33.00
12 Size - - $35.00

No. 706
17 Jewels, Hunting and Open Face
16 Size

17 jewels; polished settings; adjusted to temperature, four positions; hardened compensating balance with timing screws; rounded arm train wheels; polished gold top center wheel; tempered and polished steel escape wheel; best quality Breguet hairspring; safety screw center pinion; micrometric screw regulator; concaved winding wheels; recoil safety click; double sunk dial; gilded screws and regulator; beautifully damaskeened in narrow striped pattern.

A watch that is an exceptionally durable and accurate timekeeper.

$30.00

Illinois SPRINGFIELD Watches

Railroad Movements

16 SIZE

Bunn Special

Made in
21 & 23 Jewels, Hunting and Open Face

Adjusted 6 Positions

Extra quality ruby and sapphire jewels; raised gold settings; accurately adjusted to temperature, six positions and isochronism; very carefully rated and timed, special quality hardened and tempered compensating balance with gold screws including mean time screws; rounded arm polished gold train wheels; double roller escapement; entire escapement cap jeweled; conical pivots; beveled and polished steel escape wheel; best quality Breguet hairspring; safety screw center pinion; Illinois superior mainspring; patent micrometric screw regulator; recoiling safety click; concaved, polished and rayed winding wheels; screws are chamfered and slots cornered; double sunk glass enamel dial; plates and bridges have chamfered edges, are nicely finished and artistically damaskeened.

The 23 jewel Bunn Special contains the Illinois Motor Barrel.

Exceptionally high grade 16 size watches for railroad or any severe service.

23 Jewels, $65.50
21 Jewels, $56.00

16 SIZE

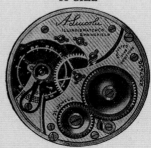

A. Lincoln

21 Jewels, Hunting and Open Face

Adjusted 5 Positions

21 ruby and sapphire jewels; gold settings; adjusted to temperature, five positions and isochronism; special quality hardened and tempered compensating balance with gold screws including mean time screws; exposed double roller escapement; sapphire roller and pallet jewels; beveled conical escape wheel; entire escapement cap jeweled; conical pivots; beveled and polished gold center wheel; patent micrometric screw regulator; best quality Breguet hairspring; patent safety screw center pinion; concaved, polished visible winding wheels; friction fitted dust band; double sunk dial; damaskeened in bright striped pattern; black enamel lettering.

A most satisfactory watch for railroad service.

$52.00

Sangamo Special

23 Jewels, Adjusted 6 Positions, 16 Size Open Face Only, Lever Setting, Sold Only as a Complete Watch

23 selected extra quality ruby and sapphire jewels, raised gold settings, accurately adjusted to temperature, SIX positions and isochronism, very carefully rated and timed, special quality hardened and tempered compensating balance with gold screws including mean time screws, gold train wheels, beveled and polished steel escape wheel, double roller escapement, one piece polished and cornered pallet and fork, gold guard pin staked in fork, selected quality oval top and bottom red ruby pallet jewels, ruby jewel pin, entire escapement cap jeweled, hand finished conical pivots, best quality Breguet hairspring, safety screw center pinion, Illinois superior mainspring, Illinois motor barrel, patent micrometric screw regulator, recoiling click, concaved and polished winding wheels, screws are chamfered and slots cornered, fitted with either glass enamel dial or nontarnishable silvered dial, heavy Arabic figures.

These movements are fitted, rerated and timed in their specially designed cases at the factory.

In 25 yr., 14k filled extra weight screw back hinged bezel case, $100.00
In 14k extra weight, solid gold jointed case, with inside cap, $185.00

Bunn

Made in
17 & 19 Jewels, Hunting and Open Face

Adjusted 5 Positions

Extra quality ruby and sapphire jewels; raised gold settings; accurately adjusted to temperature, five positions and isochronism; very carefully rated and timed; special quality hardened and tempered compensating balance, with gold screws including mean time screws; rounded arm polished gold train wheels; double roller escapement; beveled and polished steel escape wheel; one piece polished pallet and fork; sapphire pallet jewels and jewel pin; best quality Breguet hairspring; safety screw center pinion; Illinois superior mainspring; patent micrometric screw regulator; recoiling click; concaved, polished and rayed winding wheels; screws are chamfered and slots cornered; double sunk glass enamel dial; plates and bridges have chamfered edges, are nicely finished and artistically damaskeened.

The 19 jewel Bunn contains the Illinois Motor Barrel.

The Standard Watches in 17 and 19 jewels for railway service.

19 Jewels, $48.00
17 Jewels, $40.00

18 SIZE

Bunn Special

21 Jewels, Hunting and Open Face

Adjusted 6 Positions

Extra quality ruby and sapphire jewels; solid gold settings; accurately adjusted to temperature, six positions and isochronism, carefully rated and timed; double roller escapement, sapphire roller and pallet jewels; polished fork and pallet; entire escapement cap jeweled; hand finished conical pivots; beveled steel escape wheel; special quality hardened and tempered compensating balance, with gold screws including mean time screws; patent micrometric screw regulator; best quality Swiss Breguet hairspring; Phillipe coil; safety screw center pinion; first quality mainspring; all steel parts highly polished; double sunk glass enamel dial; damaskeened in bright spotted pattern.

$48.00

Sangamo Special

Montgomery Dials Furnished Without Extra Charge

Waltham Watches

Illustrations on This Page Reduced to 3/5 Size

PREMIER MAXIMUS
Special 16 Size

The Premier Maximus Watch is never spoken of in terms of equality with any other watch. It is universally recognized as the crowning achievement of timepiece construction.

The Premier Maximus Watch receives the most exacting tests known to watchmakers. During these tests, which cover a period of one year, these famous watches are submitted to extremes of temperature; also to every position that the watch can be subjected to as a pocket timepiece.

14 K. HEAVY GOLD CASE $620.00
Fitted with Gilded, Silvered or Enameled Dials

Twenty-three of the finest diamond, ruby and sapphire jewels it is possible to obtain; three pairs of diamond caps; balance, pallet and escape pivots running on diamonds; jeweled main wheel bearings; plate jewels in raised gold settings.

Adjusted with the utmost accuracy to variations in temperature, isochronism and six positions.
Delivered from factory in Sterling Silver Casquet De Luxe, with two extra main springs and extra crystal.

COLONIAL "A" SERIES

| Washington Carved | Washington Fancy | Frodsham Plain | Flat Center Carved |

$250.00 Complete Watch
Description
MOVEMENT:—21 J. Riverside Maximus. Adjusted to temperature, isochronism and five positions.
DIAL:—Silver or Gold with Raised Gold Figures.
CASES:—14 K. Green Gold Washington Carved. 14 K. Green Gold Washington Fancy. 14 K. Green Gold Frodsham Plain. 14 K. Green Gold, White Gold or Green and White Gold, Flat Center Carved.
Price $300.00

$175.00 Complete Watch
Description
MOVEMENT:—19 J. Riverside. Adjusted to temperature, isochronism and five positions.
DIAL:—Silver or Gold with Raised Gold Figures.
CASES:—14 K. Green Gold Washington Carved. 14 K. Green Gold Washington Fancy. 14 K. Green Gold Frodsham Plain. 14 K. Green Gold, White Gold or Green and White Gold, Flat Center Carved.
Price $210.00

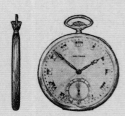

| Plain Case | Display Box | Raised Gold Figures |

$225.00 Complete Watch
Description
MOVEMENT:—21 J. Riverside Maximus. Adjusted to temperature, isochronism and five positions.
DIAL:—Silver or Gold with Raised Gold Figures.
CASES:—14 K. Yellow or Green Gold, Plain Polished.
Price $272.00

$150.00 Complete Watch
Description
MOVEMENT:—19 J. Riverside. Adjusted to temperature, isochronism and five positions.
DIAL:—Silver or Gold with Raised Gold Figures.
CASES:—14 K. Yellow or Green Gold, Plain Polished.
Price $180.00

ALL WATCHES ON THIS PAGE ARE TIMED IN CASES AT FACTORY BEFORE SHIPPING
All Watches on this page delivered in Attractive Display Boxes

Plate 427 – 429. The ads shown here and on the next two pages, from the same C. B. Norton wholesale catalog, show Waltham watches.

Waltham Watches

EIGHTEEN SIZE
(NICKEL)

P. S. BARTLETT
Open Face only. Adjusted to temperature.
17 Jewels....................$24.50

SIXTEEN SIZE
(NICKEL)

MAXIMUS	VANGUARD	CRESCENT ST.
Hunting and Open Face, Pendant or Lever Setting. Adjusted to temperature, isochronism and positions; double roller; steel escape wheel; gold train; fine ruby and sapphire Jewels.	Pendant or Lever Setting. Adjusted to temperature, isochronism and positions; double roller; steel escape wheel; fine ruby and sapphire jewels.	Pendant or Lever Setting. Adjusted to temperature, isochronism and five positions; double roller; steel escape wheel; fine ruby and sapphire jewels.
23 Jewels, 6 positions, Inner-terminal hair spring with winding Indicator, Open Face only....$135.00	23 Jewels, 6 positions, Inner-terminal hair spring with winding Indicator, Open Face only....$80.00	21 Jewels, Winding Indicator, Open Face only...................$63.00
23 Jewels, 5 positions............. 129.00	23 Jewels, 5 positions 74.00	21 Jewels............................. 58.00

RIVERSIDE	ROYAL	P. S. BARTLETT
Open Face only, Pendant or Lever Setting. Adjusted to temperature, isochronism and five positions; double roller; steel escape wheel; fine ruby and sapphire jewels.	Open Face only, Pendant or Lever Setting. Adjusted to temperature and three positions; double roller; steel escape wheel.	Hunting and Open Face, Pendant or Lever Setting. Adjusted to temperature; steel escape wheel; sapphire pallets.
19 Jewels..........................$52.00	17 Jewels $31.00	17 Jewels............................$28.40

No. 625	No. 620	No. 610
Hunting and Open Face, Pendant Setting.	Hunting and Open Face, Pendant Setting.	Hunting and Open Face, Pendant Setting.
17 Jewels.............................$25.80	15 Jewels...........................$21.60	7 Jewels............................$13.50

For Full Figured Luminous Dial and Hands add $5.00
For Dot Luminous Dial and Hands add $2.80

EVERYTHING NEEDED BY JEWELERS.

Waltham Watches

TWELVE SIZE
(NICKEL)

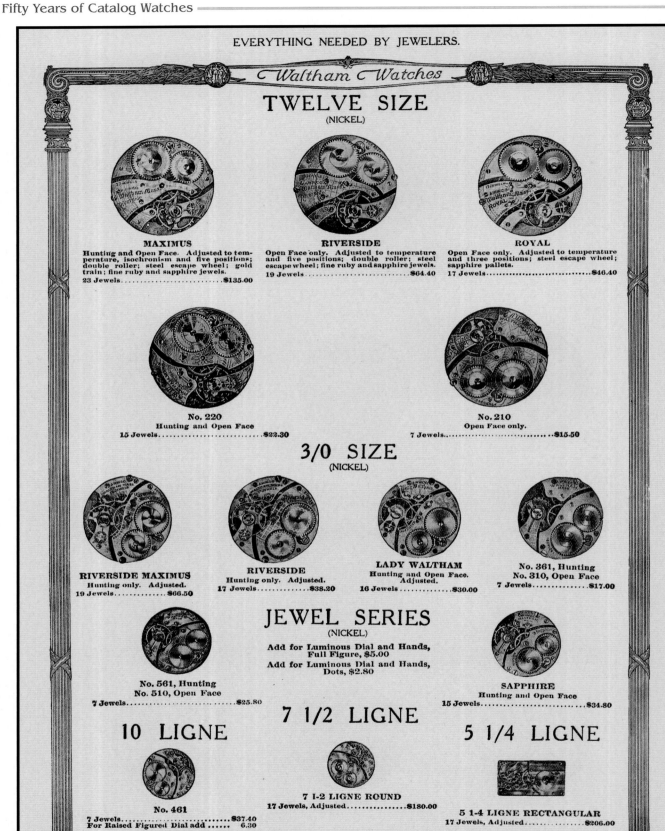

MAXIMUS

Hunting and Open Face. Adjusted to temperature, isochronism and five positions; double roller; steel escape wheel; gold train; fine ruby and sapphire jewels.

23 Jewels.........................$135.00

RIVERSIDE

Open Face only. Adjusted to temperature and five positions; double roller; steel escape wheel; fine ruby and sapphire jewels.

19 Jewels............................$64.40

ROYAL

Open Face only. Adjusted to temperature and three positions; steel escape wheel; sapphire pallets.

17 Jewels............................$46.40

No. 220

Hunting and Open Face

15 Jewels............................$22.30

No. 210

Open Face only.

7 Jewels............................$15.50

3/0 SIZE
(NICKEL)

RIVERSIDE MAXIMUS

Hunting only. Adjusted.

19 Jewels.............$66.50

RIVERSIDE

Hunting only. Adjusted.

17 Jewels.............$38.20

LADY WALTHAM

Hunting and Open Face. Adjusted.

16 Jewels.............$30.00

No. 361, Hunting
No. 310, Open Face

7 Jewels.............$17.00

JEWEL SERIES
(NICKEL)

Add for Luminous Dial and Hands, Full Figure, $5.00

Add for Luminous Dial and Hands, Dots, $2.80

No. 561, Hunting
No. 510, Open Face

7 Jewels.........................$25.80

SAPPHIRE

Hunting and Open Face

15 Jewels.........................$34.80

7 1/2 LIGNE

10 LIGNE

No. 461

7 Jewels.........................$37.40
For Raised Figured Dial add 6.30

7 1-2 LIGNE ROUND

17 Jewels, Adjusted...............$180.00

5 1/4 LIGNE

5 1-4 LIGNE RECTANGULAR

17 Jewels, Adjusted.............$206.00

All Waltham Complete Watches Are Cased and Specially Timed In Their Cases at the Factory

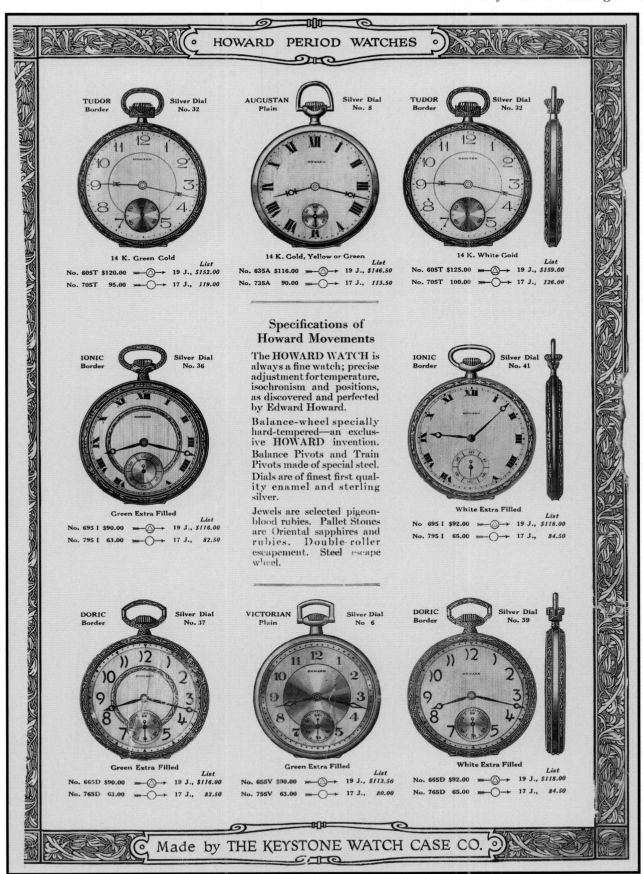

HOWARD PERIOD WATCHES

TUDOR Border	Silver Dial No. 32

14 K. Green Gold

			List
No. 605T	$120.00	19 J.,	$152.00
No. 705T	95.00	17 J.,	119.00

AUGUSTAN Plain	Silver Dial No. 8

14 K. Gold, Yellow or Green

			List
No. 635A	$116.00	19 J.,	$146.50
No. 735A	90.00	17 J.,	113.50

TUDOR Border	Silver Dial No. 32

14 K. White Gold

			List
No. 605T	$125.00	19 J.,	$159.00
No. 705T	100.00	17 J.,	126.00

Specifications of Howard Movements

The HOWARD WATCH is always a fine watch; precise adjustment for temperature, isochronism and positions, as discovered and perfected by Edward Howard.

Balance-wheel specially hard-tempered—an exclusive HOWARD invention. Balance Pivots and Train Pivots made of special steel. Dials are of finest first quality enamel and sterling silver.

Jewels are selected pigeon-blood rubies. Pallet Stones are Oriental sapphires and rubies. Double-roller escapement. Steel escape wheel.

IONIC Border	Silver Dial No. 36

Green Extra Filled

			List
No. 695 I	$90.00	19 J.,	$116.00
No. 795 I	63.00	17 J.,	82.50

IONIC Border	Silver Dial No. 41

White Extra Filled

			List
No. 695 I	$92.00	19 J.,	$118.00
No. 795 I	65.00	17 J.,	84.50

DORIC Border	Silver Dial No. 37

Green Extra Filled

			List
No. 665D	$90.00	19 J.,	$116.00
No. 765D	63.00	17 J.,	82.50

VICTORIAN Plain	Silver Dial No 6

Green Extra Filled

			List
No. 655V	$90.00	19 J.,	$113.50
No. 755V	63.00	17 J.,	80.00

DORIC Border	Silver Dial No. 39

White Extra Filled

			List
No. 665D	$92.00	19 J.,	$118.00
No. 765D	65.00	17 J.,	84.50

Made by THE KEYSTONE WATCH CASE CO.

Plates 430 and 431. The C. B. Norton ads on this page and the next show Howard watches.

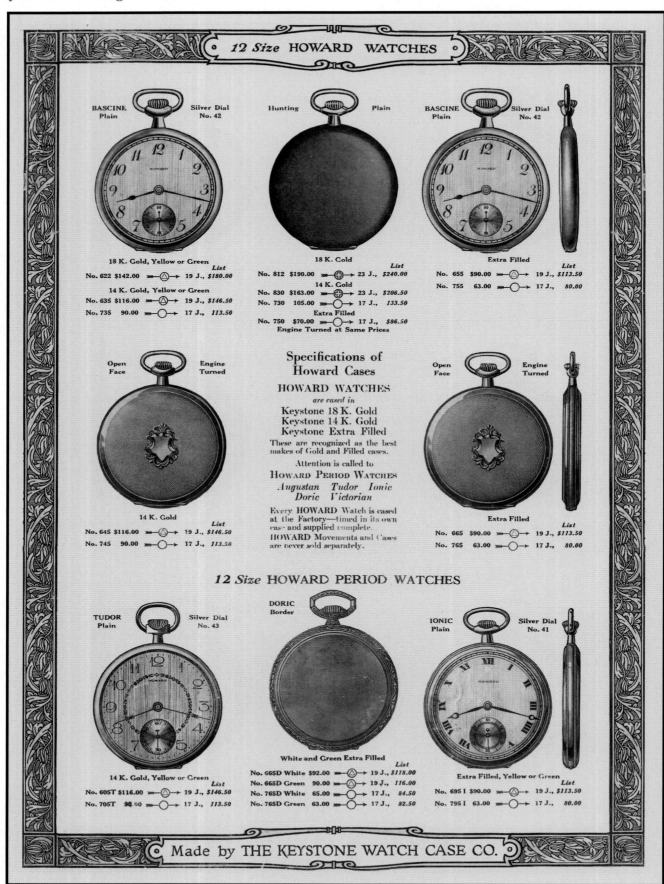

12 Size HOWARD WATCHES

BASCINE Plain — Silver Dial No. 42

18 K. Gold, Yellow or Green
                                                    List
No. 622 $142.00 ⟶ 19 J., $180.00

14 K. Gold, Yellow or Green
No. 635 $116.00 ⟶ 19 J., $146.50
No. 735   90.00 ⟶ 17 J., 113.50

Hunting — Plain

18 K. Gold
                                              List
No. 812 $190.00 ⟶ 23 J., $240.00

14 K. Gold
No. 830 $163.00 ⟶ 23 J., $206.50
No. 730 105.00 ⟶ 17 J., 133.50

Extra Filled
No. 750 $70.00 ⟶ 17 J., $86.50
Engine Turned at Same Prices

BASCINE Plain — Silver Dial No. 42

Extra Filled
                                              List
No. 655 $90.00 ⟶ 19 J., $113.50
No. 755 63.00 ⟶ 17 J., 80.00

Open Face — Engine Turned

14 K. Gold
                                              List
No. 645 $116.00 ⟶ 19 J., $146.50
No. 745   90.00 ⟶ 17 J., 113.50

Specifications of Howard Cases

HOWARD WATCHES
are cased in
Keystone 18 K. Gold
Keystone 14 K. Gold
Keystone Extra Filled
These are recognized as the best makes of Gold and Filled cases.

Attention is called to
HOWARD PERIOD WATCHES
*Augustan   Tudor   Ionic
Doric   Victorian*

Every HOWARD Watch is cased at the Factory—timed in its own case and supplied complete.
HOWARD Movements and Cases are never sold separately.

Open Face — Engine Turned

Extra Filled
                                              List
No. 665 $90.00 ⟶ 19 J., $113.50
No. 765 63.00 ⟶ 17 J., 80.00

12 Size HOWARD PERIOD WATCHES

TUDOR Plain — Silver Dial No. 43

14 K. Gold, Yellow or Green
                                              List
No. 605T $116.00 ⟶ 19 J., $146.50
No. 705T   90.00 ⟶ 17 J., 113.50

DORIC Border

White and Green Extra Filled
                                                    List
No. 665D White $92.00 ⟶ 19 J., $118.00
No. 665D Green 90.00 ⟶ 19 J., 116.00
No. 765D White 65.00 ⟶ 17 J., 84.50
No. 765D Green 63.00 ⟶ 17 J., 82.50

IONIC Plain — Silver Dial No. 41

Extra Filled, Yellow or Green
                                              List
No. 695 I $90.00 ⟶ 19 J., $113.50
No. 795 I 63.00 ⟶ 17 J., 80.00

Made by THE KEYSTONE WATCH CASE CO.

Elgin High Grade Watches

Twelve-size Elgin Movements

No. 344, Htg., } Nickel
No. 345, O. F.,

PENDANT Winding and Setting. Seventeen jewels (settings). Ruby and sapphire balance and center jewels. *Double-roller escapement.* Exposed pallet stones. Cut expansion balance. Breguet hair spring, with micrometric regulator. Exposed winding wheels. Patent recoiling click and self-locking setting device. Sunk-second dial. Plates damaskeened.
Jewels   Price $25.20

No. 314, Htg., } Nickel
No. 315, O. F.,

PENDANT Winding and Setting. Fifteen jewels (settings). Ruby balance jewels. Exposed pallet stones. Cut expansion balance. *Double-roller escapement.* Breguet hair spring, with micrometric regulator. Exposed winding wheels. Patent recoiling click and self-locking setting device. Sunk-second dial. Plates damaskeened.
15 Jewels   Price $21.30

No. 301, Htg., } Nickel
No. 303, O. F.,

PENDANT Winding and Setting. Seven jewels (settings). Ruby balance jewels. Exposed pallet stones. *Double-roller escapement.* Cut expansion balance. Breguet hair spring, with polished regulator. Exposed winding wheels. Patent recoiling click and self-locking setting device. Sunk-second dial. Plates damaskeened.
7 Jewels   Price $14.90

Streamlines

$100 Streamline

2-Size Extra Thin — exceptional timekeeping quality in a slender model. G. M. Wheeler Movement. 17 Jewels, 6 Adjustments. Embossed Sterling Silver Dial. Streamline bow and pendant. 14 K Solid Gold Engraved Cap Case, in Green Gold.................$118.80

$100 Streamline

12-Size Extra Thin—exceptional timekeeping quality in a slender model. G. M. Wheeler Movement. 17 Jewels, 6 Adjustments. Embossed Sterling Silver Dial. Streamline bow and pendant. 14 K Solid Gold engraved Cap Case, in White Gold.................$118.80

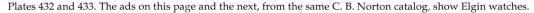

Plates 432 and 433. The ads on this page and the next, from the same C. B. Norton catalog, show Elgin watches.

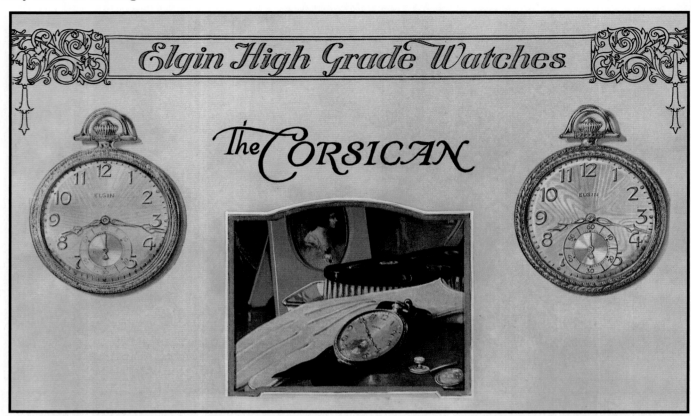

Elgin High Grade Watches

The CORSICAN

Elgin High Grade Watches

Elgin Builds a New Watch
for Railroad Service
$55.00

THE ELGIN RAILROAD WATCH *is the result of*
years of study of the railroad man's requirements.

Plates 434 and 435.

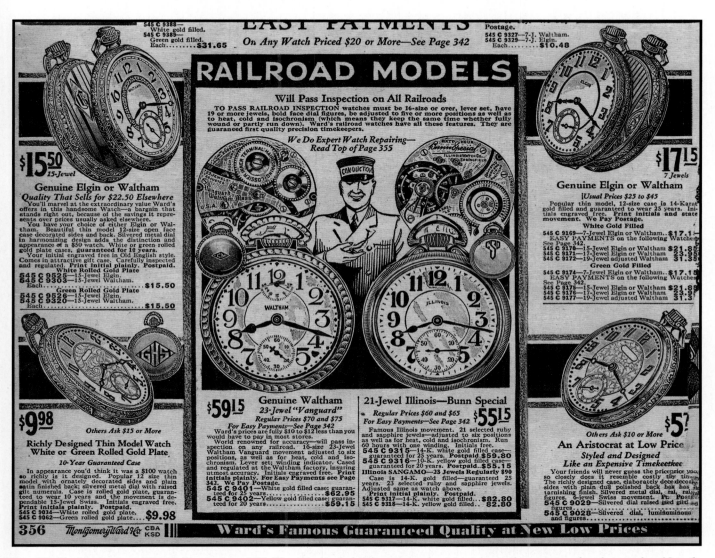

Plate 436. The Montgomery Ward fall and winter 1931/32 catalog included five pages of wristwatches and two pages of pocket watches. Note the prices for the Bunn Special.

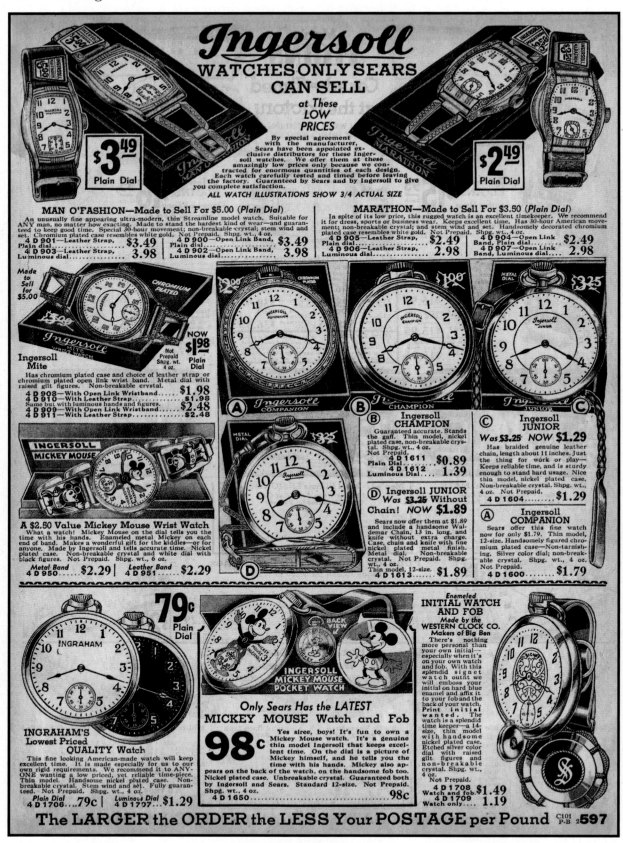

Plate 437. The 1933/34 Sears Roebuck catalog included these pocket watches. By comparing the price of the Mickey Mouse watch and fob at the bottom of the page to the price of the Mickey Mouse wristwatch, you can get an idea of how much more popular wristwatches were than pocket watches.

JUBILEE SPECIALS

Tremendous Savings on These Famous Walthams

Everyone knows the Famous Name of Waltham stands for beauty, accuracy and dependability in watches. To celebrate our 50th Anniversary we are offering guaranteed Waltham Pocket watches at unheard of low prices. Prices that save you from $5.00 to $10.00. These watches are the last word in style, design and quality. In beautiful gift boxes. Shipping weight, each, 9 ounces.

$14.95 9-Jewel
10-K Gold Filled Cases
9 or 17-Jewel Movements
Regular $19.50 and $27.50 Values

Only the finest workmanship and materials are used in assembling these Waltham watches. Modern design case with engraved edge and dull satin-like finished back and bezel. Thin, small, 12-size. 10-K white or yellow gold filled case. State choice. Your monogram beautifully engraved on case as illustrated without extra charge. Print plainly initials wanted. The fancy dial is in perfect harmony with the pierced hands. Fully guaranteed Jubilee values—sensational Jubilee values.

9-Jewel Waltham
4 D 928......$14.95

17-Jewel Waltham
4 D 929......$17.95

9 or 17-Jewel Movements
Embossed Chrome Plated Cases
Regular $14.95 and $18.95 Values
$9.98 9-Jewel

A fine quality WALTHAM watch in the popular small, 12-size. Looks like white gold and should be much higher priced. Fancy dial matches the embossed case perfectly. Shipping weight, 9 ounces.

17-Jewel Waltham
4 D 936..........$12.98
9-Jewel Waltham
4 D 935..........$9.98

IT'S AN ELGIN!
$14.75 7-Jewel

If you are familiar with watches, you will know the name Elgin is your guarantee of a good timepiece. It is one of America's foremost watches. Thin model, 12-size watch with handsomely engraved chromium plated case with your initials engraved on back. PRINT initials wanted. The assorted dials are easily read and right up to the minute in style. In gift box. Shpg. wt., 9 oz.

15-Jewel Elgin
4 D 1022..........$17.50
7-Jewel Elgin
4 D 1021.......... 14.75

7-JEWEL MOVEMENT
AMERICAN MADE
—$10.00 VALUE
$6.98

10-K Rolled Gold Plate

A large, special purchase of these guaranteed STANDARD watches enables us to sell at this low price. Handsomely engraved cases with fancy dials—Popular 12-size (small). Gift box included. Shipping wt., 9 oz.

4 D 1327—White Gold......
4 D 1328—Green Gold......$6.98

Popular Thin Model—12-Size Watches
Usually Sold Elsewhere for $8.50
Sensationally Priced at only $4.95

A very popular American made Standard watch already in the pockets of thousands of men. Engraved chromium plated cases resembling white gold come in assorted designs with modern dials. Fully guaranteed 7-jewel movement. Gift Box. Shipping weight, 9 oz.
4 D 1332.....$4.95

Neat American made Standard model of very swanky appearance. Attractive, assorted dials and cases that are beautifully engraved and sure to please. Has regular Standard feature—low crown and pull-out stem set. The 7-jewel movement is fully guaranteed. Shipping weight 9 ounces.
4 D 1331.....$4.95

23-Jewel 16-Size Railroad Watches—$70 Value
Guaranteed to Pass All Railroad Inspections—Adjusted to temperature and 6 positions—10-K Yellow Gold Filled assorted cases—60-hour mainsprings. Shipping weight, each, 11 ounces.

Illinois Movement
Cash or Easy Payments.
4 D 1330..........**$52.50**
Terms: $5 Down, $6 a Month.

Waltham Movement
Cash or Easy Payments.
4 D 926..........**$39.95**
Terms: $4 Down, $5 a Month.

23-Jewel Waltham in Stainless Steel Case
4 D 925—Cash or Easy Payments..........**$34.95**
Terms: $4 Down, $5 a Month. Use Easy Payment Order Blank.

15-Jewel Standard
An American made 16-size (medium size) watch. Attractive chromium plated case resembles white gold. A guaranteed timepiece. Gift box. Shpg. wt., 11 oz.
4 D 1326.....$6.95

New Lapel Watch!
Black or Crystal colored Catalin case, leather chain and button to match. Guaranteed movement. In gift box. State color. Shipping weight, 9 ounces.
4 D 1205   4 D 1206
7-Jewel.$7.95 17-Jewel.$9.95

Waltham and Elgin
Sturdy, Medium 16-Size Watches
$13.95 9-Jewel Waltham

These fully guaranteed watches are adjusted to keep accurate time. They are especially recommended for street railway men, brakemen, etc. who want a regulation size railroad watch but one that is not required to pass the minutest railroad inspection. The everlasting stainless metal cases resemble white gold and are embossed on front and back. Cases may vary slightly. Each in gift box. Shpg. wt., 11 oz.

Elgin Movements
4 D 1031—7-Jewel.....$14.25
4 D 1032
15-Jewel......$17.00
4 D 1033
17-Jewel......$18.00

Waltham Movements
4 D 919—9-Jewel.
4 D 920—21-Jewel. **$13.95**
Cash..............$23.95
Easy Payments......26.45
Terms: $3 Down, $4 a Month.
Use Easy Payment Order Blank

Expert Watch Repairing
Prompt Reliable Work Fully Guaranteed

All of our repair work is done by expert watch makers in a modern up-to-date shop. This work is guaranteed to satisfy and save you money. Simply print your name and address plainly on a tag and attach to your watch. Pack the watch carefully and address the package to your nearest Sears, Roebuck and Co. MAIL ORDER HOUSE. Send by insured mail. An estimate will be sent you at once . . . before work is begun.

JEWELERS' TOOL AND MATERIAL CATALOG
If you are interested in "Watch Makers' and Jewelers' Tools and Materials," write for Circular K8912D. Send orders from watchmakers' catalog to *Chicago ONLY*.

WALDEMAR WATCH CHAINS
Guaranteed Watch Chains—Each link securely soldered together, assuring strength and long wear. Neat designs. Shpg. wt., ea., 3 oz.

"Boulevard" Pierced Links
10-K heavy gold filled quality. Fancy, yet in good taste.
4 D 1925 Yellow Gold...$2.89
4 D 1926 White Gold...$2.89

10-K Solid Gold Streamline
Very attractive chain, with pierced links. Finest quality and reasonably priced.
4 D 1912 Yellow Gold $6.95
4 D 1922 White Gold $6.95

"Virginia Curb Links." The popular interwoven flat chain. Neat, attractive.
10-K Solid
4 D 1913..$7.95 Yellow Gold
10-K Yellow Gold Plated
4 D 1914 89c

Swanky "Modern." Correct beyond question. Engraved design on long slender links. Makes an attractive pattern, extremely popular.
White Gold Plate 4 D 1905....59c
Yellow Gold Plate 4 D 1927....59c

"Alpha" Slender Links. An unusual engraved design, conservative, though modern. 10-K rolled gold plate quality priced low.
White 4 D 1915....98c
Yellow 4 D 1903....98c

"Empire" Fancy Links. Floral design, engraved on narrow long links. Fine detail.
Yellow Gold Filled 4 D 1906..$1.98
White Gold Filled 4 D 1916..$1.98

BELT AND VEST CHAINS
New styles in serviceable, good looking chains. Guaranteed quality. Shpg. wt., each, 4 oz.

Initial Belt Chain. Modern design with hand engraved initial. Length, 8½ in. for belts up to 1½ inches wide. Heavy 10-K Yellow or White gold plate. State choice.
4 D 1956—Print initial.......$1.29

"Dickens" Vest Chain. 12-inch chain, with charm clasp.
Yellow Gold Shell Guaranteed Quality 4 D 1954 $1.89
Extra Heavy Yellow Rolled Gold Plate 4 D 1962 $2.98

"Colonel" Vest Chain. 11-in. long. Center charm clasp.
Heavy 10-K Yellow Gold Plate 4 D 1952..$1.98
14-K Heavy Yellow Gold Filled 4 D 1960..$4.95

716 · SEARS-ROEBUCK ✲

Plate 438. By 1936/37, the Sears Roebuck catalog contained seven pages of wristwatches and only two partial pages of pocket watches.

Plate 439. The 1939 Sears Roebuck catalog still had seven pages of wristwatches, but the pocket watches had shrunk down to one and three-fourths of a page.

Plate 440. Another page from the same catalog. The price of the Waltham Vanguard had gone down to as little as $35.95, and this included a free monogram.

Plate 441. The 1946 Montgomery Ward catalog had seven pages of wristwatches and only one-half page of pocket watches. Most of the wristwatches were Swiss. Number 4 is a Patek Philippe priced at $435.00.

18 Size 10 Kt. Rolled Gold Plate Yellow S.B. and S.B. Watch Cases

Pocket Watch Cases are available now, in the sizes and quality illustrated, and you may order them with the assurance of getting prompt delivery.

The quantity is still limited however, and we suggest you replenish your stock, so you can take care of the demands.

No. 507 . . . . $13.60
18 Size 10 Kt. Yellow Rolled Gold Plate
S.B. & S.B. Engraved

No. 508 . . . . Case only $12.70
18 Size 10 Kt. Yellow Rolled Gold Plate
S.B. & S.B. Plain Polished

16 Size, 10 Kt. Yellow Gold Filled Screw Bezel and Screw Watch Cases

Railroad Model. Dust Proof

No. 509 . . . . $19.75
16 Size 10 Kt. Yellow Gold Filled
S.B. & S.B. Butler Back

No. 510 . . . . Case only $19.75
Size 10 Kt. Yellow Gold Filled
S.B. & S.B. Butler back

No. 511 . . . . $21.70
16 Size 10 Kt. Yellow Gold Filled
S.B. & S.B. Engine Turned

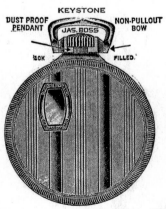

No. 512 . . . . $23.05
16 Size 10 Kt. Yellow Gold Filled
S.B. & S.B. Engraved

No. 513 . . . . $23.05
16 Size 10 Kt. Yellow Gold Filled
S.B. & S.B. Engraved

No. 514 . . . . $23.05
16 Size 10 Kt. Yellow Gold Filled
S.B. & S.B. Engraved

PRICES SUBJECT TO CHANGE WITHOUT NOTICE

Plate 442. The 1950 Benjamin Allen & Co. catalog did not include any pocket watches, but it did have six pages of watch cases for those whose watches needed recasing. It also included two pages of timers.

1900s U.S. WATCH COMPANIES CHRONOLOGICAL LISTING

The United States had gone through some bad financial times in the 1890s. Yet neither that nor the fact that the watch business had become saturated with watch companies could stop a few optimistic people from going into the business. Let's take a brief look.

APPLETON WATCH CO.
Appleton, Wisconsin
1901 – 1903
Watches with this name were actually made by the Remington Watch Company with machinery purchased from the Cheshire Watch Company. Remington made the same type of movements that Cheshire had made. Consequently Appleton had a short life.

SUFFOLK WATCH CO.
1901 – 1905
In 1901, the Columbia Watch Company was purchased by Suffolk. Instead of making inexpensive jeweled watches as its predecessor did, it concentrated on making duplex watches simular to Waterbury's. It was later absorbed by Waltham, which was later purchased by the Keystone Watch Case Company.

SOUTH BEND WATCH CO.
South Bend, Indiana
1903 – 1929
In 1903, this company purchased the Columbus Watch Company and moved the equipment to South Bend Indiana. It specialized in making good quality railroad watches.

ANSONIA CLOCK CO.
watches, 1904 – 1930
This old, established clock company started making dollar-type watches in 1904. Russia purchased the company in 1930, in order to establish watchmaking in that country.

BANNATYNE WATCH CO.
Waterbury, Connecticut
1905 – 1911
E. INGRAHAM
Bristol, Connecticut
1911 – 1971
This company was started by Archibald Bannatyne, who had been employed by the Waterbury Watch Company. He designed and patented his own dollar watch. In 1911, the company was purchased by the E. Ingraham company. It continued to make watches with the Bannatyne patent.

MANISTEE WATCH CO.
Manistee, Michigan
1908 – 1912
This was the last American watch company to be founded in the U.S. that did not form out of, or have connections with, another company. Unfortunately, though it tried to make inexpensive jeweled movements, neither its watches nor its prices could compete with the those of the large factories.

DUDLEY WATCH CO.
Lancaster, Pennsylvania
1920 – 1928
William Wallace Dudley (1851 – 1938) had worked for Illinois, Waltham, Trenton, South Bend, and Hamilton watch companies before going into business for himself. His goal for his new company was to make a pocket watch that he believed every Mason would want to own. His Masonic watch had bridges that were cut in the form of Masonic symbols. His factory produced the plates, and the barrels and other parts were bought from other companies such as Waltham and Hamilton. Some parts were also imported from Switzerland. Unfortunately, not all Masons could afford the watch. Some that could afford it did not feel as enthusiastic about it as Dudley had expected. By this time, many had switch to the new wristwatches. Dudley's company was forced to go into receivership in just three years. The J. W. Baker Company took over receivership of the company in 1925 and in 1929 sold it to the J. W. Apple Company. J. W. Apple held on to it until 1935. At that time, the company was purchased by the X-L Watch Company, and the machinery and inventory was moved to New York. The X-L in carnation remained in business until 1968. Dudley Masonic watches are very collectible.

TWENTIETH CENTURY TIMELINE

1900 — Many watches had metal dials in gold and silver.

1901— Queen Victoria died in England.

1901 – 1910 — Edward VII was King of England.

1901 — U.S. Watch Co. of Waltham was purchased by the Keystone Watch Case Company.

1903 — Columbus Watch Company was sold to the South Bend Watch Company.

1903 — Mrs. Emmeline Pankhurst, a British suffragette, formed the Women's Social and Political Union.

1903 — New York Standard was purchased by Keystone.

1905 — Non-Magnetic Watch Company of America went out of business.

1906 — Labor Party formed in Britain.

1906 — San Francisco suffered a severe earthquake.

1906 — International Exhibition of Milan.

1906 — The name Westclox appeared on Western Clock Company watches.

1908 — Ingersoll purchased the Trenton Watch Company.

1909 — Robert Peary reached the North Pole.

1909 — Henry Ford began assembly-line production of automobiles in the U.S. He had begun his career as a watch repairman, at 14 years of age.

1910 – 1936 — George V was King of England.

1911 — Roald Amundsen (Norwegian) reached the South Pole.

1912 — The Titanic sank.

1913 — The steel foundry of Imphy, in France, produced an alloy it named elivar. This alloy did not expand or contract when exposed to changes in temperature.

1914 – 1918 — World War I was fought in Europe.

1914 — "Antique" Breguet-style hands became popular.

1914 — Radium-filled (glow in the dark) hands appeared on the scene.

1914 — New England Watch Company was sold to R. H. Ingersoll and Brothers of New York.

1915 — Seth Thomas Watch Company went out of business.

1915 — Rockford Watch Company Ltd. went out of business.

1917 — United States entered the war.

1918 — U.S. government passed the Standard Time Act, using railroad time zones as their model.

1919 — The League Nations was formed in Paris by the Treaty of Versailles.

1922 — Ingersoll closed.

1922 — Waterbury Watch Company bought Ingersoll Brothers.

1925 — New York Standard went out of business.

1925 — America and the Switzerland dominatd the watch manufacturing market.

1927 — Illinois Watch Company closed its factory and was purchased by Hamilton Watch Company.

1927 — Charles Lindberg made the first solo transatlantic flight.

1929 — The Wall Street Stock market crashed. This was the beginning of a worldwide depression.

1929 — Richard Byrd (American) flew over the South Pole.

1930 — Hampden Watch Company closed.

1930 — Howard Watch Company went out of business.

1930 — Russia purchased the Hampden Watch Co. and the Ansonia Watch Co. in order to start a watch industry.

1933 — The end of Prohibition in the United States.

1934 – 1945 — Adolph Hitler was Fuhrer of Germany.

1936 — Switzerland surpassed America in the production of watches.

1936 — U.S. signed the Reciprocal Trade Treaty. This lowered the duties on Swiss watches by 50%.

1936 — Edward VIII abdicated the throne for "the woman I love."

1939 – 1945 — World War II fought.

1941 — Pearl Harbor, Hawaii, attacked by the Japanese Air Force.

1941 — The United States entered the war.

1944 — Waterbury Clock Company became part of what later became the U.S. Time Corporation; U.S. Time is the maker of Timex.

1945 — United Nations was formed.

1948 — North American Treaty Organization was formed.

1950 — Waltham went out of business.

1956 — New Haven Watch Company closed.

1958 — The Piezoelectric quartz watch was invented.

1964 — Elgin Watch Company went out of business.

1969 — Ball Watch Company closed.

1969 — Hamilton produced its last American Railroad Watch.

1982 — Swatch Watch was formed.

TWENTIETH CENTURY WATCHES

Plate 443. Circa early 1900s.

Pendant watch, green enamel, open faced with matching fluer-de-lis pin.
$1,150.00.
Courtesy of Glenn Smith, Dealer.

Plate 444. Haas Neveux Ii Cie., Geneve, No. 20552, made for Van Cleef & Arpels, circa 1900.
Very fine, rare, and elegant platinum and enamel, keyless, slim, jump-hour digital Art Deco dress watch with digital perpetual calendar.

Case. Three-piece, "bassine," polished, monogrammed back. **Dial.** Silver, marred, eccentric jump-hour aperture at the lower part, above aperture for Arabic digital minutes, above that an apertures for digital days of the week, date, and months. **Movement.** 40.6 mm (18"), rhodium-plated, "fausses cotes" decoration, 18 jewels, straight-line lever escapement, cut bimetallic compensation balance with blued-steel flat balance spring.
Signed on dial, case punched with the maker's trademark, same number on the movement and case.
Diam. 46 mm. **$17,940.00.**
Photo and description courtesy of Antiquorum Auctioneers, 14 Jun 2003.

Plate 445. Circa early 1900s.

Skeletonized watch by the New England Watch Co., duplex.
$950.00.
Description and watch courtesy of Aaron Faber Gallery.

Plate 446. Circa 1900.

Swiss, lady's open-faced enameled pendant watch, blue and gold with dark blue **dial**.
$675.00.
Description and watch courtesy of Jack Harvey.

Plate 447. Circa 1900s.
Waltham, size 18, 14K multicolored gold, boxed hinge hunting case watch, P. S. Bartlett, model #83.

Number of Jewels: 17; movement #9549987. Mint unused condition.
$3,500.00.
Description and watch courtesy of Jeff Rosen, Solvang Antiques Center.

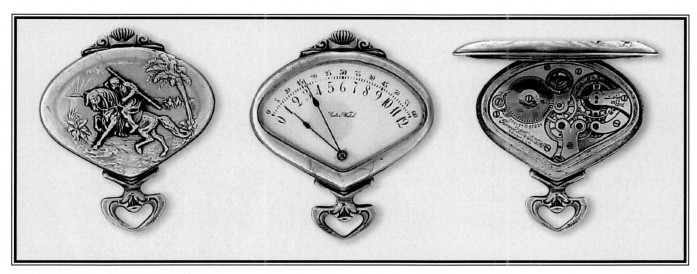

Plate 448. Circa 1900.
Good large Swiss silver sector watch by Record Watch Co.

The hands on this watch traverse the arc of the white enamel **dial** (small repair at hole) and then snap back to begin again. Handsome **case** back with a repoussé equestrian scene. Gilt 15-jewel lever **movement.**
Width, 59 mm. **$4,250.00.**
Photo and description courtesy of Stephen Bogoff, Antiquarian Horologist.

Plate 449. Circa 1900.

Illinois, size 18, model #6, Bunn Special. Number of Jewels: 21; serial number 1536023. Made for Non-Magnetic Watch Co. of America, gothic-style **dial**.
$550.00.
Photos and description courtesy of Edward Ueberall, Collector/Dealer.

Plate 450. 1900.

Lovely 18K gold, diamond, and enamel bezel wind ball watch. Black, white, and gold **case**, the bezel, bale, and center set with approximately 231 tiny diamonds. White enamel **dial** with hairlines. 15-jewel lever **movement**.
Diam. 21 mm. **$3,250.00.**
Photo and description courtesy of Stephen Bogoff, Antiquarian Horologist.

Plate 451. Patek Philippe & Cie., No. 97645, made for Tiffany &. Co., circa 1900.
Very fine and rare, 18K gold, keyless, split-seconds chronograph watch. Accompanied by an Extract from the Archives.

Case. Four-body, "bassine," with unusual double bezel construction, chronograph safety bolt at 11 o'clock, gold hinged cuvette.
Dial. White enamel, radial Roman numerals, outer minute ring, outermost chronograph ring with red five-minute/seconds Arabic markers. Blued-steel spade hands. **Movement.** 35 mm (15½"), nickel. half-plate, 25 jewels, straight-line calibrated lever escapement, cut bimetallic compensation balance with Breguet balance spring, split mechanism under the dial.
Dial, case, and movement signed by the retailer.
Diam. 46 mm **$6,325.00.**
Photo and description courtesy of Antiquorum Auctioneers 19 Mar 2003.

Plate 452. Circa 1900.
Lovely Swiss 18K gold, diamond, and precious stone lady's antique pendant watch.

Case back with a dragonfly against high-relief foliage. White enamel **dial** with hairlines, nickel 16-jewel **movement.**
Diam. 27 mm. **$2,500.00.**
Photo and description courtesy of Stephen Bogoff, Antiqarian Horologist.

Plate 454. Circa 1900.

Gunmetal quarter-repeater antique pocket watch. White enamel **dial** (faint hairline) with gold hands. Bright gilt 15-jewel lever movement. **Case** in particularly fine condition. Loud, clear tone.
Diam. 52 mm. **$1,125.00.**
Photo and description courtesy of Stephen Bogoff, Antiquarian Horologist.

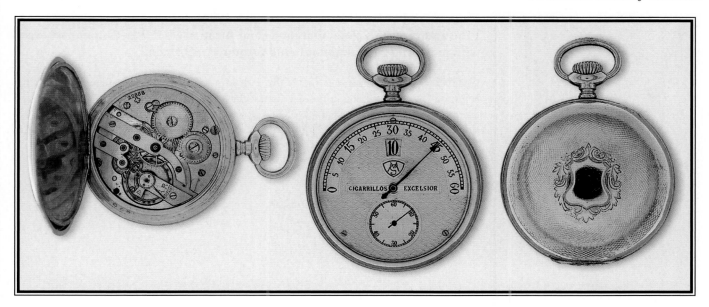

Plate 455. Circa 1900.
Swiss slim gold-filled Modernista jump-hour sector antique pocket watch.

Silver **dial** with black minute hand that traverses the upper sector and then snaps back to 0 when the hour jumps within the window. Remarkably enough, these watches were given away as premiums with the purchase of cigarettes, and the brand is on the dial. The back of the gold-filled engine-turned **case** centered with a blank shield. Nickel 15-jewel lever **movement**. Since these watches were originally given away, they were not highly valued and are almost always found in much poorer condition than this excellent example.
Diam. 50 mm. **$1,200.00.**
Photo and description courtesy of Stephen Bogoff, Antiquarian Horologist.

Plate 456. Circa 1900. Fine and lovely Swiss, Art Nouveau, 14K gold hunting case antique pocket watch by Borel Fils & Cie.

The gold **dial** with a minor scratch and attractive signs of age. Only slight wear to the high points of the handsome substantial cast **case** with a lion amidst foliage set with a large diamond. Fancy pendant and bow. Nickel 17-jewel lever **movement**. A very good example of Art Nouveau case making.
Diam. 49 mm. **$5,000.00.**
Photo and description courtesy of Stephen Bogoff, Antiquarian Horologist.

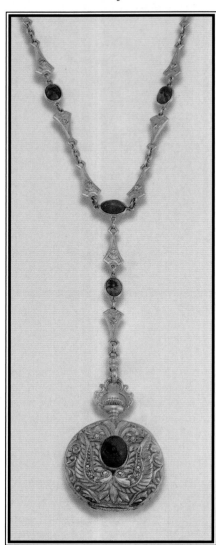

Plate 457. M & Co., Geneva, circa, circa 1900.
Fine and rare, 18K gold, diamond- and turquoise-set, keyless pendant watch with matching gold, diamond- and turquoise-set chain.

Case. four-body, "bassine et filets," back decorated in relief with diamond-set wings, centered by a cabouchon turquoise, band chased with laurel leaf pattern, gold hinged cuvette. **Dial.** Off-white enamel, blue Arabic numerals, outer minute paillon ring, subsidiary sunk seconds Louis XV gold hands. **Movement.** 22 mm (10"), rhodium-plated, 18 jewels, straight-line lever escapement, cut bimetallic compensation balance with Breguet balance spring.
Case signed.
Diam. 27 mm. **$3,220.00.**
Photo and description courtesy of Antiquorum Auctioneers, 19 Mar 2003.

Plate 458. Circa early 1900s.

New York Standard 16 size, 7 jewels, chronograph, very nice silverode screwback open-face **case**, single sunk porcelain **dial** with blue spade hands including sweep second, ¾-plate nickel **movement**, micrometric regulator.
$425.00.
Photo and description courtesy of OldWatch.com.

Plate 459. Schumacher & Co., San Francisco, No. 5716, Swiss, circa 1900.
Fine 14K gold split-seconds chronograph watch with 30-minute register.

Case. Four-body, "bassine," polished, gold hinged cuvene. **Dial.** White enamel, Breguet numerals, outer minute divisions, outermost seconds divided into fifths, minute register at t 2 o'clock, subsidiary sunk seconds. Blued-steel spade hands. **Movement.** 37 mm, rhodium plated, "fausses cotes" decoration, straight-line lever escapement, cut bimetallic compensation balance with Breguet balance spring, swan neck micrometric regulator, split-seconds mechanism under the dial.
Signed on dial and movement by the retailer.
Diam. 47 mm. **$1,973.00.**
Photo and description courtesy of Antiquorum Auctioneers, 14 Jun 2003.

Plate 460. B. Louis Elisee Piguet, No. 2762, made probably for the Russian market, circa 1900. Very fine and important 18K gold, hunting-cased, keyless, double-train, astronomical, carillon Grande Sonnerie clock-watch, with minute-repeating phases of the moon perpetual calendar, and chronograph with instantaneous center 60-minutes register.

Case. Six-body, massive, "bassine et filets," engine-turned, gold hinged cuvette over glazed go-to bezel for viewing the movement. **Dial.** White enamel, double-sunk, radial Roman numerals, outer minute track, outermost chronograph track divided into fifths, five-minute/seconds Arabic markers, four subsidiary sunk dials for days of the week, date, months of the four year leap cycle and subsidiary seconds concentric with phases of the moon aperture. Blued-steel spade hands. **Movement.** 45 mm, (20"), frosted gilt, Mairet tandem winding system, 35 jewels, straight-line calibrated lever escapement, cut bimetallic compensation balance with blued steel Breguet balance spring, carillon on three gongs and three hammers, carillon/silence lever at 12 o'clock protruding from under the bezel, repeating activated by a small push-button at 6 o'clock on the band.
Signed on the movement under the dial, engraved with Brandt's patent number, case punched with Le Locle guarantee mark.
Diam. 59 mm. **$118,560.00.**
Photo and description courtesy of Antiquorum Auctioneers, 14 Jun 2003.

Plate 461. Charles Frodsham, AD. Fmsz, By Appointment to the Queen, late of 84 Strand, 115 New Bond St., London, No. 08858, hallmarked 1900 – 1901.
Very fine 18K gold, keyless, hunting-cased minute-repeating watch.

Case. Four-body, front cover with coat-of-arms and motto "Dum Spiro Spero" (While I breathe, I hope), engraved initials on the back, gold hinged cuvette. swiveling anti-theft pendant. **Dial.** Off-white, by Willis, Roman numerals, outer minute track, subsidiary sunk seconds. **Movement.** 42 mm (19mm), ¾-plate, frosted gilt, fusee and chain, 31 jewels, lateral counterpoised lever escapement, cut bimetallic compensation balance with gold temperature screws and gold quarter nuts, diamond endstone, blued steel double overcoiled Breguet balance spring, double roller, repeating on gongs through activating slide in the band. Dial and movement signed. Case punched with Harrison Mill Frodsham mark. Dial signed by Willis.
Diam. 51 mm. **$6,900.00.**
Photo and description courtesy of Antiquorum Auctioneers, 21 May 2003.

Plate 462. Circa 1901.

Elgin, size 0, model #2, grade 269, number of jewels: 7, serial number 9511506. Multicolor lady's gold-filled watch.
$350.00.
Photos and description courtesy of Edward Ueberall, Collector/Dealer.

Plate 463. Circa 1901.

Elgin, size 18, model #8, B. W. Raymond. Jeweled motor barrel, RR grade, typical RR-style **dial**. Number of jewels, 19. Serial number 9496356.
$375.00.
Photos and description courtesy of Edward Ueberall, Collector/Dealer.

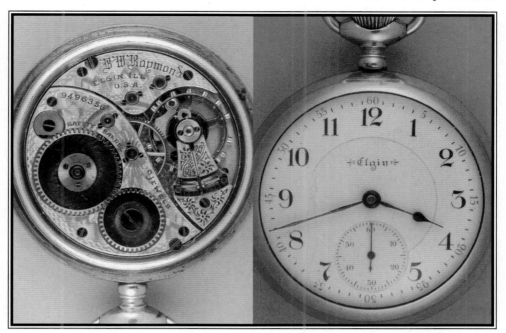

Plate 464. Circa 1902.

18 size, Illinois, Bunn Special, 24 jewels, #1605978. A worn case.
$3,500.00.
Description and watch courtesy of Father Bradly Offutt, Collector.

Plate 465. Circa 1902.

16 size, 23 jewel, Hamilton 950, in a bar with crown **case**, finger bridge **movement**. Near mint condition.
$1,000.00 – 2,000.00.
Description and watch courtesy of Father Bradly Offutt, Collector.

Plate 466. Circa 1902.

Howard L 16 size, series XII, split plate, 17 jewels, nice correct 18K solid gold triple-hinged Roy open-face **case**, double sunk porcelain **dial**, Arabic numerals, blue correct Howard hands, beautifully damaskeened ¾-plate nickel **movement**, adjusted, gold jewel settings, micrometric regulator (701118).
$3,500.00.
Photo and description courtesy of OldWatch.com.

Plate 467. Circa 1902.

Illinois 18 size, Bunn Special, 24 jewels, railroad grade, excellent yellow-gold-filled, triple hinged open-face **case**, double sunk porcelain **dial**, Gothic Arabic numerals, blue spade hands, lever set, beautifully damaskeened full-plate nickel **movement**, marked adjusted, jeweled mainspring barrel, gold jewel settings, micrometric regulator (1543286).
$1,800.00.
Photo and descriptions courtesy of OldWatch.com.

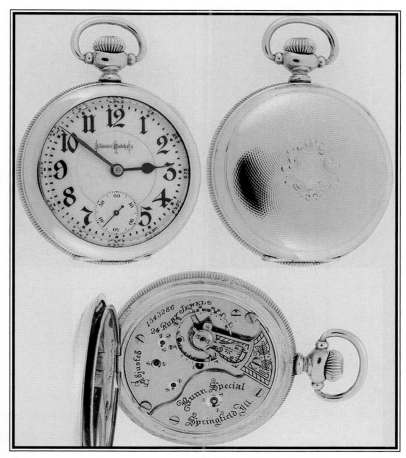

Plate 468. Circa 1902.

Illinois 18 size, Bunn Special, 21 ruby jewels, railroad grade, very nice 14k solid gold hunting **case**, double sunk porcelain **dial**, Arabic numerals, blue spade hands; lever set, nickel beautifully damaskeened full-plate two-tone **movement**, gold jewel settings, double roller, marked adjusted (1539553).
$1,950.00.
Photo and description courtesy of OldWatch.com.

Plate 469. Circa 1903.

Hamilton 16 size, 960, 21 jewels, railroad grade, white-gold-filled Hamilton railroad model, marked "Stiff Bow" **case**, double sunk porcelain **dial**, Arabic numerals, blue spade hands, lever set, nickel ¾-plate bridge model, gold jewel settings, full gold train, marked adjusted micrometric regulator (324658).
$1,150.00.
Photo and descriptions courtesy of OldWatch.com.

Plate 470. Circa 1903.

Illinois, size 16, model #5, grade Sangamo, number of jewels: 21, Serial number 1567464. TuTone wavy pattern damaskeening, Gothic-style dial. Accepted for RR service.
$550.00.
Photos and descriptions courtesy of Edward Ueberall, Collector/Dealer.

Plate 471. Circa 1903.

Waltham 18 size, Dominion Railway, 17 jewels, railroad grade, very nice nickel silver open-face **case**, double sunk porcelain multicolored "Dominion Railway" 24-hour Canadian Railroad with train on the **dial**, Arabic/Roman numerals, blue spade hands, full plate, nickel, model 83, Appleton Tracy **movement**, gold jewel settings, adjusted, micrometric regulator (12553712). **$4,500.00.**

Photo and description courtesy of OldWatch.com.

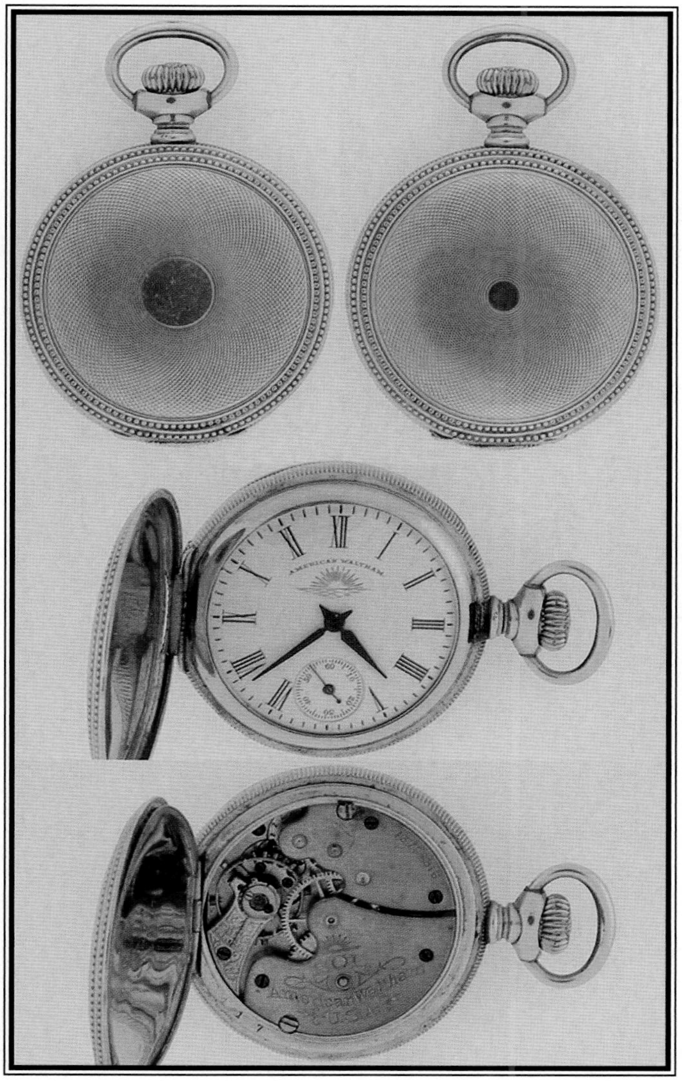

Plate 472. Circa 1903.

Waltham 0 size, Sol model 91, seven jewels, very nice yellow-gold-filled hunting case, single sunk porcelain **dial** with a sun on it, Roman numerals, blue spade hands, ¾-plate gilt **movement**, marked "Sol," with a sun micrometric regulator (13724516). **$245.00.**

Photo and description courtesy of OldWatch.com.

Plate 473. Circa 1903.

Illinois, size 18, model #6, grade 65, number of jewels: 21, serial number 1683183. Reason for this marking, "1908 Special," also seen as "1905 Special," isn't known.
$900.00.
Photos and description courtesy of Edward Ueberall, Collector/Dealer.

Plate 474. Circa 1904.

Waltham, size 0, number of jewels: 7, serial number 129331443. Lady's 14K gold with multicolor fancy **dial**.
$875.00.
Photos and description courtesy of Edward Ueberall, Collector/Dealer.

Plate 475. Circa 1904.

14K yellow gold. Number of jewels: 23, Riverside Maximus **movement**, serial number 13006435, original Riverside Maximus **dial**.
$1,800.00.
Description and watch courtesy of Penny Steiner.

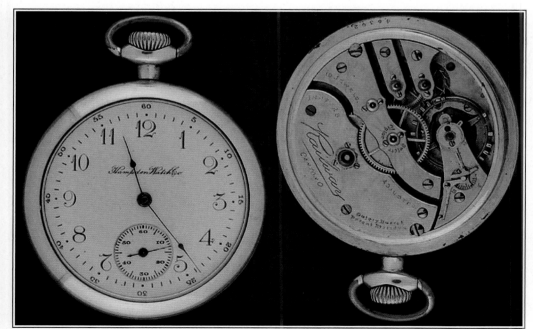

Plate 476. Circa 1904.

Hampden 16 size Railway, 19 jewels, railroad grade, nice yellow-gold-filled open-face case, single sunk porcelain **dial**, Arabic numerals, blue spade hands, lever set, beautifully damaskeened nickel bridge **movement** with gold inlay, marked "Railway," gold jewel settings, marked adjusted, gold center wheel, jeweled mainspring barrel, micrometric regulator (1897926).
$450.00.
Photo and description courtesy of OldWatch.com.

Plate 477. Circa 1904.

Hamilton 18 size, 940 two-tone, 21 jewels, railroad grade, "Hamilton"-marked salesman sample display **case**, Excellent double sunk porcelain **dial**, Arabic numerals, blue spade hands, beautiful full-plate nickel two-tone **movement**, lever set, marked adjusted, screw-down gold jewel settings, micrometric regulator (412311).
$1,200.00.
Photo and description courtesy of OldWatch.com.

Plate 478. Circa 1904.

Ball Elgin 18 size, grade 331, Commercial Standard, 16 jewels, yellow-gold-filled **case** with locomotive on the back, Ball Watch Co. single sunk porcelain **dial**, full-plate nickel **movement** with circular damaskeening, marked "Commercial Standard," gold jewel settings, micrometric regulator (11854162).
$1,150.00.
Photo and description courtesy of OldWatch.com.

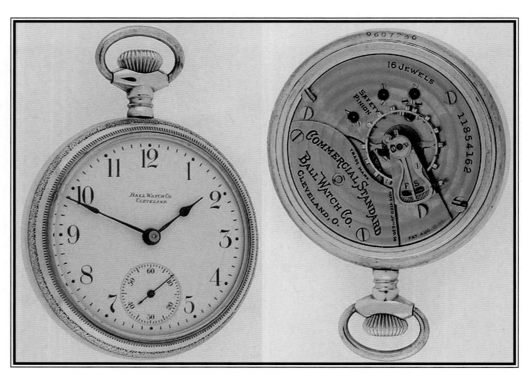

Plate 479. Circa 1905.

14K multicolored gold hunting **case** with shield on the front and a diamond on the back, stem wind, stem set, Keystone Howard, number of jewels: 17, **movement** serial number 89108.
$2,850.00.
Description and watch courtesy of Jack Harvey, Dealer.

Plate 480. Agassiz, Swiss, No. 115569, made for Tiffany & Co., circa 1905. Very fine 18K gold, diamond-set keyless pendant watch with matching gold chain.

Case. Four-body, "bassine," deeply chased and engraved with scrolling, back centered with good size diamond, gold hinged cuvette, swivel pendant. Gold ribbon-knot chain. **Dial.** Light cream-green enamel with raised white enamel cartouches for gold paillon Breguet numerals, outer minute ring. Louis XV gold hands. **Movement.** 20.3 mm (9"), nickel plated, "fausses cotes" decoration, 18 jewels, straight-line lever escapement, cut bimetallic compensation balance, Breguet balance spring. Movement signed. Dial signed by the retailer.
Diam. 26 mm. **$4,140.00.**
Photo and description courtesy of Antiquorum Auctioneers, 19 Mar 2003.

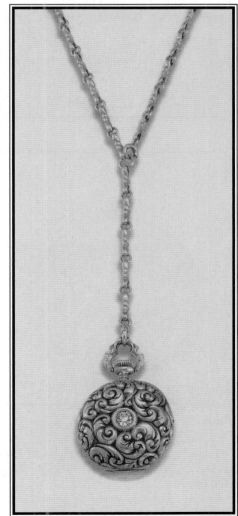

Plate 481. Ulysse Nardin, Lode, Suisse, No. 12165, especially made for a important Argentinian customer in 1905, with painted miniature on the cuvette. Very fine 18K gold, keyless, split-seconds chronograph watch with 30-minute register.

Case. Four-body, "bassine," back with champleve blue, red, and green enamel initials, polished, gold hinged cuvette fitted with enamel portrait of a young lady. **Dial.** White enamel, red Arabic numerals, 24-hour inner red Arabic ring (13 − 24), outer minute track, outermost chronograph ring with pulsometer scale (base 30), sunk minute register at 12 o'clock, subsidiary sunk seconds. Spade blued-steel hands **Movement.** 22″, adjusted by Edouard Matthey Tissol, nickel, "fausses cotes" decoration, 25 jewels, straight-line lever escapement, cut bimetallic compensation balance with Breguet balance spring, swan neck micrometric regulator, visible split-seconds mechanism. Dial and case signed.
Diam. 55 mm. **$6,900.00.**
Photo and description courtesy of Antiquorum Auctioneers, 19 Mar 2003.

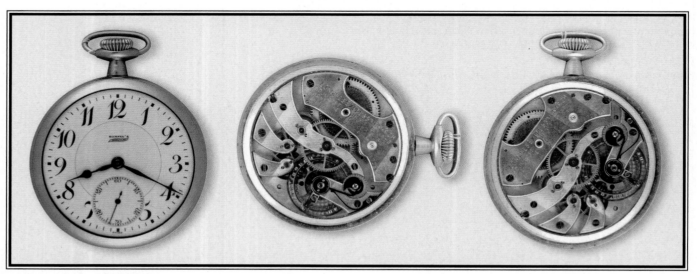

Plate 482. Circa 1905.

Longines, size 16, model #19.95, grade Express Monarch, number of jewels: 21, serial number 1972808. Longines **movement** for RR service, private label for "Bichsel's, Sedalia, MO."
$550.00.
Photos and description courtesy of Edward Ueberall, Collector/Dealer.

Plate 483. Circa 1905.

Tavannes, size 16, number of jewels: 21, serial number 12170990. Imported from Switzerland into U.S. and Canada, fits standard 16 size cases.
$350.00.
Photos and description courtesy of Edward Ueberall, Collector/Dealer.

Plate 484. LeCoultre Swiss, retail by Cartier, Paris. Produced circa 1905.
Fine, very thin 18K yellow gold dress watch. Accompanied by a Cartier box.

Case. Three-body, solid, polished, case back with enameled initials. **Dial.** Silver guilloche Sun Ray pattern with painted Arabic numerals, auxiliary seconds dial. Breguet blued-steel hands. **Movement.** LeCoultre ebauche, 17", gilt brass, 19 jewels, straight-line lever escapement, cut bimetallic compensation balance with screws, blued-steel flat balance-spring.
Case numbered "1458."
Diam. 46 mm. **$2,300.00.**
Photo and description courtesy of Antiquorum Auctioneers, 19 Mar 2003.

Plate 485. Circa 1905.

Hamilton 18 size, 946, 23 jewels, railroad grade, excellent yellow-gold-filled open-face **case**, double sunk porcelain Montgomery **dial**, Arabic numerals, blue spade hands, lever set, beautiful full-plate nickel with gold inlay, marked adjusted, gold jewel settings, jeweled mainspring barrel, micrometric regulator (442208). **$1,800.00.**
Photo and description courtesy of OldWatch.com.

Plate 486. Circa 1905.

18 size, 21 jewels, Ball made by Hamilton Watch Co., all Ball watches should be in Ball cases. But this one is not. If it were in a Ball case, it would be worth $1,000.00.
$700.00.
Description and watch courtesy of Father Bradly Offutt, Collector.

Plate 487. Circa 1905.

Zenith, size 18, Superior, number of jewels: 21, serial number 1644845. Made by Zentih Swiss for Canadian RR market. Few, if any, in U.S. RR services.
$800.00.
Photos and description courtesy of Edward Ueberall, Collector/Dealer.

Plate 488. Circa 1906.
Patek, Philippe &. Cie., Geneve, No.1 35521, case No. 243005. Fine and rare 18K gold keyless lady's pendant watch with unusual caliber.

Case. Four-body, "bassine", engine-turned, gold hinged cuvette. **Dial.** White enamel, by Pierre Reymond, Roman numerals, outer minute track with five-minute Arabic markers, subsidiary sunk seconds. Blued steel "spade" hands. **Movement.** 27 mm., cal. 12, frosted gilt, 15 jewels, straight line lever escapement, cut bimetallic compensation balance with Breguet balance spring
Signed on dial and case, movement numbered.
Diam. 30 mm. **$2,332.00.**
Photo and description courtesy of Antiquorum Auctioneers, 14 Jun 2003.

Plate 489. Circa 1906.

South Bend, size 16, model #1, grade 295, number of jewels: 21, serial number 480389. Marginal minute dial.
$1,400.00.
Photos and description courtesy of Edward Ueberall, Collector/Dealer.

Plate 490. Longines, Swiss, No. 1955190, circa 1906.
Very fine 18K gold and enamel, diamond-set fob watch with matching brooch.

Case. Four-body, "bassine," back with translucent imperial blue and olive green enamel separated by opaque white enamel with gold leaves and applied white gold diamond-set floral appliqué, gold hinged cuvette. Matching brooch with translucent olive green enamel with applied white gold diamond-set appliqué. **Dial.** Champagne, Breguet numerals, outer minute track, subsidiary seconds. Blued-steel Breguet hands. **Movement.** 22 mm (9¾"). Frosted gilt, 16 jewels, straight-line lever escapement, cut bimetallic compensation balance with flat balance spring.
Signed on dial and movement, case and movement with the same serial number.
Diam. 28 mm; length with the brooch, 68 mm. **$2,691.00.**
Photo and description courtesy of Antiquorum Auctioneers, 14 Jun 2003.

**Plate 491. Girard-Perregaux, La Chaux-de-Fonds.
Produced in the 1900s.
Fine, small, hunter-cased, keyless, 18K yellow gold, enamel and diamonds
watch. Accompanied by a yellow and white gold chain set with nine faceted,
round diamonds.**

Case. Four-body, solid, polished and brushed, hinged covers, front with floral and geometrical pattern, enamel motif and set with five faceted, round diamonds, hinged gold
cuvette with inscription. **Dial.** off-white enamel with painted Arabic numerals, outer gold
dot minute ring, sunk subsidiary seconds, Louis XV pink gold hands. **Movement.** Cal.
12", rhodium-plated, "fausses cotes" decoration, 15 jewels, straight-line lever escapement,
cut bimetallic compensation balance with screws, blued-steel flat balance spring.
Dial, case, and movement signed.
Diam. 31 mm. **$1,388.00.**
Photo and description courtesy of Bonhams and Butterfields, San Francisco, 24 Jun 2003.

Plate 492. Circa 1907.

Waltham 12 size, 15 jew-
els, very nice two-tone
open-face white/rose
gold-filled **case**, single
sunk porcelain **dial** Arabic numerals, blue moon
hands, ¾-plate nickel
movement, gold center
wheel, srew down jewel
settings, micrometric regulator (16343476).
$225.00.
*Photo and description cour-
tesy of OldWatch.com.*

Plate 493. Circa 1907.

Waltham, size 18, mModel 1892, Vanguard. Wind indicator, fig. eight-style regulator. Number of jewels, 23. Serial number 16126232.
$3,100.00.
Photos and description courtesy of Edward Ueberall, Collector/Dealer.

Plate 494. Circa 1907.

Vacheron Constantin, Swiss, 40mm size, 21 jewels, excellent solid gold 18k triple-hinged open-face **case** single sunk porcelain **dial** marked "Vacheron Constantin," Arabic numerals, straw hands, beautiful bridge, "Vacheron Constantin"–marked nickel **movement** with Wolf Teeth winding gears, gold jewel settings, marked adjusted, micrometric regulator (300178).
$4,000.00.
Photo and description courtesy of OldWatch.com.

Plate 495. Circa 1907.

Waltham, size 16, model #1899, Crescent Street, number of jewels: 21, serial number 16106127. TuTone private label, buyer and meaning of "Special W.C." unknown.
$650.00.
Photos and description courtesy of Edward Ueberall, Collector/Dealer.

Plate 496. Circa 1907.

Illinois, size 16, Sangamo. Ariston private label for Marshall Field & Co., Chicago, in original walnut presentation box. Number of jewels, 21. Serial number 2017009.
$1,450.00.
Photos and description courtesy of Edward Ueberall, Collector/Dealer.

Plate 497. Patek Philippe, Geneve gold pocket watch, 1908. Retailed by Shreve & Co.

Case. 18k yellow gold, circular, open face. **Dial.** White enamel, black Arabic numerals, sunk auxiliary seconds dial, yellow Louis XVI hands. **Movement.** Nickeled, 18 jewels, lever escapement, cut bimetallic screwed balance wheel, adjusted to: heat, cold, isochronism, and five positions, Breguet balance spring.
Signed "Patek Philippe" on case, movement. Signed Shreve & Co. on dial, movement.
Diam. 44 mm. **$1,500.00 – 2,000.00.**
Photo and description courtesy of Bonhams and Butterfields, San Francisco, 24 Jun 2003.

Plate 498. Circa 1908.

Manistee Watch Co. 16 size, 17 jewels, yellow-gold-filled hunting **case**, double sunk porcelain **dial** with multicolored blue Arabic numerals, blue spade hands, beautifully damaskeened nickel ¾-plate **movement**, gold jewel settings, gold center wheel, micrometric regulator (34017) - 1912. **$850.00.**
Photo and description courtesy of OldWatch.com.

Plate 499. Circa 1908.

14K multicolored gold, boxed-hinge hunting **case** with shield on front and large elk on the back. Rockford, number of jewels: 17, double roller, stem wind and stem set. Serial number 788610. **Dial** with Arabic numbers.
$3,975.00.
Description and watch courtesy of Jack Harvey, Dealer.

Plate 500. Circa 1909.

18 size, yellow-gold-filled, Elgin, grade 349, 21 jewels. A more common watch. #14,087,188.
$300.00.
Description and watch courtesy of Father Bradly Offutt, Collector.

Plate 501. Circa 1909.

Elgin, size 16, model #6, grade 290, number of jewels: 7, serial number 14873885. Man's dress hunting case with multicolor **case** and fancy **dial**.

$600.00.

Photos and description courtesy of Edward Ueberall, Collector/Dealer.

Plate 502. Circa 1909.

Hamilton, size 18, model #1, grade 940, number of jewels: 21, serial number 683182. Popular 18 size 21-jewel **movement** made for railroad service.

$400.00.

Photos and description courtesy of Edward Ueberall, Collector/Dealer.

Plate 503. Circa 1909.

Hamilton, size 16, number of jewels: 17, serial number 735100. Medium-grade Hamilton, pendant set.
$275.00.
Photos and description courtesy of Edward Ueberall, Collector/Dealer.

Plate 504. H. R. Ekegrin, Geneva, No. 78961, made for J. E. Caldwell & Co., Philadelphia, circa 1910.
Very fine and rare platinum, keyless, minute-repeating dress watch in original fitted box accompanied by platinum chain.

Case. Four-body, "bassine et filets," with flat monogrammed back, platinum hinged cuvette. **Dial.** Matte silver, applied yellow gold Breguet numerals, outer minute dot divisions, subsidiary sunk seconds. Gold Breguet hands. **Movement.** 38 mm, rhodium plated, 29 jewels, straight-line lever escapement, cut bimetallic compensation balance with Breguet balance spring, swan neck micrometric regulator, repeating on gongs through activating slide in the band.
Signed on dial, case, and movement.
Diam. 47 mm. **$11,661.00.**
Photo and description courtesy of Antiquorum Auctioneers, 16 Jun 2003.

Plate 505. Circa 1910.

Howard, size 16, grade 5, number of jewels: 21, serial number 1090304. Howard Montgomery **dial** with 24 hour figures for use in Canada.
$325.00.

Photos and description courtesy of Edward Ueberall, Collector/Dealer.

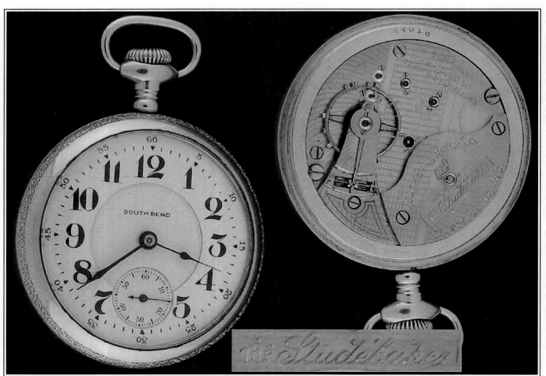

Plate 506. Circa 1910.

Southbend 18 size, 329, the Studebaker, 21 jewels, railroad grade, yellow-gold-filled open-face screw-back **case**, double sunk porcelain **dial**, Arabic numerals, blue spade hands, beautiful damaskeened nickel full-plate **movement** with gold inlay, marked "329" and "The Studebaker," gold jewel settings, double roller, adjusted five positions, micrometric regulator (634006).
$1,600.00.

Photo and description courtesy of OldWatch.com.

Plate 507. Circa 1910.
Fine and beautiful Swiss Invar 18K gold, hunting-case, minute-repeating grande and petite sonnerie clock-watch antique pocket watch in original box with release button.

The substantial **case** fully and deeply engraved on both covers and extending on the band. Fine white enamel **dial** with bold numerals and gold spade hands. Lever at the bezel to select silence or automatic strike either hours and quarters (petite sonnerie) or hours and quarters at every quarter (grande sonnerie). Button in the band for minute repeater on demand. Gold and glazed dust covers over the first-quality nickel 32-jewel tandem-wind **movement** jeweled to the center and the hammers. The original wooden box with button to sound the repeat without opening the box. A beautiful and complicated watch in wonderful condition. Diam. 55 mm. **$30,000.00.**
Photo and description courtesy of Stephen Bogoff, Antiquarian Horologist.

Plate 508. Marvin, Swiss, circa 1910.
Fine and amusing 18K gold and cloisonné enamel keyless dress watch.

Case. Three-piece, sharp edges, back decorated in cloisonné enamel in opaque and iridescent enamels in yellow, green, red, orange, and black, depicting a stream with water plants and a large applied gold realistically-painted lady bug, the bezels, pendant, and bow with champlevé blue and green stripes, wide pendant smoothly integrated with the case and bow. **Dial.** Silver with champlevé Arabic numerals, outer minute track, subsidiary sunk seconds. Blued-steel Roman hands. **Movement.** 36 mm, (16"). Rhodium plated, 16 jewels, straight-line lever escapement, cut bimetallic compensation balance with blued-steel Breguet balance spring.
Signed on dial, case, and movement.
Diam. 45 mm. **$11,512.00.**
Photo and description courtesy of Antiquorum Auctioneers, Nov 2002.

Plate 509. Patek Philippe & Cie., Geneve, No. 146188, case No. 249586, made for Gondolo & Labouriau, Relojoeiros, Rio de Janeiro, circa 1910.
Very fine 18K gold keyless Chronometro Gondolo.

Case. Four-body, "bassine," engine-turned back with engraved initials, gold hinged cuvette. **Dial.** White enamel with Roman numerals, outer minute track with five-minute Arabic markers, sunk subsidiary seconds. Gold spade hands. **Movement.** 45 mm (20"), cal. 180, gilt brass patented bridge caliber, 21 jewels, gold train, straight line moustache lever escapement, cut bimetallic compensation balance with blued-steel Breguet balance spring, Wilmot's patented micrometric cam regulator.
Signed on the dial, case, and movement.
Diam. 48 mm. **$3,408.00.**
Photo and description courtesy of Antiquorum Auctioneers, 14 Jun 2003.

Plate 510. Swiss, gold minute-repeating pocket watch. Circa 1910.

Case. 14K yellow gold, circular, open face. **Dial.** White enamel. black Arabic numerals, sunk auxiliary seconds dial, yellow Louis XVI hands. **Movement.** Nickeled, highly jeweled through hammers, lever escapement, bimetallic screwed balance wheel, Breguet balance spring.
Diam. 48 mm. **$1,527.00.**
Photo and description courtesy of Bonhams and Butterfields, San Francisco, 24 Jun 2003.

Plate 511. Circa 1910.

Gallet, size 18, number of jewels: 21, serial number 126835. Private label for T. Eaton Department store in Canada.
$475.00.
Photos and description courtesy of Edward Ueberall, Collector/Dealer.

Plate 512. Circa 1910.

Elgin, size 18, model #8, Father Time, number of jewels: 21, serial number 15644036. Winding indicator with free sprung regulator.
$1,150.00.
Photos and description courtesy of Edward Ueberall, Collector/Dealer.

Plate 513. Circa 1910.

Swiss, size 16, number of jewels: 21, serial number 38456. High grade Swiss private label for J. Jessop & Sons, San Diego, CA. Actual manufacturer unknown.
$475.00.
Photos and description courtesy of Edward Ueberall, Collector/Dealer.

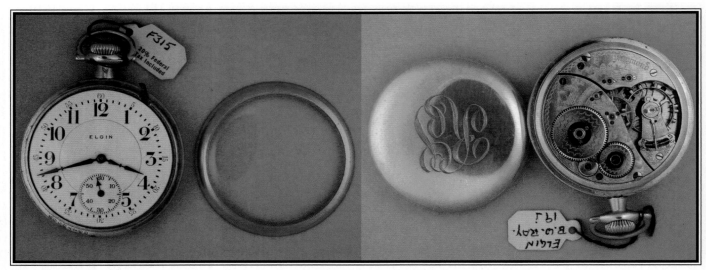

Plate 514. Circa 1910.

Elgin, size 18, model #15, grade 372, number of jewels: 19, serial number 15291819. B. W. Raymond (one of Elgin's founders, was mayor from Chicago).
$350.00.
Photos and description courtesy of Edward Ueberall, Collector/Dealer.

Plate 515. Circa 1910.

Elgin, size 18, model #8, grade 390, number of jewels: 21, serial number 15900332. B. W. Raymond with Montgomery **dial**.
$550.00.
Photos and description courtesy of Edward Ueberall, Collector/Dealer.

Plate 516. Circa 1910.

Elgin, size 18, model #8, grade 390, number of jewels: 21, serial number 15768745. Engraved "No. 349," several examples seen, reason unknown for marking.
$575.00.
Photos and description courtesy of Edward Ueberall, Collector/Dealer.

Plate 517. Staehli & Brun, Swiss, No. 14414, circa 1910.
Fine and very rare 14K gold keyless watch with special patented beat adjustment carriage and special regulator.

Case. Four-body, "bassine," back centered with imperial blue enamel initials, gold hinged cuvette. **Dial.** White enamel, double sunk, Breguet numerals, outer minute track, subsidiary sunk seconds. Blued-steel spade hands. **Movement.** 41 mm, rhodium plated, 21 jewels, adjusted to five positions and temperature, straight-line lever escapement, Cut bimetallic compensation balance with Breguet balance spring, patented concave rack-and-pinion micrometric regulator, special tourbillon-like cage for beat adjustment. Signed on the movement.
Diam. 50 mm. **$3,588.00.**
Photo and description courtesy of Antiquorum Auctioneers, 14 Jun 2003.

Plate 518. Circa 1911.

Illinois, size 16, model #5, grade Sangamo, number of jewels: 23, serial number 2327660. Made as private label for Sears Roebuck & Co., TuTone plates.
$2,000.00.
Photos and description courtesy of Edward Ueberall, Collector/Dealer.

Plate 519. Circa 1911.

Elgin, size 18, model #8, grade 214, number of jewels; 23. Serial number 16602080. Veritas-Grade winding indicator.
$3,250.00.
Photos and description courtesy of Edward Ueberall, Collector/Dealer.

Plate 520. Circa 1909.

Studerbaker, yellow gold filled, Montgomery **dial**, #643814, by South Bend. **$1,200.00 – 1,400.00.** *Description and watch courtesy of Father Bradly Offutt, Collector.*

Plate 521. Patek Philippe & Cie., Geneve, No. 162442, case No. 268123, circa 1912.
Fine 18K gold and enamel keyless pocket watch.

Case. Four-body, "bassine," with flat back and faceted bezels decorated with champlevé blue enamel Spanish pattern, knurled band, gold hinged cuvette. **Dial.** White enamel, Arabic numerals, outer minute divisions, subsidiary sunk seconds. Blued-steel Breguet hands. **Movement.** 38 mm, maillechort, "fausses cotes" decoration, 18 jewels, straight-line calibrated lever escapement, cut bimetallic compensation balance with Breguet balance spring. Signed on dial, case, and movement.
Diam. 46 mm. **$4,485.00.**
Photo and description courtesy of Antiquorum Auctioneers, 14 Jun 2003.

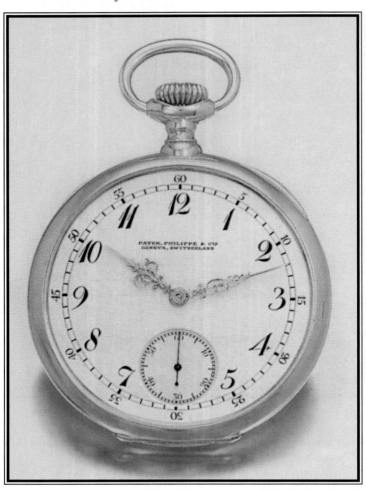

Plate 522. Patek Philippe & Cie., Geneve, No. 160343, case No. 270143, circa 1912.
Very fine 18K gold, keyless pocket watch in original fitted box, accompanied by original certificate.

Case. Four-body, all hinged, "bassine," polished, with monogrammed back, gold hinged cuvette. **Dial.** White enamel, Breguet numerals, outer minute track with five-minute Arabic markers, subsidiary sunk seconds. Gold Louis XV hands. **Movement.** 42 mm, cal. 180, frosted gilt, 20 jewels, straight-line calibrated lever escapemen, cut bimetallic compensation balance with Breguet balance spring, Wilmot patented micrometric cam regulator.
Signed on dial, case, and movement.
Diam. 49 mm. **$3,767.00.**
Photo and description courtesy of Antiquorum Auctioneers, 14 Jun 2003.

Plate 523. Patek Philippe & Cie., Geneve, No. 157332, case No. 402619, circa 1912.
Very fine 18K gold, keyless, minute-repeating presentation dress watch.

Case. Four-body, "bassine," polished with monogrammed back. **Dial.** White enamel, Breguet numerals, outer minute track, subsidiary sunk seconds. Blued-steel Breguet hands. **Movement.** 40 mm (18"), rhodium plated, 31 jewels, eight adjustments, straight-line calibrated lever escapement, cut bimetallic compensation balance with Breguet balance spring, swan neck micrometric regulator, repeating on gongs through activating slide in the band. Signed on dial, case, and movement.
Diam. 47 mm. **$10,764.00.**
Photo and description courtesy of Antiquorum Auctioneers, 14 Jun 2003.

Plate 524. Patek Philippe & Cie., Geneve, No. 157424, case No. 406135, circa 1912.
Very fine and rare 18K gold keyless double train trip minute-repeating dress watch.

Case. Four-body, "bassine," polished with monogrammed back, gold cuvette with concealed hinges. **Dial.** Gilt, matte and guilloche, champlevé Breguet numerals, outer minute crack, subsidiary sunk seconds, blued-steel Breguet hand **Movement.** 40 mm (18"), nickel. "fausses cotes" decoration, two-crain, 33 jewels, straight-line calibrated lever escapement, cut bimetallic compensation balance. Breguet balance spring, tandem winding, repeating on gongs by tripping the gold push-piece in the crown.
Signed by the retailer on dial, case, and movement.
Diam. 48 mm. **$28,704.00.**
Photo and description courtesy of Antiquorum Auctioneers, 14 Jun 2003.

Plate 525. Circa 1912.

Illinois, size 16. Private label Pennsylvania Special, TuTone **movement** in factory Illinois display case. Number of jewels, 21. Serial number 2395811.
$3,150.00.
Photos and description courtesy of Edward Ueberall, Collector/Dealer.

Plate 526. Circa 1912.

Howard 16 size, series 0, 23 jewels, correct E. Howard Watch Co., Boston yellow 14k solid gold hunting **case** with Jurgensen lips, nice double sunk **dial**, blue spade hands, nickel bridge **movement**, gold jewel settings, marked adjusted, micrometric regulator (1057322).
$2,200.00.
Photo and description courtesy of OldWatch.com.

Plate 527. Circa 1913.

Rockford, size 18, model #9, grade 950, number of jewels: 21, serial number 908002. Only 18 size winding indicator made by Rockford, 200 made.
$6,100.00.
Photos and description courtesy of Edward Ueberall, Collector/Dealer.

Plate 528. Circa 1913.

Illinois 18 size, Bunn Special, 23 jewels, jeweled barrel, railroad grade, excellent yellow-gold-filled open-face **case**, double sunk porcelain Montgomery **dial**, Arabic numerals, blue spade hands, lever set, wonderfully damaskeened full-plate nickel **movement** with gold inlay, marked jeweled barrel, adjusted temperature and six positions, gold jewel settings, double roller, jeweled mainspring barrel, micrometric regulator (2507648). **$1,400.00.**
Photo and description courtesy of OldWatch.com.

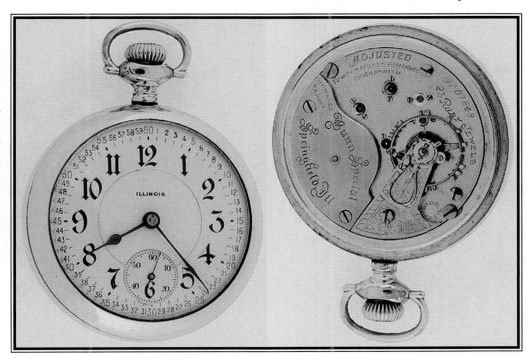

Plate 529. Circa 1913.

Hamilton, size 16. TuTone movement with special "adjusted for RR Service" **dial**. Number of jewels, 21. Serial number 1136513.
$2,650.00.
Photos and description courtesy of Edward Ueberall, Collector/Dealer.

Plate 530. Circa 1914.

Waltham, size 16, model #1908, Vanguard, number of jewels: 23, serial number 19063298. Gold center wheel, diamond stone. **$750.00.**
Photos and description courtesy of Edward Ueberall, Collector/Dealer.

Plate 531. Circa 1914.

English 16 size Mark V, 15 jewels, Royal Flying Corp., base metal case with World War I Royal Flying Corp markings, black face, **dial** marked "30 HOUR/NON-LUMINOUS/MARK V/CC 798," white hands, ¾-plate gilt movement, pressed jewels, micrometric regulator (622109). World War I. The watch has no bow because it was fitted in a special holder on the instrument panel of the aviator's plane. An interesting note: If the plane crashed and the pilot survived, he was to remove the watch from the wreck and turn it in. If he didn't do this, he was subject to a court martial! **$550.00.**
Photo and description courtesy of OldWatch.com.

Plate 532. Circa 1914.

Howard 12 size, series 8, 23 jewels, correct hinged E. Howard Watch Co., Boston, white 14K solid gold open-face **case**, nice single sunk **dial**, fleur-de-lis hands, nickel bridge **movement**, gold jewel settings, adjusted five positions, micrometric regulator (1265694). **$750.00.**
Photo and description courtesy of OldWatch.com.

Plate 533. Circa 1915.

Watham gold-filled case, Vanguard, 23 jewels, **movement**, with five positions, adjusted, serial number 20147126. **$750.00.**
Description and watch courtesy of Aaron Faber Gallery.

Plate 534. Audemars Freres, "Horlogers de Sa Majeste l'Empereur de Russie par l'ancienne Maison Aude mars fondee 1811," Brassus & Geneva, No. 32947, circa 1915.

Very fine 18K gold, hunting-cased, keyless, astronomical, minute-repeating watch with perpetual calendar, moon calendar, and phases of the moon.

Case. Five-body, "bassine," engine-turned, gold hinged cuvette. **Dial.** White enamel, Roman numerals. Outer minute track, four subsidiary sunk dials for days of the week, date, months of the four-year leap cycle and subsidiary seconds concentric with phases of the moon aperture. Blued-steel spade hands. **Movement.** 45 mm (20"), rhodium plated, "fausses cotes" decoration, 29 jewels, straight-line calibrated lever escapement, cut bimetallic compensation balance with Breguet balance spring, rack-and-pinion micrometric regulator, lever set, repeating on gongs through activating slide in the band.
Signed on dial and case.
Diam. 57 mm. **$25,226.00.**
Photo and description courtesy of Antiquorum Auctioneers, 14 Jun 2003.

Plate 535. Circa 1915.
Good Swiss Vacheron & Constantin 18K gold antique pocket watch.

Coat-of-arms and monogram on the back of the substantial plain polish **case** shows some wear. Enamel **dial** with gold hands and the name of the retailer. Fine 21-jewel eight adjustment **movement** with micrometer regulator and wolf's-tooth winding.
Diam. 50 mm. **$1,075.00.**
Photo and description courtesy of Stephen Bogoff, Antiquarian Horologist, 6 Aug 2003.

Plate 536. Swiss, gold five-minute repeater pocket-watch, circa 1915.
Retailed by Tiffany & Co.

Case. 18k yellow gold, circular, open face. **Dial.** White enamel, black Roman numerals, sunk auxiliary seconds **dial,** blued-steel spade hands. **Movement.** Nickeled, highly jeweled, lever escapement, cut bimetallic screwed balance wheel, Breguet balance spring.
Signed "Tiffany & Co." on case, dial, movement.
Diam. 49 mm. **$2,585.00.**
Photo and description courtesy of Bonhams and Butterfields, San Francisco, 24 Jun 2003.

Plate 537. Frankfeld Freres, Geneva, No. 7310, made for Dreicer & Co., New York, circa 1915.
Very fine 18K gold, keyless, very slim minute-repeating watch.

Case. Three-piece, "bassine," polished, milled for the repeater slide. **Dial.** Silver, champlevé Roman numerals, outer minute track, subsidiary seconds, blued-steel Breguet hands. **Movement.** 41 mm (18"), nickel, "fausses cotes" decoration, 29 jewels, five adjustments, straight-line lever escapement, cut bimetallic compensation balance with blued-steel flat balance spring repeating on gongs through activating slide in the band.
Dial, case, and movement signed.
Diam. 48 mm. **$3,450.00.**
Photo and description courtesy of Antiquorum Auctioneers, 21 May 2003.

Plate 538. Circa 1917.

Omega, size 18. Top of the line Omega, with diamond balance endstones, probably made for the South American market. Number of jewels, 23. Serial number 2362227.
$1,550.00.
Photos and description courtesy of Edward Ueberall, Collector/Dealer.

Plate 539. Circa 1917.

Omega, size 18, DDR, number of jewels: 23, serial number 2361979. Sold under the Brandt name in Canada.
$1,350.00.
Photos and description courtesy of Edward Ueberall, Collector/Dealer.

Plate 540. Circa 1918.

Patek Philippe Chronometro Gondolo, 55mm, 20 jewels, excellent 18K solid gold, hinged, Chronometro Gondolo "PP Co."–marked triple-hinged **case**, also marked on the dust cover: "Chronometro Gondolo Fabricado expressamente para Gondolo & Labouriam Relojoeiros Rio De Janeiro," single sunk porcelain **dial** marked "Chronometro Gondolo," Roman numerals, gold spade hands, beautiful gilt **movement** marked "Patek Philippe," wolf teeth winding gear, micrometric regulator (180291).
$6,500.00.
Photo and description courtesy of OldWatch.com.

Plate 541. Circa 1918.

Waltham, size 16, model #1908, open face, star micrometer regulator, not marked adjusted. Number of jewels, 17.
Serial number 21334118.
$175.00.
Photos and description courtesy of Edward Ueberall, Collector/Dealer.

Plate 542. Circa 1919.

Illinois, size 16, number of jewels: 15, serial number 3229481. Medium quality man's watch in silveroid (nickel silver) **case**. Metal factory **dial** with purple hands.
$165.00.
Photos and description courtesy of Edward Ueberall, Collector/Dealer.

Plate 543. Circa 1919.

Waltham 16 size, Royal model 1908, 17 jewels, very nice yellow-gold-filled hunting case, single sunk porcelain **dial**, Roman numerals, blue spade hands, ¾-plate nickel **movement**, marked adjusted, gold jewel settings, gold center wheel, micrometric regulator (23055647).
$495.00.
Photo and description courtesy of OldWatch.com.

Plate 544. Circa 1927.

Lindberg dollar watch made by Ingraham Watch Co., chrome plated on brass with the matching fob.
$700.00.
Description and watch courtesy of David Strudler.

Plate 545. Omega, Swiss, No. 7033788, circa 1920.
Very fine 18K gold and enamel Art Deco keyless dress watch.

Case. Three-piece, 12-sided, deeply chased bezels with translucent imperial blue enamel foliage, band with foliate decoration matching the bezels, monogrammed in the back. **Dial.** Silvered, matted, champlevé Arabic numerals, outer minute track, chased ring in the center with floral pattern. Elaborate gold hands. **Movement.** 23 mm, rhodium plated, "fausses cotes" decoration, 15 jewels, straight-line lever escapement, cut bimetallic compensation balance with Breguet balance spring.
Signed on dial, case, and movement.
Diam. 46 mm. **$3,230.00.**
Photo and description courtesy of Antiquorum Auctioneers, 16 Jun 2003.

Plate 546. Patek Philippe & Cie., Geneve, No. 180455, case No. 401232, made for Bunde & Upmeyer Co., Milwaukee, Wisconsin, circa 1920.
Very fine and very rare 18K gold keyless dress watch with blue sapphire jewels.

Case. Four-body, "bassine," polished, gold hinged cuverre. **Dial.** White enamel, radial Arabic numerals, outer minute track, subsidiary sunk seconds. Blued-steel cathedral hands. **Movement.** 38 mm (I Too), patented cal. 210, nickel, oil stone finish, 18 blue sapphire jewels, straight-line calibrated lever escapement, cut bimetallic compensation balance with Breguet balance spring.

Signed on dial, case, and movement; case and movement signed also by the retailer.

Diam. 45 mm. **$23,322.00.**

Photo and description courtesy of Antiquorum Auctioneers, 14 Jun 2003.

Plate 547. Circa 1920.
Fine, thin, elegant 14K gold Art Deco open-face minute repeater.

Substantial plain polish **case** with slide in the band to activate the repeat. First-quality 33-jewel **movement** with capped escapement, jeweled to the center and the hammers, and stamped with two Geneva seals, which is a sign of very high quality. Matte silver **dial** with bright silver minute markers and applied gold baton markers. A most handsome watch, in particularly fine condition with loud, clear tone.

Diam. 45 mm. **$3,500.00.**

Photo and description courtesy of Stephen Bogoff, Antiquarian Horologist, 6 Aug 2003.

Plate 548. Haas Neveux & Co., Geneve., No. 70299, circa 1920.
Fine and very rare 18K gold and enamel Art Deco keyless dress watch.

Case. Three-piece, massive, knife edge with black enameled band, back decorated with ramolaye floral and foliate decoration over a black ground, the bezel with pink and green floral decoration over a black ground. **Dial.** Silver matte with applied gold Breguet numerals and sunk subsidiary seconds. Gold Breguet hands. **Movement.** 16", rhodium plated, "fausses cotes" decoration, with Seal of Geneva quality mark, 18 jewels, straight-line lever escapement, cut bimetallic compensation balance with Breguet balance spring.
Signed on the dial, trademark on the case.
Diam. 51 mm. **$8,073.00.**
Photo and description courtesy of Antiquorum Auctioneers, 14 Jun 2003.

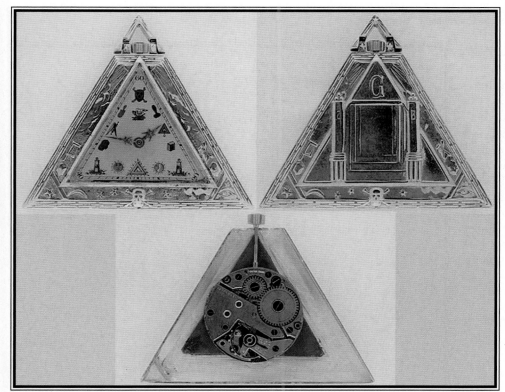

Plate 549. Circa 1920s.

Swiss Masonic triangle, 15 jewels, excellent sterling silver Masonic triangle **case** measuring 55 mm per side, beautiful multicolored Masonic **dial**, gold hands. This is a nice example of a hard-to-find watch.
$2,200.00.
Photo and description courtesy of OldWatch.com.

Plate 550. "Le Phare," Le Lode, No. 8286, circa 1920.
Fine 18K gold, hunting-cased, keyless astronomical minute-repeating watch with full calendar, phases of the moon, and chronograph.

Case. Six-body, "bassine et filets," polished, gold hinged cuvette over glazed gold bezel for viewing the movement. **Dial.** White enamel, Arabic numerals, outer minute track, outermost seconds divided into fifths, aperture at 9 o'clock for days of the week, another at 3 for months, sub-dial at 12 for date, and phases of the moon aperture concentric with subsidiary seconds. Gilt Louis XV hands.
Movement. 50 mm (22"), frosted gilt, straight-line lever escapement, monometallic balance with self-compensating Breguet balance spring, repeating on gongs by depressing activating push button in the band.
Case punched with Le Locle gold guarantee mark.
Diam. 58 mm. **$4,664.00.**
Photo and description courtesy of Antiquorum Auctioneers, 14 Jun 2003.

Plate 551. Unsigned, Swiss, No.1917, circa 1920.
Fine silver hunting-cased keyless minute-repeating watch with chronograph.

Case. Five-body, massive, "bassine," polished, silver hinged cuvette. **Dial.** White enamel, Breguet numerals, outer minute divisions, outermost seconds divided into fifths, subsidiary sunk seconds. Blued-steel Breguet hands. **Movement.** 45 mm, rhodium plated, 32 jewels, straight-line lever escapement, cut bimetallic compensation balance with Breguet balance spring, repeating on gongs through activating slide in the band. Case punched with Le Locle guarantee marks.
Diam. 56 mm. **$2,691.00.**
Photo and description courtesy of Antiquorum Auctioneers, 14 Jun 2003.

Plate 552. Patek Philippe & Cie., Geneve, No. 199054, case No. 503946. Produced in the early 1920s. Fine 18K yellow gold keyless dress watch.

Case. Three-body, solid, polished, case back engraved with geometrical pattern. **Dial.** Matte silver with applied yellow gold Arabic numerals, outer minute graduation, auxiliary seconds dial, Breguet yellow gold hands. **Movement.** Cal. 18½", rhodium plated, "fausses cotes" decoration, 19 jewels, straight-line lever escapement a moustache, cut bimetallic compensation balance with screws, blued-steel Breguet balance-spring, micrometer regulator.
Dial, case, and movement signed.
Diam. 46 mm. **$2,300.00.**
Photo and description courtesy of Antiquorum Auctioneers, 19 Mar 2003.

Plate 553. Patek Philippe & Cie., Geneve, No. 803660, case No. 409239, produced in the early 1920s.
Very fine and elegant, 18K yellow gold gentleman's dress watch with a mother-of-pearl dial.

Case. Three-body, solid, polished. **Dial.** Mother-of-pearl with applied yellow gold Arabic numerals, auxiliary seconds dial, Breguet yellow gold hands. **Movement.** Cal. 18, frosted gilt, 15 jewels, straight-line lever escapement, cut bimetallic compensation balance with screws, blued-steel Breguet balance spring.
Dial, case, and movement signed.
Diam. 46 mm. **$3,680.00.**
Photo and description courtesy of Antiquorum Auctioneers, 19 Mar 2003.

Plate 554. Agassiz, Swiss, lady's platinum, diamond, and sapphire pendant watch, circa 1920.

Case. Platinum, bezel set with diamonds, oval, back of case and chain set with diamonds and sapphires. **Dial.** Silvered, black Arabic numerals, blued-steel Breguet hands. **Movement.** 18 jewels, lever escapement, cut bimetallic screwed balance wheel, six adjustments, Breguet balance spring, estimated total diamond weight: 2.20 cts.
Signed "Agassiz" on movement.
Width of bezel: 16 x 22 mm. **$3,818.75.**
Photo and description courtesy of Bonhams and Butterfields, San Francisco, 24 Jun 2003.

Plate 555. Tiffany & Co., No. 75389.
Produced in the 1920s.
Fine and unusual, platinum and diamonds gentleman's dress watch.

Case. Three-body, polished and brushed. **Dial.** Black enamel with pavé-set diamond indexes, the quarter hours also set with baguette diamonds, concentric minute graduation on matte silver reserve. Spade blued-steel hands. **Movement.** Cal. 11," set in a black enamel ring, rhodium plated, "fausses cotes" decoration, 19 jewels, straight-line lever escapement, cut bimetallic compensation balance with screws, blued-steel Breguet balance spring.
Dial and movement signed.
Diam. 42 mm. **$4,830.00.**
Photo and description courtesy of Antiquorum Auctioneers, 21 May 2003.

Plate 556. Bredillard, France, movement by Dreicer & Co., Swiss, No. 1273, circa 1920.
Very fine and rare amethyst, gold, and platinum, diamond-set, keyless, heart-shaped fob watch with matching diamond-set brooch.

Case. Single heart-shaped piece of amethyst, platinum diamond-set bezel and ribbon-shaped pendant with hinged diamond-set ring, brooch of diamond-set gold and platinum ribbons with gold pin. **Dial.** Silver, matted, champlevé Arabic numerals, outer minute track, center with black champlevé enamel floral pattern. **Movement.** 16.5 mm (7¼"), nickel, 18 jewels, straight-line lever escapement, cut bimetallic compensation balance with blued-steel Breguet balance spring.
Signed inside the case, movement signed by Dreicer.
Diam. length 58 mm, width 32 mm. **$5,756.00.**
Photo and description courtesy of Antiquorum Auctioneers, Nov 2002.

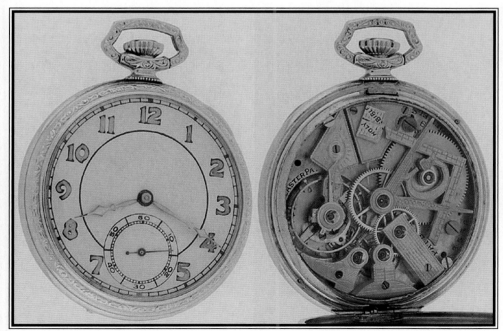

Plate 557. Circa late 1920s.

Dudley 12 size, Model 2, 19 jewels, very nice white-gold-illed flip-open back **case** with movement display, unsigned **dial**, luminescent Arabic numerals, luminescent hands, beautiful Masonic tools of the trade and silver Bible **movement**, gold jewel settings, jeweled mainspring barrel, micrometric regulator (3558).
$4,250.00.
Photo and description courtesy of OldWatch.com.

Plate 558. Agassiz, Swiss, lady's platinum, diamond pendant watch, circa 1920, with box.

Case. Platinum, bezel set with diamonds, square, winding crown with diamond, back of case pave-set with diamonds, with platinum necklace set with diamonds. **Dial.** Textured, silvered, black Arabic numerals, blued-steel Breguet hands. **Movement.** rhodiumed, 18 jewels, lever escapement, cut bimetallic screwed balance wheel, five adjustments, Breguet balance spring.

Signed "Agassiz" on movement. Signed "Tiffany & Co." on interior watch case, movement.

Width of bezel: 25 mm. Estimated total diamond weight: 40.00 cts. **$23,375.00.**

Photo and description courtesy of Bonhams and Butterfields, San Francisco, 25 Jun 2002.

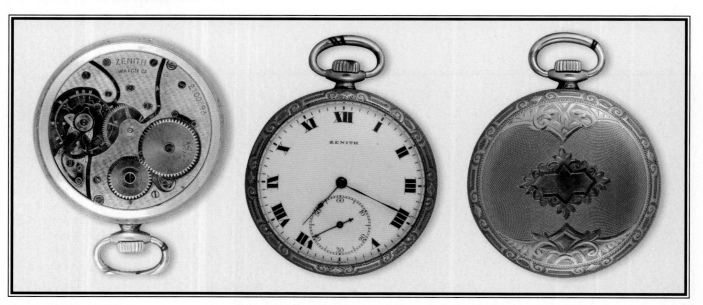

Plate 559. Circa 1920.

Zenith, size 12. Medium grade man's dress watch, well-known Swiss maker. Jewels, 15. Serial number 2100593.
$225.00.
Photos and description courtesy of Edward Ueberall, Collector/Dealer.

Plate 560. Circa 1920.
Fine and lovely Swiss Gubelin, 18K red gold, wandering-hour antique Art Deco pocket watch.

The watch made by the inventor, Robert Cart, who made virtually identical watches for Breguet. This example in red gold is rare, and the **dial** is particularly bold and attractive. The dial center rotates with the arrow holding the jump-hour aperature and pointing to the minute. Plain polish **case** with satin back. First quality rhodium 19-jewel **movement**. An elegant dress watch in particularly fine condition throughout.
Diam. 45 mm. **$12,000.00.**
Photo and description courtesy of Stephen Bogoff, Antiquarian Horologist, 6 Aug 2003.

Plate 561. Audemars Piguet, Brassus and Geneva, No. 27972, made in 1921.
Very fine and rare 18K gold, keyless, slim dress watch with unusual dial.

Case. Three-piece, matted back, bezel and band engraved with oak leaf wreath, pentagonal pendant. **Dial.** Silver, heavy, darkened, applied gold radial Roman numerals on matted recessed ring, outer minute dot divisions, center with Relaborate applied filigree oak leaf and scrolling pattern, subsidiary seconds. Gold baton hands, engraved with leaf pattern. **Movement.** 37 mm, rhodium plated, "fausses cotes" decoration, gold train, straight-line lever escapement, cut bimetallic compensation balance with blued-steel flat balance spring.
Signed on dial and movement, case incused with the serial number.
Diam. 43 mm. **$2,302.00.**
Photo and description courtesy of Antiquorum Auctioneers, Nov 2002.

Plate 562. North & Sons Ltd., Late Nicole, Nielsen & Co., 14 Soho Square, London, No. 12542, retailed by J. M. Dempster Ltd., Sydney, hallmarked 1922 – 1923.
Fine 18K gold keyless chronograph watch with 60-minute register.

Case. Four-body, "bassine et filets," polished, gold hinged cuvette, swivel pendant. **Dial.** Off-white enamel, Roman numerals, outer minute ring, outer-most chronograph scale with five-minute/seconds Arabic figures, subsidiary sunk seconds at 3 o'clock, minute register at 9 o'clock. **Movement.** 44 mm, frosted gilt, ¾ plate, 20 jewels, lateral calibrated lever escapement with the lift on the pallets, cut bimetallic compensation balance with gold screws, Breguet balance spring, chronograph work under the dial.
Movement signed. Dial signed by the retailer.
Diam. 55 mm. **$2,760.00.**
Photo and description courtesy of Antiquorum Auctioneers, 21 May 2003.

Plate 563. Circa 1923.

Waltham Vanguard, 23 jewels, adjusted six positions, #25341784. **Dial** has red standards, Lossier inner ring, terminal hairspring, 14K gold-filled "J. BOSS" **case**.
$875.00.
Description and watch courtesy of Aaron Faber Gallery.

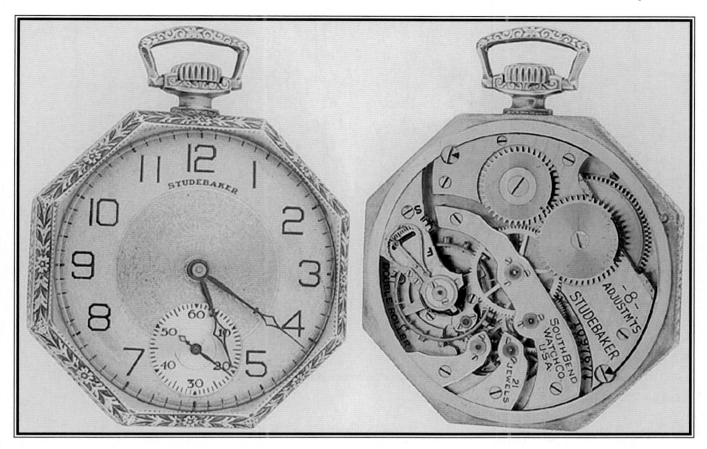

Plate 564. Circa 1923.

South Bend 12 size Studebaker, 21 jewels, very nice yellow-gold-filled open-face **case**, fancy double sunk "Studebaker"-marked **dial**, Arabic numerals, blue open diamond crossbar hands, beautifully damaskeened nickel bridge **movement**, screw down jewel settings, gold center wheel, double roller, marked adjusted eight positions, micrometric regulator (1097671). This is a very nice watch. **$550.00.**

Photo and description courtesy of OldWatch.com.

Plate 565. Circa 1923.

Illinois, Bunn special adjusted temperature, six positions, motor barrel, 23 jewels, #4137297, case — Fahys Montauk, 10K yellow-gold-filled case. **$1,275.00.**
Description and watch courtesy of Aaron Faber Gallery.

Plate 566. Circa 1924.

Elgin 16 size, B. W. Raymond 478, 21 jewels, railroad grade, very nice "Elgin R.R."–marked yellow-gold-filled open-face screwback **case**, single sunk porcelain **dial**, blue spade hands, lever set, ¾-plate nickel **movement**, gold jewel settings, micrometric regulator, adjusted 5 positions (27505594).
$475.00.
Photo and description courtesy of OldWatch.com.

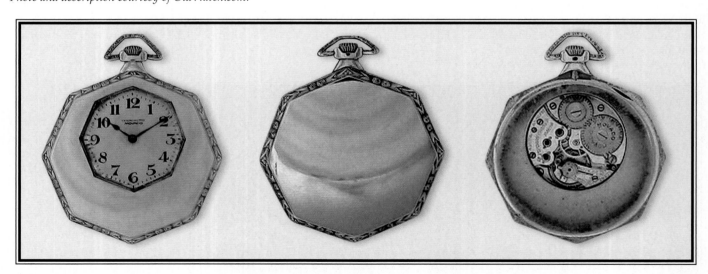

Plate 567. Circa 1925.
Unusual and attractive Movado Swiss Art Deco 18K yellow gold octagonal antique pocket watch with eccentric octagonal dial.

Original **dial**, 15 jewels Chronometro Movado **movement**. Cast and chased bezels and bow.
Diam. 45 mm. **$2,000.00.**
Photo and description courtesy of Stephen Bogoff, Antiquarian Horologist.

Plate 568. Gruen Watch Co., No. 9220, circa 1925. Very fine and rare lavishly-decorated platinum, sapphire- and diamond-set "Precision Extra" pendant watch with matching brooch.

Case. Two-body, oval, the back centered with a diamond- and sapphire-set rosette, small diamond-set pendant with additional ogival link set with diamonds and sapphires. Matching oval brooch. **Dial.** Silver with champlevé radial Arabic numerals, outer minute track, engine-turned center. Blued-steel Breguet hands. **Movement.** 20.5 x 14 mm, nickel, "fausses cotes" decoration, 18 jewels, all adjustments, straight line lever escapement, cut bimetallic compensation balance with Breguet balance spring, punched with Seal of Geneva quality mark, platinum dust cap. Signed on dial and movement.
Diam. 33 x 18 mm; length with brooch, 75 mm.
$13,800.00.
Photo and description courtesy of Antiquorum Auctioneers, 14 Jun 2003.

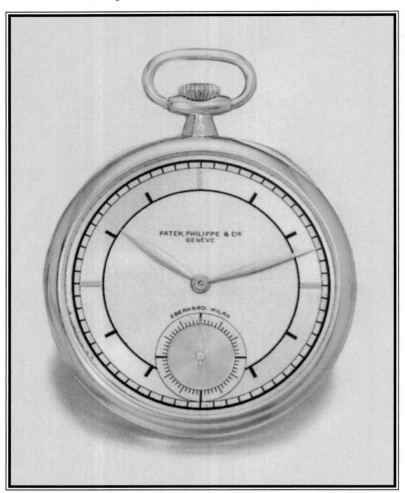

Plate 569. Patek Philippe & Cie., Geneve, No. 807290, case No. 289231, made for Eberhard, Milan, circa 1925.
Fine 18K gold, keyless pocket watch with three-tone dial.

Case. Three-body, "bassine," polished. **Dial.** Silver, applied gold indexes for quarter hours, outer minute divisions, matte center. Hour, minute chapters, and center in three different silver hues, subsidiary sunk seconds. Gold "feuille" hands. **Movement.** 40 mm, frosted gilt, 16 jewels, straight-line moustache lever escapement, cut bimetallic compensation balance with Breguet balance spring.
Signed on dial, case, and movement.
Diam. 47 mm. **$2,691.00.**
Photo and description courtesy of Antiquorum Auctioneers, 14 Jun 2003.

Plate 570. Circa 1925.

Elgin, size 16, model #19, grade 472, number of jewels: 21, serial number 28965360. Wind indicator in factory B. W. Raymond case.
$1,100.00.
Photos and descriptions courtesy of Edward Ueberall, Collector/Dealer.

Plate 571. Cartier, Paris, Art Deco, platinum/diamond pocket watch, circa 1925.

Case. Platinum, faceted rock crystal, circular, open face, with 14k white gold chain with pearls. **Dial.** Textured, white, black indexes and diamond-set Roman numerals, blued-steel Breguet hands. **Movement.** European Watch & Clock Co., rhodiumed, 19 jewels, lever escapement, cut bimetallic screwed balance wheel, eight adjustments, flat balance spring. Signed "Cartier" on dial. Signed "European Watch & Clock Co." on movement. Diam. 45 mm. **$11,750.00.**
Photo and description courtesy of Bonhams and Butterfields, San Francisco, 25 Jun 2002

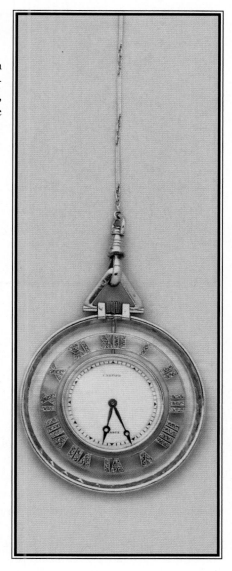

Plate 572. Circa 1925. Fine Swiss Movado 18K gold and enamel oval Art Deco antique pocket watch.

Plain polish **case** with the bezels and bow beautifully enameled in blue, black, and red. Silver **dial** with blue hard enamel numbers and Deco hands. Nickel 15-jewel, four-adjustment **movement** with precision regulator. Diam. 42 mm. **$2,600.00.**
Photo and description courtesy of Stephen Bogoff, Antiquarian Horologist.

Plate 573. Circa 1926. Rolex 9K gold open-face antique pocket watch.

White enamel **dial** with blued steel hands and the name of the retailer. Nickel damakeened 17-jewel, three-adjustment lever **movement** with precision regulator. Plain polish **case** with some wrinkles in the back cover.
Diam. 44 mm. **$1,100.00.**
Photo and description courtesy of Stephen Bogoff, Antiquarian Horologist.

Plate 574. Vacheron & Constantin, Geneve, No. 385104, case No. 251502. Produced circa 1927. Very fine and rare, keyless, 18K yellow gold gentleman's dress watch with chronograph.

Case. Four-body, "bassine," polished, engraved on the cuvette: "G Julio 1927," monogram on the case back, gold hinged cuvette. **Dial.** White enamel with painted Arabic numerals, outer minute track with chronograph divisions, outermost pulsometer graduation for 30 pulsations. Spade yellow gold hands.
Movement. 18", frosted gilt, 20 jewels, straight-line lever escapement, cut bimetallic compensation balance, blued-steel Breguet balance spring.
Dial, case, and movement signed.
Diam. 51 mm. **$3,450.00.**
Photo and description courtesy of Antiquorum Auctioneers, 21 May 2003.

Plate 575. Circa 1927.

South Bend 16 size, 227, 21 jewels, railroad grade, very nice Dueber 14k gold-filled screw-back open-face **case**, South Bend metal railroad **dial**, Arabic numerals, blue spade hands, lever set, beautifully damaskeened ¾-plate nickel **movement**, gold jewel settings, double roller, adjusted to temperature and five positions, micrometric regulator (1219719).
$495.00.
Photo and description courtesy of OldWatches.com.

Plate 576. Cortebert, Swiss, No. 593157, case No. 1544182, circa 1928.
Very fine and very rare 18K two-tone gold and enamel keyless Art Deco designed, most likely, for Barcelona Exhibition of 1929.

Case. Three-piece, square with canted corners, white gold bezels, back cover in yellow gold with champlevé raised green, red, blue, and black geometrical design with Egyptian accent, large yellow gold bow engraved in laurel leaves, smoothly extending from the band, yellow gold hinged stand for making it a desk clock. **Dial.** Silver, two-toned, following the shape of the case, applied white gold Breguet numerals over matted and whitened background, outer minute track, brushed square center, subsidiary seconds. White gold cathedral hands. **Movement.** 35 mm (15½"), rhodium-plated, 17 jewels, five adjustments, straight-line lever escapement, cut bimetallic compensation balance with gold screws, blued-steel Breguet balance spring, gold wheel train.
Signed on the dial.
Diam. height 50 mm, width 42 mm. **$4,428.00.**
Photo and description courtesy of Antiqourum Auctioneers, Nov 2002.

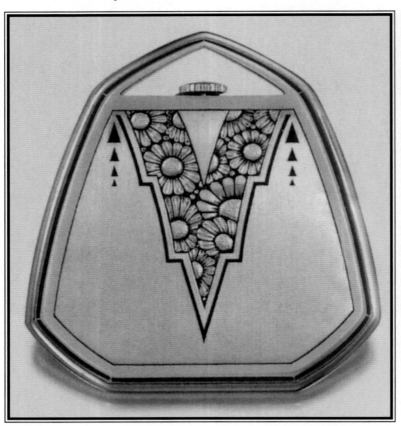

Plate 577. Cortebert, Swiss, No. 593158, case No. 1544181, circa 1928.
Very fine and very rare 18K two-tone gold and enamel keyless Art Deco Chevalier Highest Quality watch, designed, most likely, for Barcelona Exhibition of 1929.

Case. Three-piece, hexagonal, asymmetrically shaped, yellow gold bezels with blue enamel champlevé stripe, back cover in white gold with black enamel sharp geometrical figure with engraved flowers inside, large white gold bow smoothly extending from the band, white gold hinged stand for making it a desk clock. **Dial.** Silver, matte and whitened, following the shape of the case, applied yellow gold Breguet numerals, outer minute track, subsidiary seconds. Gold cathedral hands. **Movement.** 35 mm, rhodium plated, 17 jewels, S adjustments, straight-line lever escapement, cut bimetallic compensation balance with gold screws, blued-steel Breguet balance spring, gold wheel train.
Signed on the dial.
Diam. height 50 mm, width 47 mm. **$4,429.00.**
Photo and description courtesy of Antiquorum Auctioneers, Nov 2002.

Plate 578. Breguet, No. 2524, completed in October 1929, sold to Monsieur L. Harrison Dulles on 22 October 1954.
Very fine and rare 18K gold keyless center seconds digital perpetual calendar dress watch.

Case. Four-piece, "bassine er filets," polished, gold hinged cuverte. **Dial.** Silver, engine turned, eccentric chapter ring with radial Roman numerals set in the lower part, aperture for days of the week, date, and months, outer seconds division. **Movement.** 17", by Victorin Piguet, "fausses cotes" decoration, 20 jewels, straight-line lever escapement, cut bimetallic compensation balance with flat balance spring.
Signed on dial and case.
Diam. 49 mm. **$15,249.00.**
Photo and description courtesy of Antiquorum Auctioneers, 14 Jun 2003.

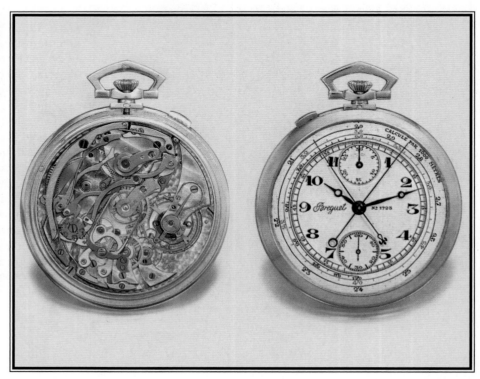

Plate 579. Bras-en-l'air Vacheron Constantin, No. 409422, case made by Verger, France, No. 12315, in 1929. Very fine and rare 18K two-colored, Art Deco, keyless "bras-en-l'air" dress watch.

Case. Three piece, Empire, white gold, polished and matte, yellow gold rims and bow. Matching black silk and bicolored gold Albert. **Dial.** Silver, marte, with an applied figure of a seated Chinese Mandarin, pointing to the hours and minutes with his arms when a push piece in the band is depressed. **Movement.** 37 mm (16⅕"), rhodium plated, 18 jewels, eight adjustments, straight-line lever escapement, cut bimetallic compensation balance with Breguet balance spring.
Signed on the movement, Verger master mark on the case.
Diam. 45 mm. **$37,674.00.**
Photo and description courtesy of Antiquorum Auctioneers, 14 Jun 2003.

Plate 580. Patek Philippe & Cie., Geneve, No. 819505, case No. 417809, made for Freccero circa 1930.
Very fine 18K gold keyless center seconds dress watch with special dial.

Case. Three-piece, "knife-edge," polished. **Dial.** Two-tone, silvered, with applied gold Arabic quarter numerals (3, 6, 9, 12) and painted indexes on a shiny ring, outer minute divisions on a marre ring separated from the seconds divisions by a shiny ring, matte center. Gold feuille hands. **Movement.** 37 mm (16½"), cal. 21 H, nickel, 17 jewels, adjusted to five positions, temperature and isochronism, straight line moustache lever escapement, cut bimetallic compensation balance with Breguet balance spring, micrometric spring regulator.
Signed on dial, case, and movement.
Diam. 45 mm. **$6,728.00.**
Photo and description courtesy of Antiquorum Auctioneers 14 Jun 2003.

Plate 581. Omega, Swiss, No. 7484545, made for the German market circa 1930. Fine and rare silver hunting-cased keyless watch for a blind person.

Case. Four-body, "bassine," polished, silver hinged cuvette. **Dial.** White enamel, radial Arabic numerals, each with enamel touch piece, 12 o'clock with three pieces, quarters with two steel spade hands **Movement.** 39 mm, rhodium plated, 15 jewels, straight-line lever escapement, cut bimetallic compensation balance with Breguet balance spring.
Signed on dial, case, and movement, case punched with Swiss and German silver marks.
Diam. 51 mm. **$1,794.00.**
Photo and description courtesy of Antiquorum Auctioneers, 14 Jun 2003.

Plate 582. Circa 1930s.

Ball Illinois 16 size Official Standard Motor Barrel, 23 jewels, very nice correct white-gold-filled official railroad standard case. Single sunk porcelain official railroad standard **dial**, Arabic numerals, correct Illinois/Ball skeleton hands, beautifully damaskeened ¾-plate nickel movement, sapphire pallets, screw-down gold jewel settings, gold center wheel, jeweled mainspring barrel, marked adjusted five positions, micrometric regulator (B800560). **$4,900.00.**
Photo and description courtesy of OldWatch.com.

Plate 583. Haas Neveux ex Co., Geneve, No. 20136, circa 1930.
Fine and elegant, 18K gold, extra flat, keyless, minute-repeating dress watch.

Case. Double-body, massive, "bassine pincee," polished, concealed hinge. **Dial.** Frosted silver with Breguet numerals and sunk subsidiary seconds. Blued-steel spade hands. **Movement.** 38 mm (17"), rhodium plated, "fausses cotes" decoration, punched with the Geneva Quality Hallmarks, 29 jewels, straight-line lever escapement, cut bimetallic balance, Breguet balance spring. Repeating on gongs with slide in the band.
Trade mark on the case.
Diam. 45 mm. **$2,875.00.**
Photo and description courtesy of Antiquorum Auctioneers, 21 May 2003.

Plate 584. Circa 1930.

Illinois 16 size, Bunn Special, 163A, 23 jewels, sixty hour, motor barrel, railroad grade, excellent white-gold-filled, 206 model, open-face **case**, lever set, double sunk porcelain **dial**, marked "Bunn Special 23J," 60 hour, six positions, Arabic numerals, blue spade hands, lever set, wonderfully damaskeened ¾-plate nickel **movement**, marked "Motor Barrel, Sixty Hour, 163A," marked "Elinvar" under the balance cock, full gold train, adjusted temperature and six positions, gold jewel settings, double roller, jeweled mainspring barrel, micrometric regulator (54572760). An excellent watch in the correct case. **$3,950.00.**
Photo and description courtesy of OldWatch.com.

Plate 585. Circa 1930s.

Hamilton, gold filled, number of jewels: 17, "safe driver watch" (original box) made as a presentation watch and never used or engraved. Maybe they had it made for a man and before he received it he had a wreck. Hamilton middle **dial**. Owner's note: metal dials originally cost more to make than porcelain dials.
$200.00.
Description and watch courtesy of Joseph Conway, Dealer/Collector.

Plate 586. Bosphorus View.
Unsigned, Geneva, made for the Islamic market, circa 1930.
Very fine and rare 18K gold and painted-on enamel, hunting-cased, jump-hour, slim pocket watch, accompanied by a matching gold and enamel key and chain.

Case. Four-body, "bassine," back cover finely painted on enamel with a view of the Bosphorus, a village in the background with a sunset behind mountains, gold and opaque white enamel scalloped frame, border in champlevé azure enamel with white enameled foliage, front with two apertures; the top one for the jump hour, the lower one for the seconds, both within a painted-on enamel rose pattern, azure background with gold and white enamel foliate and floral decoration, pendant and bow en suite, gold and enameled hinged cuvette entirely decorated with floral motifs of blue enamel on a flinque ground. Chain of five gold and enamel links terminated with Breguet-type gold and enamel chain. **Dial.** White enamel, top with jump hour aperture (Islamic numerals), eccentric minute track with 15-minute Islamic numerals, subsidiary sunk seconds. Gold counterpoised lozenge hand. **Movement.** 38 mm (17"), gilt brass, early bridge caliber, cylinder escapement, three-arm gilt balance with flat balance spring.
Diam. 48 mm. **$13,283.00.**
Photo and description courtesy of Antiquorum Auctioneers, Nov 2002.

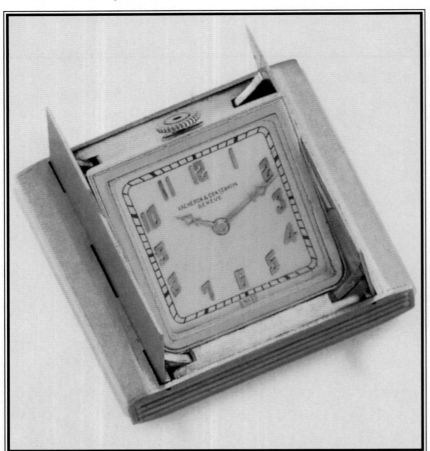

Plate 587. Vacheron & Constantin, Geneve, No. 415978, case by Verger Freres, No. 12092, circa 1930.
Fine and rare 18K two-tone gold, keyless, "montre a volets" purse watch.

Case. Solid, with yellow gold thumb bars and white gold sprung shutters, matted front and back, polished edges, fluted top and bottom. Yellow gold movement housing. **Dial.** Matted gilt with applied upright Arabic numerals, outer minute ring. Cathedral gold hands. **Movement.** 20.5 mm (9"), rhodium plated, 15 jewels, straight-line lever escapement, cut bimetallic compensation balance adjusted to temperature and three positions, blued-steel flat balance spring. Dial and movement signed. Case signed by the case maker.
Diam. 40 x 31 mm. **$2,760.00.**
Photo and description courtesy of Antiquorum Auctioneers, 19 Mar 2003.

Plate 588. Circa 1930.

Illinois, size 16, model #14, grade 163, Bunn Special, number of jewels: 23, serial number 5375531. Late Illinois **movement**, assembled by Hamilton in green GF gold-filled "Bunn Special" model **case**.
$2,950.00.
Photo and description courtesy of Edward Ueberall, Collector/Dealer.

Plate 589. Haas Neveux & Co., Geneve, No. 20132, circa 1930.
Fine and elegant 18K gold, extra flat, keyless, minute-repeating dress watch.

Case. Double-body, solid, "bassine pincee," polished, concealed hinge, the back engraved with a small monogram, a dedication dated April 21, 1933, engraved inside. **Dial.** Two-tone silver with Breguet numerals and sunk subsidiary seconds. Spade blued-steel hands. **Movement.** 38 mm (17"), rhodium-plated "fausses cotes" decoration, stamped with the Geneva Quality Hallmark, 29 jewels, straight-line lever escapement, cut bimetallic balance, Breguet balance spring. Repeating on gongs through activating slide in the band.
Trademark on the case.
Diam. 46 mm. **$3,450.00.**
Photo and description courtesy of Antiquorum Auctioneers, 21 May 2003.

Plate 590. Patek Philippe & Cie., Geneve, retailed by Walser Wald, No. 880692, case No. 616386. Produced in the late 1930s.
Very fine keyless, 18K yellow gold, gentleman's dress watch.

Case. Three-piece, "bassine et filets," solid, polished and brushed. **Dial.** Matte silver with applied yellow gold baton indexes. Baton yellow gold hands. **Movement.** Cal. 17½" stamped with the Geneva Quality Hallmark, rhodium-plated, "fausses cotes" decoration, 18 jewels, straight-line lever escapement, cut bimetallic compensation balance with gold screws adjusted to heat, cold, isochronism and five positions, blued-steel Breguet balance spring, swan neck micrometer regulator.
Dial, case, and movement signed.
Diam. 45 mm. **$2,300.00.**
Photo and description courtesy of Antiquorum Auctioneers, 21 May 2003.

Plate 591. Circa 1930.

Hamilton 16 size, 992, 21 jewels, railroad grade, excellent white-gold-filled, marked "Hamilton," railroad model, screw-back open-face **case**, double sunk Montgomery porcelain **dial**, Arabic numerals, blue spade hands, lever set, beautifully damaskeened ¾-plate nickel **movement** with gold inlay, adjusted five positions, gold center wheel, gold jewel settings, micrometric regulator, Double Roller (2411325).
$495.00.
Photo and description courtesy of OldWatch.com.

Plate 592. Circa 1933.

16 size, B. W. Raymond with up/down wind indicator, adjusted six positions.
$2,600.00 – 2,800.00.
Description and watch provided by Father Bradly Offutt, Collector.

Plate 593. Circa 1933.

Hamilton 16 size, 992E, 21 jewels, railroad grade, yellow gold-filled bar over crown **case**, Original double sunk porcelain **dial**, Arabic numerals, blue spade hands, lever set, ¾-plate nickel **movement**, gold center wheel, gold jewel settings, double roller, adjusted five positions, marked "Elinvar," micrometric regulator (2653642). **$950.00.**

Photo and description courtesy of OldWatch.com.

Plate 594. Zenith, Swiss, circa 1935.
Fine agate and yellow-gold-filled keyless dress watch.

Case. Single piece of striped red agate with white bands, gold-filled reeded bezel and pendant. **Dial.** White enamel, Arabic numerals, outer minute track, outermost 24-hour scale (13 to 24), subsidiary sunk seconds. Blued-steel Breguet hands. **Movement.** 39.3 mm, rhodium plated, damaskeened in a geometrical pattern, 17 jewels, straight-line lever escapement, cut bimetallic compensation balance, blued-steel Breguet balance spring, earn-type patented regulator. Diam. 50 mm. **$886.00.**

Photo and description courtesy of Antiquorum Auctioneers, Nov 2002.

Plate 595. Circa 1935.

Waltham Riverside, #28898991, adjusted temperature, jeweled main wheel, 21 jewels, and scepter case with a train engraved on the back.
$975.00.
Description and watch courtesy of Aaron Faber Gallery.

Plate 596. Unsigned, Geneva, circa 1935.
Fine 18K gold and enamel keyless Art Deco pendant watch.

Case. Hexagonal, elongated, central stripe with gold flowers with blue enamel center on black enamel background, sides with a dark red champlevé enamel with gold spiderweb design, triangular pendant with black and blue enamel terminated with a gold ring. **Dial.** Champagne, Arabic numerals, outer minute track. Blued-steel Scotties hands. **Movement.** 20 mm (9"), rhodium plated, 15 jewels, straight-line lever escapement, cut bimetallic compensation balance with blued-steel flat balance spring.
Diam. 38 x 30 mm. **$3,001.00.**
Photo and description courtesy of Antiquorum Auctioneers, Nov 2002.

Plate 597. Zenith, Swiss, circa 1935.
Fine agate and yellow-gold-filled keyless dress watch.

Case. Single piece of striped red agate with white bands, gold-filled reeded bezel and pendant. **Dial.** White enamel, Arabic numerals, outer minute track, outermost 24-hour scale (13 to 24), subsidiary sunk seconds. Blued-steel Breguet hands. **Movement.** 39.3 mm (17½"), rhodium plated, damaskeened in a geometrical pattern, 17 jewels, straight-line lever escapement, cut bimetallic compensation balance, blued-steel Breguet balance spring, cam-type patented regulator. Diam. 50 mm. **$1,594.00.**
Photo and description courtesy of Antiquorum Auctioneers, Nov 2002.

Plate 598. Breguet, Paris, No. 3290, circa 1935.
Very fine two-tone 18K gold and silver, keyless, lever pocket chronometer, winner of gold medal and Bulletin de Premiere Classe in Besan on, with original gold medal and original Bulletin de Marche.

Case. Four-body. "Empire". polished with reeded band, bezels with silver edges, gold hinged cuvette, silver bow. **Dial.** Silver, engine-turned center and outer border, champlevé radial Roman numerals, outer minute dot divisions, subsidiary seconds. Blued-steel Breguet hands. **Movement.** 44 mm (19½"), rhodium plated, "fausses cotes" decoration, 19 jewels, straight-line lever escapement, Guillaume anibal-brass cut bimetallic compensation balance, Breguet balance spring, wolf-tooth winding wheels, viper's head punch mark.
Signed on dial, case, and movement.
Diam. 52 mm. **$13,282.00.**
Photo and description courtesy of Antiquorum Auctioneers, 21 May 2003.

Plate 599. Vacheron & Constantin, Geneve, No. 408144, made for Charlton & Co., case by Verger, France, No. 12062, circa 1935.
Very fine and elegant 18K two-tone gold keyless Art Deco dress watch.

Case. Three piece, massive, "variee," with pink gold knife-edge, white gold bezel back and bow. **Dial.** Silver with applied cubic Arabic numerals, blued-steel Breguet hands. **Movement.** 33.75 mm (15"), rhodium plated, with polished bridges, the plate with spotted decoration, 18 jewels, straight-line lever escapement, cut bimetallic balance, eight adjustments, Breguet balance spring.
Signed on the dial, case, and movement.
Diam. 44 mm. **$6,973.00.**
Photo and description courtesy of Antiquorum Auctioneers, 14 Jun 2003.

Plate 600. Circa 1939.

Rolex 16 size, cal. 540, military, 15 jewels, very nice Dennison, silver, open-face, hinged **case,** single sunk black porcelain **dial** marked "A.19407," luminscent Arabic numerals, blue luminscent hands, ¾-plate nickel **movement,** micrometric regulator. **$950.00.**
Photo and description courtesy of OldWatch.com.

Plate 601. Circa 1940.

Waltham, Premier, 21 jewels, Riverside, adjusted temperature, jeweled main wheel, #30498685, case is Waltham Premier Keystone Victory, 10K rolled gold plate.
$525.00.

Description and watch courtesy of Aaron Faber Gallery.

Plate 602. Patek Philippe & Cie., Geneve, No. 137885, case No. 2601742, Ref. 781, circa 1940.
Very fine and extremely rare 18K gold, keyless, astronomical, split-seconds chronograph dress watch, with 30-minute register, perpetual calendar and phases of the moon, with visible split-seconds mechanism.

Case. Three-piece, massive, "bassine," polished. **Dial.** Silver with gold indexes, outer minute/seconds track with five-minute/seconds Arabic markers, four subsidiary sunk dials for days of the week, months, phases of the moon concentric with minute register, and subsidiary seconds concentric with date. Gold dauphine hands. **Movement.** 40 mm (18"), rhodium plated, "fausses cotes" decoration, 29 jewels, straight-line calibrated lever escapement, cut bimetallic compensation balance with Breguer balance spring, swan neck micrometric regulator, split mechanism on the back plate.
Signed on dial, case, and movement.
Diam. 51 mm. **$101,498.00.**

Photo and description courtesy of Antiquorum Auctioneers, 14 Jun 2003.

351

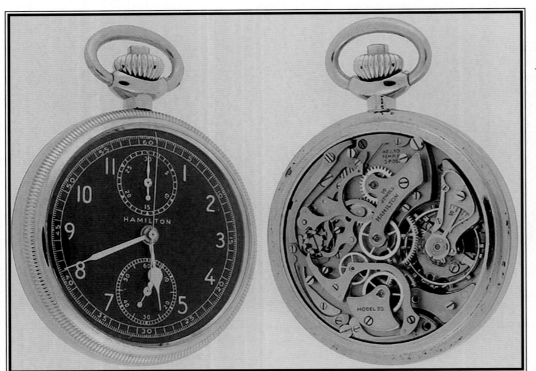

Plate 603. Circa 1940s.

Hamilton 16 size, model 23, 19 jewels, U.S. Navy Navigation and chronograph, keystone base metal **case**, black-face **dial** with white hands including sweep second, ¾-plate nickel **movement**, pressed jewels micrometric regulator, marked "Model 23," adjusted to three positions and temperature, also marked "19 Jewels (P23227)." **$750.00.**

Photo and description courtesy of OldWatch.com.

Plate 604. Patek Philippe & Cie., Geneve, No. 891329, case No. 420805. Produced in the late 1940's.
Very fine and thin, keyless, 18K yellow gold gentleman's dress watch.

Case. Two-body, polished, stepped bezel. **Dial.** Pink with applied gold and black painted round and baton indexes, auxiliary seconds dial. Baton yellow gold hands. **Movement.** Cal. 17", rhodium-plated, "fausses-cotes" decoration, 18 jewels, straight-line lever escapement, cut bimetallic compensation balance, flat balance spring.
Dial, case, and movement signed.
Diam. 47 mm. **$1,495.00.**
Photo and description courtesy of Antiquorum Auctioneers, 21 May 2003.

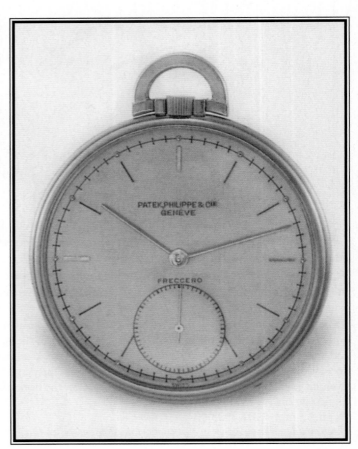

Plate 605. Circa 1940s.

Hamilton 12 size, model 922, 23 jewels, excellent gold-filled "Hamilton"-marked open-face **case**, single sunk fancy **dial**, Arabic numerals, blue open diamond/cross bar hands, circular damaskeened bridge nickel **movement**, gold jewel settings, adjusted five positions, jeweled mainspring barrel, micrometric regulator (3001208).
$425.00.
Photo and description courtesy of OldWatch.com.

Plate 606. Circa 1941.

Hamilton, size 16, grade 4 992B, number of jewels: 22, serial number 4C 14043. Made for U.S. Military during WWII. Note, 24 hour black dial, sweep second hand, and **movement** hacks (stops) when setting.
$550.00.
Photo and description courtesy of Edward Ueberall, Collector/Dealer.

Plate 607. Circa 1942.

Elgin 16 size, Type A-13 U.S. Army ordinance, grade 387, 17 jewels, correct nickel **case** with all the military markings, single sunk porcelain Montgomery **dial**, Arabic numerals, blue spade hands, ¾ nickel **movement**, screwed-down jewel settings, Elginium hairspring micrometric regulator (41433523). The Army ordered several of these to use as field watches during World War II. **$595.00.**

Photo and description courtesy of OldWatch.com.

Plate 608. Circa 1943.

Hamilton 16 size, 3992B, Navigation Master watch, 22 jewels, British military World War II, with hack, correct keystone base, metal open-face screw-back **case** with military marks on the back, with "Broad Arrow" and "H S 3," one-piece porcelain **dial**, Arabic numerals, black spade hands with sweep second, pendant set, ¾-plate nickel **movement**, gold jewel settings, adjusted temperature and six positions, Elinvar hairspring, marked "U.S. Govt.," micrometric regulator (3C844).
$1,900.00.
Photo and description courtesy of OldWatch.com.

Plate 609. Circa 1945.

Waltham 12 size, Colonial R, 21 jewels, yellow-gold-filled **case**, single sunk **dial**, Arabic numerals, gold hands, ¾-plate nickel **movement**, Elinvar hairspring, micrometric regulator (32334967). The last run of the 21 jewel Colonial R watches! **$245.00.**
Photo and description courtesy of OldWatch.com.

Plate 610. Circa 1949.

Elgin B. W. Raymond, H630521, eight adjustments, 21 jewels, keystone 10K gold filled, cased and timed by Elgin National Watch Co. **$675.00.**
Description and watch courtesy of Aaron Faber Gallery.

Plate 611. Circa 1950s.

Delaware, size 16, number of jewels: 17, no serial number. Modern Swiss **movement** used on some Canadian RRs in 1950s and 1960s.
$225.00.
Photos and description courtesy of Edward Ueberall, Collector/Dealer.

Plate 612. Circa 1950s.

Unitas, size 16, model #6500, Grade Bedforde 429, number of jewels: 21, serial number 10236. Used in service on western Canadian RRs, although may not have been authorized for service.
$325.00.
Photos and descriptions courtesy of Edward Ueberall, Collector/Dealer.

Plate 613. Circa 1952.

Hamilton 16 size, 4992B, 22 jewels, U.S. military Korean, railroad grade, with hack, correct base metal open-face screw-back **case** with military marks on the back, black 24-hour **dial**, white spade hands, sweep second, ¾-plate nickel **movement**, gold jewel settings, adjusted temperature and six positions, Elinvar hairspring, micrometric regulator (4C110256). A Korean War military watch, we purchased this watch from the Navy watchmaker who serviced it during the Korean Conflict!
$595.00.
Photo and description courtesy of OldWatch.com.

Plate 614. Circa 1958.

Shirley Temple-dial watch made by Westclock.
$400.00 – 500.00.
Description and watch courtesy of J. D. Miller.

Endnotes

CHAPTER I

1. Landes, *Revelation in Time*, 1983.

2. Gahton and Thomas, "Philip Melachthon's Watch — Dated 1530," *NAWCC Bulletin*, December 2002, pages 736 – 737.

CHAPTER II

3. *Horology*, "The Evolution of Forms," page 210.

4. Jean Rousseu, "The Shaped Watch," *Antiquorum Auction Catalogue*, June 14, 2003.

5. Edward P. Hamilton, "Dating Old Watches," *Horology*, December 1938.

6. *History of Timelines*, page 129.

7. *Antiquorum Auction Catalogue*, Sandberg Collection, page 408.

8. *World's Timeline*, page 133.

CHAPTER III

9. Bruton, *The History of Clocks and Watches*, page 116.

10. Bruton, *The History of Clocks and Watches*, page 25.

11. Jaquet and Chapuis, *The Swiss Watch*, page 120.

12. Bruton, *The History of Clocks and Watches*, page 116.

13. Cuss, *Antique Watches*, page 130.

14. *Antiquorum Auction Catalogue*, November 2002, pages 33.

15. *NAWCC Bullitin*, Supplement 20, spring 1994, page 24.

16. Bell, *Answers to Questions about Old Jewelry*, page 487.

17. *Antiquorum Auction Catalogue*, March 31, 2001, watch #8.

18. Crom, *NAWCC Bullitin*, 1993, page 144.

19. Crom, *NAWCC Bullitin*, 1993, page 144.

20. Jaquet and Chapuis, *The Swiss Watch*, page 88.

21. *Antiquorum Auction Catalogue*, November 2002, page 100.

22. Bailey, *Two Hundred Years of American Clocks & Watches*, page 125.

CHAPTER IV

23. Bailey, *Two Hundred Years of American Clocks and Watches*, page 193.

24. Harrold, *NAWCC Bulletin*, spring 1984, page 14.

25. Harold, "American Watchmaking," *NAWCC*, 1984, page 16.

26. Bailey, *Two Hundred Years of American Clocks and Watches*, page 195.

27. Harold, "American Watchmaking," *NAWCC*, 1984, page 32.

28. Bailey, *Two Hundred Years of American Clocks and Watches*, page 201.

29. Bailey, *Two Hundred Years of American Clocks and Watches*, page 206.

30. Harold, "American Watchmaking," *NAWCC*, 1984, page 126.

31. Bell, *Answers & Questions About Old Jewelry, 1840 – 1950*, 2003, page 10.

32. Partridge and Bettmann, *As We Were, Family Life*, 1850 – 1900, page 114 – 116.

33. Harold, "American Watchmaking," *NAWCC*, October 2002.

34. Harold, "American Watchmaking," *NAWCC*, 1984, page 110.

35. Jaquet and Chapuis, *The Swiss Watch*, page 176.

36. Bell, *Answers & Questions About Old Jewelry, 1840 – 1950*, 1999, page 12 – 13.

37. Jaquet and Chapuis, *The Swiss Watch*, page 188.

38. Cutmore, *Watches, 1850 – 1980*, page 51.

39. Cutmore, *Watches, 1850 – 1980*, pages 84 – 85.

40. Cutmore, *The Pocket Watch Hand Book*, pages 107 – 108.

41. Cutmore, *The Pocket Watch Hand Book*, page 77.

42. Ehrhardt, *American Pocket Watch*, 1982, page 8.

43. Jaquet and Chapuis, *The Swiss Watch*, page 172.

44. Harold, "American Watchmaking," *NAWCC*, 1984, page 46, 92.

CHAPTER V

45. Wesolowski, Z. M., *Military Timepieces 1880 – 1990*, page 24.

Bibliography

Abbott, Henry G. *Antique Watches and How To Establish Their Age*. Chicago, IL: George K. Hazlitt & Co., 1897.

Allix, Charles, and Peter Bonnert. *Carriage Clocks*. Woodbridge, Suffolk, Great Britain: Antique Collectors' Club Publishers, 1989.

Bell, C. Jeanenne. *Answers & Questions About Old Jewelry, 1840 – 1950,* 6th Edition, Iola, WI: Krause Publications, 2003.

Benis, Dr. Anthony. *Four Hundred Years Of Watchmaking, An Historic Exhibition* (Commemorative Catalog). New York, NY: Rolex Watch U.S.A., 1974.

Baillie, G.H., C. Clutton, and C. A. Ilbert. *Britten's Old Clocks and Watches and Their Makers*. New York, NY: Bonanza Books, 1956.

Bailey, Chris H. *Two Hundred Years of American Clocks & Watches*. Englewood, NJ: Prentice-Hall, 1975.

Britten, F. J. *The Watch & Clock Makers' Handbook, Dictionary and Guide*. Brooklyn, NY: Chemical Publishing Company, 1938.

Bruton, Eric. *Clocks and Watches*. Great Britain: Paul Hamlyn Publishing Group, Feltham, 1968.

_____. *Dictionary of Clocks and Watches*. New York, NY: Bonanza Books.

_____. *History of Clocks and Watches*. New York, NY: Cresent Books, 1989.

Camm, F. J. *Watches Adjustments and Repair*. Brooklyn, NY: Chemical Publishing Company.

Cardinal, Catherine. *Catalogue des montres du Musee du Louvre*. Paris, France: 1984.

_____. *Watchmaking In History, Art and Science*. Lausanne, Switzerland: Scriptar S.A., 1984.

Chapiro, Adolphe. *Catalogue de l'horlogerie et des instruments de precision*. Paris, France: Musee National de la Renaissance, Chateau d'Ecouen, 1999.

Cooke, J., A. Kramer, and T. Roland-Entwistle. *History's Timeline*. New York, NY: Cresent Books, 1981.

Criss, David. *Collector's Price Guide to American Pocket Watches*, 5th edition. Imlay City, MI: Criss Coin Enterprises, 1984.

Crom, Dr. Theodore R. *Horological Wheel Cutting Engines, 1700 – 1900*. Hawthorne, FL: T. R. Crom Published, 1970.

_____. *Horological Shop Tools, 1700 – 1900*, Hawthorne. FL: T. R. Crom Published, 1980.

_____. *Horological & Other Shop Tools, 1700 – 1900*, Hawthorne. FL: T. R. Crom Published, 1987.

_____. *Trade Catalogues 1542 – 1842*, T. R. Hawthorne. FL: T. R. Crom Published, 1989.

_____. *An Eighteenth Century English Brass Hardware Catalogue*. Hawthorne, FL: T. R. Crom Published, 1994.

_____. *Early Lancashire Horological Tools & Their Makers*. Hawthorne, FL: T. R. Crom Published, 1994.

Cuss, T. P. Camerer. *The Camerer Cuss Book of Antique Watches*. Suffolk, Great Britain: Antique Collectors' Club, 1987.

Cutmore, Max. *Watches, 1850 – 1980*. Newton Abbot, Devon, England: David & Charles, Brunel House, 1989.

_____. *Collecting & Repairing Watches*. Newton Abbot, Devon, England: David & Charles, Brunel House, 1999.

Cutmore, M. *The Pocket Watch Handbook*. Newton Abbot, Devon, England: David & Charles, Brunel House, 2002.

Daniels, George. *English & American Watches*. New York, NY: Abeland-Schuman, 1967.

Ehrhardt, Roy. *American Pocket Watches, Encyclopedia and Price Guide*, volume one. Kansas City, MO: Heart of America Press, 1982.

_____. *American Pocket Watches, Identification and Price Guide, Book 2*. Kansas City, MO: Heart of America Press, 1980.

Ehrhardt, Roy and Bill Meggers. *Railroad Watches, Identification and Price Guide*. Umatilla, FL: Heart of America Press, 1995.

Fried, Henry B. *Cavalcade of Time, A Visual History of Watches.* Dallas, TX: The Zale Corporation, 1968.

Good, Richard. *Watches in Color.* Dorset, England: Blandford Press LTD, 1978.

Harrold, Michael C. "American Watchmaking, A History of the American Watch Industry, 1850 – 1930." *NAWCC Bulletin*, Supplement No. 14, Spring 1984.

_____. "Charles Rood and Henry Cain, Origins of the Hamilton Watch Company." *NAWCC Bulletin*, October 2002.

Illinois Watches And Their Makers. Springfield, IL: Illinois Watch Company, 1999.

Jagger, Cedric. *The Worlds Great Clocks & Watches.* England: Galley Press, 1977.

Jaquet, Eugene and Alfred Chapuis. *Technique and History of the Swiss from Its Beginnings to the Present Day.* Boston, MA: Boston Book and Art Shop, 1953.

Johnson, Chester. *Clocks and Watches.* New York, NY: The Odyssey Library, 1964.

Landes, David S. *Revolution In Time.* Cambridge, MA:Belknap Press, 1983.

Langone, John. "The History of Time." Washington, D.C.: National Geographic, 2000.

Leibe, Frankie. *Watches, A Collector's Guide.* London, England: Miller's, 1999.

Leonardi, Leonardo and Gabriele Ribolini. *Pocket Watches.* San Francisco, CA: Chronicle Books, 1994.

Lippincott, Kristen. *The Story of Time.* London, England: Merrell Holberton.

Meis, Reinhard. *Pocket Watches, from the Pendant Watch to the Tourbillon.* West Chester, PA: Schiffer Publishing, 1987.

Partridge, Bellamy and Otto Bettmann. *As We Were, Family Life In America, 1850 – 1900.* New York, NY: Whittlesey House Publishers, 1946.

Pearsal, Ronald. *A Connoisseur's Guide to Antique Clocks & Watches.* Todtri Productions Limited, 1997.

Priestley, Philip T. "Early Watch Case Makers of England, 1631 – 1720." *NAWCC Bulletin*, Supplement No. 4, 2002.

Priestley, Philip T. "Watch Case Makers of England, A History and Register of Gold & Silver Watch Case Makers of England: 1720 – 1920." *NAWCC Bulletin*, Supplement No. 20, Spring 1994.

Schroeder, Bill. *1976 – 1977 Antique Watches With Current Values.* Paducah, KY: Collector Books, 1976.

Shugart, C. *The Complete Guide to American Pocket Watches.* Cleveland, TN: Overstreet Publications, 1981.

Stork, Leonard W. "Collector's Weekly." *W. G. Crook Illustrated Catalogue*, 1888.

Tait, Hugh. *Clocks and Watches.* London, England: British Museum Publications, 1983.

Terrisse. Sophie Ann. *Prestigious Watches.* New York, NY: BW Publishing, 1997.

This Fabulous Century, Sixty Years of American Life, 1920 – 1930, volume 3. New York, NY: Time-Life Books, 1969.

Ullyett, Kenneth. *Watch Collecting.* Chicago, IL: Henry Regenery Company, 1970.

Wesolowski, Z. M. *Military Timepieces, 1880 – 1990.* Wiltshire, England: The Crowood Press Ltd., 1999.

William, James. *The Magic City.*

Willsberger, Johann. *Clocks & Watches.* New York, NY: The Dial Press, 1975.

Winter-Jensen, Anne and Claude Lepaire. *Clock and Watch Museum, Geneva.* Geneva, Switzerland: Art and History Museum of Geneva Publishers, 1990.

Index

COLLECTOR BOOKS
informing today's collector

www.collectorbooks.com

For over two decades we have been keeping collectors informed on trends and values
in all fields of antiques and collectibles.

This is only a partial listing of the books on antiques that are available from Collector Books. All books are well illustrated and contain current values. Most of these books are available from your local bookseller, antique dealer, or public library. If you are unable to locate certain titles in your area, you may order by mail from COLLECTOR BOOKS, P.O. Box 3009, Paducah, KY 42002-3009. Customers with Visa, MasterCard, or Discover may phone in orders from 8:00 a.m. to 4:00 p.m. CT, Monday – Friday, toll free 1-800-626-5420, or online at www.collectorbooks.com. Add \$6.00 for postage for the first book ordered and 60¢ for each additional book. Include item number, title, and price when ordering. Allow 14 to 21 days for delivery.

1-800-626-5420   Fax: 1-270-898-8890

www.collectorbooks.com

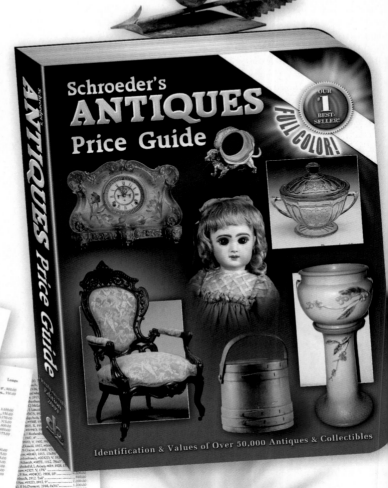